Mastering VMware vSphere 6.5

Leverage the power of vSphere for effective virtualization, administration, management and monitoring of data centers

Andrea Mauro
Paolo Valsecchi
Karel Novak

BIRMINGHAM - MUMBAI

Mastering VMware vSphere 6.5

First published: December 2017

Production reference: 1141217

Published by Packt Publishing Ltd.
Livery Place
35 Livery Street
Birmingham
B3 2PB, UK.

ISBN 978-1-78728-601-6

www.packtpub.com

Credits

Authors
Andrea Mauro
Paolo Valsecchi
Karel Novak

Copy Editors
Safis Editing
Dipti Mankame

Reviewers
Wouter Kursten
Jan Marek

Project Coordinator
Judie Jose

Commissioning Editor
Gebin George

Proofreader
Safis Editing

Acquisition Editor
Meeta Rajani

Indexer
Rekha Nair

Content Development Editor
Devika Battike

Graphics
Tania Dutta

Technical Editor
Swathy Mohan

Production Coordinator
Shraddha Falebhai

About the Authors

Andrea Mauro has 20 years of experience in IT, both in the industry and the academic world. He currently works as a solution architect in an Italian IT company (founded in 2000). He is responsible for infrastructure implementation, architecture design, upgrades, and migration processes.

He is a virtualization and storage architect, specializing in VMware, but also Microsoft, Citrix, and Linux solutions. His first virtualized solution in production was built around ESX 2.x several years ago.

He is a VMware Italian User Group founder and board member, VMTN community moderator, vBrownbag and Backup Academy contributor, and a passionate blogger.

His professional certifications include not only several VMware certifications (VCP3/4/5/6-DCV, vSAN 2017 Specialist, different VCAP, VCIX6-DCV, VCIX-NV, VCDX3/4/5/6-DCV), but also other vendor-related certifications (MCITP, MCSA, MCSE, NPP, CCA, EMCIE, EMCSA, VMCE, VMCA). He is also a VMware vExpert (2010-17), Nutanix NTC (2014-17), and Veeam Vanguard (2015-17), and he was a Microsoft MVP (2014-16).

> *I would like to thank my wife and my son for their patience (this book has taken a lot of my free time for three long months), my friends from the VMUG.IT for their support, the co-authors Paolo and Karel for their support, without which this book would not have been possible (at least not with the proposed deadline), and Scott S. Lowe for his words and suggestions.*

Paolo Valsecchi has worked in the IT industry for more than 20 years, and he currently works as a system engineer mainly focused on VMware vSphere, Microsoft technologies, and backup/DR solutions. His current role involves covering all of the tasks related to ensuring the IT infrastructure availability and data integrity (implementation, upgrade, and administration).

He holds the VMware VCP5-DCV, Veeam VMCE professional certifications, and he has been awarded the VMware vExpert title (2015-17) and the Veeam Vanguard title (2016-17).

> *A big thanks to Andrea and Karel for including me in this project, my family for their support and patience during this hard work, and all the people who supported me during this adventure.*

Karel Novak has 16 years of experience in the IT world. He currently works as a senior virtual infrastructure engineer at Arrow ECS, the Czech Republic, responsible for implementation, design, and complete consultation of VMware and Veeam. As an instructor of advanced VMware and Veeam, he has delivered many courses.

He specializes in VMware DCV and NSX and of course Veeam. He has been using VMware for 10 years and Veeam from the first version. He is the VMware User Group Leader for the Czech Republic, and Veeam User Group Czech Republic founder and unofficial Leader.

He is a VMware vExpert 2012-2017, VMware vExpert NSX 2016-2017, and a Veeam Vanguard 2015-2017.

His highest certifications are VCI-Level2, VCIX6-NV, VCIX6-DCV, VMCT-Mentor, and VMCA. He is also a VMware Certification Subject Matter Expert.

I must say thank you to Andrea and Paolo for this opportunity. Thank you to my amazing wife who supports me in all my projects. Thank you to all those around me who support me in all the activities that I do.

About the Reviewers

Wouter Kursten is a virtualization engineer, blogger, vExpert (2016 and 2017), and VMUG speaker from the Netherlands. He has been building, but mostly maintaining, VMware environments for several years. He has experience with VMware vSphere, Horizon View, Thinapp, App-V, Citrix Xenapp, and repackaging applications. You can find him on Twitter as @Magneet_NL. He currently works for Detron in the Netherlands.

He has also worked on Packt videos, including *Designing and Deploying VMware Horizon View 7, Learning App Volumes, Managing a Horizon 7 Environment* (in development).

Jan Marek is an IT consultant and architect with more than 10 years of proven experience. His professional career includes training and speaking-related activities as well. He focuses primarily on products in the area of private cloud and infrastructure services, specifically Microsoft Hyper-V, VMware vSphere, System Center, Windows Server, Active Directory, and Microsoft App-V. To prove his knowledge, he has passed many Microsoft certifications—MCSE, MCSA, MCITP, MCTS, MS, and MCT. For his speaking-/writing-related activities, he was awarded with the Microsoft Most Valuable Professional (MVP) in the Cloud and Datacenter Management category. His daily work includes architecture work, consultancy, engineering, and training delivery.

www.PacktPub.com

For support files and downloads related to your book, please visit www.PacktPub.com.

Did you know that Packt offers eBook versions of every book published, with PDF and ePub files available? You can upgrade to the eBook version at www.PacktPub.com and as a print book customer, you are entitled to a discount on the eBook copy. Get in touch with us at service@packtpub.com for more details.

At www.PacktPub.com, you can also read a collection of free technical articles, sign up for a range of free newsletters and receive exclusive discounts and offers on Packt books and eBooks.

https://www.packtpub.com/mapt

Get the most in-demand software skills with Mapt. Mapt gives you full access to all Packt books and video courses, as well as industry-leading tools to help you plan your personal development and advance your career.

Why subscribe?

- Fully searchable across every book published by Packt
- Copy and paste, print, and bookmark content
- On demand and accessible via a web browser

Customer Feedback

Thanks for purchasing this Packt book. At Packt, quality is at the heart of our editorial process. To help us improve, please leave us an honest review of this book's Amazon page at https://www.amazon.com/dp/1787286010.

If you'd like to join our team of regular reviewers, you can e-mail us at customerreviews@packtpub.com. We award our regular reviewers with free eBooks and videos in exchange for their valuable feedback. Help us be relentless in improving our products!

Table of Contents

Preface

This book will provide the knowledge of vSphere 6.5 required in order to build, manage, and simply better understand such environments.

Using real-world scenarios, this book acts as a reference guide and possible baseline for each virtualization project based on VMware vSphere. Written by VMware vExperts and certified people, this book is an indispensable guide for each vSphere professional.

This book tries to fill the gaps in existing documentation, which in some cases is too in depth, with an organic approach and overview.

This book will quickly move from the design and plan to the deployment and management aspects of vSphere 6.5, considering its new features and capabilities. Then, we will explain the fundamentals in a fast-paced manner, which will help you by deep diving into the advanced functionalities. Toward the end, we will cover advanced vSphere security features, business continuity, availability, data protection, high availability, monitoring, patching, upgrading, and troubleshooting techniques.

What this book covers

This book is structured in three main parts, starting with a high-level approach, then going in deep on configuration and management aspects, and finally with some aspects related to the maintaining.

Part 1 – From the Basics to Design

Chapter 1, *Evolution of VMware vSphere Suite*, provides a general overview of all the products, solutions, and features of the vSphere 6.5 suite, comparing the evolutions with the previous releases. Also, this chapter explains the reasons to choose (and why not to choose) vSphere 6.5 compared with previous versions or other products. Finally, it includes a general overview of all the products, solutions, and features in other VMware products and different suites that could be complementary or where vSphere represents an infrastructural foundation.

Chapter 2, *Design and Plan a Virtualization Infrastructure*, explains how to approach a virtualization project using reference architectures and best practices, from the analysis of requirements, constraints, and risks to the different types of design (conceptual, logical, and physical). Network and storage aspects are discussed, as well as different vCenter Server and ESXi design and planning aspects. Three different scenarios are used as examples—SMB, Enterprise, and ROBO.

Chapter 3, *Analysis and Assessment of an Existing Environment*, explains how to analyse and assess an existing physical or virtual environment in order to gain the data needed to plan a migration, upgrade, or improvement. Different tools and approaches will be described as ways to reach this goal.

Part 2 – From Deployment to Management

Chapter 4, *Deployment Workflow and Component Installation*, starts with network and storage requirements, host and environment preparation, and then the different ways to install ESXi, including Auto Deploy and other solutions for deploying the host part. It also details the deployment of PSC, vCenter Server, and other components, including vCSA solutions and specific features and capabilities of the new version, 6.5.

Chapter 5, *Configuring and Managing vSphere 6.5*, describes the different ways to manage a vSphere 6.5 infrastructure, including the new HTML5 clients, with an introduction to the scripting and automation tools. ESXi, vCenter, VMware cluster-related configuration, and management topics are also covered in this part.

Chapter 6, *Advanced Network Management*, is dedicated to virtual networking, both with standard and distributed virtual switches and covers the design, management, and optimization of the virtual networks. A brief introduction to new network trends, including NV, NFV, SDS, and how NSX could improve a vSphere environment is also given.

Chapter 7, *Advanced Storage Management*, is dedicated to the storage part of a virtual infrastructure. Starting from local block-based storage and moving on to shared block storage with FC, FCoE, and iSCSI protocols and NFS-based NAS storage. For each of them, we consider different optimization techniques, integration, and storage features provided by vSphere. Other types of storage architectures are also considered, especially HCI solutions. Storage caching and new types of storage, such as virtual NVMe devices, are also covered.

Chapter 8, *Advanced VM and Resource Management*, introduces the practices and procedures involved in configuring and managing of VMs in a vSphere infrastructure. Different types of VM provisioning are considered, including templates, Content Library, VA, and vApps. This chapter will also provide a comprehensive view of vSphere resources management, including reservations, limits, and shares, and how to balance and optimize them in your environment. Finally, we discuss the different migration techniques to move your workload across different environments.

Part 3 – Maintain a Virtual Infrastructure

Chapter 9, *Monitoring, Optimizing, and Troubleshooting*, covers the native tools used for monitor and troubleshoot performance and other issues in order to improve the VM and the workloads. The chapter focuses on monitoring different critical resources, such as computing, storage, and networking across the ESXi hosts, the resource pools, and clusters. Other tools, such as vRealize Operations and third-party tools, are also briefly described.

Chapter 10, *Securing and Protecting Your Environment*, explains that, in addition to the security and hardening aspects of vSphere, the new 6.5 version introduces some new, important features related to this aspect, such as VM Encryption, Encrypted vMotion, Secure Boot Support for VMs, and Secure Boot Plus Cryptographic Hypervisor Assurance for ESXi. In addition, vSphere 6.5 introduces audit-quality logging for vSphere events.

Chapter 11, *Lifecycle Management, Patching, and Upgrading*, explains that with vSphere 6.5, administrators will find significantly more powerful capabilities for patching, upgrading, and managing the configuration of the VM using Update Manager and host profile features. We will also cover the upgrade path and consideration to upgrade or migrate your VM.

Part 4 – Match Your Business Continuity and Service Levels

Chapter 12, *Business Continuity and Disaster Recovery*, describes what's behind normal operation and maintenance in order to define your business continuity requirements and match your expected service levels. Availability, SLA, data and system protection, disaster recovery, and other basics concepts are described in this chapter, with a brief introduction of SRM and SR as a solution for DR.

Chapter 13, *Advanced Availability in vSphere 6.5*, focuses on specific availability (and resiliency) solutions in vSphere, including the new vSphere High Availability (HA) features, proactive HA, vSphere Fault Tolerance (FT), and other solutions, such as guest clustering.

`Chapter 14`, *Data and Workloads Protection*, provides some information on how to save your configuration, data, and workload from your virtual infrastructure. VMware is discontinuing VMware vSphere Data Protection (VDP), a general-purpose backup product included with vSphere, making the related ecosystem the proper way to manage those aspects.

What you need for this book

This book assumes a basic level of VMware vSphere and virtualization knowledge in order to understand all the concepts.

This book requires the following minimum software components: VMware vSphere 6.5 U1, VMware vCenter Server 6.5 U1, and other optional software.

 This book was written in late 2017 (from August to November) using the vSphere 6.5 Update 1 version as a reference. New updates or patches may change some of commands, settings, behaviors, or considerations, so be sure to always verify the release notes of each update.
When applicable, we have used the vSphere Client (the new HTML5 client), but it is still incomplete; for this reason, in some parts of this book, the vSphere Web Client is used instead of the vSphere Client.

The best way to practice without the need for software licenses or hardware components is to try the VMware Hands-on-Labs (`https://labs.hol.vmware.com/`), which cover different products and technologies. The first ones that you should use, if you are new to new features of vSphere 6.5, are:

- HOL-1710-SDC-1 - Introduction to vSphere v6.5
- HOL-1710-SDC-6 - What's New: vSphere 6.5

If you prefer your own lab, there are several hints which type of hardware, if using a big server, with all nested VM and hosts, or a cloud service, for example, Ravello (which can also host nested ESXi). There are also suggestions on how to deploy all software components. One interesting way is using AutoLab (`http://www.labguides.com/autolab/`), but version 2.6 does not support vSphere 6.5; or just look on the blogs of Alan Renouf and William Lam, where you can found some powerful scripts to build an entire vSphere 6.5 (also with vSAN and NSX!).

Who this book is for

To make use of the contents of this book, a basic prior knowledge of VMware vSphere and virtualization is expected.

This book is for users such as data center administrators and IT architects who have already worked with the VMware vSphere platform, perhaps previous versions, and want to know more about vSphere 6.5.

The audience will be technical and focused on the architecture and may be VMware Certified Professionals (VCPs) or higher.

Conventions

In this book, you will find a number of text styles that distinguish between different kinds of information. Here are some examples of these styles and an explanation of their meaning. Code words in text, database table names, folder names, filenames, file extensions, pathnames, dummy URLs, user input, and Twitter handles are shown as follows: "We used the command Get-VM to retrieve a list of running VMs in the vCenter Server instance."

A block of code is set as follows:

```
Get-VM | Select-Object Name,NumCPU,MemoryMB,PowerState,Host | Export-
CSV VMinfo.csv -NoTypeInformation
```

Any command-line input or output is written as follows:

```
ppm install XML-LibXML
```

New terms and **important words** are shown in bold. Words that you see on the screen, for example, in menus or dialog boxes, appear in the text like this: "Right-click on the host once again and select the **All vCenter Actions** | **Remove from Inventory** option"

Warnings or important notes appear like this.

Tips and tricks appear like this.

Reader feedback

Feedback from our readers is always welcome. Let us know what you think about this book-what you liked or disliked. Reader feedback is important for us as it helps us develop titles that you will really get the most out of. To send us general feedback, simply e-mail feedback@packtpub.com, and mention the book's title in the subject of your message. If there is a topic that you have expertise in and you are interested in either writing or contributing to a book, see our author guide at www.packtpub.com/authors.

Customer Support

Now that you are the proud owner of a Packt book, we have a number of things to help you to get the most from your purchase.

Downloading the color images for this book

We also provide you with a PDF file that has color images of the screenshots/diagrams used in this book. The color images will help you better understand the changes in the output. You can download this file from https://www.packtpub.com/sites/default/files/downloads/MasteringVMwarevSphere6.5_ColorImages.pdf.

Errata

Although we have taken every care to ensure the accuracy of our content, mistakes do happen. If you find a mistake in one of our books-maybe a mistake in the text or the code-we would be grateful if you could report this to us. By doing so, you can save other readers from frustration and help us improve subsequent versions of this book. If you find any errata, please report them by visiting http://www.packtpub.com/submit-errata, selecting your book, clicking on the **Errata Submission Form** link, and entering the details of your errata. Once your errata is verified, your submission will be accepted and the errata will be uploaded to our website or added to any list of existing errata under the Errata section of that title. To view the previously submitted errata, go to https://www.packtpub.com/books/content/support and enter the name of the book in the search field. The required information will appear under the **Errata** section.

Piracy

Piracy of copyrighted material on the Internet is an ongoing problem across all media. At Packt, we take the protection of our copyright and licenses very seriously. If you come across any illegal copies of our works in any form on the Internet, please provide us with the location address or website name immediately so that we can pursue a remedy. Please contact us at copyright@packtpub.com with a link to the suspected pirated material. We appreciate your help in protecting our authors and our ability to bring you valuable content.

Questions

If you have a problem with any aspect of this book, you can contact us at questions@packtpub.com, and we will do our best to address the problem.

1
Evolution of VMware vSphere Suite

VMware vSphere 6.5 is the latest version of the most used enterprise virtualization platform. A good understanding of this product and its features is crucial for a successful implementation.

In this chapter, we provide a better understanding of the VMware product portfolio, vision, and evolution, learn what's new in vSphere 6.5, and introduce the different solutions, features, and editions of vSphere. Also, some hints have been provided for choosing the right editions and version of vSphere and choosing when to upgrade to vSphere 6.5 and when not to upgrade.

Finally, there is a general overview of all the products, solutions and features in other VMware products, or different suite, where vSphere represents an infrastructural foundation, or where those products could be complementary to vSphere.

This chapter will cover the following topics:

- VMware product portfolio
- What's new on vSphere 6.5 and vSphere limits
- Why you should upgrade to vSphere 6.5 and why not
- Features and editions of vSphere 6.5
- VMware vSphere as an infrastructure pillar (with a brief overview of VMware products that require vSphere, including containers)
- Overview of other VMware products that could be useful with vSphere

VMware and vSphere background

When we talk about VMware, most of you; probably will think about virtualization, and when we talk about virtualization, the first name that probably comes to mind will be **VMware vSphere**. VMware's history is strictly related to virtualization, as it was the first commercially successful company to virtualize the x86 architecture (in the late 1990s), making a new era and a new wave in **information technology (IT)** possible.

IT historical waves were the mainframe, the PC, the network; now they are followed by virtualization and cloud computing shown as follows:

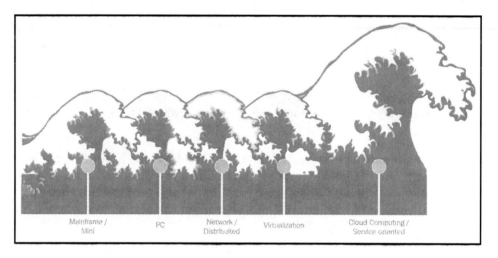

IT waves

Although the first commercial virtualization product from VMware was **Workstation**—which was targeted at the client-side server; virtualization, first with GSX, and then with ESX/ESXi, has rapidly grown in importance in just a few years. Server virtualization has become real and accessible to most, but more importantly, it has brought so many advantages (also from an economic point of view) and improved to such a level as to make the virtualization first approach the norm. The VMware vSphere suite includes ESXi (the evolution of ESX Server) for the virtualization layer and vCenter Server for the management layer.

VMware vSphere leverages the power of virtualization to transform data centers into simplified cloud computing infrastructures and enables IT organizations to deliver flexible and reliable IT services. VMware vSphere virtualizes and aggregates the underlying physical hardware resources across multiple systems and provides pools of virtual resources to the data center.

Compute virtualization is only the first step; in order to move to a real cloud computing infrastructure, you will not only need to compute resources abstraction (provided by virtualization), but also operation automation and agility (both of them only partially obtainable through virtualization). Finally, this approach should be applied not only to the compute part but also to the other resources, such as storage, networking, and security.

In 2012, former VMware CTO Steve Herrod explained this vision with the new concept of the **software-defined data center (SDDC)**, where all infrastructure elements (computing, networking, storage, and security) are virtualized and delivered as a service using a cloud computing model:

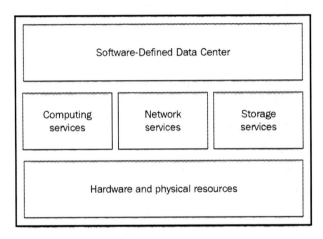

Software-defined data center

Virtualization is no longer the final destination of the digital transformation journey; it has become the starting point, an essential requirement, and a foundation for digital businesses. VMware has addressed these needs by extending both its product portfolio and its vision.

VMware has grown its product portfolio with several other products (some of them from important acquisitions, such as Nicira in 2012) in order to accelerate the digital transformation of its customers through a software-defined approach to business and IT. With more than 500,000 customers globally, VMware remains a proven leader not only in virtualization, but also in all technologies related to digital transformation.

But what is digital transformation and why is it so important? All enterprises (but potentially all companies) are becoming digital businesses by using digital technology to drive innovation and new business models. Digital transformation is all about creating new possibilities for the business.

As defined in *Gartner, 2016 CEO Survey: The Year of Digital Tenacity, Analyst: Mark Raskino, April 20, 2016:*

> "*50% of CEOs expect their industries to be substantially or unrecognizably transformed by digital.*"

VMware's vision is to help the digital transformation of those companies by providing flexibility, freedom, and control for the IT infrastructure and services. But the vision has slightly changed through the years. In 2015, VMware's vision was *one cloud, any application, and any device*, where the one-cloud model was totally based on VMware products and solutions (using the vSphere platform as a common platform).

According to VMware's vision at the time, by having a common platform both on-premises and on the public part, it would have been possible to build a hybrid cloud model, in order to have full portability of your workloads. Unfortunately, the vCloud Air project (an IaaS public cloud service offered by VMware) has not gone as expected (and on May 8, 2017, this asset was sold to OVH), so this vision has changed.

During VMworld 2016, VMware has announced a more realistic vision: *any device, any application, any cloud*. Not only one cloud, but now any cloud:

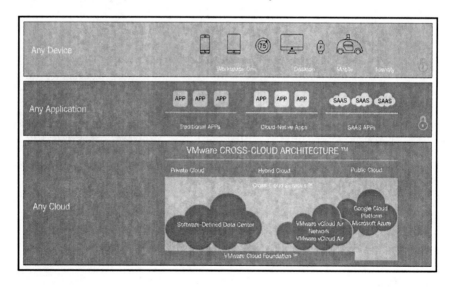

VMware vision: any device, any application, any cloud

Image source: https://www.vmware.com/radius/vmworld-2016-pat-gelsinger-keynote-recap/

VMworld 2017 has confirmed this vision, where vSphere remains the foundation of the underlying infrastructure, at least for the on-premises part, and a new suite has been introduced—**VMware Cloud Foundation**.

VMware Cloud Foundation is VMware's unified SDDC platform for the hybrid cloud and it's based on VMware's compute, storage, and network virtualization technologies to deliver a native integrated software stack that can be used on-premises for private cloud deployment or run as a service from the public cloud with consistent and simple operations.

The core components of VMware Cloud Foundation are VMware vSphere, **Virtual SAN (vSAN)** for the storage part, and NSX, for the network and security part. VMware Cloud Foundation also comes with VMware SDDC Manager that automates the entire system life cycle and simplifies software operations as described in the following figure:

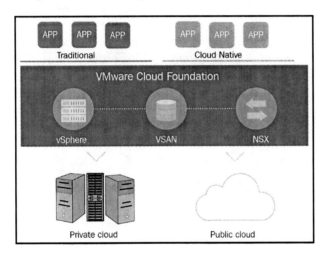

VMware Cloud Foundation

In addition, it can be further integrated with VMware vRealize Suite (added in version 2.3), VMware Horizon, and VMware Integrated OpenStack. The idea behind the any-cloud vision is to still have a common part (the VMware Cloud Foundation) to provide resources interoperability and mobility for building an effective hybrid cloud.

Cloud Foundation was released in September 2016 and is actually on version 2.3 (released on December 2017). For the private cloud, you can buy pre-assembled and configured integrated systems directly from different vendors (Dell-EMC with the vxRack SDDC, Fujitsu with PRIMEFLEX, HPE with Synergy, to give some examples) or you can build, assemble, and image with help from a partner or VMware PSO.

This book will not cover the Cloud Foundation deployment or upgrade path, but will be focused on the specific part of vSphere 6.5 (that is one of the pillars of Cloud Foundation).

For the public cloud, VMware has built some important and strategic partnerships to provide interoperability with VMware Cloud Foundation, initially with IBM (`https://www. ibm.com/cloud-computing/solutions/ibm-vmware/`) and then also with Amazon AWS (`https://www.vmware.com/cloud-services/vmware-cloud-aws.html`) with a service sold and supported by VMware as an on-demand, elastically scalable solution. The second one, according to the demos, seems the most promising due to the seamless integration with the vSphere management interface.

VMware Cloud on **Amazon Web Services (AWS)**, actually only available in the US, is a vSphere-based cloud service offered directly by VMware, but with resources and hosting on AWS. The new service will bring our enterprise-class SDDC software to the AWS cloud. And during VMworld EU 2017, other cloud solutions based on VMware vSphere provided by VMware's partners were also announced. The first is **VMware HCX** (`https:// cloud.vmware.com/vmware-hcx`) that provides application mobility and a cross-cloud infrastructure, initially with IBM and OVH (probably in late 2017). Similar, in the results, to VMware Cloud on AWS, but not sold directly from VMware and more compatible with previous vSphere versions (seems from 5.5). Second, the provider partner program has changed its name and there is a new **VMware Cloud Verified** status for selected partners.

VMware vSphere as a Cloud Foundation

VMware vSphere remains an important piece of VMware's vision, not only as a cloud OS or an infrastructure part, but also a universal application platform that supports both traditional and next-generation applications (the so-called cloud-native applications). While these two worlds are vastly different, both require infrastructure with the scalability, performance, and availability capabilities needed to meet key business objectives.

VMware vSphere 6.5 also lets you run applications from any cloud, including your data center or in public cloud environments. For this reason, vSphere 6.5 is not only the heart of the SDDC, it's also the foundation of VMware's cloud strategy. vSphere 6.5 is available in both the private cloud and as a service through a public cloud. The new products or solutions, such as VMware Cloud Foundation, VMware Cloud on AWS, and vSphere Integrated Containers, are all built on vSphere 6.5.

To run any application, vSphere 6.5 expands its workload coverage model by focusing on both scale-up and scale-out next-generation applications that are increasingly built using evolving technology building blocks such as containers.

Virtual Machine (VM) versus containers

A container image is a lightweight, standalone, executable package of a piece of software that includes everything needed to run it—code, runtime, system tools, system libraries, and settings.

Containers and VMs have similar resource isolation (maybe you can argue that virtualization provides better isolation) and allocation benefits, but function differently because containers do not include the operating system part (or at least not the kernel part of it) and containers are more *light*, so potentially more portable and efficient.

Docker's website describes in detail the differences between containers and VMs, starting with the architectural difference:

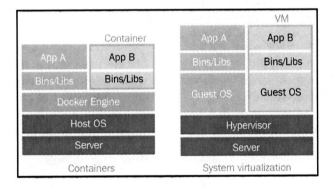

Containers versus VMs

For more details on containers, refer to `https://www.docker.com/what-container`.

Container technologies have become ubiquitous in the modern data center; their advantages for application packaging are undeniable. Developers are leading the change, adopting container technologies at a rapid rate, and demonstrating their advantages by bringing both new and updated applications to market sooner. One approach in order to solve these challenges could be **Containers as a Service (CaaS)** to all developers, providing them with better agility but, at the same time, also providing the level of standardization and governance necessary to run containers in production.

So which is best, or why have containers not replaced virtualization yet? There is not a simple answer; for sure, containers are lighter when compared to VMs, but on the other hand, not all applications can run in a container. Put simply, legacy applications will still require VMs, while new applications designed with modern approaches are the ideal candidates to run on containers.

 Initially, containers were only possible for Linux-based applications (and some specific lightweight, minimal Linux distributions such as CoreOS and VMware Photon OS were born specifically to support Linux containers) but, starting with Windows Server 2016, Windows applications can also be containerized (of course, with no portability across these two different platforms).

In the vSphere 6.5 release, VMware introduced **vSphere Integrated Containers (VIC)**, a platform to bring containers into an existing vSphere environment in a simple and easy way. With VIC, it is possible to deliver an enterprise container infrastructure that provides not only agility for developers (by using the containers) but also full control for vSphere operations teams, where containers can now be managed with the same concepts and skills as *normal* VMs, without requiring any changes in processes or tools.

VMware VIC is structured into the following different components:

- **VIC Engine**: Enterprise container runtime for vSphere that allows developers who are familiar with Docker to develop in containers and deploy them alongside traditional VM-based workloads on vSphere clusters. vSphere admins can manage these workloads through vSphere Web Client in a way that is familiar to them.
- **Virtual Container Host (VCH)**: This is basically a vSphere resource pool used for controlling and consuming some container services, with an isolated Docker API endpoint and a private network. Multiple VCHs can be deployed in an environment, depending on business requirements.
- **vSphere Web Client plugin**: Administrators interact with VIC through vSphere Web Client, gaining the ability to manage and monitor VIC by means of a plugin. A wizard is available that enables the creation of VCHs.

- **Photon OS**: This is a small-footprint container runtime for the containers, running on a VM. VIC will run each individual container on a dedicated VM (in order to have the best isolation and security enforcement) with PhonOS on each VM. In order to provide agility during VM provisioning, the new Instant Clone Technology (introduced in vSphere 6) will be used to deliver all VMs very quickly and efficiently.

- **VMware Harbor**: Enterprise container registry that stores and distributes container images. Harbor extends the Docker distribution open source project by adding the functionalities usually required by an enterprise, such as security, identity, and management.

- **VMware Admiral**: Management portal that provides a UI for dev teams to provision and manage containers. Cloud administrators can manage container hosts and apply governance to their usage, including capacity quotas, and approval workflows. Advanced capabilities are available when integrated with vRealize Automation.

For more details on the following architecture overview, you can visit the related VMware blog at https://blogs.vmware.com/cloudnative/:

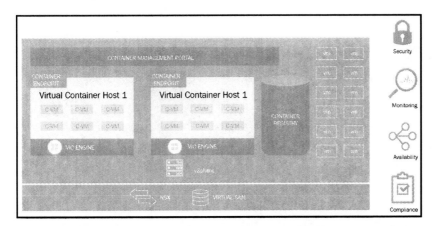

VMware VIC

Using VIC, vSphere administrators can provide a full Docker compatible interface to their developers, using the existing vSphere infrastructure with native capabilities and features, including VMware NSX for security and VMware vSAN for storage. The new version 1.2 (released in September 2017) adds a native Docker container host, from a unified management portal.

Customers with current vSphere Enterprise Plus or vSphere Operations Management Enterprise Plus licenses can download the VIC installation packages below.

Other parts, such as Photon OS, are free and available for everybody. It's also interesting to notice that Photon OS Linux is becoming the platform for the VMware virtual appliance, first with the vCenter Server Virtual Appliance, then with NSX controllers (with NSX-v 6.3.3.), and probably with more in the near future.

For more information, see the following:

- *vSphere Integrated Containers – Technology Walkthrough:* `https://blogs.vmware.com/vsphere/2015/10/vsphere-integrated-containers-technology-walkthrough.html`
- *vSphere Integrated Containers 1.1 Delivers New User Experience Enhancements*: `https://blogs.vmware.com/cloudnative/2017/04/18/vsphere-integrated-containers-1-1-delivers-new-user-experience-enhancements/`
- *vSphere Integrated Containers v1.2 Introduces Support for Native Docker Container Hosts*: `https://blogs.vmware.com/cloudnative/2017/09/12/vsphere-integrated-containers-v1-2/`

VMware vSphere as an infrastructure foundation

If virtualization has become mainstream and we are living in a post-virtualization era (that is, the cloud computing wave), does this imply that virtualization is now less important and that hypervisors are just a commodity service? Several experts think so and VMworld 2014 and 2015 may have confirmed this (there were no new vSphere products or features announced, except vSAN and other vSphere related products).

Also, other hypervisors (for example, **Hyper-V** or **Nutanix AHV**) have grown really fast both in features and in market share, although VMware vSphere still remains the main solution on-premises (we will not consider public clouds or service providers where KVM, Xen, Hyper-V are the most used platforms).

But the platform is still relevant, at least for VMware, and with vSphere 6.5, they brought attention back to the infrastructure part; vSphere is still needed by several VMware products as a core infrastructure component. Let's see a brief description of some of these products and how they require a vSphere platform.

Storage platform

Since 2014, VMware has also become a storage vendor with an interesting solution called vSAN—a software-based solution to build **Hyper-Converged Infrastructure (HCI)** systems. With more than 8,000 customers acquired in only a few years and lot of releases, vSAN is the HCI solution that is growing fastest.

But the interesting part is that vSAN is a native vSphere storage solution, that seamlessly extends local storage on each host, making a shared and resilient storage system, and creating a hyper-converged platform that simply works with most of the vSphere skills and all the existing tools, software solutions, and hardware platforms.

For more details about vSAN and HCI, see Chapter 7, *Advanced Storage Management*.

Network and security platform

VMware has begun to include network and security capabilities in a virtualized computing environment based on vSphere with the vCloud Networking and Security product.

With the Nicira acquisition, this product has been replaced by NSX, a network virtualization solution (or network overlay solution) that enables the creation of entire networks in software and embeds them in the hypervisor layer, abstracted from the underlying physical hardware. All network components can be provisioned in minutes, without the need to modify the application or the physical environment.

NSX-V is tightly integrated with vSphere components requiring both ESXi (used both as a data plane and also for hosting some NFV and VMs used as a control plane) and vCenter (NSX manager is paired with it and the management interface is just an extension of vSphere Web Client). Although, there is also an NSX edition for Linux systems (NSX-T), for NSX-V, the vSphere platform is the foundation.

For more details about NSX, *see* Chapter 6, *Advanced Network Management*.

Cloud platform

Cloud computing is the new wave after virtualization and VMware vSphere lacks a true multi-tenant support and partial automation and agility.

For this reason, VMware has several products for cloud management, addressed at private or public cloud scenarios. The most important VMware cloud-capable solutions are **vCloud Director (vCD)** and **vRealize Automation (vRA)**. VMware vCD was the first product (if we exclude Lab Manager, which was not truly multi-tenant) to bring full cloud capabilities to vSphere.

Actually, this product is still present, but it is reserved only for service providers willing to build and sell public cloud services as part of the VMware **vCloud Air Network (vCAN)** program based on top of the vSphere platform; these offerings are inherently hybrid-aware and ideal for enterprise-class organizations that want to extend their VMware-based private cloud into the public one.

In 2012, VMware acquired DynamicOps, a provider of cloud automation solutions that enable provisioning and management of IT services across heterogeneous environments. VMware vRA is a product of this acquisition and enables IT automation through the creation and management of personalized infrastructure, application, and custom IT services (XaaS). This IT automation lets you deploy IT services rapidly across a multi-vendor, multi-cloud infrastructure. In this case, the underlying infrastructure could be vSphere-based (probably the most common choice) but vRA can be extended to orchestrate and automate other non-VMware hypervisors and clouds, making possible a true multi-vendor and multi-cloud approach.

Of course, there are other types of cloud management platform (such as OpenStack), but in this case, VMware vSphere could be just a possible choice, not necessarily the main one.

End-user computing platform

Horizon 7 provides a streamlined approach to delivering, protecting, and managing **Virtual Desktop Infrastructure (VDI)** and applications while containing costs and ensuring that end users can work anytime, anywhere, across any device.

The Horizon for view part (related to VDI) is tightly integrated with VMware vSphere, requiring both vCenter Server (that is managed by the View Manager and is needed to perform provisioning and VM management) and ESXi (that is used to host the VDIs). There are some exceptions, such as if you are using manual pools of dedicated (and pre-provisioned) VMs.

Also, note that there are now some new offers, such as Horizon Cloud on Microsoft Azure (`https://blogs.vmware.com/euc/2017/10/vmware-horizon-cloud-on-microsoft-azure-now-available.html`).

Container platform

Containers do not require virtualization at all, because they can run on bare metal. And you can use different solutions for managing and deploying them.

But in the VMware vision, VMware vSphere is used to provide a CaaS solution with two different approaches:

- Using VIC (previously described), useful if you have containers that you need to put into production and use your existing production VM monitoring systems to monitor individual containers
- Using vRA to deploy VMs (with Photon OS or Core OS) that can host multiple containers

Both approaches have a similar infrastructure and only the management part is different depending on whether you have vRA for cloud management, orchestration, and automation.

And of course, vSphere may be not needed at all, because containers can run on bare metal or other platforms, and be managed by other tools. Also, in this case, VMware can still be present, because Linux-based containers still need an operating system to run on, and VMware Photon OS could be a possible option.

For more information, see *Choosing a Container as a Service (CaaS) Solution* at `https://blogs.vmware.com/services-education-insights/2017/07/choosing-container-service-caas-solution.html`.

Other VMware products complementary to vSphere

VMware has a plethora of other products for different segments and some of them could be interesting to adopt in a vSphere environment, for example:

- **vRealize Operations**: This is a monitoring tool used to improve application performance, prevent business disruptions, and make IT more efficient. There is also a specific SKU of vSphere Essentials Plus that includes the operations component. We will describe some of its features in `Chapter 9`, *Monitoring, Optimizing, and Troubleshooting.*

- **vRealize Log Insight**: This is useful to collect logs from different sources (not necessarily only ESXi hosts) and analyze that data. VMware users with a supported vCenter Server license (version 5.x or 6.x) are entitled to a 25-OSI pack of *vRealize Log Insight for vCenter Server* (see `http://kb.vmware.com/kb/2144909`). We will describe some of its features in `Chapter 9`, *Monitoring, Optimizing, and Troubleshooting.*

- **Site Recovery Manager**: This product is an orchestrator to simplify the site disaster recovery plan in a single-click procedure, with the capability to test it in safe mode and to handle not only the fail-over procedures (planned or unplanned) but also fail-backs. This product is designed to manage only **disaster recovery** (DR) for vSphere environments. We will describe some of its features in `Chapter 12`, *Business Continuity and Disaster Recovery.*

- **VMware Integrated OpenStack (VIO)**: This is a VMware supported OpenStack distribution that makes it easier for IT to run a production-grade OpenStack-based deployment on top of their existing VMware vSphere infrastructure.

What's new on vSphere 6.5 and vSphere limits?

Even if VMware vSphere seems a minor release, there are many improvements, and changes that could be considered in the same way as a new release with new functionalities and new limits.

What's new in 6.5?

VMware vSphere 6.5 became **generally available (GA)** on November 15, 2016, several years after the initial release of version 6.0 (GA was on March 12, 2012), bringing several new features and improvements to the vSphere platform.

At a high level, the new version focuses on the following four main areas of innovation:

- **Simplified customer experience**: There are several improvements in **vCenter Server Appliance (vCSA)** features and capabilities, with a new modern and truly multi-platform client (finally HTML5-based) and a simple REST based API for automation and integration
- **Comprehensive built-in security**: It uses the well-known policy-driven approach also used for security aspects at scale to secure data, infrastructure, and access
- **Universal app platform**: Following the VMware vision, vSphere 6.5 could be a single platform to support any application on any cloud as discussed previously
- **Proactive data center management**: It has become predictive in order to address potential issues before they can become serious issues

At a technical level, the different improvements are as follows:

- **Scale enhancements**: There are new configuration maximums to support even the largest application environments (see the next paragraph for the different numbers).
- **VMware vCSA**: This is now the preferred type of vCenter and the core building block for vSphere. Not only does it now have the same features as the Windows version, but it has new specific functions—a native vCenter Server high availability solution, native vCenter Server backup and restore, migration tool from existing vCenter Server (also in a previous version) to vCSA.
- **VMware vSphere Update Manager (VUM)**: In vSphere 6.5, it has been fully integrated with vCSA. This integration eliminates the additional resources required for another VM, OS license, and database dependencies of the previous architecture. Integrated VUM leverages the vPostgres installation that is part of vCSA, but the data is stored using a separate schema.
- **VMware Tools**: There are several improvements (such as digital signed ISO), but also some changes in supported OS and supported levels, including a bifurcation of VMware Tools for legacy and current guests.
- **REST APIs**: These are simple, modern developer-friendly APIs to integrate your vSphere environment in other management platforms. Also, other CLIs have been extended and improved.

- **vSphere Client**: This is a new HTML5-based GUI, similar to the VMware Host Client, that ensures fast performance, cross-platform and multi-OS compatibility. Note that the vCenter installer is now also supported on Microsoft Windows, macOS, and Linux operating systems without the need for any plugins.

- **Content library**: This was introduced in vCenter 6.0, but with some limitations. Now it's possible to mount an ISO directly from the content library, apply a guest OS customization specification during VM deployment, and update existing templates.

- **Security at scale**: This is a new policy-driven security framework that makes securing infrastructure operationally simple using the same approach as the already existing policy-driven storage.

- **Encryption**: VM-level encryption protects unauthorized data access both at rest and in motion.

- **Audit-quality logging**: There is enhanced logging that provides forensic information about user actions.

- **Secure Boot**: This protects both the hypervisor and guest operating system by ensuring images have not been tampered with and preventing loading of unauthorized components.

- **Proactive HA**: There is high availability capability that utilizes server health information and migrates VMs from degraded hosts before a problem occurs.

- **Cross-Cloud vMotion**: Live migrates workloads between VMware-based clouds.

- **Virtual Volumes Replication**: Extends **Virtual Volumes (vVols)** support (introduced in v6.0) with native array vVols replication.

- **Virtual NVM Express (NVMe) and others new controllers**: With hardware version 13, you can use NVMe, SATA, SCSI, and IDE controllers in a VM.

 All these features will be discussed in upcoming chapters of this book.

For more information, see the following links:

- https://www.packtpub.com/virtualization-and-cloud/mastering-vmware-vsphere-65-video

- https://blogs.vmware.com/vsphere/launch

- https://blogs.vmware.com/vsphere/2016/10/introducing-vsphere-6-5.html

- https://featurewalkthrough.vmware.com/#!/vsphere-6-5

- https://www.vmware.com/content/dam/digitalmarketing/vmware/en/pdf/
  whitepaper/vsphere/vmw-white-paper-vsphr-whats-new-6-5.pdf
- https://blogs.vmware.com/vsphere/2017/07/vsphere-6-5-update-1-hood.
  html
- http://blogs.vmware.com/vsphere/2016/10/whats-new-in-vsphere-6-5-
  vcenter-server.html
- http://blogs.vmware.com/vsphere/2016/10/whats-new-in-vsphere-6-5-
  security.html
- http://blogs.vmware.com/vsphere/2016/10/whats-new-in-vsphere-6-5-host-
  resource-management-and-operations.html

What's new with vSphere 6.5 Update 1?

VMware vSphere 6.5 Update 1 was released on August 2, 2017, and it adds some bug fixes, new features, and also a key additional change in the support and license of vCenter Server:

- **vCenter Server Foundation can now manage and support four ESXi hosts**: Although three hosts could be enough for smaller environments, VMware has received feedback that three host environments were too small in some **small and medium-sized business (SMB)** cases. For this reason, vSphere 6.5 Update 1 is now increasing the number of hosts that vCenter Server Foundation will support from three hosts to four.
- **vSphere 6.5 general support has been extended**: VMware understands that upgrading infrastructure can be a lengthy process. One consideration for whether or not to upgrade is how long the new product will be supported. VMware wants to make the customer's decision to upgrade easier by extending general support for vSphere 6.5 for a full 5 years. This means that support for vSphere 6.5 will now end on November 15, 2021.
- **Upgrade path**: Direct upgrade from vSphere 6.0 Update 3 is now a supported path (more details on the upgrade path will be provided in Chapter 11, *Lifecycle Management, Patching, and Upgrade*).
- **Adds full support for ESXi on Mac Pro 6,1 hardware**: Many customers and home lab users like to use Mac hardware in order to virtualize macOS in an officially supported manner. VMware vSphere 6.5 Update 1 adds full support for ESXi on Mac Pro 6,1 hardware. So, if virtualizing macOS is your thing, you can now do it with the latest hardware and without workarounds.

Also, there are some interesting enhancements, including the following:

- vSphere Client now supports 90% of general workflows and features; the new HTML5-based vSphere Client can now support up to 90% of general workflows. This is welcome news as VMware pushes towards 100% parity between the various clients (considering also that Adobe has recently announced the end of Flash Player support by the end of 2020).
- There is a new version of vSAN 6.6.1 with new capabilities, such as VUM support in order to manage vSAN software upgrades easily.
- VMware vSphere 6.5 Update 1 is required to enable VMware Cloud on AWS.
- New limits for vCenter Server in Linked Mode (see next paragraph, in the numbers specific for vCenter Server).

For more information, consult the release notes at `https://docs.vmware.com/en/VMware-vSphere/6.5/rn/vsphere-esxi-651-release-notes.html`.

Configuration maximums

As usual, the maximum numbers are published in a specific document and grouped by types. The vSphere 6.5 configuration maximums guide has already been updated with the new 6.5 U1 numbers (`https://docs.vmware.com/en/VMware-vSphere/6.5/vsp-esxi-vcenter-server-651-configuration-maximums-guide.pdf`). The most interesting numbers, as compared to the previous versions are described in the following paragraphs.

VM

With this new version of vSphere, there is a new version of the VM virtual hardware (version 13). Some limits and features (virtual RAM, NVMe controllers) are available only with the new virtual hardware 13; other limits are also valid for previous versions of virtual hardware. For more details refer to *VMware vSphere Virtual Machine Administration* guide at `https://docs.vmware.com/en/VMware-vSphere/6.5/com.vmware.vsphere.vm_admin.doc/GUID-789C3913-1053-4850-A0F0-E29C3D32B6DA.htm`.

The following table summarizes some of the maximums numbers for each VM in the different version of vSphere:

	vSphere 4.0	vSphere 4.1	vSphere 5.0	vSphere 5.1	vSphere 5.5	vSphere 6.0	vSphere 6.5
Virtual CPU	8	8	32	64	64	128	128
Virtual RAM	255 GB	255 GB	1 TB	1 TB	1 TB	4 TB	6128 GB
Max VMDK size	2 TB – 512 B	2 TB – 512 B	2 TB – 512 B	2 TB – 512 B	62 TB	62 TB	62 TB
Virtual SCSI adapters	4	4	4	4	4	4	4
Virtual SCSI target	60	60	60	60	60	60	60
Virtual NICs	10	10	10	10	10	10	10
Virtual NVMe adapters	NA	NA	NA	NA	NA	NA	4

Table 1.1: Maximums numbers for each VM in the different version of vSphere

Those limits can change if you are using VMware FT to protect your VMs and the real limits, in this case, will be lower. More details will be provided in Chapter 13, *Advanced Availability in vSphere 6.5*.

Host ESXi 6.5

ESXi hosts limits remain mostly the same from version 6.0 but, of course, new hardware and new devices are now supported. Scalability remains quite similar compared with version 6.0, as summarized in the following table :

	vSphere 4.0	vSphere 4.1	vSphere 5.0	vSphere 5.1	vSphere 5.5	vSphere 6.0	vSphere 6.5
Logical CPU	64	160	160	160	320	480	576
Physical RAM	1 TB	1 TB	2 TB	2 TB	4 TB	12 TB	12 TB
NUMA nodes	NA	NA	8 nodes	8 nodes	16 nodes	16 nodes	16 nodes
Virtual CPU	512	512	2048	2048	4096	4096	4096
VMs	320	320	512	512	512	1024	1024
LUNs (iSCSI/FC)	256	256	256	256	256	256	512*
NFS mounts	64	64	256	256	256	256	256
LUN size	64 TB	64 TB	64 TB	64 TB	64 TB	64 TB	64 TB

Table 1.2: Scalability comparison with different versions

* The official document reports 512, but the Disk.MaxLUN advanced settings report 1024 on a ESXi 6.5 host.

In most cases, there is 2x increase from vSphere 5.5.

vCenter Server 6.5

The vCSA version of vCenter Server will now have the same limits as the Windows installable version (also with the embedded DB). And finally, the vCSA is now the first choice (the Windows version will be deprecated in the next releases), including some new features available only for it. The following table summarizes the different numbers from the different versions of vCenter Servers:

	vSphere 4.0	vSphere 4.1	vSphere 5.0	vSphere 5.1	vSphere 5.5	vSphere 6.0	vSphere 6.5
Hosts per vCenter	300	1000	1000	1000	1000	1000	2000
Hosts per data center	100	400	500	500	500	500	200
Hosts per cluster	32	32	32	32	32	64	64
VMs per cluster	1280	3000	3000	4000	4000	8000	8000
Powered on VMs	3000	10000	10000	10000	10000	10000	25000
Registered VMs	4500	15000	15000	15000	15000	15000	35000
Linked vCenter Servers	10	10	10	10	10	10	15

Table 1.3: Different numbers from the different versions of vCenter Servers

There is a 2x increase as compared to previous vCenter Server 6.0.

Some numbers have been increased with vSphere 6.5 Update 1 when you are using more vCenter in Linked Mode (that defines a vSphere domain):

- **Maximum vCenter Servers per vSphere domain**: 15 (increased from 10)
- **Maximum ESXi hosts per vSphere domain**: 5,000 (increased from 4,000)
- **Maximum powered on VMs per vSphere domain**: 50,000 (increased from 30,000)
- **Maximum registered VMs per vSphere domain**: 70,000 (increased from 50,000)

Why you should upgrade to vSphere 6.5 and why not?

Despite the number, vSphere 6.5 does not represent a minor release of vSphere 6.0 but a new major release (the same considerations were possible with vSphere 5.0, 5.1, and 5.5). For this reason, you have to plan carefully whether to upgrade and how to upgrade. Finally, with vSphere 6.5 Update 1, it is possible to upgrade from vSphere 6.0 Update 3 (this was not supported in the previous version of 6.5).

Customers who are still on vSphere 5.5 will need to be at least on vSphere 5.5 Update 3b in order to upgrade to vSphere 6.5 U1.

There are several changes but also new features and scalability properties that make vSphere 6.5 interesting for new environments, but also for existing customers.

Existing 6.0 customers already have the right license keys, while 5.x customers will need to have an active subscription in order to upgrade their 5.x license keys to version 6.x.

The main consideration to make with regard to the upgrade is that each new product (it does not matter whether it is a major or a minor release) brings new features, new code, and potentially maybe also new bugs (and the history of vSphere 5.1 and 6.0 has demonstrated that early adopters came across some issues). Of course, upgrading might also fix some existing bugs. But the maturity of a new release might not be the same as the previous versions. So, before upgrading, evaluate the new release by first using it in a dev or test environment or wait a few months to see the first feedback from the community and reported issues, and how and when they have been solved. Some prefer to wait for the first Update 1 version and, finally, it is here. To be honest, the code of the initial 6.5 release already seemed to be more mature than that of version 6.0 in its infancy.

You also have to consider all third-party code, included drivers or services, and kernel modules (for example, PernixData FVP is not compatible with 6.5) or switch extensions (after vSphere 6.5 Update 1, customers using third-party virtual switches such as the IBM DVS 5000v, HPE 5900v, and Cisco Nexus 1000v will need to migrate off of those switches prior to upgrading to any future release), vCenter plugins or integration with external software, for example, backup products. For third-party switches see KB 2149722—*Discontinuation of third party vSwitch program* at `https://kb.vmware.com/kb/2149722`.

Remember also that vSphere may be just a foundation of a bigger solution and architecture (as described before); in this case, you have to check every piece of software and hardware to match the compatibility and supported version.

 More details on the upgrade procedure will be provided in `Chapter 11`, *Lifecycle Management, Patching, and Upgrade*.

Why upgrade?

There can be several reasons to upgrade vSphere to the latest version:

- **Extend the support and the life cycle of the product**: VMware vSphere 5.5 will have an extended support and will reach end of general support in September 2018, VMware vSphere 6.0 on March 2020, and vSphere 6.5 on November 15, 2021.
- **Have a new product**: It provides new features but also new hardware (and other new software) may require or have some benefit from this version.
- **New infrastructure functions**: Such as the new high availability features; we will discuss all those functions in upcoming chapters.
- **New security functions**: Some are really cool and unique, but data at rest protection using encryption could also be possible not only at hypervisor level (in this case only with 6.5) but also at storage level (also vSAN now has this capability).
- **Storage benefits**: If you are using vVols, you can now have a native replication support (of course, if your storage vendor supports it in vSphere 6.5). If you are using vSAN, the only way to upgrade it and have new features is to upgrade vSphere.
- **New web client (vSphere Client)**: Finally, we have an HTML5 client (not 100% complete, but very close, at least for operational tasks) for the vCenter Server graphical management. For the ESXi host, there was already (starting from 6.0 Update 2). Note that you can add both the HTML5 clients to the previous version using Flings software (`https://labs.vmware.com/flings`).
- **New vCSA**: The new virtual appliance for vCenter is definitely the first choice, due to the full capabilities and also for the new functions.

Why shouldn't you upgrade?

There can be few reasons to skip the upgrade to vSphere 6.5 which are as follows:

- *Is it compatible?* You may have a software or hardware part that does not support this version. Note that from the next version of vSphere, several generations of servers will probably no longer be supported (for example, if you install ESXi 6.5 on a Dell 11g, it reports that the next version of ESXi will no longer support that processor).
- *Does it support existing servers?* vSphere 6.5 drops the support to some old hardware and software. vSphere 6.5 no longer supports the following processors—Intel Xeon 51xx series, Xeon 30xx series, Xeon 32xx series, Xeon 53xx series, Xeon 72xx/73xx series.
- *Do you really need the new functions?* If you are involved in a digital transformation, you will probably need the new platform (AWS for vSphere or vSphere for integrated containers management require the new version). But for SMBs, most of the new functions are not usable or useful yet.
- *Can you really use the new functions?* Most of the new features are only for the Enterprise Plus edition (see the next paragraph for more details about the different editions).
- *Is it mature and stable enough?* As mentioned previously, vSphere 6.5 seems a better code compared to previous version 6.0 (or also 5.1) when it was released in GA. Also, it has already been used in production environments for more than 6 months, with few bugs.

Features and editions of vSphere 6.5

VMware vSphere is licensed in different ways and different packages and bundles, usually identified by a **stock keeping unit** (**SKU**) code. There are some bundles (like vSphere with Operations Management Enterprise Plus), OEM, ROBO and VDI specific SKU, or other license models (such as ELA) that we will not consider and describe.

For more details, you can consult the official VMware (vSphere) licensing page at `https://www.vmware.com/support/support-resources/licensing.html`.

For VMware vCenter Server, the licensing model is quite simple per instance and with three different editions:

Product feature	vCenter Essential	vCenter Foundation	vCenter Standard
Host manageable	Max 3 ESXi with Essential or Essential Plus	Max 4 ESXi Standard or Enterprise	Unlimited ESXi Standard or Enterprise
vCenter **High Availability (HA)**	Not available	Not available	Only for the vCSA
vCenter Backup and Restore	Not available	Not available	Only for the vCSA
Linked Mode	Not available	Not available	X

Table 1.4: vCenter features across different editions

For ESXi, the license is entitled per socket (except in some specific bundle or SKU, such as ROBO or VDI) and there are different editions with different features.

Note that since June 30, 2016, the ESXi Enterprise, vSphere with Operations Management Standard/Enterprise editions are no longer available. Customers who already own Enterprise versions are not yet affected (their current editions will continue to be supported through the EOA of vSphere 6):

Product feature	ESXi Essential Plus	ESXi Standard	ESXi Enterprise Plus
VMware Integrated OpenStack	Not available	Not available	Support is sold separately
VIC	Not available	Not available	X
vMotion	X	+Cross-vSwitch	+Cross-vSwitch / Cross-vCenter / Long Distance / Cross-Cloud
Storage vMotion	Not available	X	X
vSphere HA	X	X	X
Proactive HA	Not available		X

vSphere FT	Not available	2-vCPU	4-vCPU
vSphere Replication	X	X	X
Virtual Machine Encryption	Not available	Not available	X
Virtual Volumes	Not available	X	X
VAAI, 3rd part multipath	Not available	X	X
Storage Policy-Based Management	Not available	X	X
DRS, DPM, Storage DRS	Not available	Not available	X
SIOC, NIOC	Not available	Not available	X
Distributed virtual switches	Not available	Not available	X
Host profile, Auto-Deploy	Not available	Not available	X

Table 1.5: Product features with different vSphere editions

For ESXi, there are also the Free Hypervisor and the Essential editions; both are quite limited in function (no cluster function at all) but do not have specific limitations on the resources at the level of a single host.

The Free Hypervisor edition does not include the VDAP API, that means no native backup capability for all the backup software that uses that interface, and does not include either the vCenter Agent, that means no way to manage from vCenter.

For SMB, there are two specific bundles—vSphere Essential and Essential Plus Kit, that combine one instance of vCenter Essential and six licenses (usable on a maximum of three hosts) of ESXi Essential or Essential Plus. Both bundles have an interesting price, making virtualization also possible for companies with budget constraints.

For enterprises, depending on the size and the business requirements, for ESXi licensing, usually Standard or the Enterprise Plus can be used.

Summary

This chapter has covered a general overview of all the products, solutions, and features of the vSphere 6.5 suite, comparing the evolution with the previous releases.

In this chapter, we have explained why you should choose (or not choose) vSphere 6.5 compared to the previous version or other products. Also, it briefly describes the different editions and licenses of vSphere.

Finally, it also includes a general overview of all the products, solutions, and features in other VMware products or different suites that could be complementary or where vSphere represents an infrastructure foundation.

Next chapter, will be focused on how to plan a virtualization project in order to build a good infrastructure.

2

Design and Plan a Virtualization Infrastructure

This chapter describes how to plan a virtualization project and build a good infrastructure, by providing an approach both for the planning and the design; from how to map business requirements to technical requirements to how to move from a conceptual design to a logical and physical design.

To support those phase, are suggested different methodologies and different documents such as best practices, reference architectures, and guidelines.

In this chapter, we will learn how to:

- Approach a virtual infrastructure project
- Understand business requirements, constraints, and risks
- Perform conceptual, logical, and physical designs
- Use best practices, reference architectures, and validate designs in the right a proper way
- Approach different scenarios—SMB, ROBO enterprise

Plan a virtual infrastructure project

A virtualization project is like every other business-related process and should follow a set of proven methodologies and a flow to manage it in the right way. In each methodology, the first step is the planning and designing part, where you must define your objectives and how to reach them properly. There are several methodologies and approaches for managing the life cycle of a product or process, but for a virtualization project, we could consider the typical **plan-do-check-act** (**PDCA**) workflow, which is based on the following four main steps:

- **Plan**: This phase establishes the objectives and processes necessary to deliver all of the results in accordance with the expected business requirements. In this phase, you will also produce a design for the solution.
- **Do**: This is the implementation phase, according to the previous plan and is usually on a subset of the environment or using a **Proof of Concept (PoC)**.
- **Check**: This phase will study the results obtained in the previous phase and compare them against the expected results in order to validate the design and improve or correct it, if needed.
- **Act**: In this phase, with the results of previous phases, the final implementation is executed and, if needed, the cycle could be reiterated, normally before the end of the lifetime of the assets, or periodically to revalidate or improve the infrastructure:

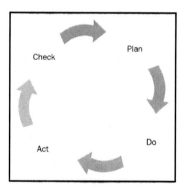

Deming Cycle (PDCA)

This approach works well for new projects on new products and technologies (at least for the customer), where a PoC might be mandatory to understand the proposed solution and verify it with all the requirements. But for virtualization projects that are a decade from mainstream, it's easy to define the expected results and the execution plan.

For this reason, a simpler workflow is usually used, based on some expected results using a well-proven technology and some recommended guidelines and design methodologies. Following a well-proven design methodology is probably the most efficient way to conduct a design and deploy virtual infrastructure in a repeatable and predictable way. In this chapter, we will discuss some of those methodologies and some design patterns.

VMware's solutions partners can also access the **Solution Enablement Toolkits (SETs)** resources that package VMware services, sales, and marketing **Intellectual Property (IP)** in a common set of tools, templates, and documents. The purpose is to enable partners to capitalize on different technologies, such as the **software-defined data center (SDDC), End-User Computing (EUC)**, and Cloud services. SETs are available in the partner central. For vSphere projects, there are the virtualization design and deploy, the virtualization design, and the vSphere upgrade kits, but there are also kits in case more VMware products are included in the same project.

One interesting source of usable methodologies is VMware's official course **vSphere: Design Workshop [V6.5]** (already updated for version 6.5) which can be found at `https://mylearn.vmware.com/mgrReg/courses.cfm?ui=www_edu&a=one&id_subject=79 170`. The design process used is based on the V-model of systems engineering and verification. The foundation of the process is a thorough set of business and technical requirements:

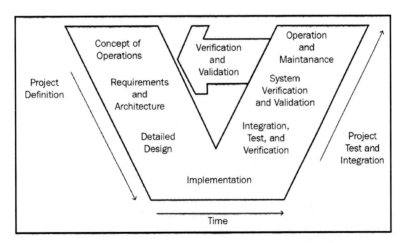

By Leon Osborne, Jeffrey Brummond, Robert Hart, Mohsen (Moe) Zarean Ph.D., P.E, Steven Conger; Redrawn by User:Slashme. - Image extracted from Clarus Concept of Operations. Publication No. FHWA-JPO-05-072, Federal Highway Administration (FHWA), 2005, Public Domain

Image source: https://commons.wikimedia.org/w/index.php?curid=10275054

This model is redefined for virtualization projects with the following phases:

- **Assess**: This phase involves defining the scope of the project and gathering all the required data for the design - not only technical data, but also data to understand customer needs and business requirements to define all project specifics.
- **Design**: In this phase, using the information gathered in the previous phase, it is possible to define a solution to meet all the requirements. This must consider the organization's goals, requirements, and constraints, as well as their best or recommended practices.
- **Deploy**: During this phase, the production environment is built and configured according to the design documents. Also, this phase can have changes and iterations.
- **Validate**: In this phase, after the solution is deployed, some tests are conducted to verify that the solution matches the design specifications, in order to validate that the solution will behave as required. This phase might be iterative if it requires additional changes to resolve configuration issues and other concerns.

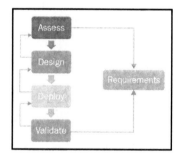

V-model of systems engineering and verification

 For a successful project, it is extremely important to understand each phase and the relationship between each phase.

For a project to be successful, you need to have customer involvement during all phases; of course, with different types of people during the different phases. For the assess and design phases, stakeholders should be involved to provide appropriate input into the design process. For the deploy and validate phases, you need the customer's operators and administrators (in all the technologies involved in the project) in order to understand the new technology and operational changes that will be needed.

Other phases, like the initial assessment and the design of the solution, will be discussed in the next chapters.

Assess

In this phase, it's really important to identify and interact with the key stakeholders, and to collect all the requirements in order to deliver a design that meets all customer and business needs. Sometimes the importance of this phase is underestimated, or it is simply not performed at all, perhaps because of time or budget constraints. This can be a huge risk for the project itself.

Also remember that, if you are providing a professional service (as a consultant or as a solution partner), you should prepare for this phase with pre-engagement planning and a kick-off in order to be prepared for the engagement. Also, if the project is handled internally, inside a customer, a successful engagement requires the right participants, defining the different roles, and good sponsors.

Tasks in the assessment phase include the following:

- Review the current state of the existing environment (if there is one)
- Learn the strengths, the weaknesses, and the pains of the customer
- Identify all the business needs in terms of requirements and constraints
- Make some assumptions for the missing input
- Perform risk management on all those pieces of information

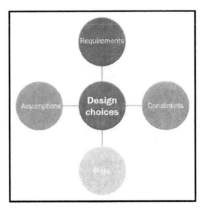

Requirements, constraints, assumptions, risks

Requirements, constraints, and assumptions

Requirements describe, in business or technical terms, the necessary properties, qualities, and characteristics of the desired solution. The customer should provide all requirements, but a good interview with the right people is needed to gain all the requirements that form the basis for the design. It's possible that different requirements may conflict with each other, or that they may change through discussion and negotiation.

Constraints are not necessarily issues or limitations; they can also be related to business processes, a business decision, a business policy, or a technical limitation. In most cases, they are mandatory requirements. Some common constraints are, for example, the usage of existing hardware (or using a specific vendor for all the hardware), or regulatory requirements. Budget restrictions and timelines could be classified as constraints (for example, if there is a mandatory milestone in the timeline) or requirements, depending on the case.

Assumptions could also be expectations about the implementation, but usually, they are related to what cannot be confirmed during the assessment or design phases. Of course, at some point, assumptions must be validated, or the respective design areas are at risk (and you must analyze their impact through risk management). All the risks must be documented and rated based on the severity of the risk and the type of impact, and must be addressed with a mitigation plan or recommendation (more details on risk analysis will be provided in Chapter 12, *Business Continuity and Disaster Recovery*).

For technical assessment, in order to gain data from the existing environment refer to Chapter 3, *Analysis and Assessment of an Existing Environment*.

 It's possible to find some conflicts in the set of requirements, constraints, assumptions, and risks. Before procedure, you have to identify how these relate to each other and consider how to resolve them; maybe by releasing a constraint, changing an assumption, or redefining a requirement.

Design

The design process is well covered in the VMware vSphere Design Workshop course. But the **VMware Certified Design Expert (VCDX)** certification also provides some useful information; the entire path of VCDX-DCV certification provides a complete VCDX methodology. This methodology is focused on how to find business needs and how to map them to design and implement decisions.

Also, if you are not VCDX certified, you can learn about this type of approach from the VCDX Boot Camp, the VCDX Blueprint, or the books and posts written by other VCDX users.

Following the VCDX methodology, or a similar one, you can have a deep look at how a large number of variables can affect the design of a virtual infrastructure. Some effects may define some creativities or risks, but also, any assumptions that are unknown or that you are unsure of should be considered risks as, depending on their probability and how critical it is, it could cause your project to fail.

The VCDX methodology is mainly based on the following phases and the relative deliverables:

- Discover the inputs (conceptual model)
- Develop the solution (logical design)
- Design the architecture (physical design)
- Determine success (validation of design)

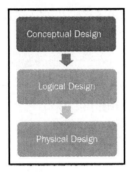

Conceptual, logical, and physical designs flow

Also, if risk management is normally under the purview of security or compliance departments, it's really important to include them in your design, considering all the **what/if** scenarios before implementing the project. Of course, some constraints may already have already been generated by some initial risk management activities.

Conceptual design

The conceptual design provides a high level of conceptual diagrams for the solution, using the data collected from the current state analysis of the existing environment (if existing), the application requirements, and the business needs and goals. All the data collected during the assessment is categorized into different categories:

- **Requirements**: This provides the business requirements that the designed solution must meet.
- **Constraints**: The conditions that provide boundaries to the design.
- **Assumptions**: Lists the conditions that are believed to be true but are not confirmed. All assumptions should be validated before the deployment.
- **Risks:** Factors that might have a negative effect on the design.

All business requirements, assumptions, and constraints must be used to support design and implementation decisions suited for mission-critical applications, considering also how risk can affect design decisions and how it can be mitigated.

From this analysis, a solution is usually defined where you should decide the number of vSphere objects, like data centers, clusters, vCenter Server, and so on.

Depending on the size of the solution, you may have some different deployment types:

Deployment type	Number of data centers	Number of vCenter Server	Number of clusters
Minimal	1	1	Single cluster
Suggested	1	2	Management + payload cluster
VMware Validated Designs (VVD) default	1	2	Management + edge + payload cluster

Table 2.1: Different deployment types

A typical conceptual design is limited to a general high-level architecture, usually with the data centers, and the interconnection between them and maybe with the cluster at an abstraction level (without the details of the hosts, the vCenter Server, and other infrastructure elements). For example, for a single site, using the suggested deployment, the concept could look as follows:

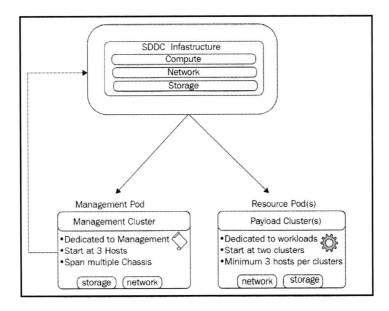

Conceptual schema

The usage of a management cluster, usually with at least three nodes (but which can potentially also start with two), is to provide security and resource isolation of management workloads from production workloads, potentially with different roles and scopes for the administrators. A management cluster is also used to simplify management, to upgrade procedures, for troubleshooting, and for dependencies. The edge cluster is a concept more related to an NSX design, where lots of virtual appliances (called NSX edge) should be deployed to provide several network services.

The production cluster or payload cluster could be one or more clusters for the different workloads. They could be differentiated with a different type of cluster, related to the life cycle of the workloads (like test or dev or productions), or isolated clusters for **Demilitarized Zone (DMZ)** purposes, or island clusters with small groups of ESXi hosts that can run workloads with special license requirements.

The usage of DMZ dedicated clusters is considered old-school, surpassed by the new network security and micro-segmentation features provided by NSX. But without NSX, it is still possible to have dedicated separated network cards for segregate networks on different physical switches, or to use different VLANs on the same physical switches.

Logical design

The logical design starts from the conceptual design and details it with all the design decisions, justifications, and implications. Typical logical design details the schema from the conceptual design by providing more information on the clusters and the different VMware components, but without going into the details of how many ESXi are used (maybe just the minimum required) or how they are sized. For example, for a single site, using the suggested deployment, the logical schema could look as follows:

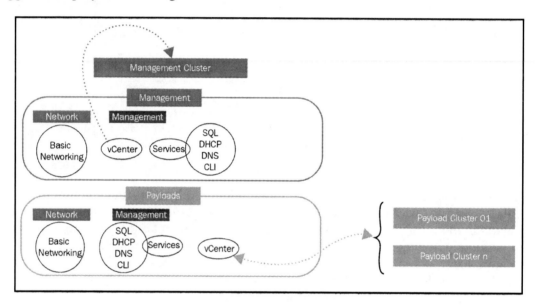

Logical schema

Also, storage and network logical diagrams are usually limited to high-level models where you can understand the logic of the architecture, but are not provided with physical details. For example, for the storage, you can see the fabric and the redundancy, but it does not provide information on the type of hardware, the number of datastores (or even just a separation between different classes of datastore), the storage vendor, and so on.

Service dependencies

The logical design must also include information about the dependencies for infrastructure and application services, in order to better understand the possible implications of a service or a component failure.

Service dependencies can be described with an entity relationship diagram with upstream and downstream dependencies:

- An upstream dependency is an entity that depends on another service
- A downstream dependency is an entity that another service depends on
- Each dependency connection must use an arrow that points to what the service depends on

These types of graphs can really help to better understand how service availability can affect other services, and it's crucial for the risk management and design processes to minimize the dependencies at the infrastructure level. For example, the usage of two different vCenter servers, both in the management cluster, is a consequence of this approach.

 One interesting VMware tool that can help in the activity of mapping services and dependencies is VMware vRealize Infrastructure Navigator (it works only on existing vSphere environments and only for VMs with running VMware Tools).

Physical design

The physical design details the logic design, where each major infrastructure component is already present, at a high level (but with the right design decisions and motivations), along with the physical layer, including the hardware and software components, the installation procedure, the configuration, and so on. Hardware sizing, for both the capacity and the performance aspects, could be assisted by the initial assessment of an existing infrastructure, as will be described in Chapter 3, *Analysis and Assessment of an Existing Environment*.

You have to size the ESXi hosts, but also the different vSphere and infrastructure components, such as the vCenter Server, or other needed virtual appliances, such as a storage management console (or server).

ESXi host

In this case you can size the ESXi hosts by considering the total required CPU and the total required RAM, define which growth margin you would like to plan (or which is required by business goals), and preserve a part for the high availability aspects (as we will discuss in Chapter 13, *Advanced Availability in vSphere 6.5*), considering not only vSphere HA, but also vSphere **Fault Tolerance** (**FT**) (if used). With the numbers, you can define a building block (or use a vendor predefined building block, like a Nutanix or vSAN ready node) for the single ESXi host and find out how many *blocks* are needed to reach the required CPU or RAM amount.

For the hosts, you can use different types of approaches for cluster design:

- **Scale-out**: More hosts in a single cluster, each mid-sized
- **Scale-up**: Fewer hosts in a single cluster, each usually with a lot of resources

More details will be provided in Chapter 4, *Deployment Workflow and Component Installation*, but usually, a trade-off between the two different approaches is used. For a traditional computer server, you mainly have to define the type of CPU, the amount of RAM, and the number and type of I/O ports.

Common processors now have a lot of cores inside (a typical number is 16, but it's growing), and considering that VMware ESXi licensing is normally per socket (except in some specific cases), you may prefer few processors with a lot of cores. In fact, the bi-processor configuration is more common for the virtualization hosts. But also remember other licenses, like the new license model for Windows Server 2016, where the number of cores is also counted.

 New server series, with the Intel **Skylake** family (https://ark.intel. com/en/products/codename/37572/Skylake), are already available on the market (such as the Dell PowerEdge Gen14 line or the HPE ProLiant Gen10 server series). The best deal is around 16 cores, but there is also the Xeon Platinum with 28 cores.

Considering that the processor could be the costliest part of a server, try to balance the performance, the budget, and the license limitations. For example, the Intel® Xeon® Platinum 8180M 2.50 GHz, 28C/56T, 10.4GT/s 3UPI, 38 MB Cache costs more than $13,000 (https://ark.intel.com/products/series/125191/Intel-Xeon-Scalable-Processors).

In a single cluster, you will need a compatible processor (at least compatible with EVC features), with no strict requirements on having the same configuration as the host. But in order to simplify resource distribution and make Host Profiles more effective, it's recommended to have hosts as similar as possible inside the same cluster.

Intel has been supplying brand new model Xeon processors (codename **Everest**) designed for customers in the finance sector, where milliseconds on a transaction are crucial because they can mean profit or loss. Server vendors are trying to gain similar features, also on traditional Xeon; for example, a new option in a 14G server called Dell **Processor Acceleration Technology (PAT)**.

About the choice between Intel or AMD: actually, there is no choice at all. The server market is dominated by Intel Xeon and it will be difficult for AMD to fill this gap in the future, considering that you need processor compatibility for vMotion mobility, inside a cluster, across clusters, across vCenters and also across clouds.

RAM memory is now reasonably cheap, and the best deal is for 16 or 32 GB modules (two **dual inline memory modules (DIMMs)** of 8 GB are costlier than one of 16). Consider that each motherboard has an optimal configuration where DIMMs work at maximum speed, and that with more per channel, the speed could decrease. Try to always match the optimal configuration suggested by the vendor (note that new Intel processors have six channels for DIMMs, instead of four as per the previous models).

Of course, there are different aspects, like the use of blade or rack or other formats (although rack is the more common format), or the type of vendor, or the presence of an out-of-band card (like iLO for HPE or iDRAC for Dell servers).

For hyper-converged infrastructure (more details will be provided in Chapter 7, *Advanced Storage Management*), the ESXi node size must also consider the required storage capacity and performance (but in those cases, you can have good sizing tools from the specific vendors). Otherwise, you have to size your external shared storage with specific vendor criteria (also, in this case, you can have good sizing tools from most of the vendors).

In both cases, you will also decide which boot device will be used, as discussed in Chapter 4, *Deployment Workflow and Component Installation*. Common choices are two hard disks in RAID 1 or a redundant SD. But new servers may also provide a SATA DOM device or a new controller card with two dual redundant M.2 sticks (this option is actually quite expensive when compared with the dual SD cards option).

For the I/O cards, it all depends on your network and storage requirements and design; we will discuss this further in the related chapters.

All hardware must be classified as VMware vSphere certified or match the VMware **Hardware Compatibility List (HCL)** between the hardware components, the firmware version, the drivers, and the proper VMware vSphere version.

Actually, there are two types of drivers—native or vmkLinux based. VMware plans to deprecate the vmkLinux APIs and associated driver ecosystem with the next release of VMware vSphere. This means that in future versions, several drivers could change.

For now, vSphere 6.5 supports I/O drivers built and certified on ESXi 5.5 (ESXi 5.5-based), on ESXi 6.0 (ESXi 6.0-based), and on ESXi 6.5 (ESXi 6.5-based). For more information, see KB 2147697—*ESXi 6.5 I/O driver information: certified 5.5 and 6.0 I/O drivers are compatible with vSphere 6.5* at `https://kb.vmware.com/kb/2147697`.

About the form factor; this is mostly dictated by the space requirements or the vendor options (for example, Cisco has a few fixed form factor options in its USC family). But also consider the flexibility in future expansion for memory and devices and cards that can easily permit scaling or extend the life cycle of a server. Blade or modular solutions could be an option, but usually make sense with a minimum number of hosts, which could vary from vendor to vendor (usually more than four hosts). For hyper-converged solutions, it is quite common to have building blocks already sized and with (few) fixed form factors.

vCenter Services

For the vCenter part, you must choose the platform (physical or virtual), the operating system (Windows-based or the appliance version), the amount of the resources, and the type of deployment (embedded or external PSC), as will be discussed in `Chapter 4`, *Deployment Workflow and Component Installation*.

Note that some deploy topologies have been deprecated, so be sure to read the KB article 2147672—*Supported and deprecated topologies for VMware vSphere 6.5* (`https://kb.vmware.com/kb/2147672`) in order to choose the right deployment type.

 Starting with vSphere 6.5, VMware recommends the usage of the vCenter Server vCSA option, with an embedded deployment (good enough for a small environment) or external PSC (if you have multiple vCenter servers and you want to use the Linked Mode feature across them).

The debate between physical and virtual remains old school, considering that almost all deployments have virtual vCenter components, but VMware still supports (though perhaps it will not, in the future) a physical installation.

Be sure to use dedicated systems for vCenter components, just because there are so many ports that are used and you can only change a few of them (anyway, avoid changing the default ports to simplify future management and troubleshooting).

Also remember that both the PSC and the vCenter Server have several dependencies both upstream and downstream (as discussed previously); be sure to analyze all of them before designing your solution, in order to understand the impact of the lack of vCenter services. More information will be provided in `Chapter 13`, *Advanced Availability in vSphere 6.5*.

There are also some good resources for vCenter design called **vCenter Server 6.5 Light Board Videos**, available at `https://blogs.vmware.com/vsphere/2017/08/vcenter-server-6-5-light-board-videos.html`

Building blocks

As discussed in `Chapter 1`, *Evolution of VMware vSphere Suite*, VMware is pushing the software-defined model, and to do so it's trying to standardize the design of the on-premises and public cloud infrastructures as much as possible. This could be done on-premises by using building blocks and common management services.

VMware Cloud Foundation is the integrated cloud infrastructure platform used to help build the SDDC VMware's vision and make hybrid clouds effective. VMware Cloud Foundation provides a dynamic software-defined infrastructure where computing, storage, networking, and security resources can easily be managed and delivered to run enterprise workloads.

The core components of VMware Cloud Foundation are—VMware vSphere, vSAN, and NSX, and the VMware SDDC Manager used to automate the entire system life cycle for the infrastructure, to simplify the operations tasks, and to provide central management for on-premises and on-cloud resources.

A VMware Cloud Foundation based solution can be designed in different ways:

- **Build your own**: Using pre-qualified ready systems; usually vSAN ReadyNode
- **As a product**: Using integrated systems where VMware Cloud Foundation software stack is preinstalled and integrated on qualified hardware (for example, VCE VxRack System 1000 with SDDC nodes)
- **As a service from the public cloud**: In this case, you can run VMware Cloud Foundation as a service managed by public cloud providers

Using integrated systems becomes more common for large deployments, and also, if not combined with VMware Cloud Foundation, this building block approach remains valuable in those cases. Several prebuild stack solutions are available on the market, such as solutions from NetApp, Cisco, and so on (many will probably shift in the future to adopt VMware Cloud Foundation). In all those cases, the entire rack solution is designed and validated to satisfy specific business requirements, pre-sized for specific performance capabilities.

How to provide good documentation

All the different design steps have some deliveries, usually in the form of a document representing the specific design and explaining the different choices. In order to realize good documents, it's really important to detail first the logical and physical designs on different technical aspects, as will be discussed later.

Then, you can start from scratch, or reuse some design patterns or templates from previous projects. Most of the projects for small environments are quite simple and almost the same; for example, ones with just a single vCenter, three ESXi nodes, and so on. In this case, a generic logical design could probably be recycled for multiple different projects.

Consider also that simplicity could be the key to a successful project; the more complicated a project is, the more complicated its documentation will be, and the more risks you can have in the deployment and implementation phase, the more complex supporting and troubleshooting it will be, and the more effort the management part will require. Of course, scripting and automation could really help in the deployment and management of complex infrastructure, and good monitoring tools could help to prevent issues and also in troubleshooting. If you still try to keep things simple and clear, you can have some advantages.

For big projects, you need something more, and usually, it's used as a building block approach with different pods (or blocks) based on some kind of reference architecture, designed from use cases or best practices.

Design areas and technologies

In your designs, you have to match all the following technology aspects to satisfy design requirements:

- **Availability**: How your solution provides a high level of services and infrastructure resiliency

- **Manageability**: How it's easy and effective to be managed, also considering automation aspects
- **Performance and scaling**: How it can run workloads effectively by matching business requirements and how it can scale if more performance is needed
- **Recoverability**: How it can be protected and restored or reactivated in the case of a fault, a data loss, or an interruption
- **Security**: How it can be protected from different types of attacks
- **Risk and budget management**: How it mitigates some possible risks, usually related to business aspects

All those aspects must be matched to each layer of the technology stack, including, from the top to the bottom:

- Workloads and applications
- Virtualization
- Compute and host
- Storage
- Networking
- Operational

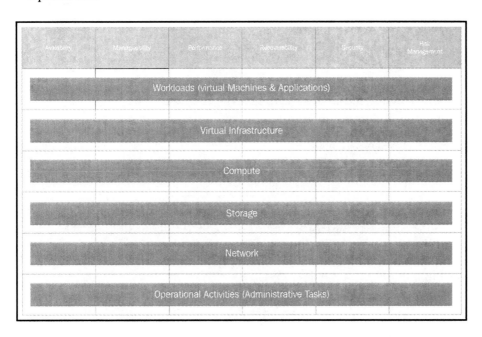

Design matrix

All of these will be discussed in the following chapters, with some specific hints for the different technologies. VMware vSphere usually stops (at higher levels) at the virtual hardware components, but you have to also consider all the details of the applications and operating systems inside each VM.

Best practices

A best practice is a method, technique, or approach that is usually generally accepted because it produces better or more reliable or repeatable results. You can consider it as a standard, suggested, or recommended way of doing some things. But it's not a law or a diktat that must be universally followed without any thought. Using best practices requires you to know the background of the best practice and how it applies to your specific situation and design.

Anyway, best practices remain a useful pattern for the design of virtual infrastructures in a proper way; as also for validating the design itself, in order to be compliance with possible future support feedback or requests.

You can find several best practices for VMware in different documents, such as:

- *Performance Best Practices for VMware vSphere 6.5:* https://www.vmware.com/ techpapers/2017/Perf_Best_Practices_vSphere65.html
- *VMware vCenter Server 6.5 High Availability Performance and Best Practices*: https:/ /www.vmware.com/content/dam/digitalmarketing/vmware/en/pdf/techpaper/ vcha65-perf.pdf

And also in several **Knowledge Base (KB)** articles, such as:

- *Best practices and advanced features for VMware High Availability:* https://kb. vmware.com/kb/1002080
- *Best practices for upgrading to vCenter Server 6.5:* https://kb.vmware.com/kb/ 2147686

Remember that there are also vendor specific best practices, like for storage or networking (but also for servers); where VMware may have a generic suggestion (such as, in storage, the multipath choice), the specific vendor will usually have more detailed information for the configuration part. For this reason, try to apply the more specific recommendations, but always check that there aren't any conflicts.

Reference architecture

Typically, a reference architecture is a business-ready design with configurations for some common virtualization cases like virtual desktops or small businesses. It could be, based on use cases, preconfigured, easy-to-order bundled solutions designed to aid in the ordering, deployment, and maintenance of a virtual infrastructure.

You can find several documents from both VMware, usually on specific products or verticals or use cases, and other vendors, where there could also be pre-packaged solutions.

For SDDC design, one of the more complete sources of documents and blueprints is **VMware Validated Designs (VVD)**.

VVD

The VVD is a pre-built end-to-end SDDC cloud infrastructure designed to perform in a predictive way, to scale, and to be reliable and resilient. More importantly, it is already pre-validated, all by matching VMware's best practices and leveraging the real-world expertise of VMware solution architects. This design is intended to be a building block for a virtual infrastructure design, valuable for large deployment, with a reduced timeframe for the implementation (and also the design phase).

Unlike specific reference architectures, which are usually focused on an individual product or purpose, the VVD gives a global overview of the full stack, with different products using a holistic approach to the design. Also, even if you don't plan to use the product in this kind of design (for example, the storage part based on vSAN), the design itself could be very valuable and good support for your project.

The VVD documentation page provides all those documents at `https://www.vmware.com/go/vvd` or `https://www.vmware.com/support/pubs/vmware-validated-design-pubs.html`.

VVD is based on a set of different VMware products with specific versions, which are included in the **VMware Customer Experience Improvement Program (CEIP)**. CEIP is an optional program that provides VMware with information on which products and features are used by the customers, and it's used to improve VMware products and features. If you don't have specific regimentation or security constraints (or concerns), you can join this program by selecting this option during product installation.

VVD is a complete multi-site and cross-cloud design, but it also supports some specific use cases. In both cases, it is optimized for integration, expansion, and Day-2 operations, as well as specific maintenance tasks like upgrades and updates.

The latest version of VDD is VMware Validated Designs 4.1 (22 Aug 2017), and already, includes:

- VMware Validated Design for SDDC
- VMware Validated Designs for Management and Workload Consolidation

For specific use cases, it includes:

- VMware Validated Design Use Cases Documentation
- VMware Validated Design for Micro-Segmentation
- VMware Validated Design for IT Automating IT

Not everything has been updated from version 4.0.x; for example, several operational aspects, such as upgrade, monitoring, backup, and so on, are still the old versions of the documents; they will probably have been updated by the time this book has been published, but be sure to check the previous document.

In the previous version, you may also find more use cases, such as, for example, VMware Validated Design for Remote Office and Branch Office 4.0.

VMware Solution Enablement Toolkits (SETs)

VVDs are documents available to both customers and partners, but for the latter there are also other types of specific documents useful for the planning, design, and implementation phases of a virtualization project.

VMware's solution partners may have access, depending on their competencies, to the SETs covering several different types of projects and different VMware products. Also, if VVDs remain the more integrated and completed documents, SETs could provide more information or specific tools, such as for the assessment part.

The more interesting SETs are:

- SDDC Assess, Design, and Deploy (actually updated to vCloud Suite 6.0)
- Virtualization Design and Deploy (already updated to vSphere 6.5)
- Operational readiness for cloud computing
- vSphere Upgrade (in this case, the related part of VVD provide better information)
- Performance and Capacity Management Design and Deploy

More and more are available (or will be available) for specific topics and use cases.

Different scenarios

There are different types of typical scenarios where most use cases can fit, but much can also depend on the type of workload and business requirements.

We will consider and discuss, at the high level, just three different cases: Enterprise, SMB, ROBO. For other, more specific examples, such as for **Virtual Desktop Infrastructure (VDI)**, there are several reference architectures, and also some specific VVDs:

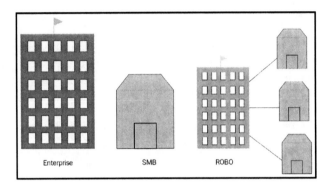

Typical company sizes

Enterprise

Large companies are usually qualified, by their size, as enterprise or corporate. Their business needs are usually very strictly defined and almost all workloads can be really business critical, including infrastructure workloads such as the vCenter Server.

The number of workloads is usually high; that probably means more payload clusters and more attention paid to performance and scaling aspects, to adapt the infrastructure to business growth. Hybrid cloud could also be used to provide more flexibility, capacity, scaling, and so on. Also, the managed data might be very big (hundreds of TBs or PBs are becoming quite common).

These kinds of organizations have grown to the point where they need dedicated, full time IT staff with specific expertise to manage specific applications or parts of the entire infrastructure; these individuals, such as storage administrator, Windows administrator, database administrator, and so on, may work on specific technology silos, but for the infrastructure part, it is becoming more common to have cross-technology capabilities, or, at least to build a shared team of people with different competencies.

Business requirements

Applications, services, and workloads are typically all (or mostly) business critical, and the infrastructure part could need a very high level of availability. For example, in a vRealize Automation private cloud, or in a VDI environment, the lack of a vCenter Server will stop the provisioning of new services or new virtual desktops, with a potentially huge impact on the business.

Possible constraints

For an enterprise, the main constraints could be related to regulations and compliance requirements, or specific laws or internal standards. But there can be a lot of other constraints, related to infrastructure or product choices, resource assignments, naming conventions, or limited capabilities in negotiating the different requirements.

Also, if budget is not a constraint, if the project size is too big or the requirements are too strict and require costly solutions, that could become a constraint.

Main risks

The main risk could be having limited visibility on the project. If you don't have time to interview all the different stockholders, that means that you don't have all the requirements (and constraints) and you may make too many assumptions based on uncertain information.

A bad timeline during project implementation could be another risk; maybe you spend too much time during the PoC, or define a design so complex that the time to implement the entire solution does not match the required time to market.

Some design decisions

Enterprise scenarios usually require a high availability level; greater than 99.99% for most workloads. Using just vSphere HA features is not enough, not for all workloads. For workloads that require a level better than 99.99%, you have to consider vSphere FT or guest clustering (building a clustered solution across VMs). Or, just design your application to provide a better resiliency and a high availability level.

Performance and scaling are also crucial, and the design needs a good initial assessment and has to consider future growth. Real-time monitoring is needed to verify the right service level, from both the availability and the performance point of view. To help in the design phase, the VVD documents provide a great example and good and validated reference architecture for most of the projects. Trying to customize too much, to adapt to specific requirements, or to deviate from the blueprints could make the design too complex and costly in terms of money or time.

In this type of project, there could also be the engagement of VMware Professional Services, at least to support the design or validate the solution.

Typically, for an enterprise, both the ESXi Enterprise Plus and vCenter Standard editions are used, but there are also specific bundles, like the vCloud suite, that include more of VMware's products. For large environments, there are specific licenses, like the **Enterprise License Agreement (ELA)**.

Note that there is one special case of enterprise environment—a multi-tenant environment, typical for service or cloud providers, but also needed in some big enterprises where different organizations need the flexibility of cloud computing, especially the ability to manage their resources in a self-provisioning way.

The VMware vCenter Server has some capabilities for multi user environments, using a role-based permission model, but cannot be considered a full multi tenant environment. As discussed in `Chapter 1`, *Evolution of VMware vSphere Suite*, in order to build a private cloud, you need some cloud management tools. VMware has two different products—vCloud Director for Service Providers or vRealize Automation for enterprises. For cloud service providers, there is a specific license model called **VMware Service Provider Program (VSPP)**.

Small or Mid-Sized Business (SMB)

An SMB is a company with a small number of employees, maybe with only a part-time individual managing its data center. As compared to an enterprise, it does not have the same budget capabilities, but still has similar business needs and requirements.

The number of employees can really vary, but for example, Gartner defines a company as an SMB if the number of employees is less than 100 (for small) or less than 999 (for medium). And there are also some criteria based on annual revenue, with less than $50 million (for small) or less than $1 billion (for medium).

The size parameters may also differ depending on the country. For example, in Italy, a small company has less than 50 employees and less than €10 million in revenue, whereas a medium company has less than 250 employees and less than €50 million. There is also the mid-market size called **Small and Midsize Enterprise (SME)**. This size organization has one or more full-time employees dedicated to managing its data centers. However, these individuals have generalist IT skills and have to manage two or more IT-related tasks (backups, databases, network, servers, support, and so on) without a specialized role.

There are also **Small Office Home Offices (SOHO)**, which are usually too small for a real virtual environment, or could be more effective using some kind of public cloud solution. Historically, SMB companies have relaxed requirements, due to the limited budget (compared to enterprise), but the digital transformation is also affecting this type of reality, in some cases more than with the enterprises. The main consequence is that now SMBs can have similar (in some cases, the same) requirements to the enterprises (like a high level of availability), but still without the same type of budget and other specific types of constraints.

They can remain more flexible as compared to enterprises regarding timing, the type of constraints, and the ability to talk directly with the C-level of the company. And, of course, the numbers, as the number of SMBs is usually much greater than the number of enterprises.

Business requirements

Requirements could be a little more relaxed compared to the enterprise scenario, but you still have to design your project with availability, reliability, performance, scalability, security, and manageability in mind.

The lack of specialized technical people makes the manageability aspect potentially much more crucial; the solution must be as simple as possible to manage, with high-level tools (like the GUI) in the hands of just a few people who have limited skills in vSphere environments.

Possible constraints

For SMBs, the budget is usually the main constraint, and you have to plan your solution carefully to consider the entire costs (included licenses) to fit in the budget. It's also possible that there is a budget spread across different years; in this case, you have to build a modular design where more parts could be added in the future to improve it (for example, the disaster recovery solution).

There can be some constraints on the devices, hardware, and software that can be used. For example, hold services must be recycled to optimize the investments.

Main risks

There can be several other risks about the locations designed for the data center, where racks may not be present at all or may not be designed for the chosen type of servers, or the uninterruptible power supply may be outdated or may not have enough power for the entire environment. Existing switches may lack in redundancy or performance (may be they have just 1 Gbps ports). Environmental conditions must be verified to validate that cooling and HVAC systems are sized well.

Some design decisions

Also, even if the public cloud is an option for SMB cases, most of them, for different reasons (one could be the lack of reliable network connectivity), are still building their own on-premises infrastructures. In SMB scenarios, a reasonable availability level could be between 99% and 99.9%, but there are some workloads that may require the higher level (or others that are not critical at all). The vSphere HA features could be enough for most cases.

Performance isn't usually a problem, due to the computing capacity of a common server today; potentially, a single host can handle all the workloads, but of course, it represents a single point of failure. For this reason, two, or more commonly three, hosts are the typical configuration. The sizing of those hosts is not usually critical and reducing the cost could also be interesting, considering single socket configurations.

For the licenses aspect, VMware has a specific bundle called **Essential Plus Kit** with limited features but an affordable price that can cover an infrastructure with up to three hosts. Other vendors have similar bundles to simplify the adoption in this scenario, or perhaps have a subscription model. In this case, the design is quite simple, because you just have to build a two or three node cluster and think about the resiliency and the recoverability aspects. The three node limits could be enough for SMBs, unless we want to also include a disaster recovery part (but you can use other licenses on the second site).

For the storage part, you can use some kind of hyper-converged solution (although, for vSAN, three hosts are just the minimum). Alternatively, use an external storage, maybe with a direct SAS connection to avoid the need for a fabric.

An interesting design option has been introduced with VMware vSphere 6.5 Update 1, through a significant change in the maximum number of hosts that the vCenter Server Foundation edition can manage now up to four nodes (not only three nodes, like in the past).

What are the possible implications of this? With four nodes, you can do interesting things that you can now plan in your design:

- **vSAN cluster**: Technically, three nodes are the minimum, but I don't like to build a vSAN cluster with only three nodes. I prefer to have four in order to plan a better resiliency.
- **vSAN two node cluster**: Does it make sense to have a cluster with just two nodes, the witness appliance on a third node, and to manage both the third node and the witness with the same vCenter? Maybe yes, or, let's say, why not? Now it can be considered.
- **Production and DR cluster managed by the same vCenter**: Also possible with three nodes, but limited to 2+1; in this case, you have more flexibility.
- **Scale out instead of scale in**: Will it make sense to have more hosts (maybe with a single processor) instead of few?

Instead, for very small environments or for very limited budgets, some other minimal solutions can be considered, if you can reduce the availability and recoverability requirements. For example, just two nodes with the Essential license (that is the cheapest one, but it does not provide any cluster functionality), one active, and one in manual standby (for each workload) with a VM based replication solution to have a minimum level of recoverability (several third-party backup solutions provide VM replication across hosts).

For an SMB scenario, there could be a risk in using licenses based per VM or instance, considering that the estimated number could increase in the future (VM spread). But if the growth could be estimated carefully, it could make sense to consider licensing based per VM or per space. Note that for VMware vSphere, the Essential Plus (or in some minor cases, the Essential) bundles remain the most popular, and they just license three bi-processor hosts.

Remote offices and branch offices (ROBO)

A ROBO is an office located on a different site or in a geographical remote area from other offices of the same company or holding. Usually, there is a headquarters that acts as the main office. Several organizations have one (or more) main office, as well as remote offices in different cities, countries, or continents. Those organizations may have, in each remote office, some local IT infrastructure and assets, usually for data locality, but also to provide local services.

Considering the size of a remote office, it's similar to a small company, because there are usually just a few servers running a few workloads to support local needs. So, they could be very similar to the SMB scenario described previously.

But in reality, if you look at the entire infrastructure, it's more similar to an enterprise scenario, with big numbers (totally), full enterprise needs, and some specific challenges.

The distributed and remote nature of this infrastructure makes it a hard case to manage, difficult to protect, and costly to operate, for a variety of different reasons, as follows:

- Limited IT budgets for each remote office, because having more remote offices acts as a multiplying factor for the total infrastructure costs.
- Lack of local IT staff at remote sites, which results in increased service-level challenges for remote IT operations, such as provisioning and configuration of servers, maintenance updates, and troubleshooting.
- Inconsistent host configurations at remote sites, which can complicate troubleshooting across a large number of remote sites.
- Life cycle challenges for the infrastructure, due to the remote nature of servers that makes it more challenging to perform activities like upgrades and maintenance.
- Limited business continuity solutions, or redundant hardware for remote sites, or in adequate backup software/hardware and/or system backup and recovery capabilities. Additionally, IT organizations do not perform comprehensive data recovery capability testing on a frequent basis.
- Limited space at remote sites poses a challenge for accommodating new servers. In addition, existing physical hosts at these sites are not efficiently utilized.

Business requirements

Each company with infrastructure located in remote and distributed sites desires, of course, to resolve the previous limitation and find a reasonable solution.

So, the basic and mandatory requirements could be:

- **Central management**: To minimize the lack of local IT staff and expertise, the solution should be easy to deploy and, more importantly, easy to manage and monitor on a large scale (depending on the number of remote offices)
- **Availability and compliance**: Deliver improved business continuity and enable proactive regulatory compliance at remote sites and branch offices
- **Data protection**: Using an affordable backup and recovery solution

But also, it would like to innovate and try to deliver:

- **Standardization**: Define and enforce configuration standards consistently across your remote sites and branch offices to minimize configuration drift
- **Repeatability**: Standardizing each office and having a baseline design and configuration for the infrastructure, in order to adopt a repeatable building block approach.
- **More agility**: To rapidly provision and manage the entire IT infrastructure
- **Infrastructures more service oriented**: The main focus should be the service and the business
- **Scalable solution**: It can work for a few workloads (in a remote office), but also with more (if needed)

Possible constraints

The budget could be the one main constraint; more are the remote offices, and much is the total cost. Also, could be complicated to find the right building block that matches the requirements and the budget constraint.

But there could also be some limitations in local IT facilities; space could be really limited, available electrical power could be capped, and for sure, UPS capacity is limited.

Also, the lack of local IT support and people must be considered for both the deployment and the maintenance of the remote infrastructure.

Main risks

This scenario could have several risks, as follows:

- The remote IT facilities are not only limited, but they lack in something; space could be a real constraint, but also a risk. For example, in the case of a migration, maybe there isn't enough space for the new systems, or rack mounting of the physical servers is not possible, for example, because the rack is not deep enough to host full-length servers.
- You have to also consider that power supplies and UPS could be insufficient in size, switches may lack in redundancy or performance (maybe they have just 1 Gbps ports), and cooling and HVAC may not be present at all.
- Actual business continuity plans could be limited and backup and recovery could be problematic, and they must be carefully addressed. Of course, this limitation in IT facilities may also mean limited physical security; in some cases, the IT facilities are not closed in a secure room or access controls are not enforced.
- Finally, one of the major risks could be related to the geographic network connection with the main (or the central) office; bandwidth or latency assumptions could be wrong and must be verified to be sure to have an effective central management and to check which kinds of services could be centralized and which must be localized.

Some design decisions

Potentially, you can centralize everything in the main office (or in a public cloud) environment. Maybe the desktop could also be centralized, using VDI or some kind of RemoteApp. From a management point of view, this solution is easy, just because all is centralized and managing and monitoring will be easier. Also, backup, data protection, and availability could be better managed.

But there can be some risks—network connectivity becomes much more critical, not only from the bandwidth point of view (where you need enough bandwidth for each service and each user), but also, because latency and reliability can impact the business continuity requirements and user experiences in the worst way. If the risk is too high, local workloads are needed at the remote offices.

In ROBO scenarios, a reasonable availability level could be between 99% and 99.9%, but there are some workloads that may require the higher level (or others that are not critical at all). The vSphere HA features could be enough for most cases.

Performance isn't usually a problem, due to the computing capacity of a common server today; a single host can potentially handle all the workloads, but of course, it also represents a single point of failure. For this reason, the two host configuration is the most typical for this scenario. The sizing of those hosts is not usually critical, and reducing the cost could also be interesting, considering single socket configurations. Fresh air cooling technology could be useful, and in some cases, also enough.

Storage is more tricky, due the budget constraints and also the possible space constraints; you still need storage with reasonable reliability and shared capabilities, in order to use a VMware cluster, but a good external storage could be costly and provide more complexity in the infrastructure (external switches, more components, and so on). Fortunately, there are some specific hyper-converged solutions for ROBO scenarios, both from VMware (vSAN for ROBO configuration, with a specific license based per VM) and other vendors (for example, StorMagic and StarWind).

In ROBO scenarios, it is usually really important to minimize the license cost of each office, in order to keep the entire project in the estimated budget. Cost per VM or space could be interesting, considering the low number of them.

The VMware vSphere ESXi licenses that are most interesting for remote offices are the ROBO SKU that are sold per VM (25 VMs SKU). ROBO advanced is around €180 per VM; that is cheaper (for few VMs) compared to ESXi Standard (around € 1000 for one socket), or the Essential Plus Kit (less than € 4500 for three hosts and six sockets). The ROBO license is independent of the number of hosts or sockets or cores, but please note that each VM counts as a license, including management VMs (like VSA or other VA).

Windows Server licenses remain per socket (and, starting with Windows Server 2016, also limit the total number of cores). With just a couple of VMs, Windows Standard edition could be considered, to limit costs.

Storage licenses depend on the type of storage; it can be included in the cost of the storage itself, but for software-based storage like vSAN or other VSA based storage, it can be licensed in different ways—per capacity (like several VSA solutions), per socket (like vSAN), or also per VM (like vSAN for ROBO).

For VMware vSAN, again, the ROBO SKU could be interesting for a small number of VMs in each remote office (around €500 per VM), compared to the other license option (starting from €2,500 per socket for the Standard edition).

Summary

This chapter has explained how to approach a virtualization project, using reference architectures and best practices, from the analysis of requirements, constraints, and risks to the different types of design(conceptual, logical, and physical). Network and storage aspects we discussed, as were different vCenter Server and ESXi design and planning aspects.

Three different scenarios have been used as examples of some design decisions—SMB, Enterprise, and ROBO.

In the next chapter, we will discuss the other phases, like the initial assessment for an existing environment, useful for planning and design.

3
Analysis and Assessment of an Existing Environment

Sometimes, you have to find a simple and effective way to analyze an existing environment; this task could become a crucial aspect of your system that must be properly planned and executed.

These are some situations in which you may need to analyze an existing environment:

- **Before planning a virtualization project**: Before starting on your virtualization journey, it is important to really understand your current IT infrastructure and how it will be impacted by the virtualization process; this is not only to clarify whether virtualization is possible but also to match or better transform the existing procedures in the new environment.
- **Before a migration**: It doesn't matter whether we are talking about an entire platform migration, a migration from one hypervisor to another, or simply a migration across vSphere (maybe different versions, in the case of a hardware refresh, or sometimes also across the same version); performing this task without good sizing and planning of the target could be really business-critical.
- **Before an upgrade**: In the case of an in-place upgrade, usually, the system is already sized. However, some minor considerations could be taken into account, such as different overheads—for example, for virtual appliances or ESXi itself. Note that upgrades require more attention and considerations, and we will cover those aspects in `Chapter 11`, *Lifecycle Management, Patching, and Upgrade*. Also, an upgrade that is not in-place just falls into the migration case.

- **On a running system**: Finding a baseline for your environment or simple document could be an important task, if it wasn't already covered during the deployment of the infrastructure. Also, it could be useful to prepare for other tasks.
- **Before an audit process**: Compliance, security, and regimentation are typical cases where you need a deep and targeted analysis of your environment, but there can be also other cases, such as a simple verification that the environment matches the business needs, or specific aspects such as performance.

Different types of analysis could be performed to achieve different goals, depending on the types of the previous cases:

- **Discover and inventory**: This is useful for capturing your assets, in order to build your documents or check the inventory. Usually, you need some detailed information from your hardware, such as firmware releases or simply the exact names and models for a device or I/O card.
- **Solution readiness**: Normally, this is related to a new virtualization project where you need to verify the effective possibility to virtualize your workloads. However, it could be useful also in any upgrade process, or in every migration, such as from a different type of hypervisor.
- **Health check or sanity check or configuration audit**: Doing a health assessment of your environment is critical in several situations, such as any migration or upgrade process. However, it could also be very useful to perform it periodically to discover wasted resources, misalignment with the documentation or with best practices from VMware or other vendors, and possible optimization or changes.
- **Risks and compliance assessment** or **audit**: This is useful when your focus is on the security or compliance aspects. Licensing validation could also fit in this case.
- **Capacity planning**: This is usually used to find out whether capacity meets the business requirements.
- **Optimization assessment**: Measuring your current performance is necessary so that you can get a good idea of how your current environment is performing. By doing this, you can ensure that you properly size your virtual hardware and can avoid any bottlenecks on your ESXi hosts. Doing this before you start your project is important so that you do not run into any surprises that can cause problems during your deployment phase.

There are also other types of analysis that could be related to the rest of the infrastructure, such as storage or network parts, that sometimes must be performed in more depth and need to be specific to the vendor, products, and solutions used. Some other analysis could be needed for other layers, such as the application layer, the database level, the network and storage level, the application architecture, and so on.

This chapter will explain how to perform the following:

- Analyze a physical environment before virtualizing it
- Assess an existing virtual environment

Analyzing a physical environment before virtualizing

Virtualization is normally used to provide workload consolidation, but this means, without the right resource management, just blending everything together; this could become a risk, like putting all your eggs in one basket without taking any precautions. In addition, all shared components of your infrastructure will most likely be affected in some way by this big change (for example, the storage or the network). Moreover, standard procedures such as monitoring, backups, patching, and administration will be also affected.

As a good practice, before virtualizing an existing environment, you need to assess all parts of your infrastructure not just the servers you plan to virtualize to uncover any potential problems or hurdles that may impact your project. The old woodworking rule *measure twice, cut once* also applies to information technology; be sure to get accurate measurements to drive the right project in the right way.

Of course, be sure to have a healthy environment before attempting to virtualize it, just to avoid incorrect measures, such as workloads with existing performance or application issues, to avoid the risk of just moving those issues to the virtual environment. Depending on the data that you collect, your conceptual and logical design (as described in the previous chapter) may remain the same, but the physical design should take account of real and objective data to be sure of a successful project. The existing environment could be physical, as was typical in the past, or mixed with some physical and virtual workloads, or already fully virtualized.

Most virtualization projects will involve migrating your current physical servers to virtual machines using a **physical to virtual (P2V)** conversion, or even better using an application/service migration to a new virtual environment. Therefore, it is important that you thoroughly understand your current environment before attempting to move it to a virtual environment. By doing this, you can ensure that you purchase properly sized server hardware for the hosts and define the correct storage, both for the capacity and the performance. For this purpose, you will need to collect some critical metrics, as discussed in the next section.

However, it's not always the technical aspects; you need to consider the licensing impact, not only for the virtual environment (for example, more hosts, more VMware licenses) but also for applications and services and operating systems where you may need new or different licenses.

Also, it's important to identify whether the old physical hardware could be reused for the virtualization; for example, for disaster recovery, or for other purposes (such as physical domain controller servers or backup server roles). In this case, you have to consider both the technical possibilities (for example, does the server have enough resources?) and the practical and organizational possibilities (is the server still supported and how much does it consume and cost during operation compared to a new server?).

Useful metrics from a physical environment

You should focus on the four general resources—processor, memory, disk, and network (that are the main elements that are virtualized). In order to have good data, you should gather these metrics for a minimum of one working week, and preferably over a one month period of time to match and discover all the different usage and peaks.

Of course, in order to have good and representative data, it's fundamental to gather those metrics during critical business cycles (such as payroll processing, batch operation, reporting, or other business processes) where performance may spike. That data and the peaks will help to right-size your environment and define the right consolidation for your workloads.

Processor metrics

Statistically, most servers have low overall CPU usage (< 25%), which is the main reason why server virtualization is so effective and used for server consolidation. But you have also to consider the peaks, which could be near 100% in some cases and, depending on how frequent they are, how long in duration, and how they are correlated, could become critical for the virtual infrastructure sizing.

CPU is usually overcommitted and depending on the workload, a 4:1 ratio between virtual and physical resource could be a reasonable target if you don't have CPU-intensive (or CPU-bound) workloads. Note that the ratio should be calculated on the physical (real) cores, not the logical processors that VMware ESXi sees, because hyper-threading could increase this number. It could be also important to define how the workload could be scale with more cores or socket and how could be dependent by the architecture (not all applications perform the same on different types of processor family) or simply the speed of the processor (some old applications just require GHz instead of cores).

For the CPU, the following table suggests the main metrics to be considered:

Metric	Description	Why it's important
% processor time (average and peaks)	Percentage of elapsed time that the processor spends to execute a non-idle thread.	Could be used to define the number of sockets and cores on the target VM, considering also a minimum hypervisor overhead. An high average value defines a workload CPU bound.
Processor queue length (average and peaks)	Number of threads in the processor queue but not currently able to use the processor resource.	This counter helps us to understand how many logical processors could be needed or whether there is a possible processor bottleneck.

Table 3.1: Main metrics to be considered in CPU

Finally, remember to compare apples with apples; a different processor may perform differently, and an application may perform differently by simply changing the type of processors.

Memory metrics

RAM could be overcommitted (assigning VMs more memory than the host physical RAM) on an ESXi host, and this was one of the historical advantages of VMware products. However, just because you can, it does not necessarily mean that you should.

Now, in most cases, it is not recommended anymore because it will degrade the performance of your environment (for example, memory ballooning or swapping also have an impact on storage). So, the right memory sizing could be really important, not only for the workload but also for high-availability aspects (we will discuss this more in Chapter 13, *Advanced Availability in vSphere 6.5*).

Note also that there are more and more workloads that are becoming more memory bound—consider, for example, all in-memory databases. In those cases, you should design the hosts carefully and maybe consider a specific cluster for those workloads (depending on the numbers and the recommended practices from the software vendor).

For memory, the following table suggests some possible metrics:

Metric	Description	Why it's important
Available free memory (average and least)	Amount of physical memory available for allocation to a process or system. It is equal to the sum of memory assigned to the standby (cached), free, and zero page lists.	This value indicates how much physical memory is not being used by your server. If you have excessive free memory then consider reducing the amount of RAM assigned to the server when moving it to a virtual host. Otherwise, a very low value defines a workload memory bound and, probably, you should increase the memory.
Pages swapped/sec (average and peaks)	Pages/sec is the rate at which pages are read from or written to disk to resolve hard page faults. This counter is a primary indicator of the kinds of faults that cause system-wide delays.	This value counts the number of times per second that the computer must access virtual memory rather than physical memory. This number normally increases as available memory decreases. Too many pages/sec can cause excessive disk activity and create a disk bottlenecks and also indicates that a system does not have enough physical memory.

Table 3.2: Some possible metrics for memory

Disk metrics

The disk can be the first bottleneck for your virtual environments; for this reason, it's very important to understand how much is used and how it is used, both for the capacity (but this could be quite easy) and for the expected performance. Using a simple **input/output operations per second (IOPS)** approach could work in several cases, but does not appropriately qualify the type of I/O and cannot always help in the storage sizing and design. Storage will be discussed in detail in `Chapter 7`, *Advanced Storage Management*.

For the disk, the following table lists some of the common metrics:

Metric	Description	Why it's important
% disk time	Percentage of elapsed time that the selected disk drive was busy servicing read or write requests.	Could be useful to identify workload that is potentially I/O bound.
Disk latency (average and peaks)	Observed latency of the disks. Warning zone of latency is typical around 10-20 ms.	High latency could mean disks or other storage bottlenecks.
Disk bytes/sec	Represent the rate of the bytes per second that are transferred to or from the disk during write or read operations.	This provides information about the throughput of the disk system and how busy it is.

Table 3.3: Some of the common metrics for disks

Network metrics

The network is usually the latest bottleneck of your virtual machines, except in the case of VMs with huge network traffic or when networks are shared between VM traffic and other types of traffics (such as IP storage, but also vMotion or FT traffic).

Depending on the **Network Interface Card (NIC)** types, you may have two different common situations for the VM traffic—dedicated NIC ports (typically for 1 Gbps ports where you may have several available ports) or shared ports (typically for 10 or more Gbps ports, where the number of ports usually is limited). Networking will be discussed in depth in `Chapter 6`, *Advanced Network Management*.

For the network, usually, the throughput is the common metric used for sizing, as described in the following table:

Metric	Description	Why it's important
Bytes total/sec	Bytes total/sec is the rate at which bytes are sent and received over each network adapter.	This counter shows the amount of traffic through your network.

Table 3.4: Common metric for network

Are all workloads good candidates to be virtualized?

Starting with vSphere 5, almost all servers and workloads can be virtualized, considering the large number of resources that you can provide to a monster VM.

However, there are some cases where you may keep a workload physical instead of migrating it to the virtual environment, as described in the following table:

Boundary condition	Why virtualize?	Why keep physical?
High-resource utilization servers	When virtualizing these types of servers, you may be able to have only one or two VMs on a host server, but you can take advantage of some of the features that virtualization offers such as snapshots, VMotion, HA, disaster recovery, and data protection, that are more difficult and costly to implement in a physical environment.	A server that has very high resource requirements may not always be as good a fit as a virtual server. Typically, these types of servers have very high CPU and memory usage and high disk and network I/O, and on a virtual host where multiple servers are competing for resources they might not perform as well.

Boundary condition	Why virtualize?	Why keep physical?
Vendor licensing models	Thankfully, most vendors today have specific license rules for virtual environments, and in some cases are also virtualization friendly (for example, with a Windows Server data center, you can run unlimited instances on a properly licensed host).	Some applications, such as Oracle, do not have virtualization-friendly licensing, and require you to license their software based on the number of physical CPUs in the host server and not the number of virtual CPUs assigned to the VM that is running the application.
Licensing restriction or limitation	There are some possible ways to accommodate these types of licensing schemes on virtual servers, such as USB redirection or specific network appliances (or Digi AnywhereUSB).	Certain applications use stricter licensing controls, such as hardware dongles (parallel/serial port/USB device keys), MAC address, or hardware serial controls.
Hardware that cannot be virtualized	Solutions are available for faxing and using modems through network connections over IP, but it's also possible to consider the PCI Passthrough feature of ESXi.	Some servers might have non-standard hardware such as a fax and modem.
Application support	Very few vendors do not support virtualization, but in those cases, you may consider keeping some physical server to reproduce the issue on them and still have the right support.	Some vendors will not provide support for their application if it is running on a virtual server.
Avoid too many eggs in the same basket	You can still consider different clusters (for example, a management cluster) or use proper QoS solutions.	Shared infrastructure could mean shared problems (for example, storage performance).

Boundary condition	Why virtualize?	Why keep physical?
Dependency or risk prevention	You can still consider different clusters (for example, a management cluster) or a different site.	Sometimes you have a circular dependency that can be a risk in case of a major failure. Dependencies are also needed to understand how power-off or power-on the entire infrastructure.

Table 3.5: To virtualize or to not virtualize

Existing tools to analyze a physical environment

For a physical environment, you need to collect all the data from the different operating systems, and then analyze and aggregate them all to right-size your ESXi hosts.

Different tools could be used but, basically, you can use standard tools provided by the different operating system, for example, **Performance Monitor** in a Windows system and `top`, `vmstat`, `sar`, and other command-line tools in a Linux system. However, using those tools is time-consuming even in a relatively small data center, because acquiring meaningful and useful inventory information requires manual aggregation of the results, and the approach is impractical in medium-to-large data centers.

VMware provides different tools or services to provide support during the initial assessment of a physical environment, with the purpose of right-sizing the new virtual environment:

- **VMware Capacity Planner**: This can help you plan for capacity optimization and design an optimal solution to achieve maximum performance. Capacity Planner is an IT capacity planning tool that collects comprehensive resource utilization data in heterogeneous IT environments, and compares it to industry-standard reference data to provide analysis and decision support modeling. This tool is limited to VMware **Professional Services Organization (PSO)** or authorized partners.
  For more information refer to the service page at `https://www.vmware.com/products/capacity-planner.html`.

- **SysTrack Desktop Assessment**: Through the use of the VMware desktop assessment service, leveraging SysTrack technology, your IT administrators gain a comprehensive understanding of the current end user environment as you evaluate Windows 10 migrations. Details on how each VMware solution would be beneficial are identified and quantitatively analyzed, resulting in the insights necessary to feel confident in moving forward with Windows 10.
  For more information refer to the service page at `https://www.vmware.com/files/microsites/latitude/index.html`.

However, there are also other tools from different vendors; third-party workload-sizing tools can also be a valid option, but the prices and capabilities of these tools vary. For example, consider the following tools:

- **Dell Performance Analysis Collection Kit (DPACK)**: This works non-disruptively in Windows, Linux, and VMware environments; customers typically allocate approximately 24 hours for data collection. The DPACK collector runs remotely and is agentless, gathering core metrics such as disk I/O, throughput, free and used capacity, and memory utilization. Then DPACK produces an in-depth analysis of server workloads and capacity requirements to help optimize data center operations and expansion.
  For more more information refer to the product page at `http://www.dell.com/en-us/work/learn/dpack`.

- **Platespin ReCon**: This was formerly known as **NetIQ PlateSpin Recon**. This is a virtualization planning tool for complex server consolidation and disaster recovery initiatives. It is really powerful and one of the first tools (excluding VMware Capacity Planner). It was also one the first to support multi-platform environments across Windows, Linux, and Unix servers.
  For more information refer to the product page at `https://www.microfocus.com/products/platespin/recon/`.

- **Quest Foglight**: This was formerly known as **Vizioncore Foglight**. This supports multiple hypervisors to drive your organization's virtual strategy across VMware, Hyper-V, and OpenStack. Additionally, Foglight can monitor Microsoft® **Active Directory (AD)**, Exchange, and Office 365, as well as the storage part.
  There's more information on the product page: `https://www.quest.com/products/foglight-for-virtualization-enterprise-edition/`.

The most interesting products are VMware Capacity Planner and Dell DPACK.

Capacity Planner

Capacity Planner is a powerful tool that automatically collects all the relevant performance metrics on each Windows server in your environment and prepares a report that you can use to determine your hardware requirements for your virtual environment. It can identify trends in your environment and make recommendations for grouping physical servers on virtual hosts. It uses the built-in Microsoft performance counters and does not require that an agent is installed on each server that will be analyzed (it uses the **Windows Management Instrumentation** (**WMI**) and the Remote Registry service). Using Capacity Planner is the best method for collecting data from your servers and reporting on it, because it was developed specifically for infrastructure assessment and data analysis and will provide consolidation estimates, recommendations, and capacity assessments.

The Capacity Planner dashboard is delivered as a web-based application that delivers rich analysis, modeling, and decision support capabilities based on the data collected from your data center. Service providers will use this interface to access pre-built report templates and create custom reports depending on the type of assessment being delivered. The analysis provided by the Capacity Planner dashboard is based on comparisons to reference data collected across the industry. This unique capability helps in guiding decisions around server consolidation and capacity optimization for your data center.

Note that, beginning with vCenter Server version 2.5, there was a *lite* version of Capacity Planner integrated into vCenter Server called **Guided Consolidation**. This utility uses a built-in wizard to discover physical systems and analyze them to prepare them to be converted into VMs. Once these systems have been analyzed, they can be converted into VMs by the built-in **VMware Converter** feature of vCenter Server 2.5. However, starting from vSphere version 5, this plugin has been removed from vCenter.

DPACK

DPACK is a software solution developed by Dell that works non-disruptively on physical systems based on Windows and Linux OS, but could also be used to collect data from VMware virtual environments.

The DPACK collector runs remotely and is totally agentless, and so without the need to modify your environment, it can gather some core metrics such as disk I/O, throughput, free and used capacity, and memory utilization. After that, DPACK produces an in-depth analysis of server workloads and capacity requirements to help optimize data center operations and expansion.

This tool is usually used to analyze both virtualization and physical data center, because it's hardware and platform-agnostic analysis service records workload characteristics, measures performance, and creates simulations from various industry-leading platforms.

All this data provides better visibility and information in order to:

- Eliminate overspending
- Speed up decision-making
- Identify opportunities for virtualization
- Increase the utility of future IT investment

This tool can reduce the guesswork involved in data center expansion and troubleshooting, and a DPACK analysis typically takes 24 hours or less to complete. For example, a storage analysis from this assessment should look as follows:

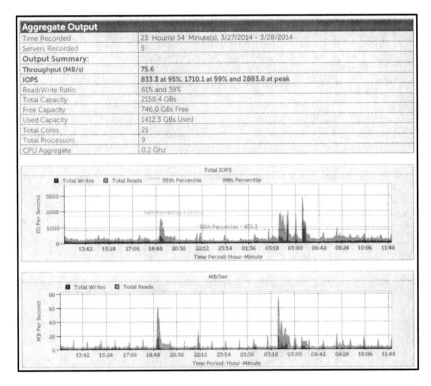

Short samples of DPACK reports

Initially, it was a service limited to Dell and selected partners, but now DPACK accounts are free and you can get one today at `http://dpack2.dell.com/register/today`.

Assessment of an existing virtual environment

For the virtualized workloads, the data is already there and can be used for the design (we will discuss later how to get and use it); maybe the greater complexity is to be found with other hypervisors, where host-related metrics could not be easily comparable with a vSphere environment. However, data collected at VM level could be good enough and quite useful.

Monitoring could be handled in the same way as with the physical environment, with the same tools and the same metrics, but it's easy to gain more information directly from your vCenter Server without having to deal with every single guest operating system. Monitoring and collecting (performance) data from a virtual environment will be discussed in depth in `Chapter 9`, *Monitoring, Optimizing, and Troubleshooting*.

But it's not all about metrics; you may also need to perform a health check or a full inventory of your environment.

Discovery and inventory

Building an inventory of your infrastructure is also very easy with the standard vSphere clients because you have a list of all your VMs or ESXi hosts with several columns (you can easily customize it with the information you want, and you can order or search your data).

Note that you can export several pieces of information, such as the hosts or the VMs list, using the vSphere Web Client and the export function in the **VMs** or **Hosts** tab:

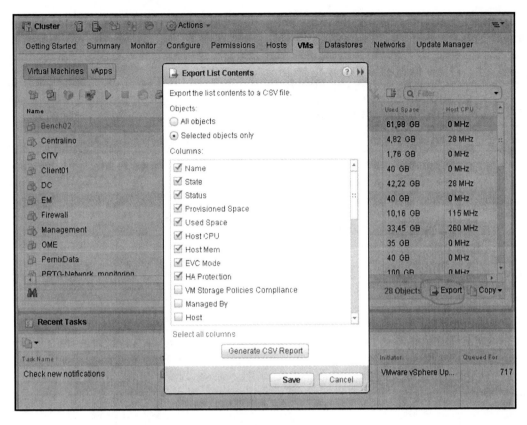

Exporting inventory data from a vSphere environment

However, if you need more detailed data, such as the firmware version of your I/O cards or the space used inside the **Virtual machine Disk (VMDK)**, this may need more effort or specific tools. One interesting case where you need a good inventory is during the upgrade procedure, where you first need to verify the **hardware compatibility list (HCL)**, with details on all hardware and their firmware and driver versions. In addition, you have to check all the software versions to ensure interoperability and guarantee the right upgrade paths. If the second task is quite easy to achieve, the first could be little more complex.

Sometimes, you can use VMware GUI or CLI functions; otherwise, you may need other tools, such as specific vendor related tools. Remember also that several servers have a specific out-of-band card (called **iDRAC** on Dell PowerEdge, **Integrated Lights-Out (iLO)** on HP ProLiant, and so on) that can also provide a lot of details about hardware configurations.

For the host's hardware details, there are some possible ways to obtain more information as follows:

Asset	How to obtain this information from VMware
Service Tag	This information is stored in the motherboard BIOS and usually can be read in the configuration/processor area
BIOS	Can be read in the configuration/processor area using the GUI
I/O cards	Some info is available from the GUI, but details on the model and the chipset are possible with specific commands, described in KB 1027206—*Determining Network/Storage firmware and driver version in ESXi 4.x and later* at `https://kb.vmware.com/kb/1027206`, or using vendor-specific management plugins for vCenter
Storage details	Vendor-specific management plugins for vCenter

Table 3.6: How to gain some hardware related details

Using good documentation to inventory your assets could be really useful for their lifecycle management. For this purpose, you can use traditional documents or spreadsheets, maybe shared in some way, or specific collaborative tools, such as SharePoint, Wiki, or custom web applications.

Health check

Doing a health check or health assessment of your current environment is critical, especially before some tasks, such as migration or upgrade. However, it can be used also during the entire life cycle of your environment, for example, to discover wasted resources, possible issues, mismatch with best practices, tools, and so on. Depending on how often your environment changes, you may need to perform this kind of task more frequently.

From a budget perspective, most companies do a deep health check on their environment every 6 or 12 months, but this may vary in each case. From a management point of view, a continuous health check would be best, but of course, in this case, you need to automate as much as possible and use the right tools. Several tools could be used to also perform other analysis, not only the health check.

Existing tools for analyzing a virtual environment

There are some VMware tools that can help by providing reports on your current environment. Most of these tools come with a 60-day evaluation period, which is enough time to get the information needed, and they are listed as follows:

- **VMware vSphere Health Check**: This is provided by VMware or partner professional services and based on a virtual appliance (or also a standalone package) that can connect to your VMware infrastructure and analyze it, with a great report generator. At this point in time, it's only available for VMware employees or selected partners. For more information refer to `https://www.vmware.com/content/dam/digitalmarketing/vmware/en/pdf/products/vsphere/consserv-vmware-vsphere-health-check-datasheet.pdf`.

- **vSphere Optimization Assessment (VOA)**: A powerful assessment tool to help optimize your vSphere environment with three analysis reports powered by vRealize Operations. For more information refer to `https://www.vmware.com/assessment/voa`.

- **VMware vRealize Operations**: The main purpose of this tool is monitoring, in a proactive way, a virtual (and in some parts also physical) infrastructure. But it can also provide some useful insight for capacity and resource planning, as also for resource optimization and resource reclaim. For more information refer to `https://www.vmware.com/products/vrealize-operations.html`.

- **vCloud Suite Assessment**: This would benefit organizations whose IT environments are predominantly or entirely virtualized and who are considering a move to the full VMware software-defined data center suite. For more information see `https://vip.vmware.com/`.

- **Virtual Network Assessment (VNA)**: This utilizes a VMware tool called **vRealize Network Insight (vRNI)** to provide a holistic view of the traffic in the data center across the virtual and physical domains, and understand how much traffic exists between VMs, applications, VLANs, and VXLANs. Identify threat planes across physical networks, virtual domains, cloud, and mobile environments.

- **vSAN Assessment**: Collect data about your existing vSphere storage environment in just one week and get the technical and business recommendations you need for a vSAN design.

- **Virtual Desktop Infrastructure (VDI) Assessment**: This is a specific assessment for a VDI environment that identifies the best candidates both for the users and the desktops; if they can be moved into a virtual desktop environment, and the order in which those groups and desktops should be virtualized to a successful VDI project.

Then, there are tools from other vendors, or also community scripts or your personal set of scripts. Note that community tools are not officially supported by VMware as they can also vary or change (there are a lot of scripts that are quite old). But scripting could be the best way to check some specific details, for example, to check whether the number of paths of each shared storage device is what you expect.

The following is a partial list of some of these tools:

- **RVTools**: Probably the most powerful and simple (you have just to connect to your vCenter or hosts) tools to inventory your environment. It also provides some health check capabilities; for more information, see `http://www.robware.net/rvtools/`.

- **VMware {code} vCheck vSphere**: A community script useful both for inventory and health check; for more information, see `https://code.vmware.com/samples/823/-vcheck-vsphere`.

- Some cloud-based monitoring tools with assessment and/or health check functions are as follows:
    - **Runecast**: `https://www.runecast.biz/`
    - **Opvizor**: `http://www.opvizor.com/`
    - **CloudPhysics**: `https://www.cloudphysics.com/`

    Most of them can also provide verification of how best practices are used and applied. The best way to learn more is just to try them, or ask for a demo.

- **Veeam ONE**: This provides advanced monitoring, reporting, and capacity planning capabilities designed to help you protect your virtual and backup environments. It also provides some useful report for the assessment of a virtual environment; for more details, see `https://www.veeam.com/one-vmware-hyper-v-monitoring-reporting.html`.

- **Turbonomic Virtual Monitor:** This is a free product that provides virtualization monitoring and reporting in an unlimited fashion across vSphere, Hyper-V, XenServer, and Red Hat Virtualization, not only for network monitoring, but also for providing insight into risk and efficiency information and potential improvements across the environment. For more information, see `https://turbonomic.com/downloads/virtual-health-monitor/`.

The most interesting and effective tools are RVTools and some assessment tools from VMware (VMware vSphere Health Check is probably the most interesting but unfortunately it cannot be directly used by customers or end users). Note that there are also situations, such as application dependency mapping, where other tools could be useful; for example, the vRealize Infrastructure Navigator.

RVTools

RVTools is a Windows .NET 4.0 application that uses the **Virtual Infrastructure Software Development Kit (VI SDK)** to display information about your virtual environments. It's a free application that can run on a server or a Windows client machine and can read information from all versions of VMware vSphere platform, from Virtual Infrastructure 3.x through vSphere 6.5 versions.

It is possible to list information about VMs, CPU, memory, disks, partitions, network, floppy drives, CD drives, snapshots, VMware tools, resource pools, clusters, ESXi hosts, HBAs, NICs, switches, ports, distributed switches, distributed ports, service consoles, VM kernels, datastores, multipath info, license info, and health checks.

The health check part may require a little tuning (for example, by default, the number of VMs per datastore is just 16, which is reasonable for old VMware infrastructure, but no more with vSphere 5 or later):

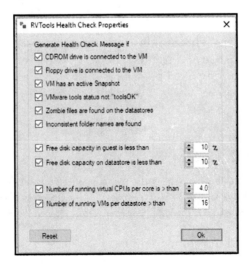

RVTools health check properties

The main pros of RVTools are that it is free, has a minimal installation, and supports all versions of vSphere. More importantly, it's able to export all that data in Excel or CVS formats.

VOA

With VOA you can proactively address the health, performance, and capacity management of the IT infrastructure and applications in your virtualized data center, as well as across heterogeneous and hybrid cloud environments, to improve efficiency, performance, and availability.

This tool can provide a different series of analytic reports that assess the configuration, performance, and capacity of your vSphere environment:

- **Configuration health**: Get a comprehensive report on vSphere configuration errors and security hardening suggestion. See a sample configuration health report at `https://www.vmware.com/content/dam/digitalmarketing/vmware/high-touch-eval/pdf/vmw-voa-phase-1-configuration-reporting-en.pdf?exp=b`.
- **Performance assessment**: It is useful to understand performance issues affecting your virtual environment and find possible bottlenecks. See a sample performance bottlenecks report at `https://www.vmware.com/content/dam/digitalmarketing/vmware/high-touch-eval/pdf/vmw-voa-phase-2-performance-reporting-en.pdf?exp=b`.
- **Capacity assessment**: This builds a customized capacity optimization report based on current usage and trends, which is useful for reclaiming underutilized resources or identifying over-provisioned VMs. See a sample capacity utilization report at `https://www.vmware.com/content/dam/digitalmarketing/vmware/high-touch-eval/pdf/vmw-voa-phase-3-capacity-reporting-en.pdf?exp=b`.

VMware vSphere Health Check

VMware vSphere Health Check is a tool only for VMware's partners (or VMware PSOs), but it can collect some data from a virtual environment, analyze the configuration, and provide a Word document with a lot of usable information structure in the following areas:

- Major findings and recommendations
- Organizational
- Operational
- Technical

- Health check assessment and recommendations
- Compute
- Network
- Storage
- Data center
- VM
- Security
- Virtual SAN

The technical recommendations section is the most interesting because it tries to check the existing configuration according to with VMware best practices and classify all the non-compliance at different priority levels, shown as follows:

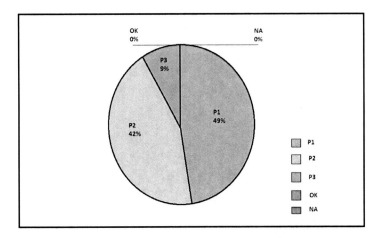

Example of VMware vSphere Health Check report

Then there is an inventory part, as with RVTools, but with the pro that it's more structured for a readable document, instead of just in some sheets in a spreadsheet.

Summary

This chapter explained how to perform an analysis and assessment of an existing physical or virtual environment, in order to gain all the data you need to plan your migration, upgrade your environment, or improve it. Different tools and approaches were described as a way to reach the goal. Specific application-level tools were not considered but must be part of a complete analysis.

Although those aspects are not specific to the vSphere version (and, in some cases, could also be generalized to other hypervisors), we also provided specific hints for VMware vSphere 6.5 editions.

The key takeaway lessons of this chapter are how to analyze a physical or virtual infrastructure, how to collect data from an existing environment to drive planning or performance analysis, and how and when to perform a health check of your environment.

With the next chapter, we are now able to start using the vSphere product, starting from the deployment of its components.

4
Deployment Workflow and Component Installation

VMware vSphere 6.5 is a sophisticated product with several components to install and set up. Understanding the correct sequence of tasks required to install and configure vSphere is the key to a successful deployment. The chapter starts by explaining the components of vSphere with their roles and services provided. We will walk-through the main aspects to consider for the preparation of a deployment plan for your environment, analyzing the criteria for hardware platform selection, storage and network requirements.

The host deployment plan will then describe the different ways to install ESXi, including Auto Deploy, and other solutions for deploying the host part. We'll also detail the deployment of **Platform Services Controller (PSC)**, vCenter Server, and other components, including the **vCenter Server Appliance (vCSA)** solution and the specific features and capabilities of the new version 6.5.

In this chapter, we will cover the following topics:

- Understanding the components used in vSphere and their role
- Preparing the deployment plan, choosing a suitable hardware platform for the ESXi environment, and defining storage and network prerequisites
- Installing ESXi hosts using different methods depending on the environment size—interactive, unattended, or automated
- Using the Auto Deploy feature to automatically install ESXi hosts
- Understanding the vCenter Server components
- Choosing a physical or virtual destination for vCenter Server
- Deploying a vCSA
- Accessing vCenter Server with the new HTML5 vSphere client

vSphere components and workflow

To provide services to the infrastructure, vSphere relies on two core components—the **hypervisor**, which is the virtualization layer for the complete environment, and **vCenter Server**, which centralizes the management of the ESXi hosts and allows administrators to automate and secure the virtual infrastructure. To complete the vSphere deployment, it is essential to know the interaction between ESXi and vCenter. Let's examine these two components to figure out their role:

- The ESXi hypervisor is the virtual platform on which virtual machines and virtual appliances run. Its main function is to provide the resources to workloads in terms of CPU and RAM. To manage the ESXi resources, ensuring performance and reliability, an additional component is necessary—vCenter Server.
- vCenter Server is a service that centrally manages ESXi hosts connected in a network and allows you to pool and manage the resources of multiple hosts. VMware vCenter Server can be installed in a virtual or physical machine with Windows Server, or deployed as a vCSA. The installation is now supported on Windows, macOS Sierra 10.12 (the installer issue due to the Sierra's security model change has been fixed with update 1), and Linux OS. Any host you plan on connecting to vCenter Server 6.5 should be running version 5.5 or above.

The vCSA is a preconfigured Linux-based (with VMware Photon OS) virtual machine that provides all services required to run vCenter Server and its components. As compared to previous versions, vCSA 6.5 has the capability of providing all services as the Windows-based vCenter Server. The latest release now integrates **vSphere Update Manager** (VUM) and you no longer need to install a separate Windows box. In a vSphere environment, vCenter Server is not an essential requirement to deploy the ESXi hosts, and virtual machines can run without it. However, advanced features available in vSphere can't be used without vCenter Server. You won't be able to provide services such as vMotion, **Distributed Resource Scheduler** (DRS), HA, FT, and Update Manager, just to mention a few.

The services required to run vCenter Server and vCenter components are now bundled in the VMware PSC, a component introduced in version 6.0 of vSphere that provides common infrastructure services for VMware products.

For a correct installation sequence, the PSC (which will be discussed later) must be always installed before deploying vCenter Server. Depending on the vSphere design, the PSC can be installed embedded in the vCenter Server or installed externally in the vCenter Server.

For a successful deployment, it is extremely important to understand the installation sequence of the involved tasks and their configuration.

A correct VMware vSphere 6.5 deployment requires a specific installation sequence to avoid problems due to missing components or services and can be summarized as follow:

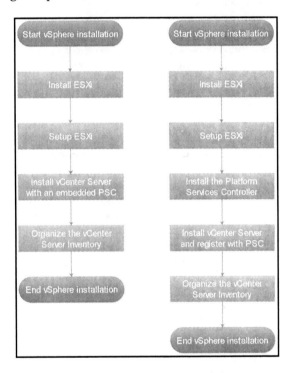

VMware vSphere 6.5 installation workflow

With a good design and following the correct workflow, the deployment procedure of vSphere 6.5 is straightforward and shouldn't raise problems. Let's have a look at the following points:

1. **ESXi installation**: In this step, you have to verify whether the chosen hardware platform is included in the HCL, and determine what installation method to use and which destination to use for booting the hypervisor.

2. **ESXi setup**: This step involves the configuration of the ESXi boot, network settings, direct console, and other settings.

3. **vCenter Server and PSC deployment**: You should identify what deployment model best fits in your environment for vCenter Server and the PSC. The vCenter Server can be deployed with an embedded or an external PSC depending on the design (multiple vCenter Server instances, for example). vCenter Server and the PSC can be installed on a Windows machine (physical or virtual) or on a vCSA. PSC appliances can be deployed on an ESXi host or vCenter Server instance.

4. **Connect to vCenter Server**: Use the integrated vSphere Web Client to complete the configuration of the vCSA or vCenter Server instance.

When the required steps are clear, let's start the vSphere deployment by examining the first core component of the infrastructure—the ESXi hypervisor.

ESXi deployment plan

A successful vSphere deployment requires an appropriate plan to avoid problems of incompatibility, performance, and instability with the commitment of remaining within the available budget.

Three main areas should be considered when planning a vSphere deployment:

- Choosing the hardware platform
- Identification of the storage architecture and protocols (NFS, iSCSI, FC, or FCoE)
- Network configuration (number of NICs, FC adapters, 1GBoE, or 10GBoE NICs)

Choosing the hardware platform

An important decision to take when planning an ESXi deployment is the choice of the hardware platform of the server. ESXi doesn't support all the hardware available on the market (storage controllers, NICs, and so on) and has some restrictions that can prevent successful installation of the hypervisor.

Only tested and supported hardware ensures that your ESXi can be installed without any problem and can operate as expected. Before purchasing the hardware for your server, it is strongly recommended you verify whether the chosen hardware platform is supported by ESXi.

To check for hardware compatibility, you can refer to the *VMware Compatibility Guide* available at the URL `https://www.vmware.com/resources/compatibility/`. The list of tested hardware is large and you can find the supported hardware from the main manufacturers, such as HP, Dell, IBM, and Cisco.

You can also use some white-box solutions but keep in mind that using a hardware platform included in the HCL ensures not only a successful ESXi deployment but also VMware technical support. When new hardware is released and certified for compatibility, the list of supported vendors is updated accordingly:

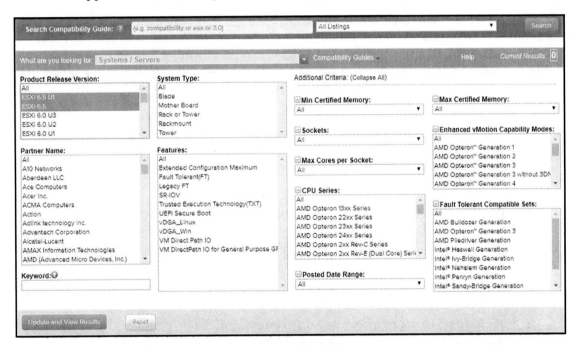

Search the Compatibility Guide available from the VMware website to check hardware for compatibility

A good practice could be to test the system for 72 hours to verify and check for possible hardware errors.

Choosing the right server for your installation is not an easy task, especially if your environment grows quickly and the business requirements change frequently. Capability, scalability, availability, and support are the elements of the server you need to evaluate carefully to be sure the final choice fits in the available budget without affecting the global design.

If you need to provide a large amount of resources to your infrastructure, a big server isn't necessarily the best choice.

In some scenarios, it is better to have more, smaller servers in a cluster to provide the required resources than a few big servers. The obvious question could be—*why are smaller servers a better choice?* Servers with more powerful CPUs and lots of RAM installed necessarily raise the costs for purchase and for support.

In the event that one ESXi fails, it's one thing to replace a server with dual CPU sockets and 128 GB of RAM; it's a different story if the server to be replaced has 6 or more CPU sockets and 512 GB of RAM. In terms of costs, the difference is enormous and often it's hard to justify the investment to the management. The challenge is to find a server that provides the amount of resources that meets the requirements but at the same time supports enough expansion (scalability) if the demand for resources grows.

Another factor you should consider is the expected performance of the server. The default hardware BIOS settings of the chosen hardware do not always ensure the best performance. To optimize performance, you should check some of the following settings on your server's BIOS settings:

- Hyperthreading should be enabled for processors that support it
- Enable turbo boost if your processors support it
- In NUMA-capable systems, disabling node interleaving (leaving NUMA enabled) will give you the best performance
- Hardware-assisted virtualization features, such as VT-x, AMD-V, EPT, RVI, and so on should be enabled
- vSphere 6.5 includes features that perform significantly better, incur significantly lower CPU load, or both, on hardware that supports Intel's **Advanced Encryption Standard New Instruction Set (AES-NI)**
- Consider whether you should disable any devices you won't be using from the BIOS
- For power management, you can choose to enable max performance or leave the control at ESXi with OS Controlled Mode

Identification of the storage architecture

Choosing a suitable storage solution is another piece of the deployment plan. You should consider what protocols will be used and their direct dependencies. For instance, a **Fibre Channel (FC)** storage device requires FC adapters to be installed on the server. vSphere supports software and hardware initiators (known also as **host bus adapter (HBA)** or converged network adapters) that add flexibility to your storage architecture design. An ESXi host may use multiple storage protocols in the same installation to support the design requirements. It is not unusual to see different ESXi installations with FC and NFS storage devices connected at the same host and, in some scenarios, also with the addition of an iSCSI storage. Storage will be discussed in detail in Chapter 7, *Advanced Storage Management*.

Defining the network configuration

For a successful deployment plan, you should consider the impact on your environment and how the deployment will integrate with the existing network infrastructure. This is another key point to keep in mind because it is strictly related to the hardware chosen for the server and the storage protocols used. Networking will be discussed in depth in Chapter 6, *Advanced Network Management*.

ESXi generates network traffic that must be controlled and sized to properly manage advanced features such as vMotion, FT, and VM traffic without congesting the network. The question could be *how many NICs should I use?*

The number of NICs supported by the server can heavily influence the network design and consequently, the overall host performance. If the server has only four slots available to accommodate the adapters and FC storage is used, the server needs to be equipped with at least two FC adapters to provide FT, taking precious slots intended for additional NICs.

Modern servers have several slots for the network adapters that may vary from 6 up to 12 or more. Often, the available budget for the hardware makes the difference.

Depending on the design of your ESXi server, general guidelines you might consider when defining the number of NICs to use are the following:

- **ESXi management network**: One NIC is required; two would be better for redundancy.
- **vMotion**: At least one NIC and due, to the amount of data involved during a vMotion process, a **Gigabit Ethernet (GbE)** must be used. More NICs can provide, more bandwidth, with the right configuration

- **vSphere FT**: It requires at least 1 GbE NIC but, depending on how many vCPU and FT enabled VMs are configured, a 10 GbE NIC could be a better choice. A second NIC is recommended for redundancy.
- **Storage**: Except for FC, which uses different adapters, NFS or iSCSI storage protocols need at least 1 GbE or, better, 10 GbE. Also, for this configuration, more NICs are recommended for redundancy and performance.
- **VM traffic**: To better distribute and balance the load, two or more GbE NICs are recommended.

If your server doesn't have enough slots for additional NICs, vMotion and ESXi Management traffic can be combined and the two NICs can handle both traffic.

When you have defined the server and the number of NICs you need for your design, the ESXi installation plan raises a new question—*how should I install ESXi?*

ESXi installation

Once you have defined the hardware platform and the storage and network setup, you are ready to deploy the ESXi host. The installation is pretty simple and takes only a few minutes. The latest release of vSphere made an important enhancement in terms of security, introducing a new feature for the hypervisor—**secure boot**. Secure boot is a solution that ensures that only trusted code is loaded by the EFI firmware before the OS boots. The trust is given by the UEFI firmware that validates the digitally signed ESXi kernel against a digital certificate stored in the UEFI firmware.

Once you have defined the design of the virtual infrastructure, you should evaluate which installation option is suitable for your environment. vSphere 6.5 offers three options to deploy ESXi:

- **Interactive**: Manually providing answers to installation options
- **Unattended**: Using installation scripts
- **Automated**: Using the vSphere Auto Deploy feature

The deployment method to adopt depends on the size of your environment and on the number of hosts to install. Interactive installation is definitively the simplest procedure you can use but requires more time if you have several hosts to deploy. Automated installation is more complex to implement but for large environments is always the preferred choice.

Once you have defined how to install ESXi, you should ask yourself the question—*where should I install ESXi?* Let's examine the available options you may consider.

Where to install ESXi?

Before installing ESXi, you need to decide where to store the ESXi files. A local disk, SD card, SAN (LUN), FC, or USB device are all possible destinations you can use for ESXi but what solution is the best and what you should use is very hard to say. The choice to make depends on your infrastructure design, network configuration, and the installed devices in your target machine.

You can use a SAN (LUN) to install your ESXi but if the server on which you are going to install ESXi doesn't have iSCSI hardware initiators, it excludes the SAN option as a booting device. An extra configuration is anyhow required to set up LUNs and zoning (zoning configuration can be avoided if is used the iSCSI boot from SAN mode). Anyhow, the use of SAN LUN creates a dependency on an external storage array that, in case of failure, makes the ESXi unusable.

Using local disks as the destination for the ESXi files is a solution that, until a few years ago, was popular in most ESXi installations because it is a cost-effective solution and doesn't require any extra configuration. If the local hard disk is your choice, I strongly recommend configuring **RAID 1** to provide fault tolerance. I won't consider the use of SSD as a booting device due to the high cost. Perhaps SSD would be a better choice for caching purposes using the HDD to boot from instead.

A valid alternative to HDD is the use of SD cards that offer better performance and compared to years ago, are now bigger and more cost-effective. To use SD cards, the target server needs to be equipped with **Secure Digital (SD)** bays but if your server has only one bay available, it won't be able to provide fault tolerance. Luckily, certain hardware manufacturers, such as Dell and HP, provide servers equipped with double bays for SD cards you can mirror like you would an HDD and fit perfectly in this installation method.

The downside of using SD cards is the requirement of some additional configuration. The scratch partition of ESXi (which will be covered in *Chapter 5, Configuring and Managing vSphere 6.5*), needs to be placed in a persistent storage (VMFS or NFS volumes attached to the server) to store `vm-support` output, which you need when you create a support bundle. Also, it's not supported for hosts with 512 GB or more, if you use vSAN.

The USB stick is another possible option you can use for ESXi installation. It is the most economical destination device but for production servers, I don't recommend its use since you don't have any redundancy in case of failure. As with SD cards, for USB sticks, no log files will be stored locally (a scratch partition needs to be configured). Although a 1 GB USB or SD device suffices for a minimal installation, it is recommended you use a 4 GB or larger device.

Did you notice that fault tolerance is a recurrent caveat for devices? Is there any reason for that? Yes, of course. Let's talk for a minute about the importance of having fault-tolerant components. What happens if you use just one device for your ESXi installation and suddenly the device fails? The ESXi simply stops working, stops providing its resources, and in a situation of a poor infrastructure design, the network services may be no longer available to users. For this reason, a good design for ESXi should consider the use of two devices configured in mirror RAID1 to provide fault tolerance and performance.

Preparing for deployment

When the destination for your ESXi has been chosen, you should decide what method to use for the ESXi deployment. Before proceeding with the installation, you can download the installation files at URL `https://my.vmware.com/web/vmware/downloads/`. The installation files are typically provided in ISO format to be easily burned to a physical CD/DVD or mounted to a server.

The installation using a physical CD/DVD can be considered old-fashioned and time-consuming, but to install the ESXi, you have also the option of using an USB flash drive, through the network using the **Preboot Execution Environment** (**PXE**) or mounting the ISO installation file (virtual CD) if your server is equipped with the remote management tool (iLO, iDRAC, IPMI, or similar). Perhaps the USB key is the fastest solution to use if your server doesn't have any integrated remote management tool since you just need to create a bootable USB key. Tools such as **UNETbootin** or **Rufus** can do that using the ISO file without burning any CDs:

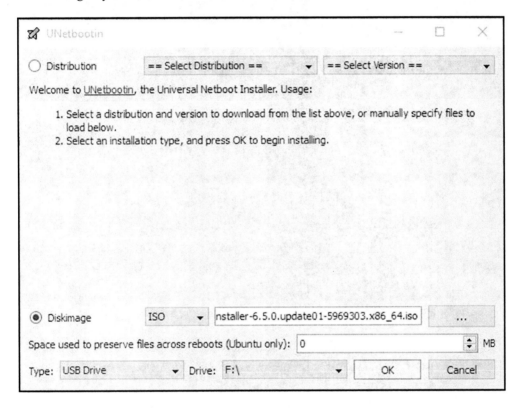

The UNetbootin tool is used to create a bootable USB key from ISO files

Some manufacturers, such as HP, Dell, and Super Micro provide servers with an integrated remote management tool that allows the use of the virtual CD feature that remains a good way to install your ESXi without the need to burn the ISO (you can sit at your desk without getting cold inside the data center):

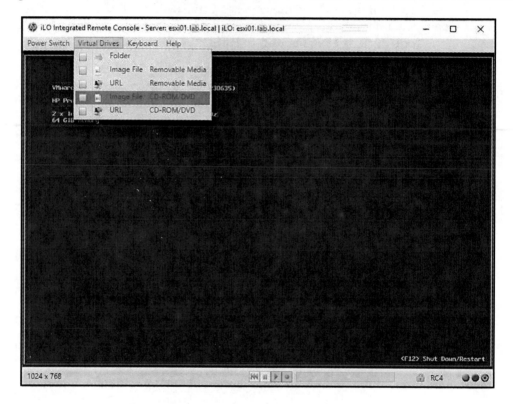

The iLO console used to mount virtual drives to install ESXi without burning a CD

Another option could be booting from the SAN (for FC storage, but it also works for FCoE and, in some cases, for iSCSI). You can deploy one ESXi on a 1 GB LUN of the storage, then stop the reboot process after the installation. At this point, you have a generalized installation of the ESXi. You just make several copies of this LUN from the SAN and then you have lots of ESXis ready (to be configured) with just one installation.

To avoid the risk of overwriting production data, disconnect all storage devices connected to the physical server you are not using as destinations for installing the ESXi.

Let's examine the three possible installation options:

Interactive installation

Interactive installation is very simple because the procedure makes use of an easy and intuitive interface that guides the user during the entire process. The installer is booted from a CD/ DVD, from a bootable USB device, or by PXE booting the installer from a location on the network. The interactive installation method best applies for small environments where the number of ESXi hosts to install is very limited. You can install ESXi in few minutes simply launching the installer from the installation media and no scripts or dedicated network configurations are required to complete the procedure. If you need to install a few ESXis, this is definitively the fastest and most straightforward option.

Depending on the ESXi installer media used (CD/DVD, USB flash drive, or PXE), remember to set the BIOS server accordingly to configure the correct boot sequence.

Perform the following steps to proceed with an interactive installation:

1. Insert the installation medium (CD/DVD, USB flash drive) and power on the server. When the server boots, the installer will display the **Boot Menu** window:

ESXi 6.5 boot menu

2. Select the ESXi installer and press *Enter*. The system loads the ESXi installer and displays the welcome screen. Press *Enter* to continue.
3. Accept the **End User License Agreement (EULA)** by pressing *F11* and continue with the installation.

4. The next screen displays the available devices on which to install the ESXi, divided into local devices or remote devices (see the following screenshot). Select the desired destination and press *Enter*. Since the disk order shown in the list is determined by the BIOS, make sure the selected device is operative. To get details of any previous ESXi installation and what VMFS datastore is detected, press *F1*:

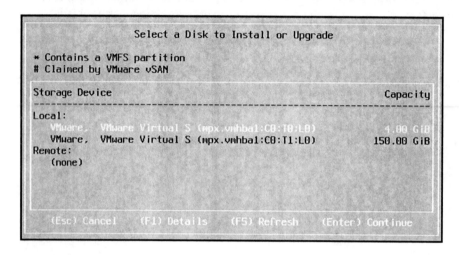

```
                Select a Disk to Install or Upgrade

 * Contains a VMFS partition
 # Claimed by VMware vSAN

 Storage Device                                          Capacity
 ------------------------------------------------------------------
 Local:
     VMware,   VMware Virtual S (mpx.vmhba1:C0:T0:L0)     4.00 GiB
     VMware,   VMware Virtual S (mpx.vmhba1:C0:T1:L0)    150.00 GiB
 Remote:
     (none)



    (Esc) Cancel     (F1) Details    (F5) Refresh    (Enter) Continue
```

Storage devices detected by the ESXi installer

 In the disk selection window, SATA disks, SD cards, SATADOM, and USB flash drives are listed as local devices, while SAN LUNs and SAS devices are listed as remote.

5. If the selected device contains a previous ESXi installation or a VMFS datastore, you have three self-explanatory choices to select:

- **Upgrade ESXi, preserve VMFS datastore**
- **Install ESXi, preserve VMFS datastore**
- **Install ESXi, overwrite VMFS datastore**

Use the arrow keys and spacebar to select an option, then press *Enter* to apply the chosen option:

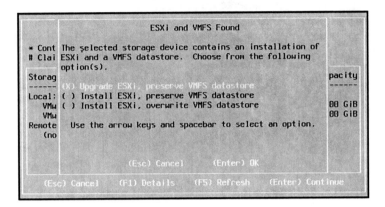

ESXi installation options

6. The keyboard layout selection is the next screen. Select your language then press *Enter*.
7. Enter the root password twice and press *Enter*. For security reasons, keep the password in a safe place.
8. During the installation, if the CPU doesn't meet certain requirements, a warning may be displayed. Press *Enter* to continue but note this warning if the current server will be used also in future releases of ESXi:

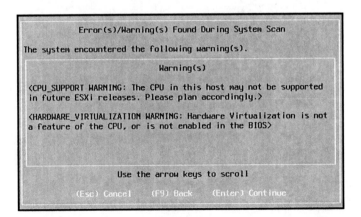

The warning displayed during the host installation if the CPU doesn't meet certain requirements

9. At the **Confirm Install** screen, press *F11* to proceed with the installation. The procedure only takes a few minutes and begins repartitioning the disk and installing the host in the selected device:

The host installation is confirmed by pressing F11

10. After the installer completes, remove the installation CD/DVD or USB flash drive and press *Enter* to reboot the host.

11. Once the host has rebooted, the procedure is complete. For new installations, or if an existing VMFS datastore is overwritten, VFAT scratch and VMFS partitions are created on the host disk (only if the destination device is not an SD card or USB stick).

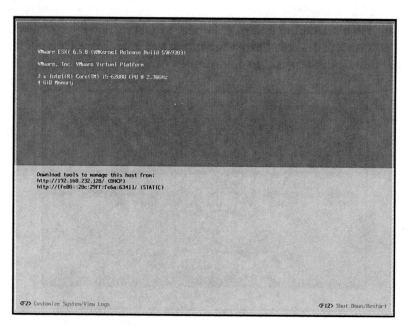

How the ESXi 6.5 screen looks when the booting has completed

By default, the ESXi is configured to obtain an IP address from a DHCP server used for its management. If your network doesn't have any DHCP server installed, the ESXi won't be able to obtain an IP address and you will need to configure it manually. The configuration of a static IP address and the post-installation configuration of the ESXi will be discussed in Chapter 5, *Configuring and Managing vSphere 6.5*.

Unattended installation

While interactive installation is very easy, you need to repeat the same steps for each server to install. If the number of hosts to install increases dramatically, the interactive installation method may not be the most suitable choice. The installation process can be automated using a script to provide an efficient way to deploy multiple hosts.

ESXi supports the use of an installation script to automate the installation process and can be useful if you want to have a consistent configuration for all hosts. Using an installation script, you can quickly deploy multiple instances of ESXi, creating **unattended installation** routines. These scripts can be saved on a USB flash drive or in a network location accessible through NFS, HTTP, HTTPS, or FTP.

The following table indicates some common boot options for unattended ESXi installation. For a complete list of supported boot options, refer to the *vSphere Installation and Setup Guide* available on the VMware website:

Boot option	Description
`BOOTIF=hwtype-MAC address`	Similar to the `netdevice` option, except in the PXELINUX format as described in the IPAPPEND option under SYSLINUX at the `syslinux.zytor.com` site.
`gateway=ip address`	Sets the default gateway to be used for downloading the installation script and installation media.
`ip=ip address`	Used to set a static IP address to be used for downloading the installation script and the installation media.
`ks=cdrom:/path`	Specifies the path of the installation script, that resides on the CD in the CD-ROM drive. The path of the script must be written in uppercase characters (for example, `ks=cdrom:/KS_CUST.CFG`).

`ks=file://path`	Performs a scripted installation with the script at `path`.
`ks=protocol://serverpath`	Specifies the script is located on the network at the given URL. Supported protocol can be HTTP, HTTPS, FTP, or NFS (for example, `ks=nfs://host/porturl-path`).
`ks=usb`	Indicates the installation script is located in an attached USB drive. `ks.cfg` must be in the root directory of the drive. Only FAT16 and FAT32 are supported. If multiple USB flash drivers are attached, the system search until the `ks.cfg` file is found.
`ks=usb:/path`	Specifies the path of the installation script that resides on the USB (for example, `ks=usb:/ks.cfg`).
`ksdevice=device`	Tries to use a network adapter device when looking for an installation script and installation media. If the script has to be retrieved over the network, the first discovered plugged-in NIC is used if not specified.
`nameserver=ip address`	Specifies a domain name server to be used for downloading the installation script and installation media.
`netdevice=device`	Tries to use a network adapter device when looking for an installation script and installation media. Device can be specified as vmnicNN name. If the script has to be retrieved over the network, the first discovered plugged-in NIC is used if not specified.
`netmask=subnet mask`	Specifies subnet mask for the network interface that downloads the installation script and the installation medium.
`vlanid=vlanid`	Used to specify the VLAN for the network card.

Table 4.1: Common boot options for unattended ESXi installation

The installation script is a text file often named `ks.cfg` that contains supported commands useful to provide the required installation options to the ESXi installer. In the installation medium, VMware included a default installation script that can be used as a reference to perform an unattended ESXi installation to the first detected disk. You can use this script as if it is suitable for your ESXi installation.

The default sample script is as follows:

```
#
# Sample scripted installation file
#
# Accept the VMware End User License Agreement
vmaccepteula
# Set the root password for the DCUI and Tech Support Mode
rootpw mypassword
# Install on the first local disk available on machine
install --firstdisk --overwritevmfs
# Set the network to DHCP on the first network adapter
network --bootproto=dhcp --device=vmnic0
# A sample post-install script
%post --interpreter=python --ignorefailure=true
import time
stampFile = open('/finished.stamp', mode='w')
stampFile.write( time.asctime() )
```

To create a custom installation script or modify the default script, you should use the supported commands available.

The following is a list of some of the commands supported in the ESXi installation script:

`accepteula or vmaccepteula`	Accepts the ESXi license agreement.
`install`	This specifies that is a fresh ESXi installation and requires additional parameters.
`--disk= or --drive=`	Specifies the disk to partition.
`--firstdisk=`	Indicates on which disk ESXi will be installed. By default, the ESXi installer chooses the disks in the following order—local disks, remote disks (network storage), USB disks. You can change the order of the disks by appending a comma-separated list to the command, for example `--firstdisk=usb, remote`
`--ignoressd`	Solid-state disks are excluded as a destination for ESXi installation.
`--overwritevmfs`	Overwrites an existing VMFS datastore on the disk before installation.
`--preservevmfs`	Existing VMFS datastore is preserved on the disk during installation.

`keyboard`	Used to specify the keyboard type.
`network`	The network command is used to specify the network parameters assigned to the ESXi.
`--bootproto=[dhcp|static]`	Command used to specify whether the ESXi obtains the network settings from a DHCP or is set as static IP.
`--device=`	Indicates the device name to assign the IP address in the form vmnicNN as in vmnic0.
`--ip=`	This parameter is used with the option `--bootproto=static` to set the IP address for the machine to be installed.
`--gateway=`	Used with option `--bootproto=static` specifies the default gateway.
`--nameserver=`	This command is used to specify the primary name server. Used with the `--bootproto=static` option.
`--netmask=`	Option used to specify the subnet mask for the installed system. Also, this option is used with `--bootproto=static`.
`--hostname=`	Sets the hostname for the installed ESXi.
`--vlanid=`	If the network infrastructure makes use of VLANs, this option assigns the VLAN to the specified NIC configured in the ESXi. The `vlanid` parameter is used with the option `--bootproto=dhcp` or `--bootproto=static`.
`rootpw`	This is a required parameter and is used to set the system root password. Use the `--iscrypted` parameter if you don't want the root password displayed in clear.
`reboot`	Optional parameter used to automatically reboot the system at the end of the installation.

Table 4.2: Commands supported in the ESXi installation script

A complete list of supported commands to use with installation scripts can be found in the vSphere *Installation and Setup Guide* you can download from VMware website at the URL https://docs.vmware.com/en/VMware-vSphere/6.5/vsphere-esxi-vcenter-server-65-installation-setup-guide.pdf.

To configure an unattended installation booting from a USB stick, perform the following steps:

1. Navigate to the installation media and edit the boot.cfg file. Replace kernelopt=runweasel with kernelopt=runweasel ks=usb:/ks.cfg. This allows the system to automatically use the script located on the USB drive. Make sure you use an editor that can handle UNIX encoding.

2. Create a ks.cfg file in the root directory of the USB device that the installer will use for the unattended installation. Edit the file and create the script. You can use the following simple script as an example:

```
vmaccepteula
rootpw mypassword
install --firstdisk —overwritevmfs
keyboard English
network --bootproto=dhcp --device=vmnic0
reboot
```

3. Save and close the file. Plug in the USB stick and power on the server.

4. To manually run the installer script when the ESXi installer window appears, press *Shift + O* to edit boot options. At the runweasel command line, type ks=usb:/ks.cfg. To specify the path to an installation script, you may also use the command ks=http://ip_address/kickstart/ks.cfg, where the IP address refers to the machine where the script resides.

5. The system will boot from the USB stick and do an unattended installation:

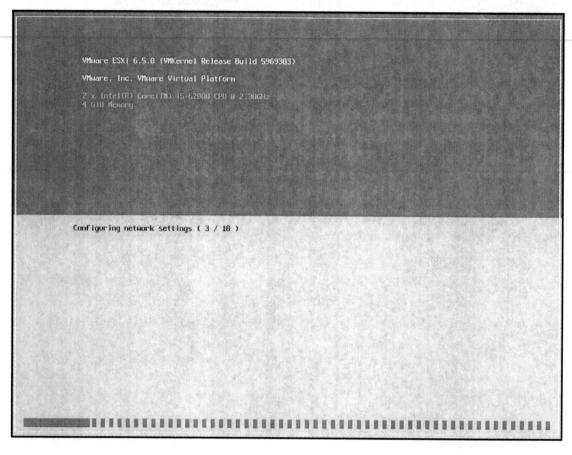

ESXi unattended installation

The main benefit of using unattended installations for ESXi is not only speeding up the installation process, but also ensuring a consistent configuration of all ESXi hosts.

Auto Deploy installation

Auto Deploy installation is a way to PXE boot your ESXi hosts from a central Auto Deploy server. This method is based on the use of master images with some set of rules to deploy ESXi with the desired specifications. Auto Deploy can also be used with the vSphere Host Profile feature (this will be detailed in `Chapter 5`, *Configuring and Managing vSphere 6.5*), to customize all ESXi hosts, ensuring a consistent configuration within the infrastructure. In a large environment, setting up the vSphere Auto Deploy feature to handle ESXi installations is the most efficient and suitable method to use.

Auto Deploy relies on several components and the configuration required is more complex. A vCenter Server must be already present in the vSphere infrastructure to provide the Auto Deploy feature. You need also a DHCP service, and a **Trivial File Transfer Protocol (TFTP)**.

The following figure outlines involved components and tasks used during vSphere Auto Deploy:

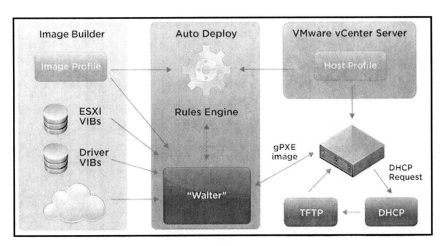

Schema of components used in vSphere Auto Deploy

The Auto Deploy feature in VMware vSphere 6.5 introduces a new graphical user interface for managing ESXi images and deployment rules that reduces complexity and helps users during the configuration. PowerCLI is still available and in version 6.5 has been enhanced with the new **script bundle** that allows administrators to add a post-deployment script once all the configurations have been applied to a stateless ESXi host:

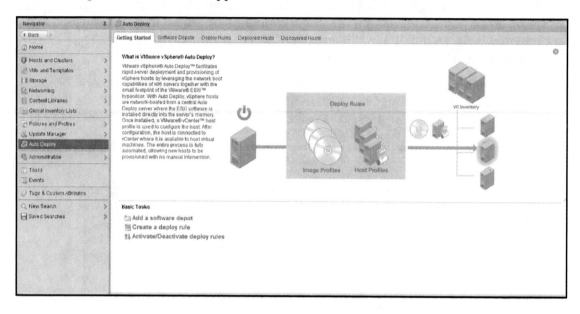

Configuration window of the vSphere Auto Deploy feature

An additional new feature of Auto Deploy is the ability to interactively deploy new hosts without first creating a rule. When a new host is PXE booted on the Auto Deploy network, it checks in with Auto Deploy for instructions. If the host doesn't match any deployment rule, it is registered as a **Discovered Hosts** waiting for commands:

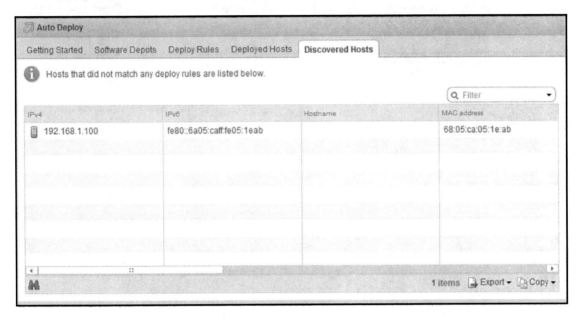

Discovered hosts with no deployment rules associated

With the new graphic, administrators can easily discover available hosts in the network and create new deployment rules or deploy without creating a rule. To deploy discovered hosts without any rule, simply select one or more hosts from the list and click the **Add to Inventory** button. A wizard will start in order to specify the parameters needed to deploy the selected hosts—ESXi image, host profile, and location.

The Auto Deploy feature is installed with the vCSA but by default is disabled. To use this functionality, you need to enable the service.

To enable the Auto Deploy feature, you should perform the following steps:

1. Go to **Home** | **Administration** | **System Configuration**.
2. In **System Configuration**, select **Services** to display the list of available services.
3. Select the Auto Deploy item and, from the **Actions** menu, select **Start** to start the service:

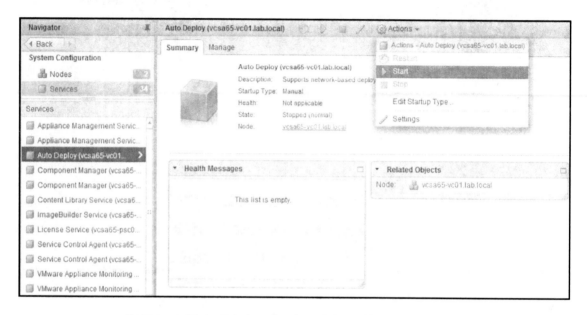

To take advantage of the Auto Deploy feature, the service must be first started from the vSphere Web Client

If both Auto Deploy and ImageBuilder services are not started, the Auto Deploy UI may not be visible in the vSphere Web Client. If the Auto Deploy service has already started, follow these steps to start the ImageBuilder service:

1. Log in to the vSphere Web Client as `administrator@vsphere.local`.
2. Go to **Administration** | **System Configuration** | **Nodes**, highlight the vCenter Server node and select the **Related Objects** tab on the right pane.

3. Right-click **ImageBuilder Service** and select **Edit Startup Type.**
4. Choose **Automatic** and click **OK**.
5. Select **ImageBuilder Service** and choose **Start**:

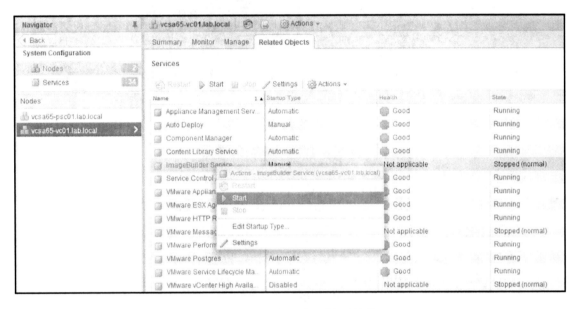

Starting the ImageBuilder Service from vSphere Web Client

6. Log out of the vSphere Web Client and log in once again. The Auto Deploy icon should now be visible.

Before digging in the installation procedure, let's see how vSphere Auto Deploy works and the configuration of the required components (DHCP, TFTP).

How Auto Deploy works

To take advantage of this deployment method, it is essential to understand how Auto Deploy works and what steps and services are involved during the ESXi deployment process. Different components interact with vSphere Auto Deploy when a fresh host boots:

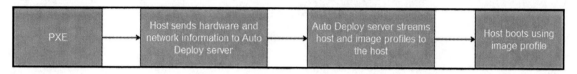

ESXi booting process using the Auto Deploy feature

The ESXi booting process through Auto Deploy feature involves the following different steps:

1. When the server first boots, the host starts a PXE boot sequence. The DHCP server provides an IP address giving instructions to the host on how to contact the TFTP server (DHCP configuration will be discussed later).
2. When the host establishes the connection with the TFTP server, it downloads the iPXE file (executable boot loader) named `undionly.kpxe.vmw-hardwired` and an iPXE configuration file.
3. During the iPXE execution, the host makes a HTTP boot request to the vSphere Auto Deploy server (this info is stored in the iPXE configuration file) to get hardware and network information.
4. The vSphere Auto Deploy server consequently queries the rules engine for information about the host and streams the components specified in the image profile, the host profile, and optional vCenter Server location information.
5. At this stage, the host boots using the image profile assigned. If a host profile has been specified, it is applied to the host.
6. The host is added to the same vCenter with which Auto Deploy is registered. If the inventory location is not specified by any rule, the host is added to the first data center displayed in the vSphere Web Client UI.
7. If the host is part of a **Distributed Resource Scheduler** (**DRS**) cluster, only when it has been added to the vCenter Server can VM from other hosts be migrated to the host.

If the host to provision is with legacy BIOS, the vSphere Auto Deploy server must have an IPv4 address since PXE booting with legacy BIOS firmware is supported only over IPv4. Using UEFI firmware, it is possible to PXE boot with either IPv4 or IPv6.

Configuring DHCP

To support vSphere Auto Deploy, the DHCP server has to be configured accordingly. First we have to define basic settings to configure a DHCP scope including the default gateway. If you want to assign a specific IP address to the host to be better identified, you can use DHCP reservation to accomplish this.

When the basic settings are ready, you need to specify two additional options:

- `Option 66`: In this option, you should specify the **Boot Server Host Name** to be used by the system.
- `Option 67`: The **Bootfile Name** must be specified. The filename `undionly.kpxe.vmw-hardwired` can be found in the **Auto Deploy** configuration tab in the **BIOS DHCP File Name** field.

If VLANs are used in your vSphere Auto Deploy environment, make sure you set up end-to-end networking properly because during the host PXE booting, the firmware driver has to tag the frames with proper VLAN IDs. Changes must be set manually in the UEFI/BIOS interface.

Configuring TFTP

To configure the TFTP server, you should **Download TFTP Boot Zip** file available in the **Auto Deploy** configuration tab and copy it into the TFTP server root folder. As the TFTP server, you can use some free tools such as SolarWind TFTP Server available at URL `http://www.solarwinds.com/free-tools/free-tftp-server` or Tftpd32 available at URL `http://tftpd32.jounin.net/`.

In the following figure, you can see a screenshot of the SolarWinds TFTP server used for Auto Deploy:

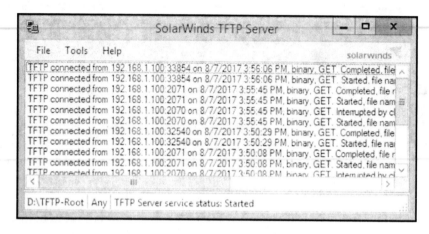

A TFTP server must be configured to allow the ESXi PXE boot

When you boot a new server, it gets the IP address from the DHCP and connects to the TFTP server through the **Option 66** and **Option 67** specified during the DHCP configuration. In the **Discovered Hosts** tab of **Auto Deploy** configuration, you will be able to see the host with an assigned IP address.

At this stage, a warning advises you that no deployment rules have been assigned. This is the new feature that comes in version 6.5—the ability to interactively deploy new hosts without first creating a rule.

Creating an image profile

Image profiles are a set of **vSphere Installation Bundles** (VIBs), a collection of files packaged into a single archive to facilitate distribution and used to boot the ESXi hosts. Image profiles are built and made available in public depots by VMware and VMware partners. You can create custom image profiles, usually cloning an existing image profile and then adding required software packages VIBs to the image created.

To create an image profile, you should add at least one software depot but you can add multiple **software depots**. A software depot can be a structure of folders and files stored on an HTTP server (online depot) or, more commonly, in the form of a ZIP file (offline depot). The software depot contains the image profiles and software packages VIBs that are used to run ESXi.

Using the new available graphic interface introduced in vSphere 6.5, you can create image profiles in an easier way without having to battle with PowerCLI. The steps are as follows:

1. Go to the **Auto Deploy** configuration page then select the **Software Depots** tab
2. Click on the green arrow to import a software depot
3. Type a name in the **Name** field and select the file to use as image then click **Upload**:

The software image used to boot the hosts is imported into vSphere depot

4. Click on **Image Profiles** to see the available image profiles defined in this software depot:

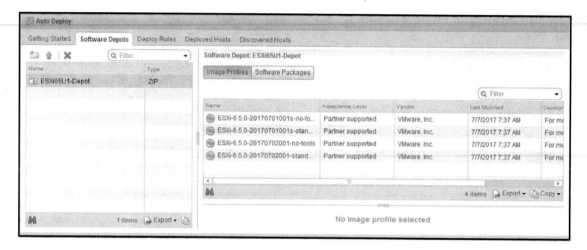

Software depots are used to store image profiles used to boot ESXi hosts

 An image profile doesn't contain any configuration (virtual switch, security settings, and so on) and you should use the vSphere Host Profile feature to store the desired ESXi configuration in vCenter Server providing the parameters to the host to provision. If syslog is not configured in the host profile, logs are lost every time the host is rebooted since they are stored in memory.

Creating deployment rules

Deployment rules are used to link the image profiles to hosts and VIBs defined in a specific image profile. To make an image profile available to hosts, VIBs are copied to the Auto Deploy server to be accessible from hosts.

To start provisioning hosts through Auto Deploy, you should define a deployment rule to apply. To create a new deployment rule, proceed with the steps as follows:

1. Select the **Deploy Rules** tab and click on the **New Deploy Rule** icon. Enter a name in the **Name** field and specify to which hosts the rule should apply. If you want to apply the rule only to specific hosts, select one or more patterns the hosts should match. In the example, we want to install the host with IP address `192.168.1.100` previously listed in the **Discovered Hosts** tab. Then click **Next**:

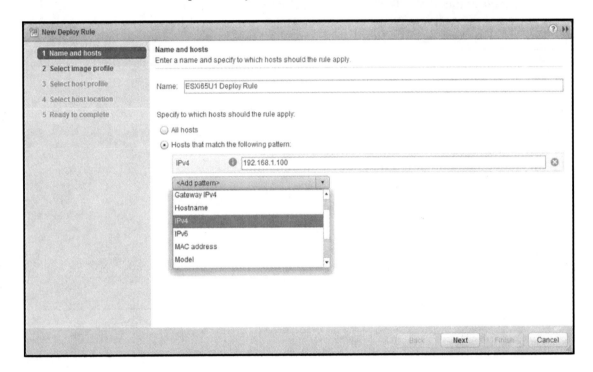

A deployment rule must be applied to a previously discovered host based on a specific pattern

2. Select the image to assign to the host then click **Next**.
3. Select the host profile to apply. If you don't have any host profiles available, flag the **Do not include a host profile** option and click **Next**.
4. Specify the location, cluster, or folder where the host should be added and click **Next**.
5. Click **Finish** to create the rule. By default, the rule is disabled and must be activated using the **Activate/Deactivate rules...** button as well as specifying the deploy rule order. To modify an existing rule, the rule must be first deactivated from the **Activate/Deactivate rules...** button to allow editing:

A deployment rule must first be enabled before it can be applied

6. Restart the host. When it boots, it should start the installation according to your configuration:

```
CLIENT IP: 192.168.1.100  MASK: 255.255.255.0  DHCP IP: 192.168.10.120
GATEWAY IP: 192.168.1.2
PXE->EB: !PXE at 9E8E:0070, entry point at 9E8E:0106
         UNDI code segment 9E8E:0BCE, data segment 90F8:5960 (611-638kB)
         UNDI device is PCI 02:01.0, type DIX+802.3
         611kB free base memory after PXE unload
iPXE initialising devices...ok


VMware iPXE Build: 4446055 (undionly.kpxe.vmw-hardwired)
iPXE 1.0.0-vmw (4750) -- Open Source Network Boot Firmware -- http://ipxe.org
Features: DNS HTTP HTTPS iSCSI TFTP AoE ELF MBOOT PXE bzImage COMBOOT Menu PXEXT


net0: 00:0c:29:55:06:68 using undionly on UNDI-PCI02:01.0 (open)
  [Link:up, TX:0 TXE:0 RX:0 RXE:0]
Configuring (net0 00:0c:29:55:06:68)............... ok
net0: 192.168.1.100/255.255.255.0 gw 192.168.1.2
net0: fe80::20c:29ff:fe55:668/64
Next server: 192.168.10.111
Filename: tramp
tftp://192.168.10.111/tramp... ok
tramp : 109 bytes [script]
https://192.168.10.40:6501/vmw/rbd/tramp... ok
/vmw/rbd/host-register?bootmac=00%3A0c%3A29%3A55%3A06%3A68..._
```

How an ESXi host console looks during the boot through PXE

The boot process of the ESXi provisioned with vSphere Auto Deploy is different compared to the interactive or unattended installation methods:

The ESXi host booting process with Auto Deploy

Auto Deploy modes

Having completed the Auto Deploy installation procedure, let's walk-through the different modes you can use to configure vSphere Auto Deploy. There are three possible installation types you can use:

- **Stateless**: The ESXi image is not technically installed but it is loaded directly into the host's memory as it boots.
- **Stateless caching**: The image is cached on the local disk, remote disk, or USB. If the Auto Deploy server is not available, the host boots from the local cache.
- **Stateful**: The image is cached on the local disk, remote disk, or USB. As compared to stateless caching, the boot order is inverted; the host boots first from local disk then from the network.

Let's have a look at the different procedures to configure Auto Deploy installations.

Stateless installation

Stateless installation follows the procedure previously seen where the host receives the configured image profile when it boots. This installation method just requires an available image profile and a deployment rule that applies to the target host.

Stateless caching installation

During the ESXi deployment through Auto Deploy, the image is cached on local disk, remote disk, or USB drive. The host is always provisioned by the vSphere Auto Deploy but if the server becomes unavailable due to bottlenecks (for example, hundreds of hosts that attempt to access the Auto Deploy server simultaneously), the host boots from the cache and attempts to reach the Auto Deploy server to complete the configuration.

The stateless caching solution is primarily intended to prevent situations where the deployment process may fail due to server congestion, a common scenario that occurs in large environments.

To enable stateless caching mode, follow these steps:

1. From vCenter Server, navigate to **Home** | **Host Profiles**.
2. Edit an existing host profile attached to hosts to provision or create a new one.
3. Under **Advanced Configuration Settings**, select **System Image Cache Configuration**.

4. From the drop-down menu, select **Enable stateless caching on the host** and click **Finish** to save the configuration. You can specify a comma-separated list of disks to use (by default, the first available will be used) using the syntax shown in *Table 4.1* to configure an unattended installation:

The host profile configuration must be modified to enable stateless caching

5. Configure the boot order from the BIOS of your server to boot from the network first then from the local disk. Reboot the host to get a fresh image.

After a successful boot, the Auto Deploy image loaded in memory is saved to the local disk. When you reboot the host and Auto Deploy is not available, the host boots from the cached image on local disk.

Stateful installation

The stateful installation method is almost the same as stateless caching mode with the exception that the boot order in the host's BIOS is inverted. Stateful installation is a method to perform a network installation because, after the first successful boot, Auto Deploy is no longer needed.

To enable stateful mode, follow these steps:

1. From vCenter Server, navigate to **Home | Host Profiles**. Edit an existing host profile attached to hosts to provision or create a new one.
2. Under **Advanced Configuration Settings**, select **System Image Cache Configuration**.
3. From the drop-down menu, select **Enable stateful installs on the host** and click **Finish** to save the configuration. You can specify a comma-separated list of disks to use (by default, the first available will be used) using the syntax shown in *Table 4.1* to configure an unattended installation:

The stateful installation feature is enabled by editing the host profiles configuration

4. Configure the boot order from the BIOS of your server to boot from the local disk first then from the network. Reboot the host to get a fresh image. During the boot process, settings stored in the host profile are applied to the host:

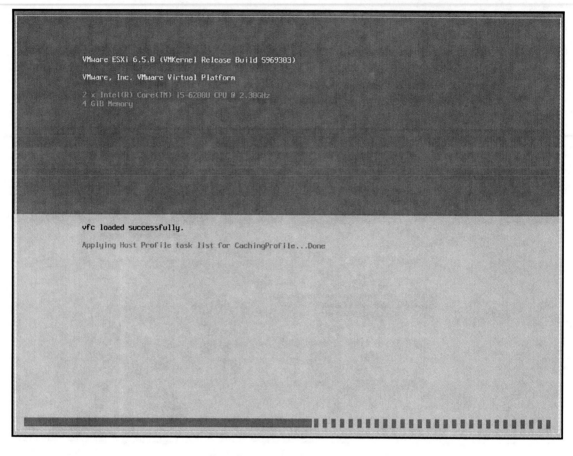

VMware ESXi 6.5.0 (VMKernel Release Build 5969303)

VMware, Inc. VMware Virtual Platform

2 x Intel(R) Core(TM) i5-6200U CPU @ 2.30GHz
4 GiB Memory

vfc loaded successfully.

Applying Host Profile task list for CachingProfile...Done

Host profile settings are applied during ESXi boot

5. When the host boots, it will enter in maintenance mode. At this stage, the settings passed with the host profile configured with Auto Deploy must be applied to the host. The host remediation action should be performed to complete the deployment process:

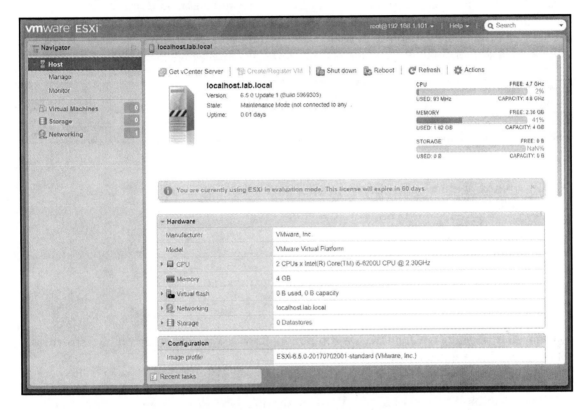

Processed host needs to be remediated to apply the selected host profile

6. Specify the IP address for the host and reboot the host. When the host boots, it will start from the local disk as a normal ESXi.

vCenter Server components

vCenter Server is a service that centralizes the management of the ESXi hosts and the VM that run on the hypervisor. This vSphere core component interacts not only with ESXi hypervisors, but also integrates with other VMware products—vRealize Automation, Site Recovery Manager, and vSphere Update Manager, just to give you some examples.

vCenter Server is not limited to act as a central management tool only. The advanced features such as **sign-on server (SSO)**, centralized authentication, vMotion, DRS, HA, and FT are all services that come into play only when vCenter Server is present in the infrastructure. With vCenter Server, you have the capability to manage resources, ESXi hosts, VM, templates, logs and stats, alarms and events, and so on. In addition, vCenter Server provides all the functionalities needed to distribute and manage the network services, ensuring the availability of resources and data protection. vSphere management will be discussed in detail in Chapter 5, *Configuring and Managing vSphere 6.5:*

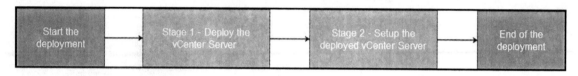

Deployment flowchart for vCenter Server

Starting from vSphere 6.0, the vCenter installation includes the deployment of two components:

- PSC
- vCenter Server

PSC

Introduced in vSphere 6.0, the PSC is a component used to provide common infrastructure services for VMware products.

The PSC is an important component in the design that provides services not only for vCenter Server or vSphere but for the VMware products in general. SSO, for example, can be shared also to other VMware products to provide a centralized user authentication (for example, vRealize Orchestrator, vRealize Automation).

Depending on your environment and the infrastructure design, vCenter Server and the PSC can be deployed in two different ways—embedded or external:

- **Embedded**: This is the preferred choice for small environments. vCenter Server can be deployed with an embedded PSC to simplify the management and, because both components are not connected over the network, outages due to connectivity and name resolution issues between vCenter Server and PSC are avoided. If the vCenter Server used is the Windows-based version, you can also save some Windows licenses. This setup, however, is resource consuming because for each product there is a PSC, that is not always required. If you install vCenter Server with an embedded PSC, you can reconfigure the setup and switch to vCenter Server with an external PSC later on:

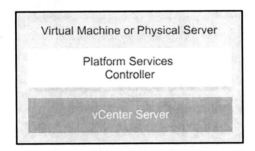

PSC and vCenter Server can be installed on a physical or virtual machine

- **External**: Installing the vCenter Server with an external PSC is a solution suitable for large environments with the benefit that shared services in the PSC instances consume fewer resources. This setup increases the management complexity and, in the event of connectivity issues between the vCenter Server and PSC, could cause some outages.

If the vCenter Server is the Windows-based version, you need additional Windows licenses:

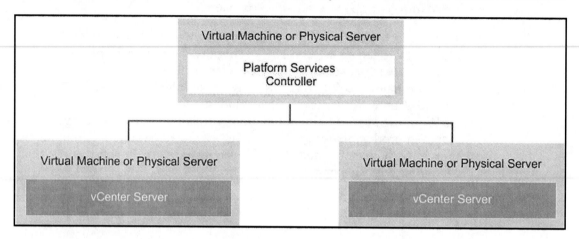

An external PSC can manage multiple vCenter Servers

Which method to use strictly depends on the requirements in terms of availability for your vCenter Server. You can have a PSC that serves multiple sites or a highly available PSC in a single cluster.

VMware recommends six high-level PSC topologies:

- vCenter Server with embedded PSC
- vCenter Server with external PSC
- PSC in replicated configuration
- PSC in HA configuration

- vCenter Server deployment across sites:

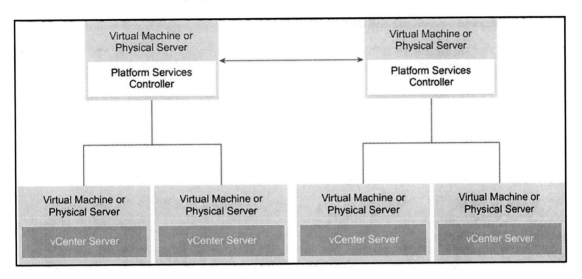

vCenter Server deployment across sites

- vCenter Server deployment across sites with load balancer

 For more information, see also KB 2147672—*Supported and deprecated topologies for VMware vSphere 6.5* at `https://kb.vmware.com/kb/2147672`. Some topologies have changed from version 5.5 and are now deprecated. The choice of the right topology depends on different aspects, such as features (do you need enhanced linked mode between multiple vCenters?), availability, scalability, physical topology, and so on.

Although a mixed environment is supported, it is recommended that you use the same platform (only appliances or only Windows-based installations) for both vCenter Server and PSC to ensure easy manageability and maintenance:

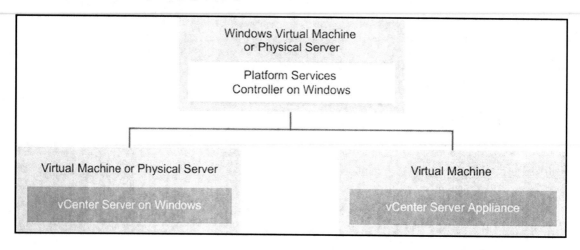

Mixed environment deployment is not a recommended design

There are three core services provided by the PSC essential for the vSphere functionality—SSO, VMware License Service, certificate management:

- **SSO**: This is a prerequisite to install vCenter Server (it cannot be installed without SSO). This service solves the problem of authentication in an environment with multiple ESXi hosts. Using a secure token mechanism, vSphere components can communicate with each other without requiring a separated authentication for each component. For each administrator who needs access to a specific server, without having a vCenter Server in your environment you need to create for each ESXi, a separate user account and grant access permissions. If the number of ESXi hosts grows, the number of accounts to manage also grows. Joining the ESXi to Active Directory to centralize the authentication can be an option (Active Directory integration will be covered in Chapter 5, *Configuring and Managing vSphere 6.5*), but adds another dependency in the infrastructure—the **Domain Controller** (**DC**). The SSO authentication service is easier to manage and more secure for the authentication against VMware products.

- **VMware License Service**: This centralizes the management of all the information related to the license of the vSphere environment and VMware products that support PSC. This capability allows licensing information between vCenter Servers not configured in Linked Mode group installed in geographically different locations to replicate every 30 seconds (by default). vCenter Servers in a Linked Mode group will be examined in detail in Chapter 5, *Configuring and Managing vSphere 6.5*.
- **Certificate Management:** This is required to communicate in a secure way with each other and with ESXi hosts, vCenter Server services make use of SSL. The **VMware Certificate Authority (VMCA)** provisions ESXi hosts and services with a certificate signed by VMCA by default.

Other services provided by PSC are as follows:

- VMware Appliance Management Service (only in appliance-based PSC)
- VMware Component Manager
- VMware Identity Management Service
- VMware HTTP Reverse Proxy
- VMware Service Control Agent
- VMware Security Token Service
- VMware Common Logging Service
- VMware Syslog Health Service
- VMware Authentication Framework
- VMware Directory Service

Additional details and configuration of PSC will be discussed in Chapter 5, *Configuring and Managing vSphere 6.5*.

Where to install – physical or virtual?

One recurrent question about vCenter Server installation is whether it should be installed on a physical server or on a VM. Technically, vCenter Server can be installed on both destinations but personally I prefer deploying on the virtual machine. Why this choice?

If you have the vCenter Server installed on a VM and the ESXi that hosts the vCenter Server fails, HA will restart the VM on another node, ensuring service availability. If a physical server with vCenter Server installed fails, you lose not only the vCenter Server but all services it provides. The best option would be having a management cluster with vCenter running on it (this perhaps makes more sense for large environments) but it would be an expensive solution the business could not afford/approve.

Another option could be placing the vCenter Server in the running cluster of your vSphere environment, a common approach for small environments. In large environments, if you need to shut down the infrastructure or perform some maintenance, it could be useful to know exactly which ESXi is hosting the vCenter Server without wasting time on research between hosts. A trick could be disabling the DRS for that VM to stop the vCenter Server being migrated around. To achieve that, you should edit the DRS setting from the vSphere Web Client. Proceed with the steps as follows:

1. Select the cluster on which your vCenter Server runs and go to the **Configure** tab (previously known as **Manage** but renamed in vSphere 6.5).
2. Under **Configuration**, select the **VM Overrides** option to disable the DRS for the vCenter Server.
3. Click **Browse...** to select the VM to process (vCenter Server) and enable **Override** in **DRS automated level**. Set the value to **Disabled:**

Override option can be used to disable DRS for a specific VM

4. Click **OK**. From now on, the vCenter Server is no longer DRS processed, remaining in the original ESXi.

VMware recommends deploying vCenter Server on a VM, suggesting the use of the vCSA. The feeling is the vCSA is replacing the Windows-based vCenter Server that will be deprecated quite soon.

vCenter Server deployment

vCenter Server can be installed on Microsoft Windows Server 2008 SP1 or later, Microsoft Windows Server 2016 included. Starting with vSphere 6.5, vCenter Server supports a mixed IPv4 and IPv6 environment. This means that you can connect vCenter Server with an IPv4 address to vCenter Server with an IPv6 address.

 Both vCenter and PSC require IP and name settings. If you use a **fully qualified domain name (FQDN)**, you will not be able to change it later (neither for vCenter and PSC). If you just use an IP (not recommended), you will not able to change it anymore.

Before proceeding with the installation, make sure all vSphere components have their clocks synchronized to avoid issues in communication between network machines due to the SSL certificates, which are time sensitive.

To avoid security problems, the use of a dedicated account for the vCenter Server service is recommended since the Windows built-in system account has more permissions on the server that vCenter Server needs. The user account configured in vCenter Server should be granted with the following permissions:

- Member of the Administrators group
- Log on as a service
- Act as part of the OS (if the user is a domain user)

Installing vCenter Server on a network drive or USB flash drive is not supported. If you use **Active Directory (AD)**, the vCenter Server cannot be installed on a **Domain Controller (DC)**.

Because vCenter Server stores the information on a database, let's analyze the criteria of database selection.

Choosing the database

Both vCenter Server and the virtual appliance require a database to store and organize server data and each vCenter Server instance must have its own database. vCenter Server 6.5 comes with a bundled PostgreSQL database that can be used if your environment has upto 20 hosts and 200 VM; for larger environments, you need an external supported database. vCenter Server 6.5 Windows-based supports Microsoft SQL Server and Oracle databases, while for the vCSA, Oracle is the only possible option.

The following table shows the supported databases in vCenter Server 6.5 Update 1 Windows version:

Database type	Configuration notes
Embedded PostgreSQL	The database is suitable for environments with up to 20 hosts and 200 VM. If you uninstall vCenter Server on Windows, the embedded PostgreSQL database is also uninstalled, and all data is lost.
Microsoft SQL Server 2008 R2 SP2 or higher	Ensure that the machine has a valid ODBC DSN entry.
Microsoft SQL Server 2012	Ensure that the machine has a valid ODBC DSN entry.
Microsoft SQL Server 2014, 2014 SP2	Ensure that the machine has a valid ODBC DSN entry.
Microsoft SQL Server 2016, 2016 SP1	Ensure that the machine has a valid ODBC DSN entry.
Oracle 11g and Oracle 12c	Ensure that the machine has a valid ODBC DSN entry.

Table 4.3: Supported databases in vCenter Server 6.5 Update 1 Windows version

For an updated list of supported databases, refer to the *VMware Product Interoperability Matrices* from VMware's website at the URL https://www.vmware.com/resources/compatibility/sim/interop_matrix.php.

Which database server type should be used for vCenter Server? Microsoft SQL Server and Oracle are both good options for vCenter Server and the choice is often driven by the platform and knowledge an organization already has. If you have an environment where Microsoft products are predominant and supported by a special contract agreement, the choice will likely be Microsoft SQL Server. If Oracle is already used in an organization, logic suggests going ahead with Oracle database.

Once you have chosen the supported database type to use with your vCenter Server, make sure you understand configuration requirements and setup to avoid problems. During the installation procedure, you must specify whether the system points to an external database or to install the embedded database, therefore the size of your environment plays an important role in this decision.

For small environments, you can also consider the use of Microsoft SQL 2016 Express Edition installed on the same server as the vCenter Server to save a Windows license and take advantage of the SQL Server knowledge you may already have. As soon as your environment grows, you can always upgrade your SQL Express Server to a full Standard or Enterprise edition at a later time.

Although Microsoft officially supports a SQL Server upgrade, I always prefer to build a fresh SQL Server installation and then migrate the vCenter Server database later on. You can find a complete vCenter Server database migration procedure in the VMware's KB 1028601—*Migrating the vCenter Server database from SQL Express to full SQL Server* at `https://kb.vmware.com/kb/1028601`.

If an external database will be used for your vCenter Server deployment, the database must be configured accordingly to work with vCenter Server and the external database can be configured manually or by using a script. Let's walk-through the setup of the external database SQL Server.

Configuring a Microsoft SQL Server database

Perhaps due to its popularity, the most common database type used with vCenter Server is Microsoft SQL Server. The installation of SQL Server is out of the scope of this book but you can find detailed information on Microsoft's website at `https://docs.microsoft.com/en-us/sql/database-engine/install-windows/install-sql-server`. Once the installation of SQL Server has been completed, you need to create the database and configure it to connect with vCenter Server.

To configure and manage the SQL database, you can install Microsoft **SQL Server Management Studio (SSCM)** (download at `https://docs.microsoft.com/en-us/sql/ssms/download-sql-server-management-studio-ssms`) for having a graphical user interface or running scripts. The vCenter Server installer package contains the example scripts at `vCenterServer\dbschema\DB_and_schema_creation_scripts_MSSQL.txt`.

Before creating the database, the connection between vCenter Server and SQL Server has some key points you should keep in mind:

- A database cannot be shared with different vCenter instances. Each vCenter Server must have its own database.
- The user account used to access the vCenter Server database should be granted the `db_owner` role.
- vCenter Server supports as authentication type both Windows and mixed-mode. The Windows authentication should be the preferred configuration to increase security. Mixed-mode should be used if you add third-party tools that support SQL authentication only. However, you can always change the SQL authentication mode from the SSCM tool.
- If a domain service account is used to run vCenter Server, the SQL Server database must be configured to allow the domain account access to SQL Server.
- If Microsoft Windows built-in system account is used to run the vCenter Server service, vCenter Server supports only **Data Source Name (DSN)** with SQL Server authentication.

When the database configuration has completed, the ODBC DSN must be created to complete the setup.

Configuring ODBC DSN

Once the SQL database configuration has been completed, you must create on the same server where the vCenter Server is installed, the ODBC DSN used by the vCenter Server to connect to the SQL Server instance that hosts the database.

Because vCenter Server requires a 64-bit Windows version, the DNS must also be configured using the 64-bit version. If not already installed, you should download and install the SQL Native Client on the vCenter Server to connect the SQL Server through the ODBC. SQL Native Client can be found also in the SQL Server installation medium.

To create the required ODBC DNS, follow this procedure:

1. Open the ODBC Data Source (64-bit) and select the **System DSN** tab.
2. Click on the **Add...** button and select **SQL Server Native Client** from the drivers list. Click **Finish**.
3. Enter name in the **Name** field (this value will be used during the vCenter Server installation to connect the database) and description in the **Description** field, then select the SQL Server where the database is stored. Click **Next**.
4. Select the correct authentication type set in the SQL Server and click **Next**.
5. Enable the **Change the default database to** option and select from the drop-down menu the vCenter Server database previously created. Click **Next**.
6. Click **Finish** to continue.
7. Click the **Test Data Source...** button to test the ODBC DSN connection with the SQL Server then click **OK** to save the configuration. The newly created System DSN is visible in the **ODBC Data Source Administrator** window:

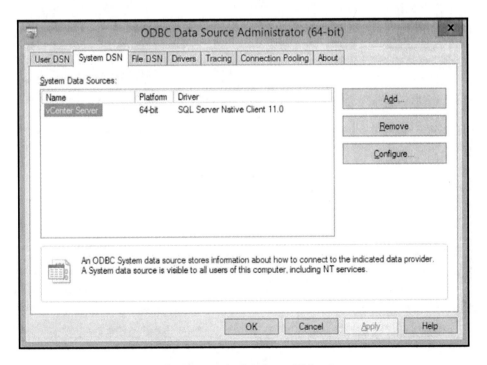

System DSN used to connect the vCenter Server to SQL Server instance

When the database and ODBC DSN have been configured, you are ready to proceed with vCenter Server installation.

Installing vCenter Server for Windows

When the database is configured and ready, you can start the vCenter Server for Windows installation procedure by double-clicking the `autorun.exe` file from the installation media.

The Windows installation wizard has been simplified and when it starts, you have the option of installing two components—vCenter Server and VUM. vSphere Update Manager will be covered in `Chapter 11`, *Lifecycle Management, Patching, and Upgrade*.

To start the installation, you should select **vCenter Server for Windows** option and click **Finish** to begin the installation process:

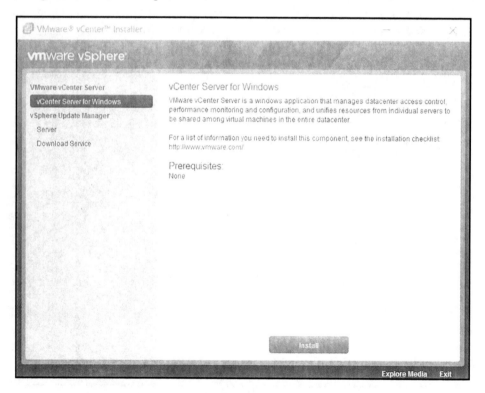

vCenter Server installation performed from the installation medium

Looking at the latest development in vCSA 6.5, it looks obvious that the VMware plan is to get rid of the Windows-based vCenter Server in favor of the vCSA. An official post published on the VMware website on August 26, 2017 has confirmed that the Windows version of the vCenter Server will be deprecated with the next numbered release. In the next version of vSphere, the Windows-based vCenter Server will be the final release. Almost a year after its release and having been tested in depth in production, vCSA 6.5 is now robust and stable enough to be the core component of the vSphere environment.

Since the installation process of the vCenter Server is almost the same for Windows and Linux-based versions, the installation procedure will be covered and explained for the vCSA.

vCSA deployment

vCSA is a prepackaged and preinstalled Photon Linux-based VM that provides vCenter and PSC services. As compared with old versions, vCSA now offers the same capabilities provided by the Windows-based version plus some exclusive services such as native high availability, native backup and restore, a migration tool, and improved appliance management.

With vSphere 6.5 Update 1, you can run the vCSA GUI and CLI installers on Microsoft Windows 2012 x64 bit, Microsoft Windows 2012 R2 x64 bit, Microsoft Windows 2016 x64 bit, and macOS Sierra. The new capabilities make the appliance complete and ready to take over the Windows-based version.

The following is a short description of new features introduced in vSphere 6.5:

- **Native high availability**: This feature, available for vCSA only, is a solution to provide HA to your vCenter. You could have the active vCSA in one data center and the passive vCSA located in a DR or secondary data center. It removes the dependency on expensive third-party database clustering solutions of RDMs.
- **VUM**: This is now embedded into vCSA. You no longer need a separate Windows VM, and an additional license.
- **New graphic**: The new **vCenter Server Appliance Management Interface (VAMI)** allows administrative management and monitoring of the vCenter appliance. Syslog configuration is now part of the VAMI as well.
- **Client Integration Plugin (CIP)**: This is now deprecated and no longer required since it has been replaced by the native web client.

- **Native backup and restore**: The process has been simplified with a new native file-based solution. Restore the vCenter Server configuration to a fresh appliance and stream backups to external storage using HTTP, FTP, or SCP protocols (vCSA only).

The installation procedure has been simplified and now vCSA and PSC installation is a two-stage process:

- **Stage 1**: Deploy OVF
- **Stage 2**: Configuration

This is a great enhancement and provides not only better validation checks, but also you can take a snapshot between stages for rollback. In addition, you can create a template for additional deployments.

Introduced with vSphere 6.0 Update 1, the Appliance Management client (accessible at the address `https://<VCSA_IP>:5480`) simplified the configuration and upgrade process. Now you can patch or upgrade the appliance through ISO or URL-based patching, simplifying the process and allowing you to save precious time:

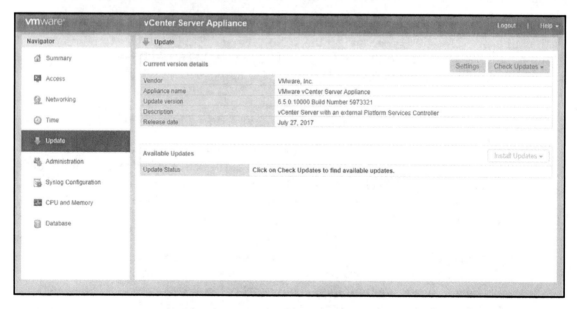

vCSA updates can be applied directly from the VAMI taking benefit of an intuitive GUI

Why deploy vCSA instead of the Windows version?

There are several reasons why you should deploy vCSA:

- Being a packaged and installed vCenter, the deployment is quick and you only need to supply a few details.
- The embedded PostgreSQL database supports up to 2,000 hosts and 35,000 VMs, and it is scalable and robust enough to be used for most environments.
- No need for extra Microsoft Windows licenses. Since VUM is now embedded, there is no need for a separate Windows box.
- Having now identical features, it's only a matter of time before VMware drops the vCenter Windows version permanently.
- vCSA 6.5 runs on Photon Linux OS and generally is a more secure OS compared to Windows.
- Less hardware to use since vCSA can be deployed only as VM. This allows you to reduce costs.

After having analyzed the reasons for making vCSA the preferred choice for your vCenter Server and the benefits it brings, let's walk-through the installation process.

Installing the vCSA PSC

As the vCSA installer with a new look, independent of a browser, now also support macOS, Linux, and Windows, then you can use the system you are more familiar with. Before proceeding with the installation, make sure you enter the new host in the DNS in order to both forward and reverse resolve. Perform the steps as follows:

1. Mount the ISO and run the installer.
2. When the main screen appears, there are four actions you can do—**Install**, **Upgrade**, **Migrate**, and **Restore**. Click on **Install**.
3. Click **Next** to begin stage 1. When prompted, accept the EULA and click **Next**.

4. As seen previously, the deployment type to use depends on the size of your environment. For this example, we are going to install vCenter Server with an external PSC. Select the option accordingly and click **Next**:

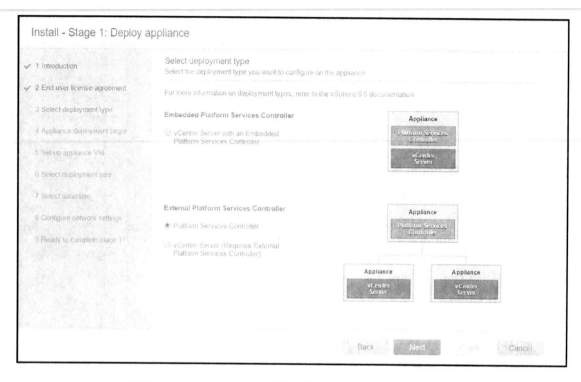

vCenter Server can be deployed with an external PSC by selecting the correct option in the installation wizard

5. Specify the ESXi target settings and the host credentials. Click **Next**.
6. Click **Yes** to accept the self-signed SSL certificate.
7. Enter the vCSA name and the root password then click **Next**.
8. Next, you need to specify storage options. Here, you have the option to enable thin-provisioned disks but this is not recommended for production environments. Click **Next**.
9. Configure the networking the vCSA appliance should use. Make sure the DNS for the IP used can both forward and reverse resolve to avoid errors. Click **Next**.
10. In the **Summary** window, click **Finish** to deploy the vCSA.
11. When the deployment completes, click **Continue**. Stage 1 is now complete.

At this point, you can take a snapshot before proceeding with stage 2. If any error should occur during stage 2, you don't have to deploy the PSC from the beginning. If you leave the installer when stage 1 has completed, you can finish the vCSA configuration by entering in your browser the address `https://<VCSA_IP>:5480`.

The installation continues with stage 2, performing the configuration of NTP and SSO services:

1. From the main screen, click **Next** to begin.
2. Time synchronization is the first option to configure to avoid communication issues with hosts. Here, you can also enable or disable SSH. Click **Next**.
3. Configure SSO, specifying a domain name, password, and site name. Click **Next**.
4. Feel free to join the **Customer Experience Improvement Program (CEIP)**. Make your choice and click **Next**.
5. In the **Summary** window, click **Finish**. This will complete stage 2 and the installation of the PSC:

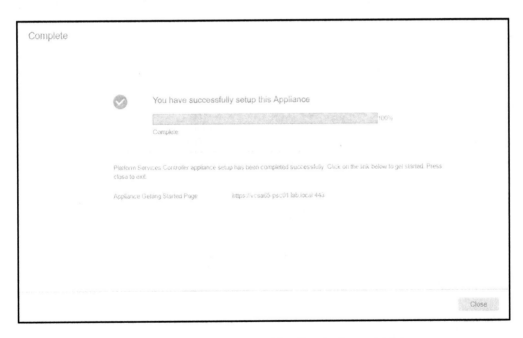

When the installation process is complete, the PSC is fully working and can be accessed via the browser

Installing the vCSA vCenter

To install the vCSA vCenter, you should run the installer once again, repeating a similar procedure to that used to deploy the PSC component:

1. During the vCenter Server deployment procedure, at step 3 click **vCenter Server(Requires External Platform Services Controller)** under **External Platform Services Controller** option and then click **Next**:

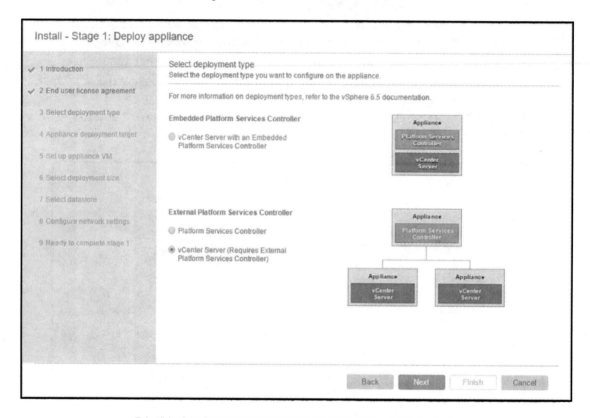

To install the vCenter Server with an external PSC, make sure a PSC is already available in the network

2. After specifying the storage options, in step 8 during stage 1 of the PSC deployment, you should specify the deployment size for the vCenter based on your environment. Make your choice then click **Next:**

Resources required for different deployment sizes					
Deployment Size	vCPUs	Memory (GB)	Storage (GB)	Hosts (up to)	VMs (up to)
Tiny	2	10	250	10	100
Small	4	16	290	100	1000
Medium	8	24	425	400	4000
Large	16	32	640	1000	10000
X-Large	24	48	980	2000	35000

Resources required based on deployment type

3. Continue the installation procedure by following the remaining steps until you complete stage 1.
4. When the stage 2 installation process begins, click **Next**.
5. Specify NTP servers in the **NTP servers (comma-separated list)** field and set **SSH access** option as **Enabled**. Click **Next** to continue the configuration.
6. In the SSO configuration page, specify the PSC appliance to connect, enter the SSO domain and SSO password then click **Next**. You can create a new, or join an existing, SSO domain.

7. In the summary, click **Finish** to complete the vCenter Server installation:

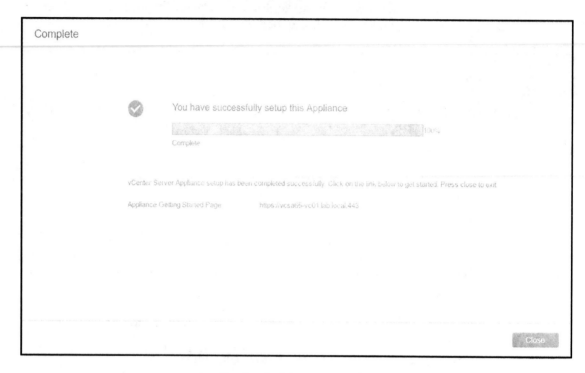

Complete

You have successfully setup this Appliance

Complete

vCenter Server Appliance setup has been completed successfully. Click on the link below to get started. Press close to exit

Appliance Getting Started Page   https://vcsa65-vc01.lab.local:443

Close

vCenter Server installation completed successfully

In vSphere 6.5, the only way to log in to vCenter is through the two integrated web clients:

- **Flash-based web client:** `https://<VCSA_IP>/vsphere-client`
- **HTML5 web client:** `https://< VCSA _IP>/ui`

Summary

For the successful deployment of VMware vSphere 6.5, understanding
all the involved steps not only ensures the correct sizing of the hardware components, but
helps to avoid potential misconfigurations.

This chapter walked-through the core components of vSphere 6.5, explaining the roles and
services provided. The ESXi host is responsible for providing resources to workloads while
the vCenter Server is used to manage hosts and resource availability. To ensure a successful
deployment, a deployment plan must be drawn up in order to define the correct hardware
platform to use, storage architecture and protocols, and network configuration.

We explained in detail the different installation methods available to users for vSphere
components to finalize the deployment. There are three ways to install ESXi hosts
depending on the environment size—interactive installation, unattended using installation
scripts, or automated that uses the vSphere Auto Deploy feature to install ESXi through
PXE. The Auto Deploy feature is the most suitable method for the deployment of a large
number of ESXi hosts, automating the process and ensuring configuration consistency
within the whole environment.

The chapter also covered the vCenter Server components and how to properly install them.
vCSA 6.5 requires the deployment of two components—the PSC (used to manage SSO,
License Service, and certificate management) and the vCenter Server. The vCenter Server
can be installed with an embedded PSC or with an external PSC. As stated by VMware, the
vCSA will replace the deprecated Windows-based vCenter Server.

Now that all the different vSphere components have been deployed, in the next chapter we
will discuss how to configure the entire virtual infrastructure.

5
Configuring and Managing vSphere 6.5

This chapter will cover the configurations required by ESXi and vCenter Server to operate in a healthy status in order to provide services and resources to a VM. It will explain how to properly set up the hypervisor, assign the correct IP address, and configure a time-synced network in order to have a working infrastructure.

This chapter will also walk-through the configuration of vCSA main parameters and features, such as **Single Sign-On (SSO)**, **Active Directory (AD)**, roles, permissions, and so on, and how to efficiently manage data centers, clusters, and hosts using the new vSphere Client (HTML5 client).

The use of PowerCLI and **vSphere CLI (vCLI)** is another important topic covered in this chapter, because time-consuming tasks can be automated and executed in seconds using scripts, reducing the workload for the IT staff.

In this chapter, we will cover the following topics:

- Configuring the main ESXi options, understanding the partition layout, and how to configure the scratch partition
- Using the vSphere Host Profile feature to get a consistent configuration of your hosts and setting up a configuration backup using CLI commands to quickly restore a failed host
- Configuring a vCSA and understanding the correct license model to apply
- Configuring and managing data centers, clusters, and hosts
- Automating some tasks using PowerCLI, vCLI scripts, and the vCenter REST API

VMware vSphere HTML5 client

The new vSphere 6.5 introduces the long-awaited HTML5-based vSphere Client that will replace the flash-based client in the next numbered release (not an update release), as stated in the post published on the VMware website on August 25, 2017.

The new client, just called vSphere Client (but in this book, we will call it HTML5 client, to clarify the type of client), comes from the vSphere HTML5 Web Client Flings project (`https://labs.vmware.com/flings/vsphere-html5-web-client`), still available if you want to add this client to a vSphere 6.0 infrastructure also. Unfortunately, the HTML5 client doesn't support all required functionalities, but the VMware team is working hard to make a full release available as soon as possible. With the release of vSphere 6.5 Update 1, HTML5 client development reached a higher step of supported functionalities, covering 90% of the workflow.

The new client is completely built on HTML5, requires no plugins, and is lighter and much faster than the flash-based client. The vSphere **Client Integration Plugin (CIP)** has been deprecated and it no longer works for connecting vSphere 6.5 components. Both the Flash and HTML5 clients are automatically installed as part of the vCenter deployment process. The HTML5 client can be accessed through `https://<VCSA_IP>/ui`:

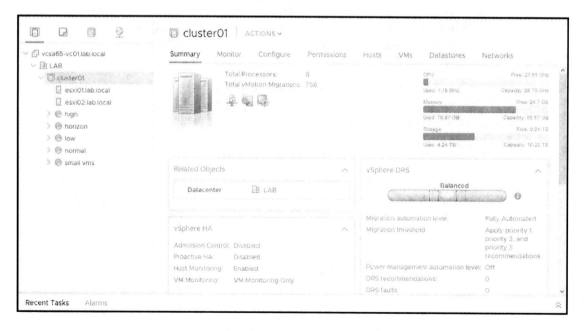

New vSphere HTML5 client introduced in vSphere 6.5

At the time of writing, the browsers supported by the vSphere HTML5 client are the following:

OS	Browser
Windows	Microsoft Internet Explorer 10.0.19 and later Mozilla Firefox 34 and later Google Chrome 39 and later
macOS	Mozilla Firefox 34 and later Google Chrome 39 and later

Table 5.1: Browsers supported by vSphere HTML5 client

The performance with Internet Explorer 11 can be slower than with other browsers, because of the rendering engine it uses.

To log in to the ESXi host, version 6.5 provides the new built-in HTML5 client available at https://<ESXi_IP>/ui</kbd>. The HTML5 client started as the Flings project (https://labs.vmware.com/flings/esxi-embedded-host-client) and was later integrated into ESXi 6.0 U2, becoming the only client in version 6.5.

ESXi configuration

When the installation of the ESXi host is complete, there is some configuration you need to do to connect the hypervisor with the network infrastructure. Let's walk-through the main settings you should configure.

Management console configuration

By default, ESXi is configured to receive the IP address for the management console through **Dynamic Host Configuration Protocol (DHCP)**. If no DHCP server is present in your network, the hypervisor doesn't obtain any IP and you won't be able to connect.

Assigning a dynamic IP address to ESXi is not a recommended configuration because management and services are linked to specific IP addresses assigned to the server. If the IP changes (after rebooting the host or for an expired lease), some services may not work as expected. If the server has multiple physical NICs installed and the DHCP assigns an IP address to an NIC linked to a wrong vSwitch, you may experience connectivity issues that will impede the correct connection to the management console and you won't be able to manage the host.

Configuring a static IP address to the ESXi management console is the recommended configuration to adopt. The ESXi management console can be configured accessing the **Direct Console User Interface (DCUI)** directly, or through the iLO, iDrac, IPMI, or similar (if your server has an integrated remote management console). Proceed with the following steps:

1. Access the ESXi console and press *F2* to **Customize System/View Logs**:

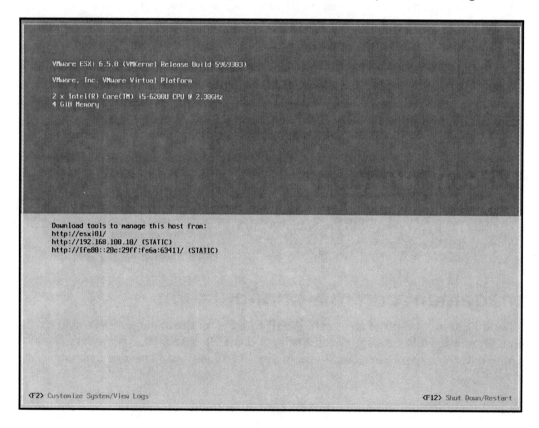

The ESXi console to access the host configuration

2. When requested, enter the root password set during the installation process.

3. Select **Configure Management Network** from the **System Customization** menu and press *Enter.*

4. Select **Network Adapters** from the **Configure Management Network** menu and press *Enter.*

5. Using the spacebar, toggle the NIC to use for the ESXi management and press *Enter.* Press *D* to see details related to the selected NIC (for example, attached vSwitch).

6. Now select **IPv4 Configuration** and press *Enter* to assign a static IP address.

7. Use the spacebar to select the **Set static IPv4 address and network configuration** option, then configure **IPv4 Address, Subnet Mask,** and **Default Gateway.** Press *Enter* to save the configuration:

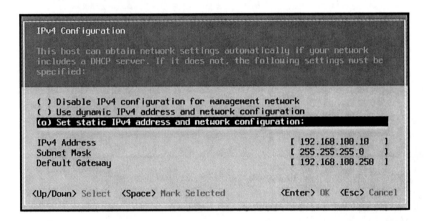

It's recommended to configure the host with a static IP address

8. Select **DNS Configuration** to specify the primary and alternate DNS servers and the hostname. Press *Enter* to confirm the settings.

9. Select **Custom DNS Suffixes** to specify the suffix to use (lab.local, for instance). Press *Enter* to confirm.

10. Press *Esc* to exit the **Configure Management Network** console. Press *Y* to apply changes when prompted.

Enabling SSH access

You may need to access the hypervisor through SSH for troubleshooting or to perform some actions using CLI commands. To access the ESXi host through SSH, you must enable the SSH protocol first, because it is disabled by default. For security reasons, it is suggested that you keep the SSH protocol disabled if not used. A warning message advises you that the SSH protocol is enabled:

SSH warning message when the protocol is enabled in the host

To enable SSH from the web console, log in to the ESXi, and right-click the host. Select **Services | Enable Secure Shell (SSH)**.

To enable SSH from the DCUI, perform the following procedure:

1. From **System Customization**, select the **Troubleshooting** option and press *Enter*.
2. Select **Enable SSH** and press *Enter* to change. SSH is now enabled.
3. The same procedure must be performed if you want to enable the ESXi Shell.
4. Press *Esc* to exit.

Configuring NTP

Time synchronization in your network should always be configured, but sometimes users underestimate its relevance because they believe that having the network time-synced is not so important. Wrong it's extremely important.

If the ESXi hosts are not in sync, you can face some communication issues between vSphere components that can cause service outage. If you use AD in your network, for example, **Domain Controllers (DCs)** and clients must be time-synced to avoid authentication problems. If the time between DCs and clients differs by more than 5 minutes, Kerberos tickets will fail and you will not be able to log in. By default, machines joined to a domain will contact the DC that holds the **Primary Domain Controller (PDC)** emulator role to synchronize the time.

VM use VMware Tools (VMware Tools will be discussed in `Chapter 8`, *Advanced VM and Resource Management*) to synchronize the time with the host. Although a VM can be time-synced with the ESXi host using VMware Tools (VMs automatically synchronize the time when specific events, such as VM vMotion, snapshot creation, and guest OS reboots, occur), it is recommended to synchronize the guest OS time with **Network Time Protocol (NTP)** source instead.

If your network is not time-synced, you may experience authentication issues between the vCenter Server and the **Platform Services Controller (PSC)**.

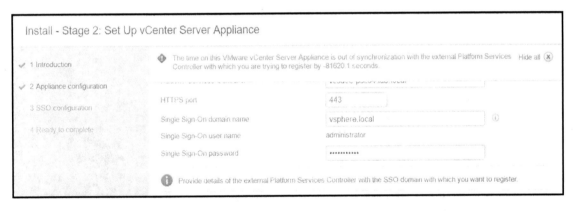

When vSphere components are not time-synced, the login procedure may fail due to communication issues between the PSC and vCenter

To keep the time synchronized, ESXi supports the NTP that you can configure through the vSphere Client. As a time source for your network, you should use a reliable external source, such as the `pool.ntp.org` project (a big virtual cluster of time servers providing a reliable, easy-to-use NTP service) or an internal source, such as a DC synchronized with an external time source.

A configuration option that could be used to synchronize the network time requires the setup of the ESXi server to point to an internal source that can be a DC configured as an NTP server, which is synchronized with an external and reliable NTP source.

Let's see how to configure an NTP in your ESXi by performing the following steps:

1. Open vSphere Client by typing the address `https://<ESXi_IP>/ui` into your favorite browser, and log in to the host.
2. In the navigator, select **Manage**. Go to the **System** tab and select **Time & date**.
3. Click **Edit settings** to open the time configuration window.
4. Select **Use Network Time Protocol (enable NTP client)** to specify the NTP parameters. Select **Start and stop with port usage** (recommended option) in the **NTP service startup policy** drop-down menu. In the **NTP servers** field, enter the NTP server to use; specify the `pool.ntp.org` NTP servers to directly point the host to an external source, or enter the AD DC that holds the PDC emulator role configured to synchronize the time to an external source, to ensure the correct time:

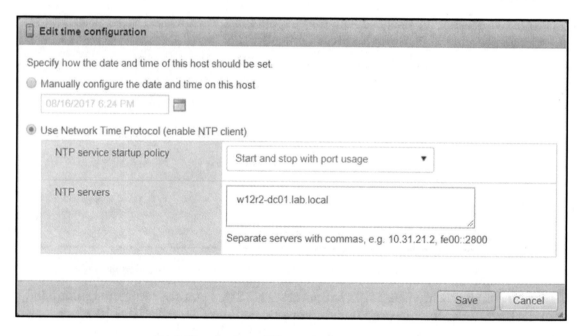

Hosts should be configured to use an NTP server to keep time-synced within the network

5. Click **Save** to save the configuration.
6. Click **Action** and select **NTP service | Start** to start the service.

The time of the ESXi host is now synchronized with a reliable NTP server.

 VMware recommends that you use NTP instead of VMware Tools time synchronization, as NTP provides more precise timekeeping on VMs.

ESXi 6.5 partition layout

Regardless of the installation method you have chosen for your host, once the ESXi has been installed on the destination device, a specific partition layout is created on the disk. It is not possible to modify the partition layout during the installation process and all the partitions are created automatically.

To identify the partition layout created by the installer in vSphere 6.5, you should use the partedUtil command, because the fdisk command was compatible with previous releases only. With the introduction of the **GUID Partition Table (GPT)** partition from ESXi 5.x, the fdisk command has been deprecated because it doesn't work anymore. To display the partition table, you need to access the ESXi console and run some specific commands.

Proceed as follows to display the partition table information:

1. SSH the ESXi and run the command ls /dev/disks -lh to identify the name of the system disk (usually, it is the only disk with more partitions):

```
[root@esxi01:~] ls /dev/disks/ -lh
total 162402208
-rw-------    1 root     root        4.0G Aug  7 18:20 mpx.vmhba1:C0:T0:L0
-rw-------    1 root     root        4.0M Aug  7 18:20 mpx.vmhba1:C0:T0:L0:1
-rw-------    1 root     root      250.0M Aug  7 18:20 mpx.vmhba1:C0:T0:L0:5
-rw-------    1 root     root      250.0M Aug  7 18:20 mpx.vmhba1:C0:T0:L0:6
-rw-------    1 root     root      110.0M Aug  7 18:20 mpx.vmhba1:C0:T0:L0:7
-rw-------    1 root     root      286.0M Aug  7 18:20 mpx.vmhba1:C0:T0:L0:8
-rw-------    1 root     root      150.0G Aug  7 18:20 mpx.vmhba1:C0:T1:L0
```

ESXi 6.5 partitions

2. Once you have identified the system disk, you can use the `partedUtil` command with the `getptbl` option to see the partition size. Looking at the previous screenshot, the partition size was already visible did you notice?

```
[root@esxi01:~] partedUtil getptbl /dev/disks/vml.0000000000766d686261313a303a30
gpt
522 255 63 8388608
1 64 8191 C12A7328F81F11D2BA4B00A0C93EC93B systemPartition 128
5 8224 520191 EBD0A0A2B9E5443387C068B6B72699C7 linuxNative 0
6 520224 1032191 EBD0A0A2B9E5443387C068B6B72699C7 linuxNative 0
7 1032224 1257471 9D27538040AD11DBBF97000C2911D1B8 vmkDiagnostic 0
8 1257504 1843199 EBD0A0A2B9E5443387C068B6B72699C7 linuxNative 0
[root@esxi01:~]
```

Use partedUtil with the getptbl command to display partition size

Looking at the preceding screenshot, the ESXi 6.5 host partition layout created by the ESXi installer can be composed of up to eight partitions. Partitions 2 and 3 may not be visible if the host is installed on SD cards or USB flash drives:

- 1 (`systemPartition` 4 MB): Partition needed for booting.
- 5 (`linuxNative` 250 MB—/`bootbank`): Core hypervisor VMkernel.
- 6 (`linuxNative` 250 MB—/`altbootbank`): Initially empty.
- 7 (`vmkDiagnostic` 110 MB): Partition used to write the host dump file in case of ESXi crash.
- 8 (`linuxNative` 286 MB—/`store`): This partition contains the VMware Tools ISO file for the supported OS.
- 9 (`vmkDiagnostic` 2.5 GB): Second diagnostic partition.
- 2 (`linuxNative` 4.5 GB—/`scratch`): Partition created to store vm-support output needed for VMware support. Not created on SD cards or USB flash drives.
- 3 (VMFS datastore): Available and unallocated space of the disk is formatted VMFS5 or VMFS, depending on the ESXi version. Not created on SD cards or USB flash drives:

| Boot Loader (4 MB) | Primary Boot Bank (250 MB) | Alternate Boot Bank (250 MB) | Core Dump Partition (110 MB) | Diagnostic Partition (2.5 GB) | Storage Partition (286 MB) | Scratch Partition (4 GB) | VMFS Datastore (XX GB) |

ESXi 6.5 partition roles, sizes, and scope

It is curious to note that some partitions are reported as Linux native, but they contain an FAT filesystem (reported also by the `dfutility`).

Boot banks

Looking at the preceding figure, you may notice that partitions 5 and 6 are named **Primary Boot Bank** and **Alternate Boot Bank**. What are these two partitions? The quick answer—a fail-safe. The ESXi system has two independent banks of memory, each of which stores a full system image. When a fresh ESXi installation is performed, partition 6 is empty.

During the system upgrade, the new version is loaded into the inactive bank of memory and the updated bank it is set to be used when the ESXi reboots. If the boot process fails for any reason, the system automatically boots from the previously used bank of memory. You can also manually choose which image to use for that boot at boot time .

Scratch partition

In the partition layout, we saw that a scratch partition is created during the ESXi installation procedure. But what is the scratch partition, exactly? The scratch partition is a 4 GB VFAT partition used for storing temporary data, including logs, diagnostic information, and system swap. Although the scratch partition is not required, VMware recommends that ESXi has a persistent scratch location available. If the scratch partition is not configured, `/scratch` is located on the **ramdisk** linked to `/tmp/scratch`.

Leaving the scratch partition on the ramdisk will affect performance and memory optimization; therefore, it is recommended to create the partition in a suitable destination.

If ESXi is installed on a destination such as an SD card or a USB stick, the scratch partition is not created. As result, an annoying warning message will be displayed in the UI that advises you to set a persistent storage for logs.

To get rid of the warning message, you have to edit the advanced settings and manually configure the scratch partition or move the logs to another location:

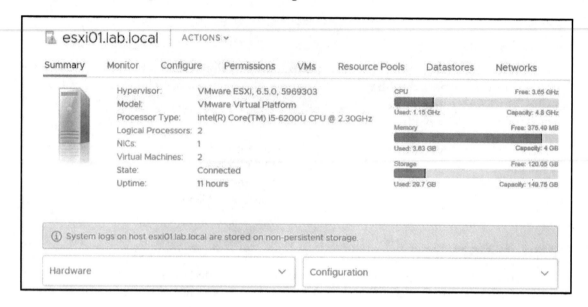

If the scratch partition is not configured, you may receive a warning message

To configure the scratch partition, it is necessary to have a VMFS or NFS volume attached to the server to host the log files, but of course you would have that anyway, for your VM to live on.

Perform the steps as follows:

1. Access ESXi using the vSphere Client and click the **Manage** item.
2. Go to the **System** tab and select **Advanced settings** to access the advanced settings.

3. In the **Search** field, type `scratch`, then press *Enter* to find the parameter key needed to modify the partition location. The **scratchConfig.CurrentScratchLocation** contains the current location of the scratch partition. Edit the key **ScratchConfig.ConfiguredScratchLocation** and enter a unique directory path for this host, for instance, `/vmfs/volumes/DatastoreUUID/DatastoreFolder`:

Scratch partition is configured in the Advanced settings

4. Reboot the host for the changes to take effect.

Messages from the VMkernel and other system components useful to identify the status of the host or potential issues are written to the log by the ESXi's syslog service, `vmsyslogd`.

To modify or configure the log location, you should perform the following steps:

1. Open the vSphere Client and select **Manage**.
2. Go to the **System** tab and click **Advanced settings** under **System**.

3. Search for the `Syslog.global.logDir` key that specifies where the logs are stored. The `/scratch` directory can be located on mounted NFS or VMFS volumes using the syntax `[datastorename] path_to_file`, where the path is relative to the root of the volume backing the datastore. An entry such as `[ts421] /lab-esxi01/logs` maps the `/vmfs/volumes/ts421/logs` path:

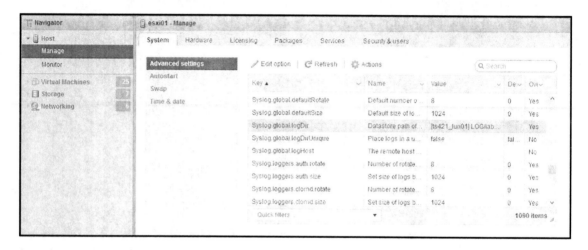

To specify where the logs should be stored, you need to edit the Advanced settings

4. Click **OK** to save the configuration. Changes to the syslog options take effect immediately.

vCSA configuration

When the deployment of the vCSA is complete, as part of the installation, vSphere Web Client and the new HTML5 client are available to access the appliance. Both clients rely on the Tomcat web service to access the appliance, and no third-party software is required. As explained in `Chapter 4`, *Deployment Workflow and Component Installation*, in vSphere 6.5, the login to the appliance can be done using both flash-based and HTML5-based web clients.

In your favorite browser, type the following addresses:

- Flash-based client (vSphere Web Client): `https://<VCSA_IP>/vsphere-client`
- HTML5 client (vSphere Client): `https://< VCSA _IP>/ui`

Basic setup using vCenter Server Appliance Management Interface (VAMI)

Let's walk-through the basic configuration you should do on your vCenter Server instance to ensure the correct functionality. The configuration of the vCSA can be easily managed using the VAMI that allows you to export logs, configure NTP, enable/disable SSH, and so on. The same configuration can also be made using the vSphere Client.

Modifying the IP address and DNS

Although you configure the IP address and DNS during the deployment process, you can further modify the parameters through the VAMI. The steps are as follows:

1. To modify the IP address and DNS, log in as root to the VAMI and select **Networking**.
2. Access the **Manage** tab and click the **Edit** button in the **Hostname, Name Servers, and Gateways** area and modify the network parameters.
3. Click **OK** to apply the new settings:

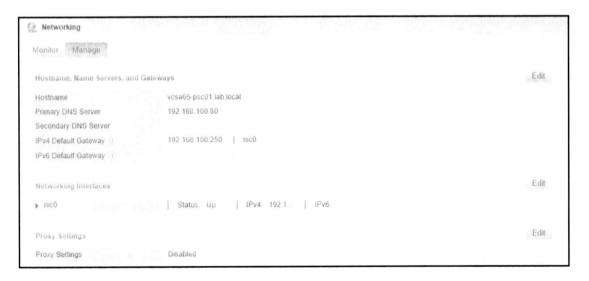

Easily modify the vCSA's network settings; the VAMI UI makes the procedure simpler

Exporting a support bundle

For diagnosing and troubleshooting purposes, you can export a support bundle that contains the log files of the running vCenter Server instance. The bundle can be submitted to VMware support for assistance or analyzed locally in your machine.

To export the log files, proceed as follows:

1. Log in as root to the VAMI and go to the **Summary** tab
2. Click on the **Create Support Bundle** button to save the bundle in .tgz format somewhere on your local machine:

To receive tech support from VMware, you need to submit a bundle you create from the Create Support Bundle button

Configuring time synchronization

We have already discussed the importance of having the network time synchronized. If vCenter Server is connected to an external PSC and the time is not synchronized, you may experience authentication issues. To avoid this problem, make sure you configure the same time synchronization source.

To configure time synchronization, follow these steps:

1. From the VAMI, go to the **Time** tab to configure the time zone and time synchronization.
2. In the **Time zone** area, click the **Edit** button to configure the correct time zone.
3. In the **Time Synchronization** area, click the **Edit** button and set the **Mode** field as NTP, then specify the NTP source servers. Click **OK** to save the setup:

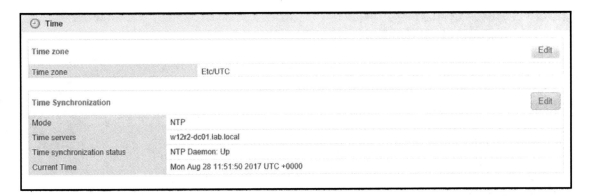

To keep the vCSA time-synced with the network, you can configure an NTP server from the VAMI

Changing the vCSA password

Changing the vCSA root password on a regular basis is not only a way to enforce security, but it's also a best practice. The steps are as follows for changing the vCSA password:

1. From the VAMI, go to the **Administration** tab to change the password.

2. Under the **Change root password** area, type the current password and enter a new one twice. Click **Submit** to save the changes:

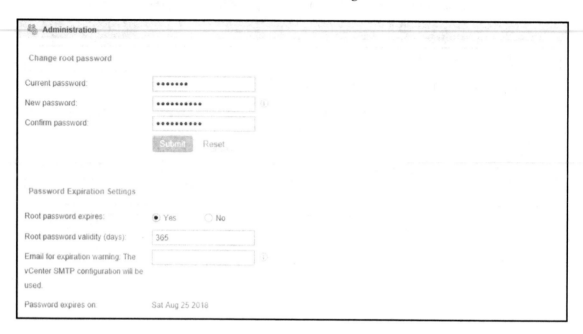

vCSA's root password should be changed on a regular basis for security reasons

Licensing

VMware vSphere 6.5 is available as a 60 day, fully working trial, to give admins the opportunity to test the product's functionalities and services provided. When the evaluation license expires, you need to insert a valid license composed of a 25-character alphanumeric string to re-enable the functionalities in ESXi and vCenter Server, avoiding service outage.

The available services are strictly related to the applied license. VMware vSphere ESXi is licensed per processor, and this means that you need a valid license key for each physical CPU installed in the physical server. The license key can be used on different servers, since it doesn't contain any server-related information and it's not tied to specific hardware. You don't have any restrictions in terms of physical cores or physical RAM, and the number of VMs you can run is unlimited if the proper license is applied.

The VMware vSphere and vSphere with Operations Management editions use the same licensing model.

VMware vSphere 6.5 comes with the three following editions:

- **vSphere Standard Edition**: This is the entry-level solution that allows basic server consolidation
- **vSphere Enterprise Plus Edition**: This edition offers all the features of vSphere and ensures application availability and business continuity
- **vSphere with Operations Management Enterprise Plus Edition**: This edition offers all the features of vSphere

In addition, there are two Essential editions provided as full kits developed for small environments that need to save costs, where you can have up to three hosts with a maximum of two physical CPUs each (each kit includes six processor licenses and one vCenter Server Essential license):

- **Essential**: This provides basic functionality only and doesn't protect the running VM in the event that one ESXi fails
- **Essential Plus**: As compared to the Essential edition, this offers services such as vMotion, vSphere HA, and **vSphere Data Protection** (**VDP**) to ensure business continuity and data protection

You can refer to `Chapter 1`, *Evolution of VMware vSphere Suite,* for additional info about licensing.

To centralize the management of ESXi hosts and VMs and enable the available services, you need one instance of vCenter Server. vCenter Server comes in the two following editions:

- **vCenter Server Essentials**: This is used for the management of vSphere Essential kits and is integrated in the bundle
- **vCenter Server Standard**: This allows you to take advantage of all the features available in vSphere, such as vSphere vMotion, vSphere HA, vSphere DRS, and so on.

Using the vCSA is the simplest method to apply and manage licensing across the infrastructure. Keep in mind that licensing is a service provided by the PSC.

If you configure the vCenter Server HA feature, you don't need to license a separate vCenter Server Standard instance for the Passive or Witness node.

To enter a new vCenter Server license, proceed with the following steps:

1. From the vSphere Web Client, go to the **Configure** tab and select the **Licensing** option. Click on the **Assign License...** button to insert a new license key.
2. Click on the green plus sign icon Create New Licenses to add a new license. In the **New Licenses** window, enter the license key and press **Next**.
3. Specify the license name and click **Next**. On the **Summary** tab, click **Finish** to save the license.
4. By default, the evaluation license is selected. Select the new license and click **OK** to apply. The license details are displayed in the **Licensing** tab:

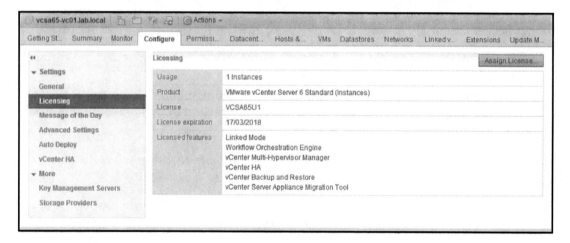

Correct license must be applied to enable the desired vSphere features

Roles and permissions

Permissions specify the privileges (tasks a user can perform) an authenticated user or group has on a specific vCenter Server object and can be assigned on different levels of a hierarchy. For example, you can assign permissions to a cluster object or to a data center object. The best practice is to assign only needed permissions, to increase security and to have a clearer permissions structure. The use of folders to group objects based on specific permissions makes the vSphere administration simpler.

There are also global permissions that are applied to a global root object to grant the user or group privileges for all objects in all hierarchies. Use global permissions carefully, because you assign permissions to all objects in the inventory.

Roles are a set of permissions you can assign to users to perform specific tasks on inventory objects. There are some default roles predefined on the vCenter Server, such as **Administrator**, **Read-only**, and **No access**, that cannot be modified. Other roles, such as network administrator, are defined as *sample* roles. You can create new roles or clone and modify existing roles. It is suggested to clone an existing profile instead of creating a new one to avoid potential security issues.

You can manage the vCSA's roles from the **Administration** menu. Follow these steps to create or modify a new role:

1. To create a new role, select the **Read-only** role and click on the clone role action icon.
2. Specify a role name and optionally, add a description, then click **OK**.
3. Select the just-created role and click the edit icon to edit the role action.
4. Enable all the actions the new role should be able to perform, then click **Next**.

5. You can modify the role name and the description of the role if needed. Click **Finish** to save the role configuration. You can navigate the **DESCRIPTION**, **USAGE**, and **PRIVILEGES** tabs to have an overview of granted permissions and to which objects the created role has been assigned:

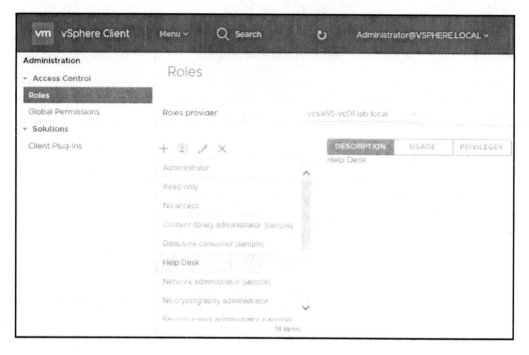

A role must be defined in vSphere to assign specific permissions to a user or group

Once a role has been defined, you need to assign the role to an authenticated user or group. Where possible, it's recommended to assign permissions to groups instead of users for better and more efficient management.

To assign a role to a user or a group, proceed with the following steps:

1. From the vSphere Client, select the object you want to assign permissions to and click the **Permissions** tab.
2. Click the add icon to access the wizard.
3. Specify the domain to use from the **User/Group** drop-down menu, then search or type the user or group name you want to use. The user or group can be a member of localos, SSO domain, AD, or other identity sources.

From the **Role** drop-down menu, select the role you want to assign to the selected user or group. It is recommended to enable the **Propagate to children** option to also apply the role to child objects. Click **OK** to save the settings:

When roles and permissions have been defined, they must be assigned to an authenticated user or group

AD integration

To assign permissions to AD users or groups to manage vCenter Server objects, you must join the PSC instance or the vCSA to the AD domain. This allows the AD users to log in to vCenter Server using the Windows session authentication **Security Support Provider Interface (SSPI)**.

The procedure to join vCenter Server to an AD domain depends on how the vCSA and the PSC have been deployed:

- If you deployed the vCSA with an embedded PSC, you need to join the vCSA to the AD domain
- If you deployed the vCSA with an external PSC, you need to join the PSC to the AD domain

The use of a **Read-Only Domain Controller (RODC)** in an AD domain to join a PSC or a vCSA with an embedded PSC is not supported. Only a writable DC must be used to join the AD domain.

To join an external PSC to the AD, follow these steps:

1. From the vSphere Web Client, log in to the PSC using the `administrator@vsphere.local` account.
2. Under **Certificates**, select the **Appliance Settings** option, then click the **Manage** tab on the right side. Click the **Join** button to enter the details to join the AD.
3. Enter the domain to join in the **Domain** field and, optionally, the **Organizational unit**. Specify the AD username in UPN format (`username@domain.com`) with the privileges to join the PSC and the password. Click **OK** to confirm.
4. When the process completes, the joined domain is listed in the **Domain** field and a new **Leave** button is displayed:

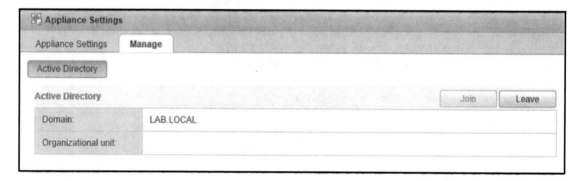

Joining the PSC to an AD domain, authenticated domain users or groups can manage vCenter Server objects

5. You need to reboot the node to enable the changes. Since a command to reboot the node is not available from the PSC GUI, you can use the command line to manually restart the service:
   1. SSH the PSC and log in as root, then run the shell command to enable the shell.
   2. Change the directory to `/bin` using the `cd /bin` command.
   3. Restart the service responsible for the VMware Identity Management Service by running the following command:

   ```
   service-control --stop vmware-sts-idmd
   ```

4. When the service has stopped, start the service again with the following command:

```
service-control --start vmware-sts-idmd
```

6. When the node has been rebooted, navigate to **Configuration** | **Identity Sources** to add the AD domain. Click **Add** to open the **Add identity source** wizard.

7. Select the **Active Directory (Integrated Windows Authentication)** option and enter the joined FQDN domain name if it's not displayed automatically.

8. Select the **Use machine account** option to use the local machine account as **Service Principal Name (SPN)**. If you expect to rename the machine, don't use this option, because it will break the authentication process. Click **OK** to confirm the specified AD domain as the new Identity Source.

9. In the **Identity Sources** tab, the joined AD domain is now displayed. Now you can assign permissions to user/group members of the AD domain:

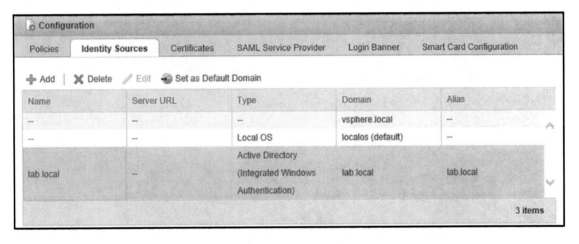

Specify the Identity Sources to assign permissions to AD users or groups

You can select the added AD domain and click on **Set as Default Domain** icon to make the new identity source the default domain.

Configuring a host with AD authentication

An ESXi host can also be joined to an AD domain to allow users and groups to manage the hypervisor. When the host is added to AD, the domain group ESX Admins is granted full administrative access to the host:

1. Log in to the host through a web console by entering the address `https://<ESXi_IP>/ui` in your favorite browser, then select the **Manage** menu.
2. Go to the **Security & users** tab and select the **Authentication** sub-menu. Click on the **Joined domain** field to join the host to the domain.
3. Enter the domain name and the credentials of an AD user with sufficient permissions to join computers to the domain. Click on the **Join Domain...** button:

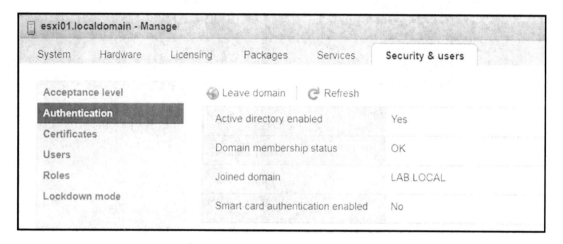

The ESXi joined to the AD domain

Installing the VMware Enhanced Authentication plugin

To allow users to log in using Integrated Windows Authentication, you need to install the VMware Enhanced Authentication plugin. This plugin replaces the CIP from vSphere 6.0.

In addition to Integrated Windows Authentication, the VMware Enhanced Authentication plugin also provides Windows-based smart card functionality. If you have the old CIP from a previous vSphere version installed on your machine, both plugins can coexist and there are no conflicts.

The installation of the plugin is simple and straightforward, as follows:

1. Using your favorite browser, open vSphere Client by typing the address of your vCenter Server, `https://<VCSA_IP>/ui`.

2. Click the **Download Enhanced Authentication Plugin** option at the bottom of the page. Save the plugin on your machine and run the installer.

3. When the installation has completed, refresh your browser. A **Launch Application** window may pop up in this step, asking for permission to run the Enhanced Authentication plugin. If the plugin doesn't work, try adding the address `https://vmware-plugin:8094` to the trusted/safe sites in your browser.

4. Enable **Use Windows session authentication** to use Windows credentials to access the vCenter Server and click **Login:**

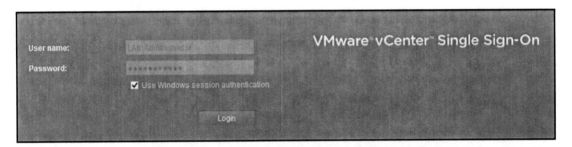

AD domain users can automatically log in to vCenter Server 6.5 using Windows session authentication

If the VMware Enhanced Authentication plugin is installed from an Internet Explorer browser, you need to disable Protected Mode and enable pop-up windows.

vCSA and PSC

As seen previously, starting from vSphere 6.0, vCenter is composed of the PSC and vCenter Server components. The PSC is a multi-master model component that provides licensing, authentication, and certificate services. If the PSC fails, these services stop working and consequently, the entire infrastructure will no longer work.

During the design of your virtual infrastructure, you should consider the option of installing and configuring two PSCs at the site to ensure availability. To ensure service availability, you may need to connect vCenter Server to another external PSC or to point the vCSA with an embedded PSC to an external PSC.

Let's see how to configure vCenter Server to point to different PSCs.

Repointing the vCSA to another external PSC

If the external PSC fails or if you want to distribute the load of an external PSC, you can configure the vCenter Server instance to point to a different PSC in the same domain and site.

The steps are as follows:

1. SSH the vCenter Server instance using the root credentials and enable the shell.
2. To repoint vCenter Server, run the following command:

```
cmsso-util repoint --repoint-psc psc_fqdn
```

   Here, `psc_fqdn` is the FQDN (the value is case-sensitive) or the static IP address of the external PSC.

3. Using the vSphere Client, log in to the vCenter Server instance to verify the instance is running and you can manage it. The vCenter Server instance is now registered with the new PSC.

Pointing the vCSA with an embedded PSC to an external PSC

If the vCenter Server instance has been deployed with an embedded PSC and you want additional vCenter Server instances in your SSO domain, you can modify the vCenter Server instance configuration to point to an external PSC. Anyway, this configuration is a one-way process only, and it's not possible to switch back to the previous configuration with an embedded PSC.

Before proceeding, take snapshots of both the vCenter Server with embedded PSC and the external PSC in order to revert if something goes wrong during the configuration.

To point the vCSA with an embedded PSC to an external PSC, you should perform the following steps:

1. SSH vCenter Server with the embedded PSC using the root credentials and enable the shell.

2. Verify that all services are running in the PSC using the following command:

```
service-control --status --all
```

The services that must be running are as follows:

- VMware License Service
- VMware Identity Management Service
- VMware Security Token Service
- VMware Certificate Service
- VMware Directory Service

3. To reconfigure vCenter Server, use the following command:

```
cmsso-util reconfigure --repoint-psc psc_fqdn --username
username --domain-name domain --passwd password
```

Here, `psc_fqdn` is the FQDN or the static IP address of the external PSC.

For instance, you can run the following command:

```
cmsso-util reconfigure --repoint-psc vcsa65-psc01.lab.local --
username administrator --domain-name vsphere.local --passwd
Password00
```

4. Using the vSphere Client, log in to the vCenter Server instance to verify the instance is running and you can manage it. If the procedure has completed successfully, the vCenter Server with the embedded PSC is now demoted and redirected to the external PSC.

Resetting the SSO password

There are some situations where you need to reset the SSO password to recover access to the PSC due to a forgotten password.

Follow this procedure to reset the SSO password:

1. SSH the PSC or vCenter Server with embedded PSC appliance as root user and enable the shell with the command `shell.set --enabled true`, then type `shell`. Press *Enter*.
2. Run the command `/usr/lib/vmware-vmdir/bin/vdcadmintool` to load the console to also manage the password reset.

3. Select the option 3. `Reset account password` and, when prompted, enter the account UPN (for example, `administrator@vsphere.local`):

```
root@vcsa65-psc01 [ ~ ]# /usr/lib/vmware-vmdir/bin/vdcadmintool


====================
Please select:
0. exit
1. Test LDAP connectivity
2. Force start replication cycle
3. Reset account password
4. Set log level and mask
5. Set vmdir state
6. Get vmdir state
7. Get vmdir log level and mask
====================

3
    Please enter account UPN : administrator@vsphere.local
New password is -
EzBE=yYL7@x{j7#LAGwO
```

The SSO password can be reset by running the command vdcadmintool in the PSC

4. A new password is generated. Use this password to log in to the system with the user you reset the password (for example, `administrator@vsphere.local`).

5. Once you are successfully logged in to vSphere Client using the password generated by the system, click **Users and Groups** under the **Single Sign-On** menu and select the **Users** tab.

6. Select the account used to log in and click the edit icon to set a new password. Enter the new password twice and click **OK** to confirm the change.

Managing data centers, clusters, and hosts

vCenter Server is a core component of the infrastructure that allows a centralized administration of hosts and VM for your environment. To ensure the maximum efficiency of the infrastructure, you need to consider how to administer VMs and their resource demands.

For optimal organization of the inventory, you need to create some virtual objects in vCenter Server to define a logical structure. The organization of the inventory requires some tasks to be performed, as follows:

- Create data centers
- Add hosts to the data centers
- Build a logical infrastructure using folders
- Set up networking (vSS and vDS)
- Configure storage system (datastore and datastore cluster)
- Create clusters (resource consolidation, vSphere HA, and vSphere DRS)
- Create a resource pool (flexible management of resources)

In vCenter Server, there are four main views available to manage the inventory:

- **Hosts and Clusters**: Clusters, hosts, resource pools, and VMs. From this view, you can manage the resource allocations of VMs and their locations.
- **VMs and Templates**: Folders, VMs, and templates. This view can be used to group VMs in a logical structure (role, location, department, and so on) using folders. You can also manage the templates from which you can deploy new VMs.

  Depending on the business requirements, you can use this view to organize the management of VMs following the organization's policies. Folders can be used as containers to assign permissions to objects, and other programs (backup applications, for instance) can use folders as logic containers for dynamic objects (for example, software such as Veeam also uses folders to manage VMs to back up):

The vCenter Server 6.5 VMs and Templates inventory view

- **Storage**: Datastore and datastore cluster. From this view, you have an overview of installed datastores in your virtual infrastructure, regardless of the data center membership. You can configure and manage all device configurations, including the datastore clusters.
- **Networking: vSphere standard switch (vSwitch)** and **vSphere distributed switch (vDS)**. Setup of services such as vMotion, vSphere FT, vSAN, and so on are managed from this view.

Creating a data center

vCenter Server is composed of a data center object that acts as a core container for all other objects. To add hosts and virtual machines to vCenter Server, at least one data center object must be created.

You can configure more than one datacenter per vCenter Server, since multiple datacenter objects within a single instance are supported. Datacenter objects are shared among the four views, allowing a better organization of the view based on the corporate policies, simplifying the management.

To create the data center object, proceed with the following steps:

1. From the vSphere Client, right-click on the connected vCenter Server and select the **New Datacenter...** option.
2. Enter a name in the **Name** field and click **OK** to create the data center object. Once the data center has been created, you can add the hosts to the inventory:

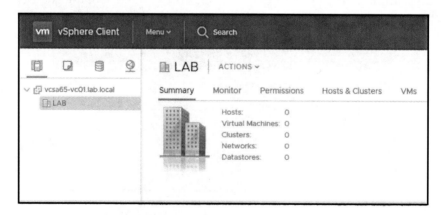

Datacenter object displayed in the inventory view

Adding a host to vCenter Server

Since the vSphere environment strongly relies on DNS, before configuring vCenter Server, make sure that name resolution is working properly in your network.

Verify that vCenter Server is able to resolve ESXi hostnames added to the inventory and that the added ESXi hosts can resolve the vCenter Server hostname used to manage them. Ensure that all the hypervisors added to vCenter can resolve the hostnames of other ESXi hosts.

To add ESXi hosts to vCenter Server, follow these steps:

1. From the vSphere Client, log in to vCenter Server to configure.
2. In the **Hosts and Clusters** view, right-click the configured data center object and select the **Add Host...** option.
3. Enter the ESXi hostname or IP address and click **Next**. In this step, it is suggested to use FQDN instead of the IP address.
4. Enter the root credentials and click **Next**. When prompted, click **Yes** to trust the host and to accept the host's certificate.
5. On the host summary page, click **Next** to continue. On this page, information related to the added host is displayed .
6. Select an available license to assign to the host. A 60-day evaluation license can be assigned if no license keys have been entered previously. Click **Next**. If you didn't purchase a vSphere Enterprise Plus license, using the 60-day evaluation license, you have all the vSphere features available to complete the configuration of the environment, taking advantage of some automatism and functionalities included in the Enterprise Plus license only. For example, you could take advantage of the Storage DRS feature to optimize the performance and resources across different storage devices in your vSphere environment.

7. Configure Lockdown mode. By default, Lockdown mode is set as **Disabled**. Select **Normal** to manage the host through the local console or the vCenter Server, or **Strict** to allow access to the host only through vCenter Server, stopping the DCUI service. Select the option you want to use and click **Next**:

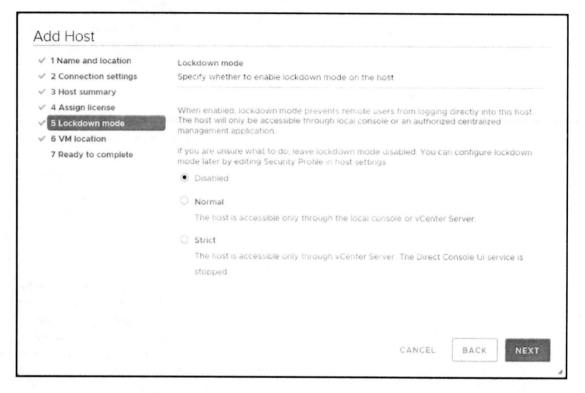

Add Host

✓ 1 Name and location
✓ 2 Connection settings
✓ 3 Host summary
✓ 4 Assign license
✓ 5 Lockdown mode
✓ 6 VM location
   7 Ready to complete

Lockdown mode
Specify whether to enable lockdown mode on the host

When enabled, lockdown mode prevents remote users from logging directly into this host. The host will only be accessible through local console or an authorized centralized management application.

If you are unsure what to do, leave lockdown mode disabled. You can configure lockdown mode later by editing Security Profile in host settings.

● Disabled

○ Normal

    The host is accessible only through the local console or vCenter Server.

○ Strict

    The host is accessible only through vCenter Server. The Direct Console UI service is stopped.

CANCEL   BACK   NEXT

Lockdown mode configuration window

8. Specify the location to which you want to move existing VMs running in the selected host and click **Next**.

9. Review your settings and click **Finish** to add the host to vCenter Server. Repeat the same procedure to add all other required hosts to this vCenter Server instance.

When you enter the root password to add the host to the vCenter, the password is used to establish a connection with the host and to install the vCenter agent. The process sets different credentials that maintain the communication and authentication between ESXi and vCenter, even if ESXi's root password is changed.

Disconnecting a host from vCenter Server

Once ESXi is connected to vCenter Server, you can always disconnect or remove the host later on. It's important to understand that disconnecting the host from vCenter Server is different from removing the host. Disconnecting a managed host from vCenter Server doesn't remove ESXi from the vCenter Inventory as well as the VM registered in the host. When the managed host is disconnected, vCenter Server suspends monitoring and management activities for that host.

It's a different story if you remove the host from the vCenter Server. Removing a managed host from the vCenter Server means the host and its VM are removed from the vCenter Inventory.

To disconnect a managed host from vCenter Server, proceed with the following steps:

1. From the vSphere Client, log in to the vCenter Server that manages the host to disconnect.
2. Right-click the managed host, select the **Connection** | **Disconnect** option, and click **OK** to confirm. Once the host is disconnected from vCenter Server, in the inventory view, the ESXi and all the VMs associated are marked as disconnected:

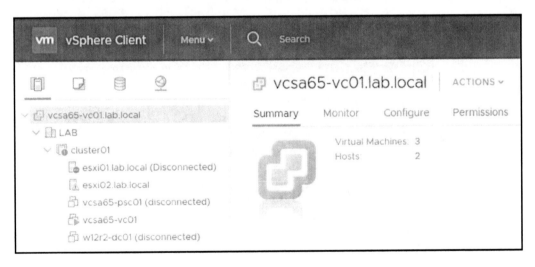

ESXi disconnected from vCenter Server

To reconnect the host, you always operate from vCenter Server:

1. Right-click on the disconnected host and select the **Connection** | **Connect** option, then click **OK** to confirm.
2. Click **Next** in the **Name and Location** tab, then enter the root credentials of the host to reconnect. Click **Next**.
3. In the host summary, click **Next**, then specify where to locate the VM in the **VM location** tab. Click **Next** to continue.
4. Click **Finish** to reconnect the host. When the procedure has completed, the disconnect label is removed from the host and its VM. The host is available to the vSphere environment again.

Removing a host from vCenter Server

Removing a host from vCenter Server stops all the vCenter Server monitoring and managing activities. You should remove the managed host while still connected in order to remove the vCenter agent as well.

To remove a managed host, follow this procedure:

1. From vSphere Client, log in to the vCenter Server that manages the host to remove.
2. Power off all running VMs and right-click on the host and select **Maintenance Mode** | **Enter Maintenance Mode**. Click **Yes** to confirm.
3. Right-click on the host once again and select the **All vCenter Actions** | **Remove from Inventory** option. Click **Yes** to confirm the removal. The host and its VM are removed from the vCenter Inventory; the license assigned to the host is removed from the vCenter list and retained by the host.

When the host has been removed, the vCenter Server is no longer able to manage the host and to access the VM, and you need to access the host directly.

Creating a cluster

A vSphere cluster is a configuration that allows the management of the added hosts pooling the available resources. Once the cluster has been created, you can move the hosts to the cluster. When hosts are added to the cluster, the cluster manages the available resources and allows you to enable the vSphere HA, vSphere DRS, and vSphere FT features available only with clusters. These features will be covered in `Chapter 13`, *Advanced Availability in vSphere 6.5*.

To create a cluster, proceed as follows:

1. From the vSphere Client, log in to the vCenter Server to configure.
2. In the **Hosts and Clusters** view, right-click on the configured data center object and select the **New Cluster** option.
3. Enter the name of the cluster and select the features you want to enable. Click **OK** to create the cluster. To better understand the available features displayed in the wizard, the HA feature provides business continuity, while DRS is used to balance the workload across the hosts.

Enhanced vMotion Compatibility (EVC) is a feature that allows VMs to vMotion across hosts with different processors in the same cluster. The caveat is that all processors must be from the same vendor (Intel or AMD), since a mixed cluster is not supported. Pay attention when you install a new ESXi server in the same cluster.

To add hosts to the created cluster, the easiest way is to drag and drop the ESXi hosts into the cluster. Alternatively, you can right-click on the hosts, select the option **Move To...**, select the target cluster, then click **OK**. You can also use scripts to automate the process of adding hosts to the cluster. If you are prompted about the resource pool management, leave the default option and click **Yes**:

Select the cluster object to have a summary of the available resources in the cluster

Removing a host from a cluster

When you remove a managed host from a cluster, the cluster loses the resources provided by the removed host, reducing the total capacity. All historical data remains in the vCenter Server database. Before removing a host from a cluster, make sure that the cluster has enough resources to provide to the workloads to avoid performance issues or, in the worst situation, service disruption.

If the vSphere DRS feature is not enabled in the cluster, make sure to migrate all running VMs to a new host using vMotion before putting the host in Maintenance Mode. If not migrated, powered off, or suspended, VMs will remain associated with the removed host:

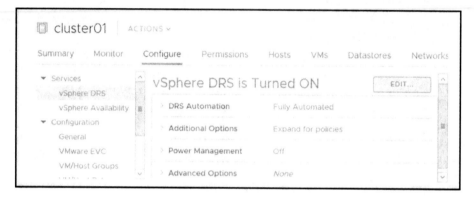

vSphere DRS configuration area

Follow these steps:

1. From the vSphere Client, right-click on the host you want to remove from a cluster.
2. Right-click the host to remove and select the **Maintenance Mode | Enter Maintenance Mode** option, then click **OK** to proceed. If DRS is enabled, powered-off (you need to enable the option) and running VMs are migrated to other hosts in the cluster.
3. When the host enters into Maintenance Mode, the host icon changes. Right-click on the host and select the **Move To...** option .
4. Select the destination (data center, folder, or a different cluster) to move the host to and click **OK**.
5. When the host has moved off the cluster, right-click on the host and select **Maintenance Mode | Exit Maintenance Mode**.

VMs in the host can now be powered on.

> If you want to move a host in a cluster from one vCenter Server to another, you can disconnect the host and move it without putting the host in Maintenance Mode.

Managing hosts

vCenter Server is a core component of VMware vSphere that centralizes host administration, offering some powerful features that simplify the management process. vCenter Server provides a single pane of glass for your environment and allows access to the installed hosts and their configurations.

To access the ESXi management area, select a host from the vSphere Client. Navigating from the available tabs, you can access the different configuration areas to set up the host matching the business requirements:

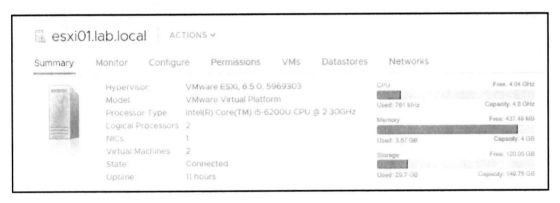

The ESXi host can be managed through vSphere Client

Let's have a look at the main areas:

- **Summary**: This displays information related to the ESXi, such as resources in use, tags, global configuration, and so forth.
- **Monitor**: From this tab, you can track issues and alarms related to configuration problems and check the host's performance information, tasks and events related to the selected host, and the hardware health, to keep the status of hardware components under control.

- **Configure**: From this tab, you can modify the host configuration. Storage configuration (storage adapters, storage devices), network settings (vSwitches, VMkernel adapters, TCP/IP), system components (host profile, firewall, security profile, and so on), and hardware changes can be done in this section.
- **Permissions**: Used to add permissions specifying users and roles.
- **VMs**: Shows the list of VMs and VM Templates registered in the selected host. Double-click on the object to access its configuration area.
- **Datastores**: Displays the list of attached storage, showing details such as status, type, storage capacity, and free space.
- **Networks**: Displays a list of virtual switches and distributed virtual switches configured in the selected host.

Using tags

A tag is a label you can apply to vCenter Server objects (datastores, VMs, hosts) to simplify the research, allowing better sorting. When a tag is created, it must be assigned to a category that groups related tags. A category also specifies whether you can assign one or multiple tags to an object. The creation and management of tags and categories is done through an intuitive configuration area, reachable from menu, then **Tags & Custom Attributes**:

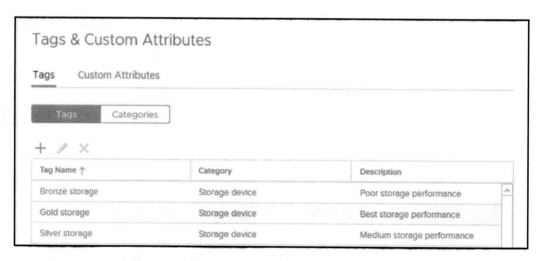

Tags can be used to categorize objects and to simplify the research

For instance, you can use tags to classify your storage devices installed in your vSphere environment. Create **Gold storage**, **Silver storage**, and **Bronze storage** tags assigned to a storage device category associated to the datastore object type. Assigning these tags to the storage devices available in your network, you can categorize storage devices based on their performance and quickly identify what storage to use based on the requirements; for example, storage used in production will have different requirements as compared to storage used for a secondary backup.

To assign a tag, right-click on an object in the vCenter Inventory and select **Tags & Custom Attributes | Assign Tag**.

Some software backup solutions make use of tags to group VM with the same backup policy (for example, RTO), making the administration easier and more straightforward.

Tasks

Tasks are activities performed by the system that occur on an object of the vCenter Inventory (power on or power off a VM, for example) and can be executed in real time or scheduled.

The task list can be viewed in the vSphere Client by selecting the **Tasks** option from the menu. The list displays all tasks that occurred to a specific object, detailing information such as the target, status, initiator, and so on. By default, tasks listed for a single object also include tasks assigned to its child objects. The list can be filtered by typing the keywords in the search field on the right.

Scheduling tasks

Tasks can be scheduled to run at specific times or at recurring intervals. A task cannot be scheduled to run on multiple objects. The available tasks you can schedule from the vSphere Web Client are the following:

- Add hosts and check compliance of a profile
- Change power state, clone, create, deploy, migrate, make a snapshot, edit resources of VMs
- Change cluster power settings
- Scan for updates
- Remediate

Tasks not included in the list can be scheduled using the vSphere API. To schedule a task, proceed as follows:

1. From the vSphere Web Client, select the object on which you want to schedule a task and select **Monitor | Tasks & Events**. Click **Scheduled Tasks** to create a new schedule.
2. From the **Schedule a New Task** drop-down menu, select the task to schedule (available tasks depend on the selected object).
3. Configure task-related options and the scheduling settings. Enter an email address to notify when the task is complete and click **OK** to save the task schedule:

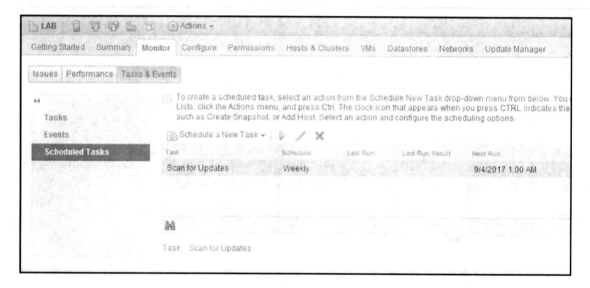

Tasks can be scheduled to run at specific time in the Tasks & Events section

Managing host profiles

Host profile is a feature of vSphere 6.5 that allows you to include the ESXi configuration in a profile (template) to ensure that all hosts installed across the infrastructure have the same configuration and are compliant with the setup policy you might have in your organization.

Generally, after completing the deployment of an ESXi host, there are several settings you should configure to ensure the host's services match your infrastructure:

- **Network configuration**: VMkernel and VM port groups creation, assigning IP to VMkernels, setup of NIC-teaming, and so on
- **Storage configuration**: NFS configuration, software iSCSI adapters, port bindings, CHAP
- **Time synchronization**: Configure and enable the NTP service
- **Enable services**: Enable services such as SSH, shell
- **Firewall**: Open specific ports required by some services

If you have just a few hosts to install, you can quickly and easily use the Interactive ESXi installation method and once, completed, manually set up the required host's parameters. If the environment to build is large and you have 100/1,000 hosts to set up, manually performing the configuration for each hypervisor is a tedious and time-consuming task and human error can occur at any moment; incorrect IP addresses assigned, wrong NIC to a VMkernel portgroup mapping, and so on.

Host profile is a solution to avoid such configuration errors. You profile a host creating a *template* containing the configuration extracted from a reference host, then you apply this template to any host of the infrastructure to ensure consistency. Once created, the host profile can be edited to change, enable, or disable properties. If a host profile is applied to a cluster, all the member hosts are affected, ensuring a consistent configuration.

Host profiles can also be used together with the Auto Deploy feature (Auto Deploy was covered in `Chapter 4`, *Deployment Workflow and Component Installation*) to fully automate the provisioning process.

The overall process can be summarized as follows:

- Set up and configure the reference host. Because the configuration will be saved to the host profile, make sure the ESXi setup is correct and verified.
- Create the master host profile, extracting the configuration from the reference host.
- Attach the created host profile to a host or cluster in order to apply the standard configuration.
- Check the compliance of processed hosts to the host profile to ensure they all have the same configuration.
- Remediate the host to apply the settings. The ESXi host attached to the selected host profile modify its configuration only at this stage.

To create a host profile, perform the following steps:

1. From the vSphere Web Client, right-click on the hypervisor used as a reference host and select **Host Profiles** | **Extract Host Profile**.
2. Enter a profile name and, optionally, a description. The description is useful to identify the scope of the profile. Click **Next** when done.
3. Click **Finish** to start the host profile creation. When the process has completed, the created profiles can be found in the **Home** | **Host Profiles** area of the vSphere Web Client:

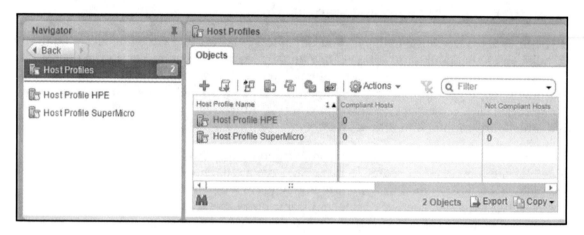

Created host profiles can be found in the host profiles area in vSphere Web Client

To apply settings saved in the profile to a host or cluster, you need to attach the created host profile. To attach the host profile, proceed as follows:

1. From the vSphere Web Client, right-click on the host to process and select the **Host Profiles** | **Attach Host Profile...** option.

2. Select the host profile to attach and click **OK**. At this stage, you can customize the host (for example, configure the IP address and DNS server) or enable the **Skip Host Customization** option to avoid host customization during the process:

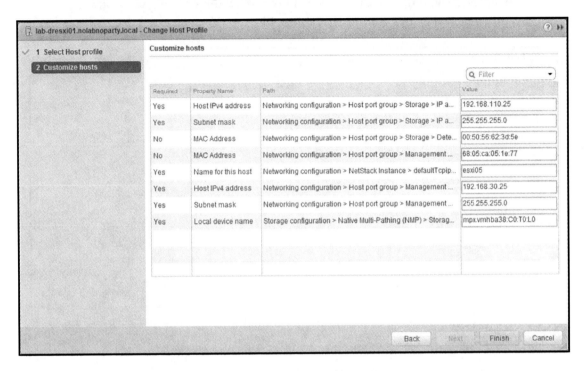

The host customization window allows you to specify the network parameters to apply to the processed host

 If you skip host customization during this process, you should edit or import host customization before you remediate the host profile.

Once a host profile is attached to a host, the configuration is not automatically applied, but you must perform a compliance check first in order to compare the current host configuration with the configuration stored in the used profile.

To run the compliance check, follow these steps:

1. Right-click on the host to check and select **Host Profiles | Check Host Profile Compliance**. If the checked host is found to be non-compliant, a warning message is displayed in the **Summary** tab:

Warning message informs you when a host is not in compliance with the attached profile

2. Settings that are non-conforming are listed in the **Host Profile Compliance** area. To apply the host profile settings to the host, click on **Remediate Host**:

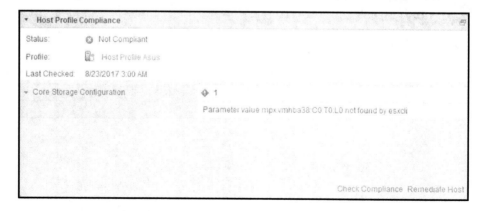

Host profile settings are applied, remediating the host

Host profiles can be modified to change some settings by editing the desired profile. To modify a host profile, proceed as follows:

1. From vSphere Web Client, go to **Home** | **Host Profiles**
2. Select the profile you want to modify from the list and click the **Edit Host Profile...** button to proceed:

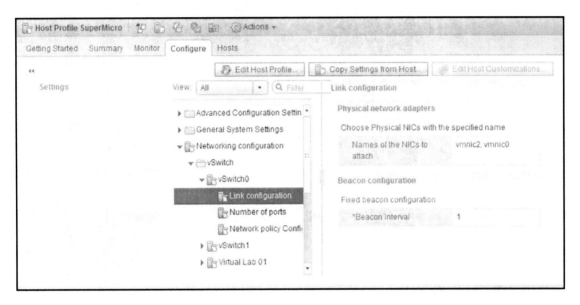

Host profile settings can be changed to meet specific requirements

vCenter Server in Enhanced Linked mode (ELM)

If you need to work with multiple vCenter Server instances or if you want to manage a number of hosts or VMs that exceed the maximum supported by a single vCenter Server instance (2,000 hosts or 25,000 powered on VMs), you can install the vCSA in ELM that allows you to connect multiple vCenter Servers together for a maximum of 15 instances.

To enable ELM, the vCenter Server instances must be registered to the same PSC in order to share roles, permissions, licenses, policies, and tags:

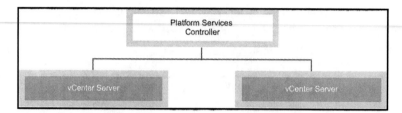

vSphere 6.5 Enhanced Linked mode

To install a vCenter Server in ELM, you must first deploy the PSC creating a new SSO domain or joining an existing SSO domain (another PSC instance must have deployed). Deploy the first vCSA with an external PSC instance pointing to the previous installed PSC. To configure a new vCSA instance in ELM, you just need to point the vCenter Server instance to the same PSC used before (repointing a vCSA to another PSC has been discussed previously in this chapter):

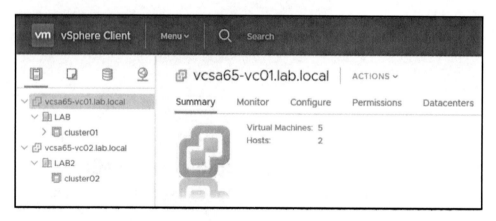

Enhanced Linked mode allows the management of multiple vCenter Servers from a single vSphere Client

Automating tasks with scripts

The administration of the vSphere environment often requires you to perform repetitive tasks that can be time-consuming, involving the same activities to be done for each component of the infrastructure, for example, migration of VMs or deploying new VMs from a template.

The chance to automate some tasks will allow you to optimize your time, improving efficiency and ensuring consistency. Manually modifying the configuration of 1,000 or more VMs, for example, will require a lot of time to complete the task, with the risk of missing some steps or making some errors. Automation can perform tasks in seconds with no errors and ensure consistency within the network, reducing the workload of the IT staff.

VMware offers some tools to automate tasks, such as PowerCLI, vCLI, **vRealize Orchestrator (vRO)**, and vSphere Web Services SDK. **vSphere Management Assistant (vMA)** has been deprecated and version 6.5 is the final release.

Perhaps the most popular tools are PowerCLI and vCLI, but of course, the optimal solution is only what is suitable for your environment and needs.

Automating with PowerCLI

The most common automation tool provided by vSphere is PowerCLI, a command-line and scripting tool built on Windows PowerShell that provides cmdlets used for managing and automating vSphere and other VMware products.

The installation process of PowerCLI has been simplified and requires running a command from the PowerShell console. To install PowerCLI, an additional Microsoft component, *PackageManagement PowerShell Modules Preview* (download available at the URL `https://www.microsoft.com/en-us/download/confirmation.aspx?id=51451`), must be installed in your system.

To install PowerCLI, follow this procedure:

1. Open the PowerShell console and run the following command:

   ```
   Install-Module -Name VMware.PowerCLI
   ```

   If you get an error, the PackageManagement PowerShell Modules Preview is not installed in the system. Double-click `PackageManagement_x64.msi` to install.

2. You are prompted to install a NuGet provider to interact with the NuGet-based repositories. Type *Y*, then press *Enter*. You may receive a warning that the used repository is untrusted; type *Y* and press *Enter* to install the module:

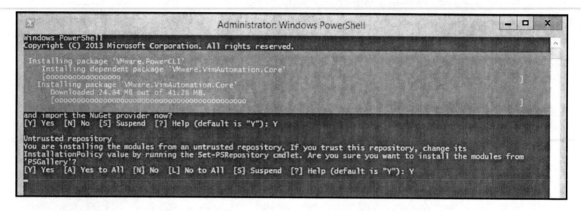

To install PowerCLI, the VMware.PowerCLI package must be installed in the PowerShell console

3. To see the installed modules, run the following command:

```
Get-Module vmware* -listavailable
```

For example, using PowerCLI, you can quickly get the list of running VMs in a specific vCenter Server instance:

1. Open the PowerShell console where the VMware PowerCLI module has been installed

2. From the console, connect the vCenter Server instance to query, then run the following command (enter the login credentials when prompted):

```
Connect-VIserver -server VCSA_fqdn
```

3. To get a list of VMs running in the selected vCenter Server instance, enter the following command:

```
Get-VM
```

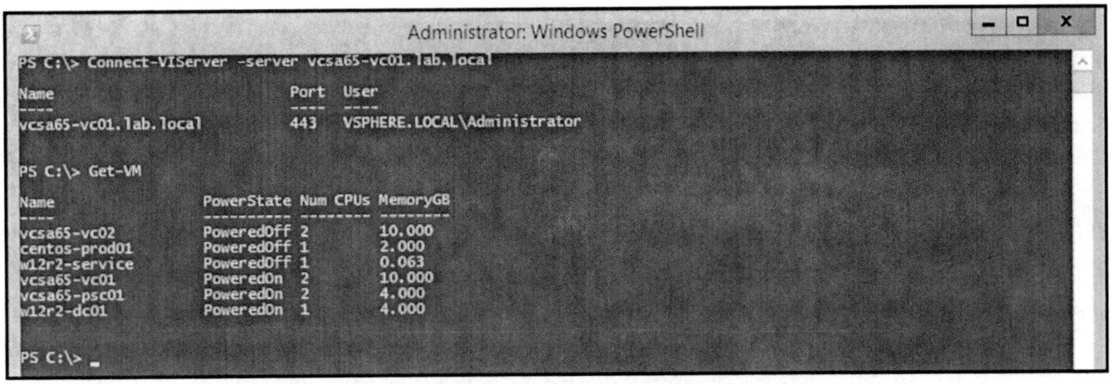

Use of PowerCLI cmdlets can be used to query the vSphere environment

Remembering all PowerCLI commands and the correct syntax is not easy for most people and the documentation or the Internet connection are not always available to help. A useful cmdlet is available in PowerShell that provides information about a specific command—Get-help. To find the correct syntax to use with a specific cmdlet, Get-help helps you to find the information you need. For example, to find what parameters can be used with the cmdlet Get-VM to retrieve the list of running VMs, you can enter the following:

Get-help Get-VM

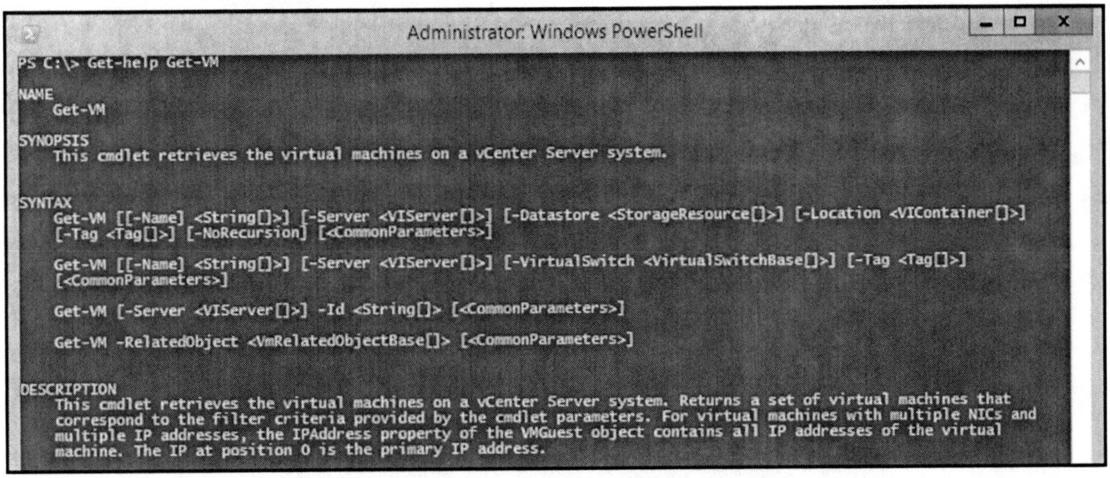

The Get-help cmdlet allows you to find the correct syntax to use for a specific command

You get a brief explanation of the command, the syntax to use, and the description. If you append -example at the end of the command, the system also displays examples of how to use the command. You can pipeline multiple PowerShell cmdlets to build a script in a single line of code.

PowerCLI script examples

Here are some of the examples of PowerCLI scripts used to perform some tasks in the vSphere environment:

- **Moving VM**: If you want to move all VMs to another host, use the following script:

```
Get-VMHost esxi01 | Get-VM | Move-VM -Destination (Get-VMHost esxi02)
```

To move a single VM to a different host, use the following script:

```
Move-VM -VM VM_name -Destination esxi01
```

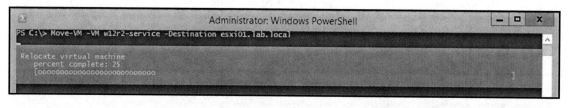

A PowerCLI cmdlet can be used to move a virtual machine to a different host

- **VM info**: Previously, we used the command Get-VM to retrieve a list of running VMs in the vCenter Server instance. You also have the option of exporting the list of VMs in a .csv file, including some properties you want to specify:

```
Get-VM | Select-Object Name,NumCPU,MemoryMB,PowerState,Host | Export-CSV VMinfo.csv -NoTypeInformation
```

To know on which host a specific virtual machine runs, use the following script:

```
Get-VMHost -VM (Get-VM -Name VM_name)
```

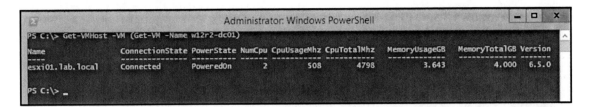

PowerCLI cmdlet can also be used to know which host a specific VM runs on

- **Configuring NTP**: We discussed the importance of having the hosts time-synced to avoid authentication issues. The following cmdlet configures the NTP server for the specific host:

```
Get-VMHost <esxi01> | Add-VMHostNtpServer -NtpServer
<NTPServer>
```

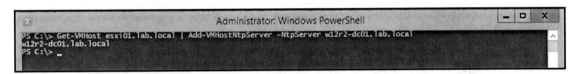

NTP server configured for a specific host using PowerCLI

Using vCLI

vCLI is a command-line administration tool built on vSphere SDK for Perl that runs common system administration commands to manage ESXi hosts and vCenter Server from any machine. The application is available to download at `https://code.vmware.com/tool/vsphere-cli/6.5`. Including **Data Center CLI (DCLI)** commands, the tool allows you to manage services in the vSphere REST API.

As compared to **vSphere Management Assistant (vMA)**, vCLI comes as a standalone installer and includes lots of command-line utilities, available in vMA. To manage the vSphere environment, vCLI is available for Windows and Linux OS. The vMA appliance that includes vCLI commands is still available in version 6.5, but has been deprecated.

vCLI version 6.5 is supported by the following OS:

- Red Hat Enterprise Linux (RHEL) 6.6, 7.1, 7.2, and 7.3 (Server) 64-bit
- Ubuntu 12.04, 14.04, 15.10, and 16.04 (LTS) 64-bit
- SLES 11 SP3 and 12 64-bit

- Windows 8 and 10 64-bit
- Windows 2008 and 2012 R2 64-bit

Version 6.5 is also compatible with ESXi 6.0 Update 3 and vCenter Server 6.0 Update 3.

Installing vCLI on Windows

In version 6.5, ActivePerl has been removed from the Windows installer. Before installing vCLI on a Windows OS, you need to separately install ActivePerl version 5.14 or later (download at `https://www.activestate.com/activeperl/downloads/`).

To install ActivePerl, double-click on the downloaded installation file and follow the instructions (it just requires you to click **Next** button a few times):

ActivePerl must be installed in the system as a requirement for vCLI

When the ActivePerl package installation has completed, you also need to install the required `XML/LibXML.pm` from the Command Prompt by running the following command:

```
ppm install XML-LibXML
```

```
C:\>ppm install XML-LibXML
Downloading XML-LibXML-2.0129...done
Downloading XML-SAX-Base-1.09...done
Downloading XML-SAX-0.99...done
Downloading XML-NamespaceSupport-1.12...done
Unpacking XML-LibXML-2.0129...done
Unpacking XML-SAX-Base-1.09...done
Unpacking XML-SAX-0.99...done
Unpacking XML-NamespaceSupport-1.12...done
Generating HTML for XML-LibXML-2.0129...done
Generating HTML for XML-SAX-Base-1.09...done
Generating HTML for XML-SAX-0.99...done
Generating HTML for XML-NamespaceSupport-1.12...done
Updating files in site area...done
 112 files installed

C:\>_
```

The XML/LibXML library is another component required to be installed

For additional information and to get a list of available commands in vCLI, check out the VMware website at `https://www.vmware.com/support/developer/vcli/`.

For example, you can quickly join an ESXi host to an AD domain using vCLI commands. Proceed by performing the following procedure:

1. Open the Command Prompt from the machine where vCLI tool has been installed

2. To add the host to the AD domain, run the following command:

    ```
    vicfg-authconfig.pl --server=<esxi_fqdn> --authscheme AD --
    joindomain <domain.com>
    ```

3. Verify the ESXi host is in the intended Windows AD domain with the following command:

    ```
    vicfg-authconfig.pl --server <esxi_fqdn> --authscheme AD -c
    ```

    To fully automate the procedure, avoiding manually entering the credentials, you can modify the script as follows:

    ```
    vicfg-authconfig.pl --server=<esxi_fqdn> --username=<ESXi_root>
    --password=<ESXi_root_password> --authscheme AD --joindomain
    <domain.com> --adusername=<Domain_Admin> --
    adpassword=Domain_Admin_password>
    ```

vCenter REST API

A new feature introduced in vSphere 6.5 is a new REST API, a more modern, simpler to use, and developer-friendly vSphere API. As compared to the capabilities provided by the vSphere API, at the time of writing, not all functions are supported by the REST API and the functionality is limited to vCSA management, Content Library and VM operations, and lifecycle. Embedded in the vCSA, there is an API Explorer that allows you to access the documentation of the new REST APIs.

Access your vCSA at the address `https://<VCSA_IP>/apiexplorer` to reach the API Explorer and click the **Select API** drop-down menu to select the available endpoints:

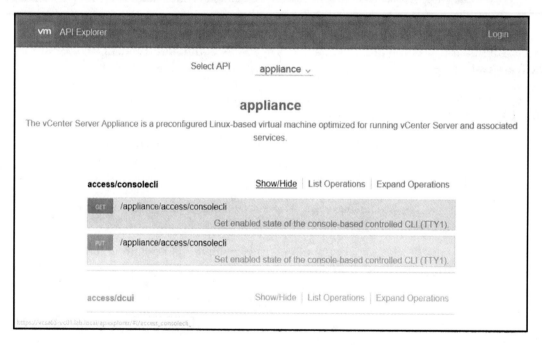

The vSphere 6.5 API Explorer

To get the complete documentation on a specific API (description, required fields, request body, and so on), click the **Show/Hide** option to expand the available sections.

Summary

A correct configuration of the vSphere components ensures business continuity and improves performance.

We discussed the ESXi installation procedures, where settings such as NTP and IP address should be configured to avoid authentication issues and accessibility problems. We also explained the scratch partition used for storing temporary data, including logs and diagnostic information. Configuring the vCSA accordingly, roles and permissions can be assigned to users or groups to manage the infrastructure on different levels and the integration with AD provides domain users with the capability to manage vSphere based on assigned roles.

The management of vSphere objects was another topic covered in the chapter, describing virtual objects to be created in vCenter Server to define a logical structure and to better organize the inventory—data centers, clusters, and resource pools. To simplify the host configuration, the vSphere Host Profile feature ensures all hosts have the same configuration settings.

The chapter ended by showing how to speed up and avoid repetitive tasks, using the PowerShell, vCLI, and REST API tools to automate some tasks using scripts or command-line commands.

The next chapter will go deep into the specific configurations related to the network infrastructure.

6
Advanced Network Management

In this chapter, we will be discussing networking from basics to NSX. Networking is a very important part of the VMware infrastructure. When you configure well, you will be a happy admin. Networking is a critical part of a server virtualization.

So, let's go networking. Wait!

In this chapter, we will cover the following topics:

- Virtual networking concepts
- Standard and distributed virtual switches
- Physical switches integrations (VLAN, LACP/link aggregation/team, network security)
- VMkernel interfaces
- Virtual switches design (numbers of virtual switches, portgroup, vmnic, vmk)
- Moving from the virtual network to NSX

Basic overview

Before starting, we fly a little bit under some network basics, starting from the multi-layered model and the encapsulation and de-encapsulation concept, through some other technical information.

OSI model

The OSI model is a conceptual model that is used to describe how data flows in a network from one device to another. We know that there are seven layers, and layer 1 is the lowest. For details, see `https://en.wikipedia.org/wiki/OSI_model`:

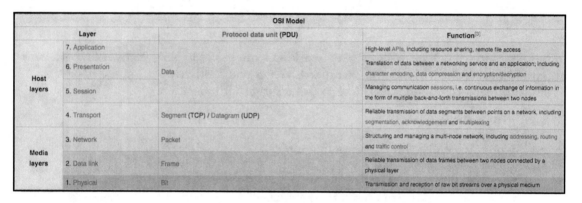

	Layer	Protocol data unit (PDU)	Function[3]
	7. Application		High-level APIs, including resource sharing, remote file access
Host layers	6. Presentation	Data	Translation of data between a networking service and an application; including character encoding, data compression and encryption/decryption
	5. Session		Managing communication sessions, i.e. continuous exchange of information in the form of multiple back-and-forth transmissions between two nodes
	4. Transport	Segment (TCP) / Datagram (UDP)	Reliable transmission of data segments between points on a network, including segmentation, acknowledgement and multiplexing
Media layers	3. Network	Packet	Structuring and managing a multi-node network, including addressing, routing and traffic control
	2. Data link	Frame	Reliable transmission of data frames between two nodes connected by a physical layer
	1. Physical	Bit	Transmission and reception of raw bit streams over a physical medium

The OSI model

Encapsulation and de-encapsulation

Information that is transmitted over the network must undergo a process of conversion at the sending and receiving ends of the communication. The conversion process is encapsulation and de-encapsulation. For details, refer to `https://en.wikipedia.org/wiki/Encapsulation_(networking)`.

Broadcasting, unicasting, and multicasting

Broadcasting transmits a packet that will be received by every device on the network. The broadcast is limited to a broadcast domain:

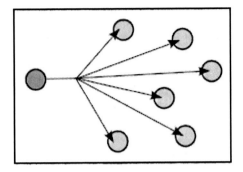

Broadcast

Unicasting specifies one-to-one transmission from one point to another point in the network:

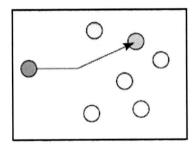

Unicast

 A free e-book, *Brocade IP Primer*, is a very good resource and can be found at https://community.brocade.com/t5/Ethernet-Switches-Routers/ Brocade-IP-Primer-eBook-Download-Now/ta-p/2905.

Multicasting specifies one-to-many where data transmission is addressed to a group or destination:

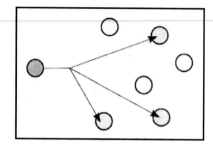

Multicast

MAC tables and MAC learning process

Physical switches use MAC tables to perform frame forwarding. Physical switches learn and build the MAC table. The switch reads the Ethernet headers and learns the MAC address of the device and makes an entry in its MAC table.

Address Resolution Protocol (ARP) can discover a MAC address that corresponds to a known IP address, in order to permit the building of the layer 2 packets. From ESXi, you can see the ARP packets with this command:

```
[root@esxi2:~] tcpdump-uw arp
tcpdump-uw: verbose output suppressed, use -v or -vv for full protocol
decode
listening on vmk0, link-type EN10MB (Ethernet), capture size 262144 bytes
15:28:23.878389 ARP, Request who-has 10.10.70.110 tell
nsxmanager.lab.local, length 46
15:28:23.879198 ARP, Request who-has esxi2.lab.local tell
labserver.lab.local, length 46
15:28:23.879316 ARP, Reply esxi2.lab.local is-at 44:a8:42:22:a3:f2 (oui
Unknown), length 28
```

On ESXi, there is a local ARP table for all the VMkernel interfaces, and you can print it with the command `esxcli network ip neighbor list`.

Maximum Transmission Unit (MTU)

The original IEEE 802.3 specifications defined a valid Ethernet frame size from 64 to 1,518 bytes. Considering that the standard Ethernet header is 18 bytes in length, then the payload for a standard frame ranges in size from 46 to 1,500 bytes. This is the **MTU**.

However, since the original Ethernet specification was defined, different IEEE standards have been developed that support additional, expanded frame types listed here as follows:

- **VLAN tagging (802.1Q)**: This is with an additional 4 bytes in the Ethernet header.
- **Provider Bridge (802.1ad)**: This is with an additional 8 bytes to the original frame to support service and customer tagging.
- **FCoE frames**: These have an MTU of 2,500 bytes.
- **Multiprotocol Label Switching (MPLS)**: This increases the maximum Ethernet frame size to 1,518 bytes + (n * 4 bytes), where n is the number of stacked labels.
- **VXLAN**: This adds another 50 bytes.
- **Jumbo frames**: These are Ethernet frames with more than 1,500 bytes of payload, typically around 9,000 bytes. They are mostly used for IP-based storage traffic.

Which is the recommended MTU? If you plan to use jumbo frames for iSCSI or NFS traffic, there is a specific KB 1007654—*iSCSI and Jumbo Frames configuration on VMware ESXi/ESX* at `https://kb.vmware.com/kb/100765`. For VXLAN traffic, their recommended MTU is 1,600.

MTU unit details can be found at `https://tools.ietf.org/html/rfc791` or `https://tools.ietf.org/html/rfc1191` or `https://en.wikipedia.org/wiki/Maximum_transmission_unit`.

Virtual LAN (VLAN)

VLAN is a broadcast domain, so you can be segmenting Ethernet broadcast domains with VLANs. Network ports might be configured with one (access or untagged mode) or multiple VLANs (trunk or tagged mode).

802.1Q trunking modifies Ethernet frames to add a numeric tag. Using this tag can forward frames to different VLANs. Native VLAN is the untagged VLAN on an 802.1Q trunked switch port. VMware vSphere supports external VLAN tagging (only at physical switch level), virtual switch VLAN tagging, and VM VLAN tagging.

All of this from the total basic networking, we will describe in the next part.

For more information, refer to Virtual LAN details at `https://tools.ietf.org/html/rfc3069`.

Transmission Control Protocol (TCP) versus User Datagram Protocol (UDP)

TCP is connection-oriented; once a connection is established, data can be sent bidirectionally, and TCP provides guaranteed delivery packets. UDP is a simpler, connectionless protocol that provides a network without the overhead of a reliability mechanism.

Some vSphere-related services are based on TCP or UDP, depending on the type of service.

For more information about UDP, see `https://tools.ietf.org/html/rfc768`.
For more information about TCP, see `https://tools.ietf.org/html/rfc793`.

IPv6

Starting with vSphere 4.1, there is support for both IPv4 and IPv6; although the IPv6 support was initially disabled by default. With vSphere 5.1, IPv6 has become enabled by default for VMkernel traffic.

It is better to keep it vSphere 6.5 enabled, also because there is a bug in ESXi 6.5 (not fixed yet with Update 1) where the ESXi host 6.5 may fail with a **Purple Screen of Death (PSOD)** when IPv6 is disabled. For more information, see KB 2150794—*ESXi 6.5 host fails with PSOD when IPV6 is disabled* at `https://kb.vmware.com/s/article/2150794`.

For guest OS, both on Linux and Windows systems, it becomes very difficult to disable it, and Microsoft itself does not recommend disabling IPv6. We do not recommend that you disable IPv6 or its components, or some Windows components may not function. Find more information at `https://support.microsoft.com/en-us/kb/929852`.

You can find more details on IPv6 at `https://www.ietf.org/rfc/rfc2460.txt`.

Virtual networking

In VMware world, we have two types of virtual switches which are classified as **vNetwork Standard Switch (vSS)** and **vNetwork Distributed Switch (vDS)**.

What is the difference between vSS and vDS? When to use vSS or vDS? The vSS is configured on every ESXi host, meaning independently on each ESXi host in your environment. The vDS managed from a vCenter Server manages at the datacenter level. This idea is better because your administration takes place all in one place.

The virtual switch is a software construct running in the VMkernel. The virtual switch provides two types of connectivity to the VM (VM port group) and the hypervisor services (VMkernel ports).

vSS

The following figure shows a basic configuration of vSS. We have three VMs with **virtual NIC (vNIC)** to connect to the VM port group (for example, VLAN 100). We have configured two VMkernel ports—one is **vmk0** for management network and another is **vmk1** for vMotion traffic. There are two physical uplinks, (pNIC) connects to vSS attaching more adapters to the same virtual switch and provides redundancy.

pNIC provides connectivity to the external physical network. vSS is a layer 2 switch. With vSS, it is possible to use 802.1Q VLAN tagging:

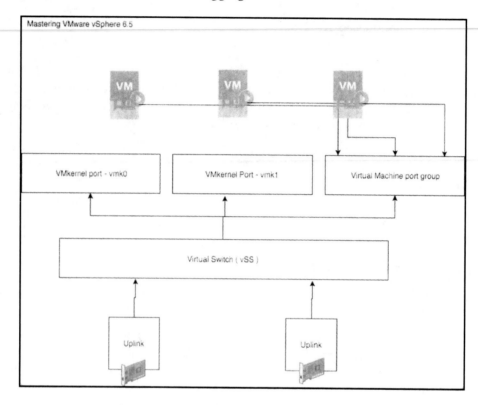

Example of vSphere standard switches

vDS

The following figure shows what your typical vDS should look like. We have a vCenter server where it is all a configured management plane. Completely create all VMkernel ports and VM port group. Very often it is a problem to understand what is uplink and what is vmnic. You must map vmnic to vDS uplink. Designation of vmnic starts from 0 and designation uplink starts from 1. The total typical example is **vmnic0** is mapped to **Uplink1**:

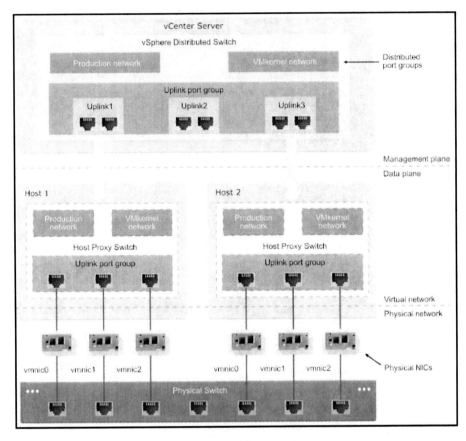

A vDS architecture

Examples of vSS and vDS in the real world are as follows:

We can use CLI, which is very old but still good, `esxcfg-vswitch -l`; this CLI shows you both a virtual switch vSS and vDS, with a lot of information:

```
[root@esxi1:~] esxcfg-vswitch -l
Switch Name        Num Ports    Used Ports    Configured Ports    MTU      Uplinks
vSwitch0           4352         10            128                 1500     vmnic0
   PortGroup Name           VLAN ID    Used Ports    Uplinks
   VM Network               0          6             vmnic0
   Management Network       0          1             vmnic0
Switch Name        Num Ports    Used Ports    Configured Ports    MTU      Uplinks
vSwitch1           4352         4             128                 1500     vmnic1
   PortGroup Name           VLAN ID    Used Ports    Uplinks
IPSstorage                   0          1             vmnic1
Switch Name        Num Ports    Used Ports    Configured Ports    MTU      Uplinks
```

```
vmservice-vswitch   4352            2              16                    1500
   PortGroup Name          VLAN ID  Used Ports  Uplinks
   vmservice-vshield-pg   0            0
   vmservice-vmknic-pg    0            1
Switch Name          Num Ports   Used Ports  Configured Ports   MTU    Uplinks
vSwitch2             4352         1              128             1500
   PortGroup Name          VLAN ID  Used Ports  Uplinks
   Space                   0            0
DVS Name             Num Ports   Used Ports  Configured Ports   MTU    Uplinks
DSwitch-SDN10GB      4352         18             512             9000
vmnic5,vmnic4
   DVPort ID            In Use       Client
   8                    0
   9                    0
   12                   1            vmnic4
   13                   1            vmnic5
   124                  1            vmk2
   168                  1            App02.eth0
   172                  1            DB01.eth0
   164                  1            App01.eth0
   212                  1            desktop-ubuntu.eth0
   180                  1            Web01.eth0\
   196                  1            edge-3-jobdata-155792-0.eth0
   135                  1            edge-3-jobdata-155792-0.eth1
   136                  1            edge-4-jobdata-155794-0.eth0
   137                  1            edge-4-jobdata-155794-1.eth0
```

The CLI that helps you audit your configuration is `esxcli`. This is used for both vSS and vDS. Consider the following two examples of `esxli`:

- First, list all vSS on a host using the following command:

```
[root@esx1:] esxcli network vswitch standard list
vSwitch0
Name: vSwitch0
Class: etherswitch
Num Ports: 5632
Used Ports: 1
Configured Ports: 128
MTU: 1500
CDP Status: listen
Beacon Enabled: false
Beacon Interval: 1
Beacon Threshold: 3
Beacon Required By:
Uplinks:
Portgroups: VM Network, EXTERN
```

```
vSwitch1
Name: vSwitch1
Class: etherswitch
Num Ports: 5632
Used Ports: 1
Configured Ports: 128
MTU: 1500
CDP Status: listen
Beacon Enabled: false
Beacon Interval: 1
Beacon Threshold: 3
Beacon Required By:
Uplinks:
Portgroups: MGMT2, MGMT, iSCSI, Prod1, Prod2, vMotion
```

- Second, list all information about vDS configuration on a host using the following command:

```
[root@esx1:~] esxcli network vswitch dvs vmware list
DELL_VDC
Name: DELL_VDC
VDS ID: 50 2c 86 06 eb 30 e4 04-95 d9 d7 d0 70 a8 d1 72
Class: etherswitch
Num Ports: 5632
Used Ports: 1
Configured Ports: 512
MTU: 9000
CDP Status: both
Beacon Timeout: -1
Uplinks:
VMware Branded: true
DVPort:
        Client:
        DVPortgroup ID: dvportgroup-18
        In Use: false
        Port ID: 3856
        Client:
        DVPortgroup ID: dvportgroup-18
        In Use: false
        Port ID: 3857
```

For a lover of GUI, of course, it is very easy to show vSS and vDS in vSphere Web Client or new vSphere Client (HTML5).

In the following screenshot, the **vSwitch0** is vSS, and after clicking on this object, you can check the VM port group and VMkernel ports:

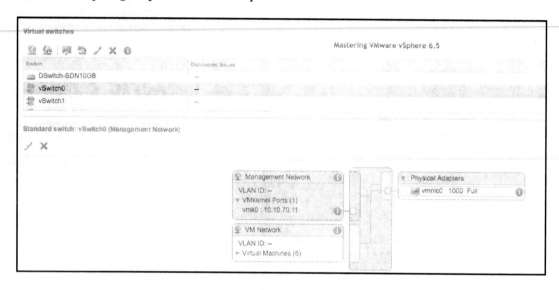

vSS and vDS from vSphere Web Client

The same configuration details are also available with the new HTML5 interface, using the vSphere Client. Basically, is the same information rearranged in a different way:

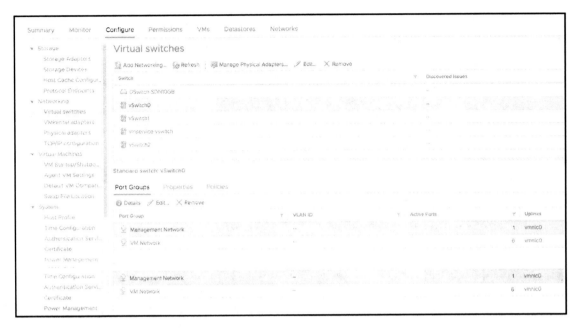

vSS and vDS from vSphere Client (HTML5)

Managing vSS

In this part, we will describe how to add, edit, and configure vSS and vDS. Working with GUI is easy, but you can use CLI of course. First, we will be working with a vSS switch. We show how it is easy to configure a new vSS.

We use first a host client direct on the ESXi host. This situation is good to know when you don't have already a vCenter Server. In this case, you need to prepare a first VM port group for the first VM. This happens typically before the deployment of vCSA (or the VM that will host the vCenter Server).

The following screenshot shows you the GUI host client where you click on **Networking** | **Virtual switches** | **Add standard virtual switch**:

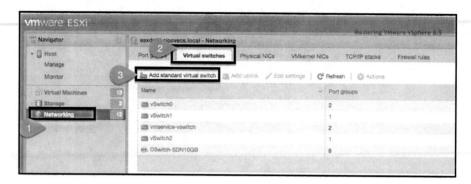

Add new virtual switch

When you create a new standard virtual switch, you have a lot of details, the vSwitch name (note that it's possible to give them a name only from the ESXi UI), the MTU, the used uplinks, the link discovery protocol (on vSS only CDP is supported), the security settings, and so on:

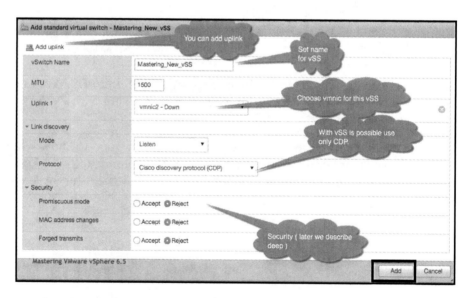

Add new virtual switch detail

You can change your setting of vSS through the **Edit settings** option:

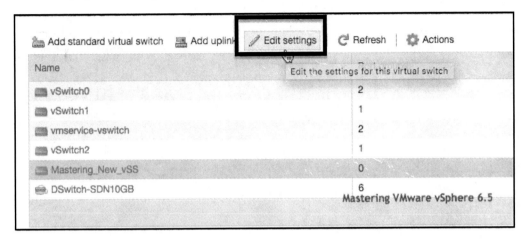

Edit vSS

We created vSS with the name `Mastering_New_vSS`, but at the moment, it is not possible to connect **virtual network interface cards (vNIC)** from a VM to vSS. *Why?* We need to configure the VM port group.

So, you click only on the next left side from the **Virtual switches** option and click on the **Port groups** option, and here you find the **Add port group** button as follows:

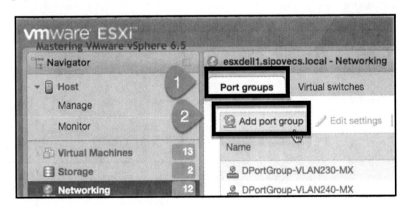

Add port group

Under the **Add port group** option, you specify a name for port group, VLAN ID tag, and the correct vSS in our case as `Mastering_New_vSS`:

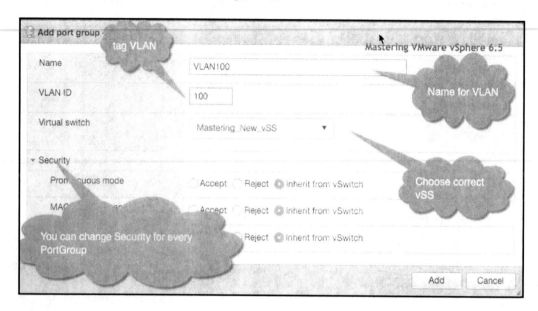

Add port group detail

Yes, we have completed the configuration of vSS with VM port group, so we can add vNIC to this VLAN100 port group:

Shows topology after add VLAN100 to vSS

If you need to, it's very easy to change a VM port group, for example, to move a VM from one network to another network. On the VM, just choose the **Edit settings** option. You have to look at the virtual network card part of VM properties and define a new port group (or also distributed port group). In the following example, the **Network Adapter 2** will be connected to the **VLAN100** port group:

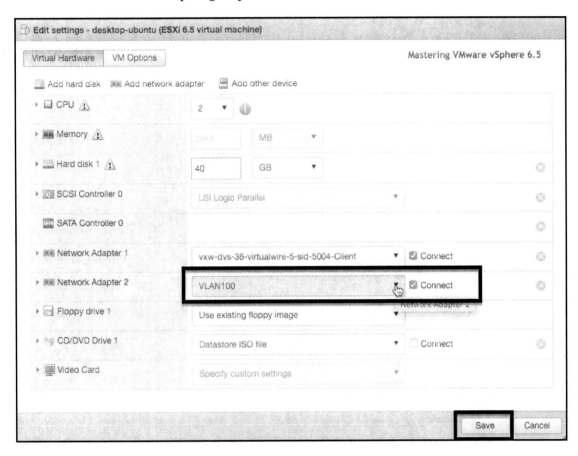

Change PG on VM

Now, we have a ready network for deploying the vCenter appliance. After deployment, we change GUI and connect to the vCenter server through vSphere Client (HTML 5) or vSphere Web Client.

After connecting to your vCenter Server, you can select one ESXi host and then choose the **Configure** tab. Then click on **Networking** | **Virtual switches** and you will see something like the following screenshot:

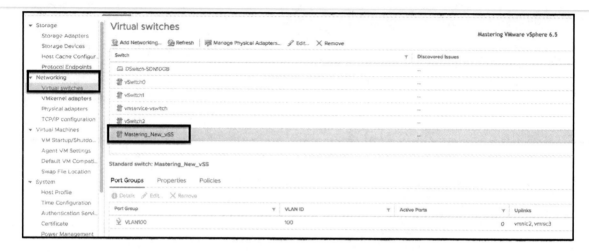

Same view in vSS from HTML5 client

What is the possible configuration and change after creating vSS? Here is the detail after clicking on the **Edit settings** option:

Edit setting on vSS

We can change settings in four tabs—**Properties**, **Security**, **Traffic shaping**, and **Teaming and failover**. The description of these tabs is as follows:

- **Properties**: Here, it is possible to change only one setting in MTU. The MTU can improve the networking efficiency. You can enable jumbo frames, and the MTU can be greater than 1,500, but you can't set the MTU size greater than 9,000 bytes. The number of ports is from vSphere 5.5 and later dynamically scaled up and down. So, it is not possible to get the vSS changed. In **Elastic** port allocation, the default number of ports is 8. When all ports are assigned, a new set of 8 ports is created:

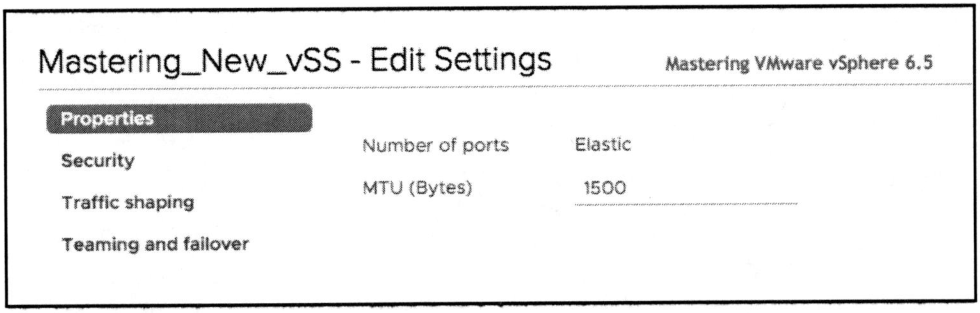

Mastering_New_vSS - Edit Settings   Mastering VMware vSphere 6.5

Properties

Security

Traffic shaping

Teaming and failover

Number of ports	Elastic
MTU (Bytes)	1500

Properties tab in Edit Settings vSS

- **Security:** This is an easy tab because here you can change three settings:

    1. **Promiscuous mode**: The options in this mode are as follows:
        - **Reject**: This is the default option. Guest OS does not result in receiving frames for another VM.
        - **Accept**: All frames passed on the virtual switch that is allowed under the VLAN policy for port group. This can be useful to detect and monitor traffic or sniffer traffic analyzer.

    2. **MAC address changes**: This provides for the following options:
        - **Reject**: Guest OS changes the MAC address of the adapter to a value different from the address in the .vmx configuration file. The switch will block the port.
        - **Accept**: This is the default option. Guest OS can change the MAC address of a network adapter, the adapter receives frames to its new address.

    3. **Forged transmits**: This is very similar to a MAC address changes option, but for outbound traffic. This provides for the following options:
        - **Reject**: The switch drops any outbound frame with a source MAC address that is different from the one in the .vmx configuration file.

- **Accept**: The switch does not perform filtering and permits all outbound frames:

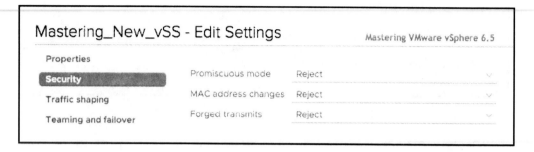

Security-Edit Settings-vSS

- **Traffic shaping**: When you need to shape traffic but with vSS, it is possible only on outbound network traffic. When you need bidirectional control, you must use vDS inbound and outbound traffic. This option is disabled by default.

When you enable the status you can set:

1. **Average bandwidth (kbit/s)**: Establish the number of bits per second to allow across a port, averaged over time. This number is the allowed average load.
2. **Peak bandwidth (kbit/s)**: The maximum number of kilobits per second to allow across a port when it is sending a burst of traffic. This number tops the bandwidth that is used by a port whenever the port is using its burst bonus.
3. **Burst size (KB)**: The maximum number of kilobytes to allow in a burst. This is useful if you want a permit whenever bandwidth peaks (bigger than the average bandwidth) for a limited time. Note that the burst is not expressed in time, but in size.

Traffic shaping tab in Edit Settings vSS

I haven't used traffic shaping for the past seven years, but it can be used for any testing and developing.

- **Teaming and failover**: This is the important part of vSS settings and it's composed of several options as follows:
    - **Load balancing**: This option determines how network traffic is distributed between the network adapters in a NIC team, according to one of these algorithm:
        - **Route based on originating virtual port (default)**: The virtual switch selects uplinks based on the VM port IDs on the vSS or vDS. This method is without extra configuration on the physical switch and has low overhead.
        - **Route based on source MAC hash**: The virtual switch selects an uplink for a VM based on the VM MAC address. To calculate an uplink for a VM, the virtual switch uses the VM MAC address and the number of uplinks in the NIC team. This method is a support for all physical switches and has low overhead.
        - **Route based on IP hash**: The virtual switch select uplinks for VMs based on the source and destination IP address of each packet. The IP-based method requires 802.3ad link aggregation support or EtherChannel.
        - **Use Explicit Failover**: No actual use load balancing with this policy. The virtual switch always uses the first uplink that is in the active adapter list. If not possible, one of the other active adapters will be used instead of the standby adapter.

- **Network failure detection:** This option is how you understand that one link is not usable. You can specify two methods for failover detection:

  - **Link status only**: This is the default option. Detect failures on a link as a removed cables problem on the physical switch.
  - **Beacon probing**: When you want to use this detection mode, you must have as a minimal for beacon probing, three or more NICs in the team. *How does it work?* It sends out and listens for Ethernet broadcast frames that physical NICs send to detect a link failure in all physical NICs in a team. ESXi hosts send beacon packets every second.

In a production environment, **Link status only** option is very often used to avoid extra traffic, but also because beacon probing requires at least three physical NICs (for the uplinks) in order to have a clear majority.

- **Notify switches:** This option is a single option (by default it's enabled) used to speed the change of the network topology at the physical switches level. When the physical port used for the VM traffic must be re-routed to a different physical port (for example, due to link failure), then the virtual switch sends notifications over the network to update the lookup tables on the physical switch. The same happens during vSphere vMotion migration.

The protocol used is **Reverse Address Resolution Protocol (RARP)**

- **Failback:** This option is another single option (again, by default it's enabled) that determines how a physical adapter is returned to active duty after recovering from a failure. By default, the adapter returns to active duty immediately.
- **Failover order**: This option specifies how the different uplinks (the physical NICs) are used:
  - **Active adapters**: This continues to use the uplink when it is up as active

- **Standby adapters**: If there are no active adapters that are up, then the next uplink from the standby adapters list will be used
- **Unused adapters**: Never use this uplink

 Of course, when you want to use IP Hash, load balancing is a very bad idea; configure some uplinks as standby uplinks.

So, we now have a basic idea about setting vSS:

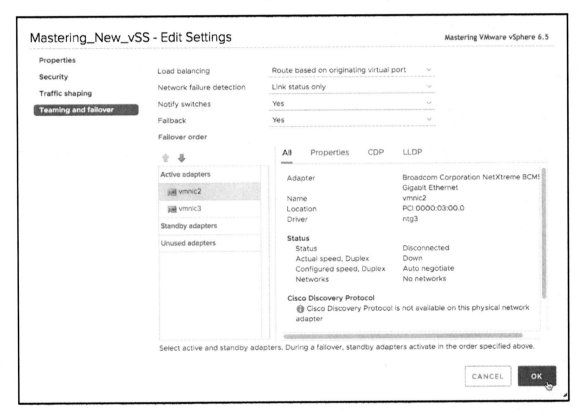

Teaming and failover option in Edit Settings vSS

We have a ready vSS. We know settings on the vSS level, but we check edit settings on the **Port Group** level. Once more, it is very easy and click on the **Edit...** button on the port group **VLAN100**, as shown in the following screenshot:

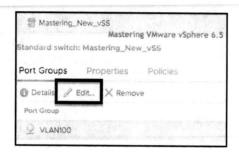

Edit Settings-Port Group-VLAN100

You will see the very same settings as on the vSS level. The different tabs on the port group level are as follows:

- **Properties**: Here it is possible to change the name of the port group and change VLAN ID, as shown in the following screenshot:

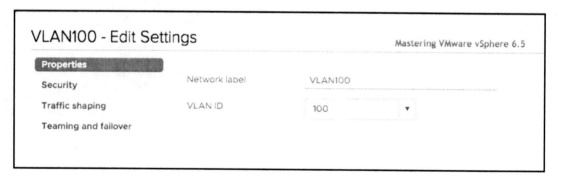

Properties-Port Group-VLAN100

- **Security**: Like the security settings described at the switch level. For each port group, it's possible to override the virtual switch configuration and have some settings that are more specific:

Security-Port Group-VLAN100

- **Traffic shaping**: Like the traffic shaping settings described at the switch level. For each port group, it's possible to override the virtual switch configuration and have some more specific settings. Useful if you need to limit bandwidth only for the specific VMs group:

Traffic shaping-Port Group-VLAN100

- **Teaming and failover**: Like the teaming settings described at the switch level. For each port group, it's possible to override the virtual switch configuration with some settings that are more specific. Used, for example to change the active uplink for a specific port group and define a different network path (at layer 2) for different VMs or different VMkernel interfaces:

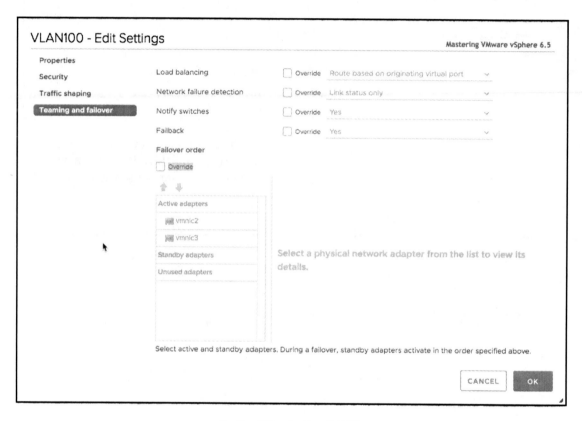

Teaming and failover-Port Group-VLAN100

All these settings are possible to list through CLI. I would like to show you some **esxcli** commands that can be useful for you in practical life. For example, consider the following two commands:

- The first command lists the details for vSS Mastering_New_vSS. You can try the next command, esxcli, as it is very easy to use in the everyday life of administrating vSphere:

```
[root@esxi1:~] esxcli network vswitch standard list -v
Mastering_New_vSS
Mastering_New_vSS
 Name: Mastering_New_vSS
 Class: etherswitch
 Num Ports: 4352
 Used Ports: 5
 Configured Ports: 1024
 MTU: 1500
 CDP Status: listen
 Beacon Enabled: false
 Beacon Interval: 1
 Beacon Threshold: 3
 Beacon Required By:
 Uplinks: vmnic3, vmnic2
 Portgroups: VLAN100
```

- The second command gets information about policy settings on vSS Mastering_New_vSS:

```
[root@esxi1:~] esxcli network vswitch standard policy security
get -v Mastering_New_vSS
 Allow Promiscuous: false
 Allow MAC Address Change: false
 Allow Forged Transmits: false
```

When you write the esxcli network command and click on *Enter*, you will see all possible commands for the network:

```
[root@esxi1:~] esxcli network
Usage: esxcli network {cmd} [cmd options]
Available Namespaces:
  firewall        A set of commands for firewall related operations
  ip              Operations that can be performed on vmknics
  multicast       Operations having to do with multicast
  nic             Operations having to do with the configuration of
Network Interface Card and getting and updating the NIC settings.
  port            Commands to get information about a port
```

```
     sriovnic                Operations having to do with the configuration of
SRIOV enabled Network Interface Card and getting and updating the NIC
settings.
     vm                      A set of commands for VM related operations
     vswitch                 Commands to list and manipulate Virtual Switches on
an ESX host.
     diag                    Operations pertaining to network diagnostics
```

In the next part, we will be describing and working with the VMkernel port.

VMkernel adapters

VMkernel port (or VMkernel adapter or interface) is used for VMkernel services when we need connecting to the physical network. VMkernel adapters are used (and needed) for IP-based storage (such as NFS or iSCSI), for vSAN, for vMotion traffic, for vSphere FT logs, for management interfaces, for vSphere Replication, for NSX-VTEP. The section with details of the VMkernel port can be found under the **Virtual switches** option in the **Networking** section:

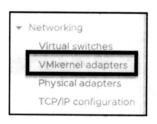

VMkernel port tab – Networking

We will create a new VMkernel port; this step is very easy but very important for the next vSphere features. Proceed with the steps as follows:

1. First step is to choose the **Add Networking...** option shown as follows:

Add Networking

2. You choose the interface type, by selecting the **VMkernel Network Adapter** option:

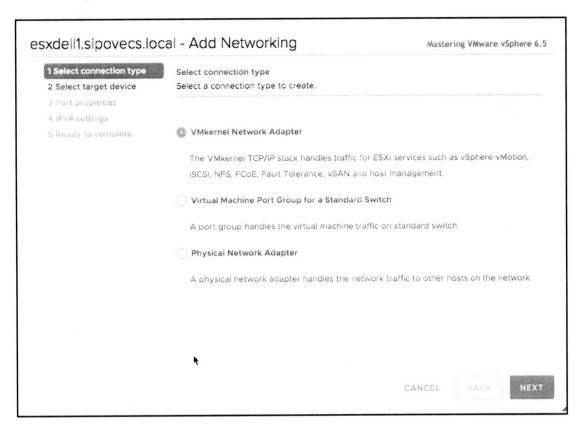

Add VMkernel Network Adapter port

3. Then you have to define where it's connected, by selecting the existing network or selecting existing vSS; otherwise, you can create a new vSS. In this case, we select an existing network:

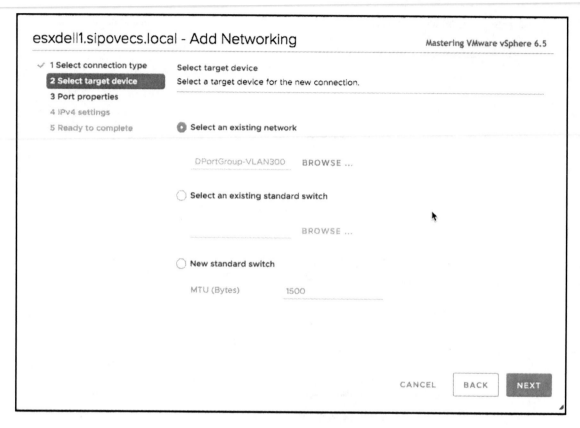

Select target device-VMKernel port-Networking

4. In this example, we have built a new VMkernel port for vMotion network traffic. For this reason, the VMkernel port will be enabled for vMotion service. You can also specify if you are using IP version v4 or v6, the required MTU, or the TCP/IP stack:

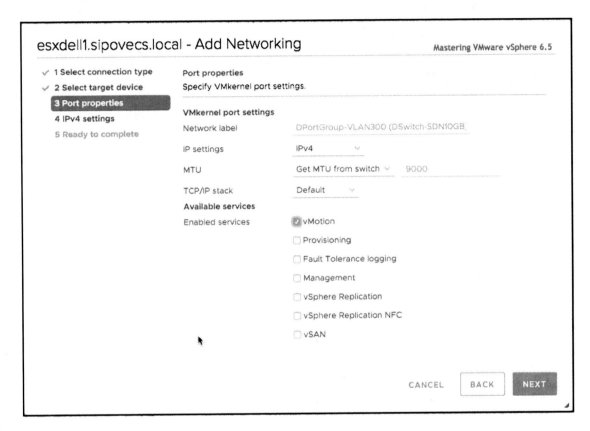

VMkernel port properties

5. In the next step, you configure IP settings as DHCP or static:

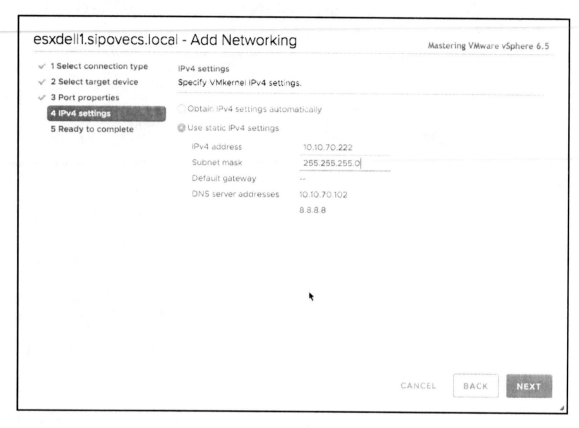

IPv4 settings

6. Now you are ready to create the VMkernel port and you can check the summary of the entire configuration on the final page shown as follows:

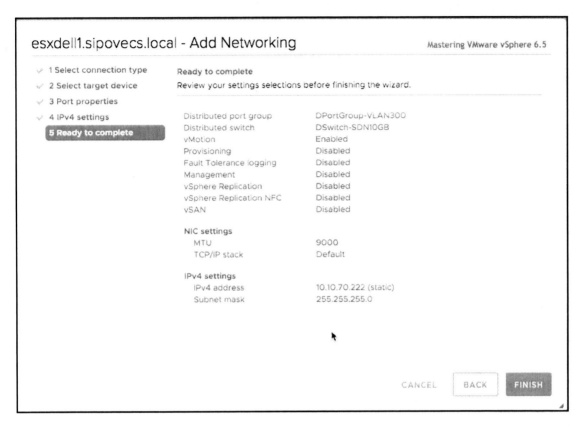

Ready to complete

7. You can monitor the process in the **Recent Tasks** area:

Status in Recent Tasks tab

Now that the new VMkernel port has been created, a new unique identifier has been assigned to it, in this example, vmk5. VMkernel names start from vmk0 (by default the management interface created during ESXi installation) and grow number by number with every new VMkernel port.

You can easily edit the settings for this new VMkernel port by using its identifier:

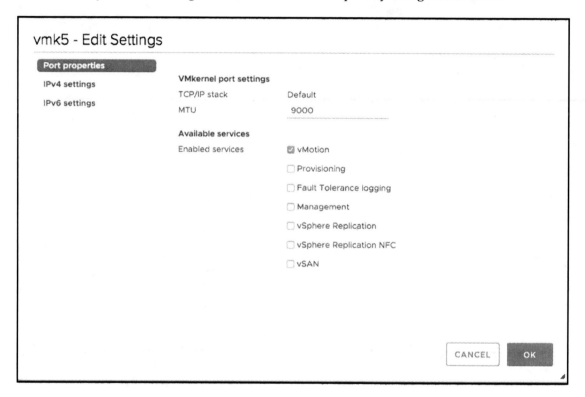

Edit settings of vmk5 interface

Physical adapters

Physical adapters (also called pNICs) are usually used as the virtual switches uplinks. You can find the detailed information about a physical network card in your ESXi host, by selecting the **Networking** section and **Physical adapters** option:

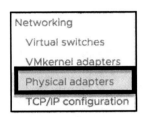

Physical adapters

You have a list of all your physical network ports (from your network cards). Each network port is named starting from vmnic0 (the first recognized network port), then vmnic1, and so on. For each port, you will have some details such as network speed, virtual switches where it's connected, the physical MAC address, the observed IP range (based on broadcast packets that are received by the interface):

Device	Actual Speed	Configured Speed	Switch	MAC Address	Observed IP Ranges	Wake on LAN Supported
vmnic0	1000 Mb	1000 Mb	vSwitch0	44:a8:42:22:a0:fe	No networks	No
vmnic1	1000 Mb	1000 Mb	vSwitch1	44:a8:42:22:a0:ff	0.0.03-255.255.255.254	No
vmnic2	Down	Auto negotiate	Mastering_New_vSS	44:a8:42:22:a1:00	No networks	No
vmnic3	Down	Auto negotiate	Mastering_New_vSS	44:a8:42:22:a1:01	No networks	No
vmnic4	10000 Mb	10000 Mb	DSwitch-SDN10GB	00:50:86:82:26:e8	No networks	No
vmnic5	10000 Mb	10000 Mb	DSwitch-SDN10GB	00:50:86:82:26:e9	No networks	No

Physical ports list

You can get the same information, in a faster way by using esxcli, it very quickly shows a list of all NICs:

```
[root@esxi1:~] esxcli network nic list
Name    PCI Device    Driver  Admin Status  Link Status  Speed  Duplex  MAC
Address         MTU  Description
------  ------------  ------  ------------  -----------  -----  ------  ---
--
------------  ----  -------------------------------------------------------
vmnic0  0000:02:00.0  ntg3    Up            Up            1000  Full
44:a8:42:22:a0:fe  1500  Broadcom Corporation NetXtreme BCM5720 Gigabit
Ethernet
vmnic1  0000:02:00.1  ntg3    Up            Up            1000  Full
44:a8:42:22:a0:ff  1500  Broadcom Corporation NetXtreme BCM5720 Gigabit
Ethernet
vmnic2  0000:03:00.0  ntg3    Up            Down             0  Half
44:a8:42:22:a1:00  1500  Broadcom Corporation NetXtreme BCM5720 Gigabit
Ethernet
vmnic3  0000:03:00.1  ntg3    Up            Down             0  Half
44:a8:42:22:a1:01  1500  Broadcom Corporation NetXtreme BCM5720 Gigabit
Ethernet
vmnic4  0000:04:00.0  ixgbe   Up            Up           10000  Full
```

```
00:10:86:82:26:e8   9000   Intel(R) 82599 10 Gigabit Dual Port Network
Connection
vmnic5  0000:04:00.1  ixgbe   Up            Up         10000  Full
00:10:86:82:26:e9   9000   Intel(R) 82599 10 Gigabit Dual Port Network
Connection
```

When you think that `esxcli` is very long, you can still use the old command `esxcfg-nics -l`:

```
[root@esxi1:~] esxcfg-nics -l
Name     PCI            Driver       Link Speed       Duplex MAC Address
MTU      Description
vmnic0   0000:02:00.0 ntg3          Up   1000Mbps     Full   44:a8:42:22:a0:fe
1500     Broadcom Corporation NetXtreme BCM5720 Gigabit Ethernet
vmnic1   0000:02:00.1 ntg3          Up   1000Mbps     Full   44:a8:42:22:a0:ff
1500     Broadcom Corporation NetXtreme BCM5720 Gigabit Ethernet
vmnic2   0000:03:00.0 ntg3          Down 0Mbps        Half   44:a8:42:22:a1:00
1500     Broadcom Corporation NetXtreme BCM5720 Gigabit Ethernet
vmnic3   0000:03:00.1 ntg3          Down 0Mbps        Half   44:a8:42:22:a1:01
1500     Broadcom Corporation NetXtreme BCM5720 Gigabit Ethernet
vmnic4   0000:04:00.0 ixgbe         Up   10000Mbps    Full   00:10:86:82:26:e8
9000     Intel(R) 82599 10 Gigabit Dual Port Network Connection
vmnic5   0000:04:00.1 ixgbe         Up   10000Mbps    Full   00:10:86:82:26:e9
9000     Intel(R) 82599 10 Gigabit Dual Port Network Connection
```

The last tab in the networking is tab **TCP/IP configuration**. *What is it?* From version vSphere 6, it is possible to separate the TCP/IP stack. You can use for better isolation for the traffic. For example, vMotion or IP Storage. The TCP/IP stack has its own memory heap, ARP tables, routing tables, and default gateway.

TCP/IP stacks

Before vSphere 6.0 the TCP/IP configuration was mainly managed by a single network stack. But now we can have multiple and different TCP/IP stacks (also called netstacks) for different VMkernel interfaces. You can verify all stacks from the **Networking, TCP/IP configuration**:

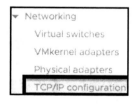

TCP/IP configuration

There are some predefined TCP/IP stacks—**Default**, **Provisioning**, and **vMotion**. In the following screenshot, you see next **vxlan** (a specific stack from NSX, that will be described later) and **IPstorage**, which I created before from CLI:

TCP/IP stacks

You can also have the same list from CLI, using the `esxcli` command:

```
[root@esxi1:~] esxcli network ip netstack list
defaultTcpipStack
Key: defaultTcpipStack
    Name: defaultTcpipStack
    State: 4660
vxlan
    Key: vxlan
    Name: vxlan
    State: 4660
IPstorage
    Key: IPstorage
    Name: IPstorage
    State: 4660
```

What you must do from CLI is a situation when you want to create a new TCP/IP stack; no options exist in the GUI clients, the only way to perform this task is from the CLI.

Consider the example; how easy is it to create the stack `Mastering_Stack`:

```
[root@esxi1:~] esxcli network ip netstack add -N Mastering_Stack
```

And once more, list all netstacks as follows:

```
[root@esxi1:~] esxcli network ip netstack list
defaultTcpipStack
    Key: defaultTcpipStack
    Name: defaultTcpipStack
    State: 4660
vxlan
    Key: vxlan
```

```
      Name: vxlan
      State: 4660
IPstorage
   Key: IPstorage
   Name: IPstorage
   State: 4660
Mastering_Stack
   Key: Mastering_Stack
   Name: Mastering_Stack
   State: 4660
```

You have to be very careful when you need to ping or list routes. You must every time specify which TCP/IP stack you want to use. For example, when we want to ping on the VMkernel port that is on another host in the TCP/IP stack vxlan (NSX), you must specify the stack.

The new `Mastering_Stack` TCP/IP stack will be also visible from the vSphere Client, as shown in the following screenshot:

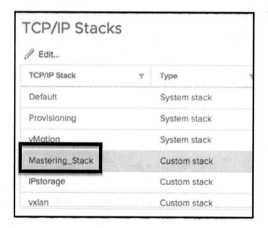

TCP/IP Stacks in GUI

When you need to check the correct connection between the two ESXi hosts, you can use `vmkping`, but specify which VMkernel interface you want to use and specify the TCP/IP stack you want to use:

```
[root@esxi1:~] vmkping ++netstack=vxlan 10.200.10.11 -I vmk2
PING 10.200.10.11 (10.200.10.11): 56 data bytes
64 bytes from 10.200.10.11: icmp_seq=0 ttl=64 time=0.232 ms
64 bytes from 10.200.10.11: icmp_seq=1 ttl=64 time=0.210 ms
64 bytes from 10.200.10.11: icmp_seq=2 ttl=64 time=0.218 ms
```

Once more, when you want information about the route table for stack vxlan, you must specify the netstack in CLI:

```
[root@esxi1:~] esxcli network ip route ipv4 list --netstack=vxlan
Network        Netmask        Gateway       Interface  Source
-----------    -------------  -----------   ---------  ------
default        0.0.0.0        10.200.10.1   vmk2       MANUAL
10.200.10.0    255.255.255.0  0.0.0.0       vmk2       MANUAL
```

One typical use case of the TCP/IP stack is to provide a different default gateway address for a specific VMkernel interface (for example, to use vMotion across datacenters). Another use case is to provide a specific routing path without the need to specify a static routing table; that is otherwise a little tricky task on ESXi, as described on KB 2001426—*Configuring static routes for vmkernel ports on an ESXi host* at https://kb.vmware.com/kb/2001426.

To provide a different default gateway for each stack, you can use both the GUI and the CLI.

- The first option used is the GUI:

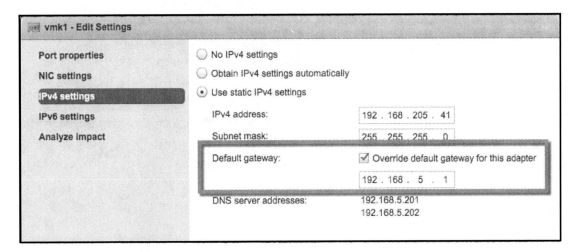

Override default getaway for VMkernel adapter

- The second option is using the CLI with the `esxcli` command:

```
esxcli network ip interface ipv4 set -i vmknic -t static -g
gateway -I IP address -N mask
```

More details on virtual networks are available in the *VMWare Networking* guide available at `https://docs.vmware.com/en/VMware-vSphere/6.5/com.vmware.vsphere.networking.doc/GUID-8BCBB25E-9A84-4322-94BC-C556DE9C2956.html`.

So many congratulations that you are an expert on vSS. We need to know more of next interesting things, so go for coffee, and we will continue with a vDS.

Managing vDS

In the most part of this chapter, we will use the new vSphere Client in HTML5, but still, there is some functionality that has not been ported on it. You can find the details at `https://docs.vmware.com/en/VMware-vSphere/6.5/rn/vsphere-client-65-html5-functionality-support.html`.

Distributed Switch	Management	<ul><li>Add and manage hosts (template mode)</li><li>Edit distributed port settings</li><li>Advanced features: NIOC, port mirror (edit sessions), traffic filtering, LACP</li><li>Import and export distributed switch and distributed port group</li><li>Manage physical network adapters for distributed switch</li><li>Health check</li><li>Topology view</li><li>Upgrade distributed switch</li></ul>

Unsupported functionality

To create a new distributed switch, using the vSphere Client, follow these steps:

1. First, we will create a vDS in the networking inventory view (1). This specific inventory view is the logical container of vDS definition and configuration. Right-click on the datacenter (in this example, SDN_PRAHA) and from the contextual menu, choose the **Distributed Switch** menu and then the **New Distributed Switch...** option as shown in the following screenshot:

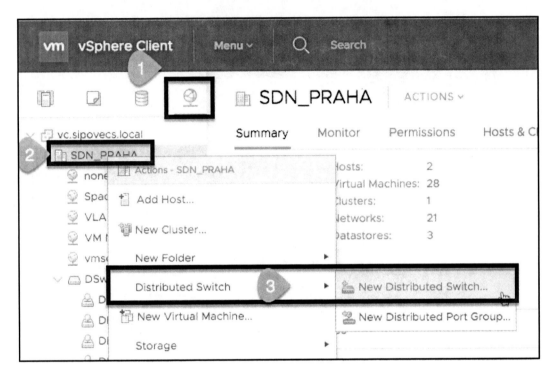

New vDS

2. The next step is to specify the name for the vDS, which in our case is `Mastering_DSwitch` as shown in following screenshot:

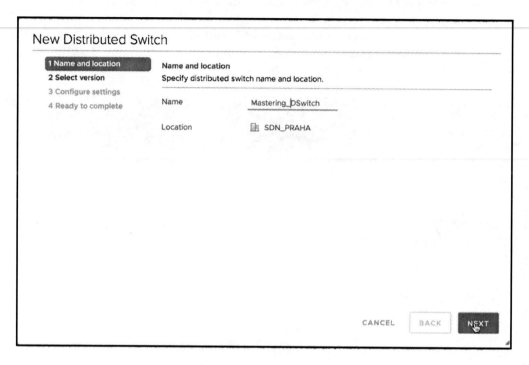

Name and location vDS

3. In the next part, we must specify the version of vDS. This step is very important because each different version has different features and enhancements, but of course, newest versions are not compatible with the previous version of ESXi and vSphere. To learn more about the features and capabilities of the different versions of vDS, you can click on the small blue icon **i** in the vSphere Client.

In this example, we used the latest version 6.5 because we have all the hosts in the latest version:

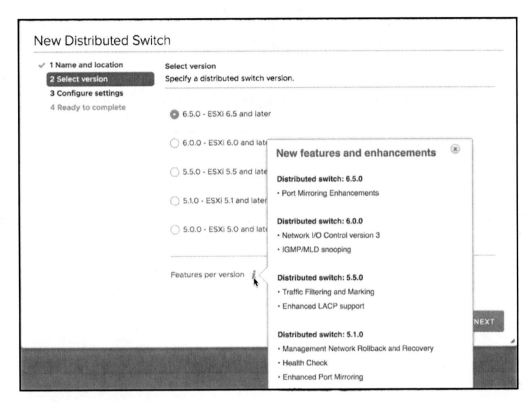

vDS versions

4. The next step is to configure the settings as follows:

- **Number of uplinks**: You can specify the maximum number of allowed physical connections to the distributed switch per host
- **Network I/O Control**: You can prioritize the access to network resources for workloads
- **Default port group**: You can set create now or create later
- **Port group name**: This is the name for the default port group

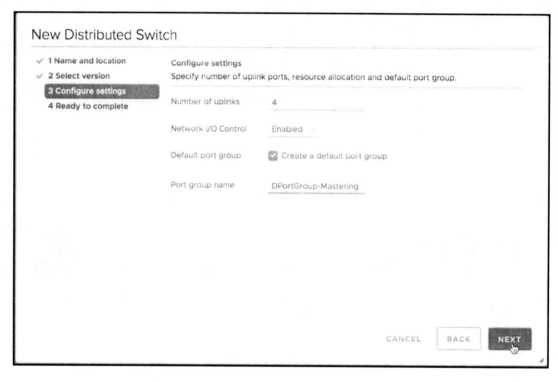

Configure settings vDS

5. Finally, you will have the summary with all the information related to your configuration, for the last check. At this point, you can click on the **Finish** button shown as follows:

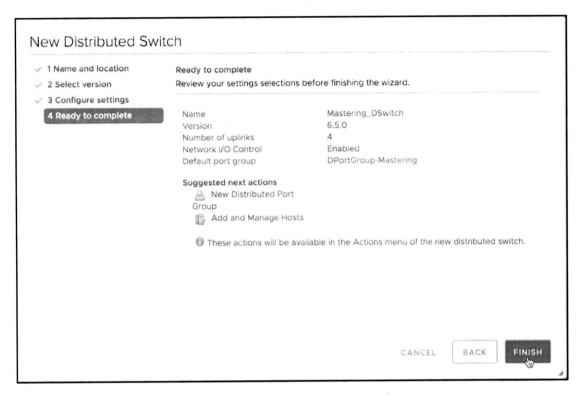

Complete vDS

OK guys, this is going to be a little bit confusing for you, but trust me at the moment vSphere 6.5 Update 1 is better used for working with vDS vSphere Web Client. *Why?* The easy answer coming is that this version is not fully ready for working with vDS. It will be very soon.

So, we will switch to the vSphere Web Client in order to configure all the available settings of a vDS.

Properties

Still, you have to work in the same network inventory view. You will see the vDS created before and you can simply select it, then choose the **Configure** tab and the **Properties** menu to see all the settings of your vDS:

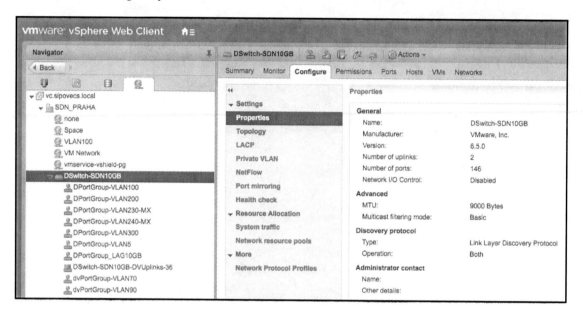

General properties vDS

You can change the settings by clicking on **Edit** in the right corner. Distributed switched settings are grouped in a general part (for the common settings) and in an advanced part (for the advanced settings):

- **General**: You can change the name of the vDS, change the number of uplinks (and their names), enable or disable network I/O control or add a description to your vDS:

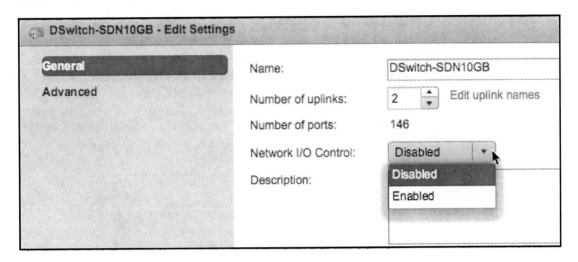

General vDS

- **Advanced**: Advanced settings include the possibility to change the MTU, multicast filtering mode, discovery protocol, and add administrator contact. Under **Multicast filtering mode**, you can set the filtering mode as follows:
    - **Basic filtering**: In basic multicast filtering mode, a vSS or vDS forwards multicast traffic for VMs according to the destination MAC address of the multicast group.
    - **Multicast snooping**: In the multicast snooping mode, a vDS provides IGMP and MLD snooping according to RFC 4541. For more details refer to `https://tools.ietf.org/html/rfc4541`.

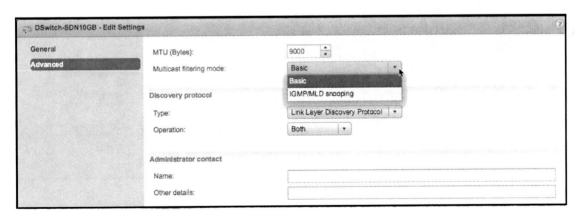

Advanced vDS

- **Discovery protocol**: There are two different supported protocols. First is **Cisco Discovery Protocol (CDP)**, proprietary from Cisco, but supported also by some other switches. The second is a vendor-neutral standard called **Link Layer Discovery Protocol (LLDP)**. Note that vSS supports only CDP. You can choose the discovery protocol, and if it is enabled you can choose also in which directory it can be used (advertise, to announce at the physical switch, or listen, to receive information from the physical switch):

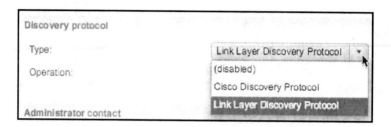

Discovery protocol

Topology

Next part of the vDS configuration and settings is the **Topology** section, where there is a view of your vDS and port groups:

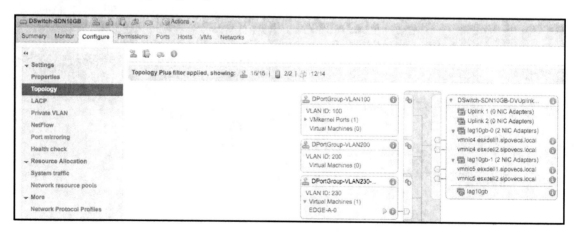

Topology vDS

This view can be very useful to check the network connections and find possible problems, such as links that are down, blocked ports, and so on.

Link Aggregation Control Protocol (LACP)

The LACP protocol is fully supported with vDS (note that it's not available for vSS). You can connect the ESXi host to physical switches by using dynamic link aggregation. LACP must be prepared correctly for the physical part of the networking. You create **Link Aggregation Groups (LAG)**, every LAG group is with two or more ports. You can create up to 64 LAGs. Information about the configuration maximum is part of Maximus vSphere 6.5 documents.

 For more information on Maximus vSphere 6.5 documents, refer to `https://www.vmware.com/pdf/vsphere6/r65/vsphere-65-configuration-maximums.pdf`.

The next part is about LACP and the configuration LAG group on vDS:

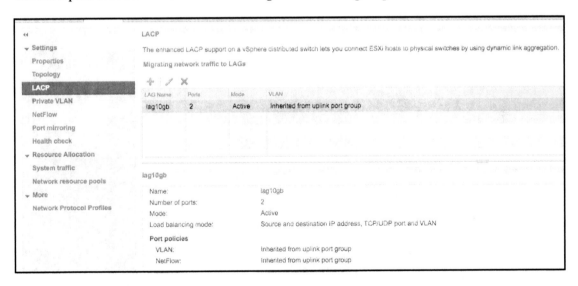

LACP settings vDS

We can check the configuration through a CLI `esxcli`; that is, information about config, stats, and so on as follows:

```
[root@esxi1:~] esxcli network vswitch dvs vmware lacp config get
DVS Name LAG Name LAG ID NICs Enabled Mode Load balance
--------------- -------- --------- ------------- ------- ------ -----------
---------------
DSwitch-SDN10GB lag10gb 438932027 vmnic4,vmnic5 true Active Src and dst ip,
port, vlan

[root@esxi1:~] esxcli network vswitch dvs vmware lacp stats get
DVSwitch LAGID NIC Rx Errors Rx LACPDUs Tx Errors Tx LACPDUs
--------------- --------- ------ --------- ---------- --------- ----------
DSwitch-SDN10GB 438932027 vmnic5 0 101136 0 3030161
DSwitch-SDN10GB 438932027 vmnic4 0 101137 0 3030164

[root@esxi1:~] esxcli network vswitch dvs vmware lacp status get
DSwitch-SDN10GB
 DVSwitch: DSwitch-SDN10GB
 Flags: S - Device is sending Slow LACPDUs, F - Device is sending fast
LACPDUs, A - Device is in active mode, P - Device is in passive mode
 LAGID: 438932027
 Mode: Active
 Nic List:
 Local Information:
 Admin Key: 15
 Flags: SA
 Oper Key: 15
 Port Number: 32773
 Port Priority: 255
 Port State: ACT,AGG,SYN,COL,DIST,
 Nic: vmnic5
 Partner Information:
 Age: 00:00:00
 Device ID: 10:0e:7e:bf:9e:c0
 Flags: FA
 Oper Key: 2
 Port Number: 2
 Port Priority: 127
 Port State: ACT,FTO,AGG,SYN,COL,DIST,
 State: Bundled
. . . . . . . . . .
```

Private VLAN

Private VLANs are used to solve limitations and segmentation broadcast domains. There exist three Private VLANs—**promiscuous**—private VLAN communicates with primary VLAN, **isolated**—communication only with promiscuous, and the last one is **community**—communication with promiscuous and with ports in the same secondary VLAN:

Private VLAN

NetFlow

In order to monitor vDS and analyze its network traffic, it's possible to use **NetFlow** for monitoring your vDS. For example, **vRealize Network Insight (vRNI)** acts as a NetFlow collector, but there are also other possible products and solutions. NetFlow configuration is really easy; you have to only configure the IP address of the NetFlow collector, as in the following example:

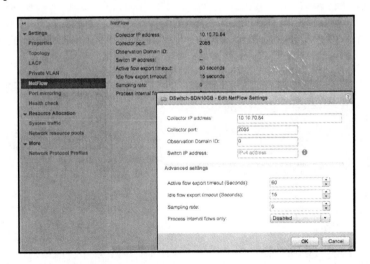

Netflow settings

Port mirroring

The next monitoring option is the port mirroring. Port mirroring sends a copy of packets from one switch port to another switch port. That data can be used from a packets capture program, for example, Wireshark (`https://www.wireshark.org`).

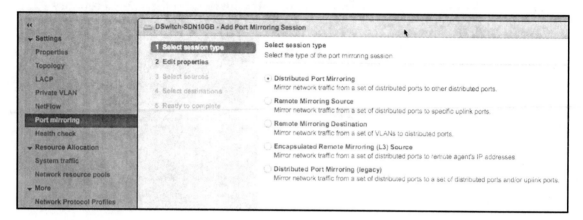

Port Mirroring settings

Health check

The health check is the next part of configuring vDS. This technology is used to monitor changes in vDS and helps with the troubleshooting process. You can check the MTU, teaming policy, and VLAN trunk. You would very fast know information about misconfiguration between the ESXi host and a physical switch:

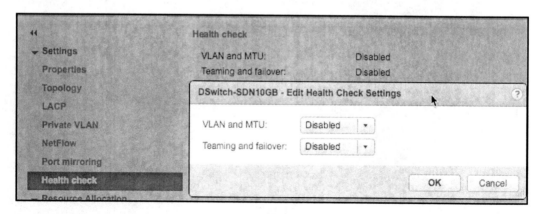

Health check settings

Network I/O Control (NIOC)

The health check is the last part of the **Settings** option, and we move to the **Resource Allocation** option where the first option is the **System traffic**. The entire network resource allocation and management is provided by a function called NIOC.

When you are using NIOC v3, you can manage the network resources, such as shares, reservations, and limits in a similar way like resource pools for computing. NIOC is a vDS only feature that allows the VMware administrator to prioritize the different type of network traffic.

Network traffic can be managed using the same resources concepts also used for CPU and memory (for example in the resources pools):

- **Limit**: The maximum bandwidth that a system traffic type can consume on a single physical network adapter
- **Shares**: From 1 to 100 reflects the relative priority of system traffic type against the other system traffic types that are active on the same physical network adapter.
- **Reservation**: The minimum bandwidth that must be guaranteed on a single physical network adapter

For example, you can configure bandwidth allocation for the traffic system features in vSphere. The total reserved system traffic types can be configured up to 75% of the total bandwidth. In the following screenshot, you can see a total bandwidth of 10 Gbps (if you are using 10 Gbps uplink), but the maximum reservation that is allowed is 7.5 Gbps:

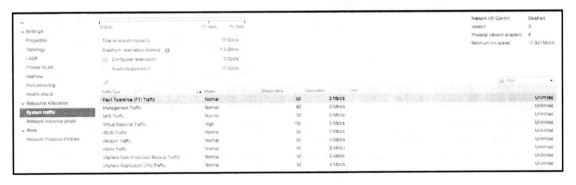

System traffic

If we enable NIOC, the reservation can be configured for the different types of network traffic. See the following example:

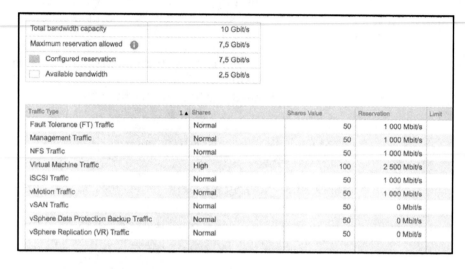

Traffic Type	1 ▲ Shares	Shares Value	Reservation	Limit
Fault Tolerance (FT) Traffic	Normal	50	1 000 Mbit/s	
Management Traffic	Normal	50	1 000 Mbit/s	
NFS Traffic	Normal	50	1 000 Mbit/s	
Virtual Machine Traffic	High	100	2 500 Mbit/s	
iSCSI Traffic	Normal	50	1 000 Mbit/s	
vMotion Traffic	Normal	50	1 000 Mbit/s	
vSAN Traffic	Normal	50	0 Mbit/s	
vSphere Data Protection Backup Traffic	Normal	50	0 Mbit/s	
vSphere Replication (VR) Traffic	Normal	50	0 Mbit/s	

Reservation settings

In **Virtual Machine Traffic**, we assign a 2.5 Gbps reservation for VMs traffic that is used in admission control. When you power on VM, then admission control verifies that the bandwidth is effectively available.

The reservation setting, **Virtual Machine Traffic** can be assigned using two options:

- The first one is using **network resource pools** that are assigned to port group. We are create the Mastering_RP1 network resource pool that will be assigned to the port group:

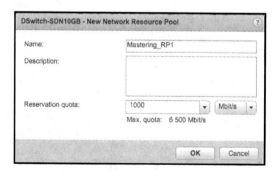

Create new network resource pool

We have configured a bandwidth reservation of 2.5 Gbps, but in the following screenshot, the **Configuration reservation** option is 10 Gbps. When you have following configuration—two hosts with 2 x 10 Gbps network card, you have the total capacity of 40 Gbps so the reservation will be in total 4 x 2.5 Gbps = 10 Gbps:

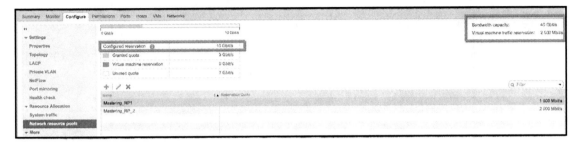

Understand reservation

Then you need to assign the network resource pool to a distributed port group. In this example, `Mastering_RP1` and `Mastering_RP_2`:

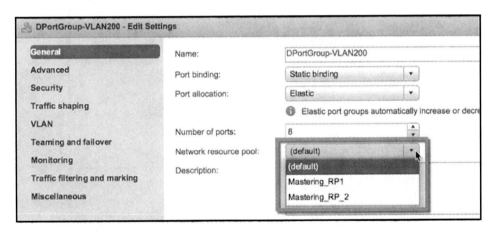

Add network resource pool to port group

- The second option, how to set reservation is the configuration on the per vNIC. Edit the VM setting and change vNIC reservation. In the following example we set 500 Mbps, only on one vNIC:

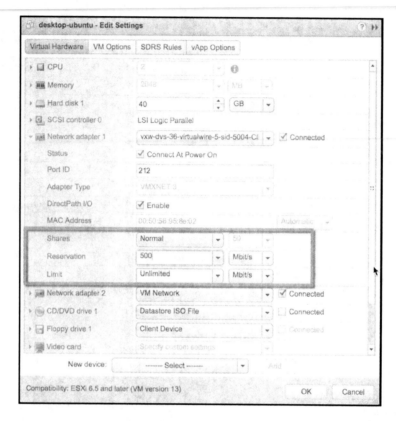

VM configuration reservation

In the following screenshot, we can see that reservation configured on the VM level that is not part of network resource pool are listed in **Virtual machine reservation** section. When the VM is connected to distributed port group with assigned a network resource pool, VM reservation will be taken from network resource pool reservation:

Detailed information about reservation for VM

In the previous screenshot you have a summary page with the following information:

- **Granted quota**: This taken from network resource pools
- **Virtual machine reservation**: This is taken from configuration VM which are not connected to the distributed port group with network resource pool assigned
- **Unused quota**: Free reservation capacity that can be used for additional resource pools or vNIC reservations

Network protocol profiles

The network protocol profiles can be used only with vApp. The network profile contains pool IPv4 or IPv6 address, which vCenter assigns to vApp:

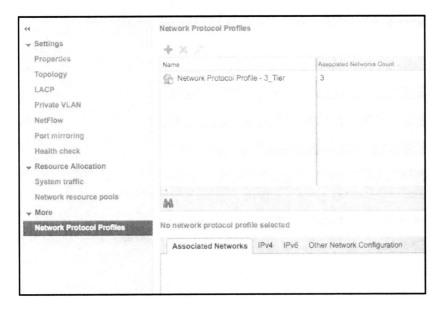

Network Protocol Profiles

So great! We understand all parts of the configuration tab. We can move to the next tabs in the main menu and look at all of them.

Ports, hosts, VMs, and networks

The other tabs relevant for the network configuration are the ports, hosts, VMs, and networks tabs and are discussed as follows:

- **Ports**: Using this tab, it is possible to view on all connect ports to vDS and find a lot of useful information on all ports. For example, it is possible to check the state of the port and other configuration-related pieces of information:

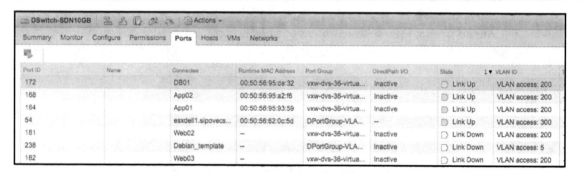

Ports detail

It's also possible to collect some runtime configuration, such as statistics, using the Start Monitoring Post State menu:

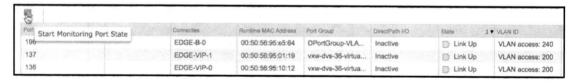

Start monitoring port state

- **Hosts**: This provides some details, such as which hosts are connected to vDS:

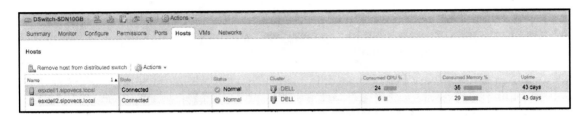

Hosts detail

- **VMs**: In this view, you can see all VMs connected to vDS:

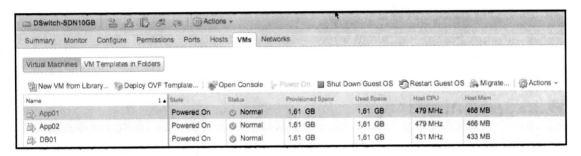

VMs detail

- **Networks**: This tab provides a list of all distributed port groups and also all the uplinks connected to the vDS:

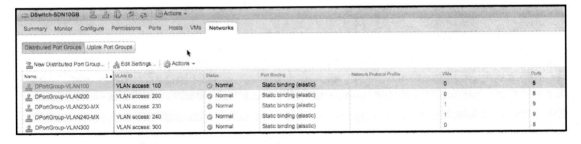

Networks detail

Now, you have the basic understanding about the network, and we can continue with NSX.

Introduction to NSX

In the last part of this chapter, we will be describing NSX technologies. This SDN part and SDDC concepts are very important for the complete path to the SDDC solution. VMware NSX is a network virtualization platform.

NSX is possible to use very fast because it is used with all vendors (physical networking) and only must be possible with a MTU set as 1,600 and higher for transport network. NSX network hypervisor reproduces a complete set of L2–L7 network services as a logical switching, routing, firewall, and load balancing in software.

NSX components

NSX architecture has three different layers—**management plane**, **control plane**, and **data plane**.

Management plane

The management plane is represented by the NSX Manager, a single component deployed as a virtual appliance starting from an OVA file. NSX Manager is a single point of configuration gateway for REST API. NSX Manager relationship is 1:1 with the vCenter server. NSX Manager provides the plugin for the vCenter Web UI. NSX Manager is important for deploying controller cluster and ESXi host preparation, last is the deployment of NSX Edge. The distributed firewall is important.

Control plane

The NSX control cluster runs **NSX Controller cluster**. NSX control cluster is a management system for control plane functions for logical switching and routing. Controller nodes are deployed as three controllers for high availability. A failed control cluster does not impact any data plane traffic.

A controller cluster is a central point for logical switching and routing. A controller cluster is important for unicast and hybrid control plane modes, and it eliminates the need for multicast support from the physical network. NSX Controller supports ARP suppression. NSX Controllers use distributed system, a slicing mechanism that helps utilize all cluster nodes. Every cluster nodes are used as a master for another logical switching and routing. Best practice for high availability is to create separate DRS rules for controller cluster VMs:

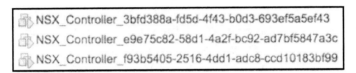

NSX Controller Cluster

A controller cluster holds three tables—MAC, ARP, and **VXLAN Tunnel Endpoint (VTEP)** table.

Control VM is the next component in the control plane part. Control VM is a virtual appliance, that is used with distributed logical routing when you want to use dynamic routing protocol as an **Open Shortest Path First (OSPF)** or **Border Gateway Protocol (BGP)**. The second use case is software L2 bridging VXLAN to VLAN.

Distributed logical router (DLR) can work without control VM only with static routing.

Data plane

NSX data plane is **NSX vSwitch**. NSX vSwitch is based on the vDS with NSX kernel modules; userspace agent is packaged in VIB and run hypervisor kernel. It provides services as a logical firewall, routing, and switching (VXLAN):

```
[root@esxdell1:~] vmkload_mod -l | grep nsx
nsx-dvfilter-switch-security9 128
nsx-traceflow 3 20
nsx-bfd 1 28
nsx-core 2 12
nsx-vdl2 7 416
nsx-vdrb 1 340
nsx-vsip 21 652
```

NSX installation

Installing NSX is really easy because you can deploy only one virtual appliance in OVA format, that is the NSX Manager. The installation and configuration steps are:

1. **Deploy NSX Manager:** Use the vSphere Web Client to deploy the virtual appliance. Assign the complete network configuration (IP address, netmask, gateway, DNS servers).

2. **Log in to the NSX Manager:** When the VM is ready, use a web browser and connect to URL NSX manager for the first configuration.

3. **Register NSX Manager with vCenter Server:** You have to configure the relationship with the vCenter server by providing the right credentials:

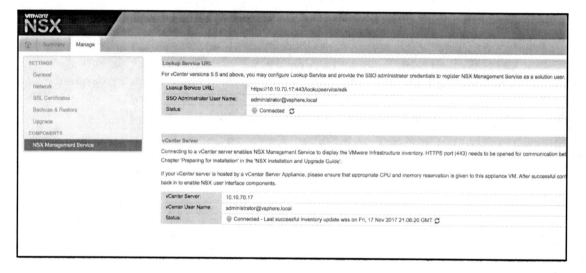

Registration page vCenter Server

4. **Back up the NSX Manager configuration:** During the first configuration NSX, it's very important to configure a backup policy, to make possible use of the future configuration restore:

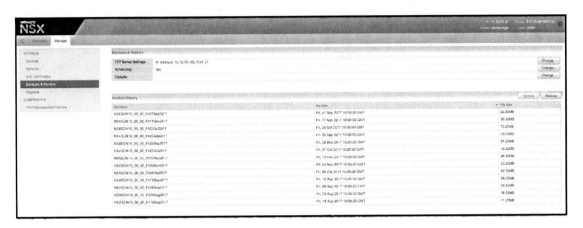

Backup configuration

5. **Deploy NSX Controllers:** At this point, you must change the UI and login with your vSphere Web Client. You can now use the new registered plugin for NSX (**Networking and Security**) shown as follows:

Plugin for NSX in vSphere Web Client

This plugin is your main administration for NSX Domain. You can still use central CLI and REST API. Go to the installation part and click on the green plus in NSX Controller nodes part. Deploy a cluster with all three controllers. You deploying three controllers is the minimum and maximum for a production environment. After deployment create the DRS anti-affinity rule.

When you want to test NSX in the lab, you can use only one controller, but *only for testing.*

Installation NSX Controller nodes

6. **ESXi host preparation**: The **Host Preparation** tab will help to add NSX VIBs on all cluster hosts:

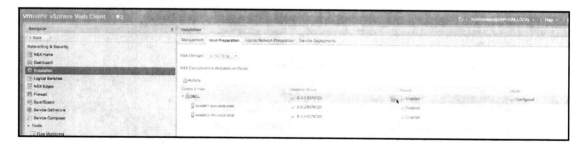

Host preparation

7. **Configure the VXLAN transport**: The next step is to configure VXLAN and VTEP, which is used for encapsulation and de-encapsulation. Each VTEP is a VMkernel interface that must have an MTU of 1,600. The MTU must be set on VMkernel, virtual switch, and also on the physical network and it's important because, during encapsulation, the VXLAN header is added to the standard layer 2 frame. VTEP configuration could be performed in the **Logical Network Preparation** tab, and it checks correct create VTEP vmk interface on every host:

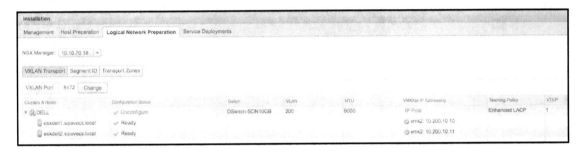

VXLAN-VTEP information

8. **Define the VXLAN segment ID range**: VXLAN packets require an ID (similar to the VLAN ID). You need to add a segment ID range, starting from 5,000; this ID is used for **VXLAN Network Identifiers (VNI)**, your logical switching:

Segment ID-VNI

9. **Define the transport zones**: The transport zone defines the boundaries for the logical switch and logical routing:

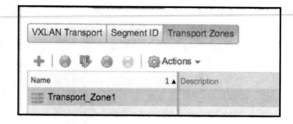

Transport Zones

Network Functions Virtualization (NVF)

Now that you are ready with the NSX basic configuration, you can start to configure the different network components, such as switch, router, firewall, gateway, and so on.

One network component is the **logical switch** or distributed switching. Each logical switch has a unique identification called VNI, starting from 5,000 (the same pool that you have set for the Segment ID). Logical switches are located on the transport zone and you can create or view the entire list in the **Logical Switches** menu:

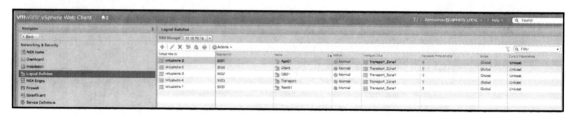

Logical Switches

Each NSX logical switch is mapped to a VM distributed port group. For example:

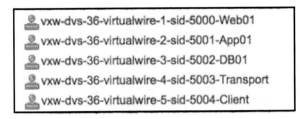

Distributed port group created by NSX

You are limited only to the maximum port group per vDS. You can connect a VM to a logical switch using the port group name (like a common vDS port group) or from the **Logic Switches** menu.

Another network component could be a layer 3 device and, in NSX, there are two different types—the Distributed **Logical Router (DLR)** and the **Edge Service Gateway**. Both of them could be created in the **NSX Edges** menu part:

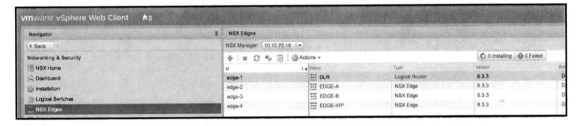

NSX Edges

When you add a new Edge, you can choose logical routing (DLR) or Edge Services Gateway. The DLR is a distributed router, optimized for east–west traffic, typically between VMs inside a cluster or a datacenter. The Edge Service Gateway is a perimeter router, optimized for north–south traffic, typically used for edge network or to connect physically to virtual networks. Other network functions could be VPN or load balancing devices. Both are just specific features of an Edge Service Gateway, that can be simply enabled, if needed.

Last network function is the **firewall**. One interesting capability of NSX is the microsegmentation in order to protect network traffic on the virtual network. Two different types of firewall are available—**distributed firewall** and **edge firewall**. Distributed firewall is part of VMkernel and works directly at virtual NIC level, so, probably, the best solution for microsegmentation:

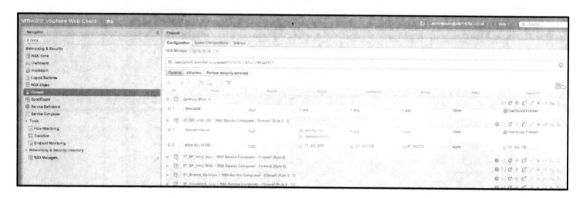

Firewall

We very quick fly under basic NSX information. For next step, a good starting point is the *VMware® NSX for vSphere Network Virtualization Design Guide ver 3.0* at `https:// communities.vmware.com/docs/DOC-27683` and of course hands-on-lab for practice.

Summary

This chapter described networking concepts and specific network configuration and features of vSphere 6.5.

Virtual networking concepts are covered, both with standard and distributed virtual switches. Also, there are some considerations about the design, the management, and the optimization of virtual networks.

Virtual networks are real and widely used, with a total number of virtual NICs that is already larger than the physical NICs number (VMware has become the biggest hardware vendor for MAC address).

However, there are new network trends, including **Network Virtualization (NV)**, **Network Function Virtualization (NFV)**, and all **Software-defined Networking (SDS)** solutions and products. VMware NSX, is an NV solution, that could really improve a vSphere environment, not only in the networking part, but also by adding a lot of new functions (using NFV), especially in the security part.

The next chapter will be focused on another important component of the infrastructural part—the storage.

7
Advanced Storage Management

Storage is usually the most critical part of a virtual infrastructure, due to the need for enough performance and capacity for the entire cluster and all the workloads inside it. In order to provide features such as vSphere **High Availability (HA)**, vSphere **Distributed Resource Scheduler (DRS)**, and other cluster-related capabilities, you need common shared storage for all the ESXi hosts of the cluster. You can also have more storage per cluster, or use the same storage for more clusters.

This chapter details the storage part of a virtual infrastructure, starting from local block-based storage and extending into shared block storage with FC, FCoE and iSCSI protocols and NFS-based NAS storage.

In this chapter, we will learn more about:

- How storage is changing with new technologies
- Which type of storage VMware vSphere can use and how to configure and manage it
- Which storage features are provided at vSphere level and at which storage level and how to use them in the right way
- Some concepts related to storage design to rightsizing for capacity and performance, but also how to configure it for better availability and resiliency
- Which kind of hyper-converged solutions are available for vSphere

Storage basics

There are different types of storage, with different protocols, different architectures, different scaling, different capabilities, and also different purposes.

In a virtual environment, you will need a resilient and reliable storage solution, with the expected performance, that can scale for the future. This can only be possible using enterprise storage products, with some exceptions for the ROBO and SMB scenarios, as discussed in `Chapter 2`, *Design and Plan a Virtualization Infrastructure*.

Enterprise-class storage can be classified in different ways, but usually different acronyms are used, such as:

- **Direct Attached Storage (DAS)**
- **Network Attached Storage (NAS)**
- **Storage Area Network (SAN)**
- **Content Addressable Storage (CAS)/Fixed Content Storage (FCS)**
- Object-based storage/cloud storage

For VMware vSphere, the first three storage classes are the most relevant and the only type of solutions actually usable for running VMs, but object-based storage could be used by other solutions (such as backup products), and maybe also by vSphere in the future.

The main difference across these different types of storage are the types of services, the different targets of usage, the performance, and how they can scale, as shown in the following table:

Storage type	Type of service	Front-end protocols	Data/access ratio	Typical usage
DAS	Block	SCSI, SATA, SAS	1:1	Local storage (inside ESXi)
SAN	Block	FC, FCoE, FCIP, iSCSI	N:1 – 1:1	Shared storage
NAS	File	SMB, NFS	1:N	File server
Object	Object	HTTP, APIs	1:Millions	Cloud storage

Table 7.1: Different types of storage

All the enterprise storage could be classified according to its architecture. A great classification is from Chad Sakac (Dell-EMC), which defines four main types of storage architecture—clustered scale-up and down, tightly coupled scale-out, loosely coupled scale-out, and distributed shared nothing. For more information, see the blog post at `http://virtualgeek.typepad.com/virtual_geek/2014/01/understanding-storage-architectures.html`.

To keep it simple, we can just focus on two different architectural models:

- **Scale-in** or **scale-up**: This is where the storage grows in capacity (and initially also in performance) by adding new disk shelves
- **Scale-out**: This is where more arrays are managed as a single *logical* storage performance, and capacity can scale by adding new arrays

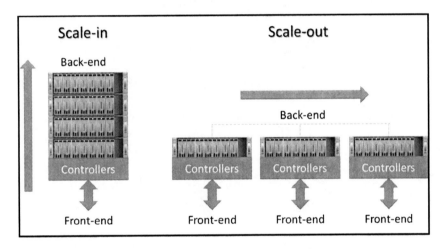

Scale-in and scale-out storage

A different point of view, more focused on the evolution of the storage market, is provided by Stuart Miniman on Wikibon (`http://wikibon.org/wiki/v/Server_SAN_Market_Definition`).

But a more simple classification could define different levels of the tiers used to classify the storage:

- **Tier 0**: This is usually not used, but sometimes define a very high-performance storage, such as the **All-Flash Array (AFA)**
- **Tier 1 or primary storage**: This is usually the main storage that corresponds to the VMware side at the different types of datastores

- **Tier 2 or secondary storage**: This is a storage not (usually) used from VMware, that stores online archives, backups, cold data, and so on
- **Tier 3**: This could be a long-term and may be offline archival storage repository, such as tapes, or copy on public cloud storage

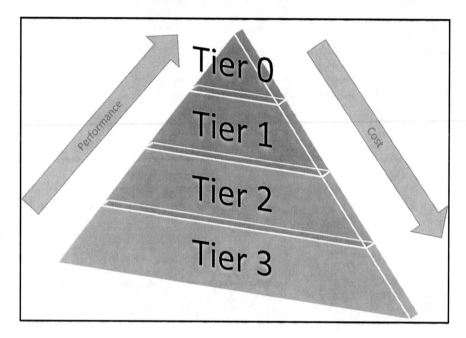

Storage tiers

The evolution of the storage world

Storage-related technologies have been changing really fast in recent years and flash memory is totally redefining the storage offering, both in the architectures, as described previously, and also on the effective components where data is stored.

Spinning disks

Just 10 years ago (but we could also say just a little over 5 years ago), the different tiers described previously were usually filled with the following types of storage:

- **Tier 0**: 15K RPM **Serial-Attached SCSI (SAS)** disks
- **Tier 1**: 10K RPM SAS disks
- **Tier 2**: 7K RPM SATA or nearline disks
- **Tier 3**: Usually tapes

Traditional **Hard Disk Drives (HDD)** were the standard components for storage arrays, and more were used both for redundancy and for increasing performance. RAID hardware was the standard at the beginning, surpassed by a more software controlled style of data management.

The typical interface and bus for those hard disks is SAS, working at 6 or 12 Gbps. SATA disks use the Serial ATA (3.0 revision works at 6 Gbps).

 There are also some new trends in the interfaces and the intelligence of big disks; for example, kinetic architecture (https://www.openkinetic.org/), where the drive can use Ethernet and provide high-level services.

Anyway, spinning disks are still relevant and used, and new improvement has been achieved to increase density, performance, and reliability; for example, the **perpendicular recording (2006)** and the **Advanced Format (2011)** technologies. The second one is quite important because it can work in two different modes—legacy 512e or native 4K. Windows has supported 4K mode since Windows 8 and Windows Server 2012, and Linux since kernel version 2.6.31. ESXi 6.5 is now supporting this new technology, but only in 512e mode.

See also KB 2091600—*Support statement for 512e and 4K Native drives for VMware vSphere and vSAN* (https://kb.vmware.com/kb/2091600).

Flash devices

Flash storage has squeezed all the traditional rotating disks into one (or just two) tiers. Also, the cost is already competitive with 15K disks (just comparing the same capacity) and it's becoming more competitive with 10K disks also.

On the other side, flash storage provides a different type of low-level technologies for the NAND chips with a decreasing cost:

NAND cell types	Bit per cell	Performance	Type of usage
Single Level Cell (SLC)	1-bit	Fastest both on read and write	Used for the write-intensive flash
Enterprise Multi Level Cell (eMLC)	2-bits	Slower (as compared to SLC) on the write operation	Used in enterprise storage for the read-intensive flash
Multi Level Cell (MLC)	2-bits	Average performance	Usually for the consumer market
Three Level Cell (TLC)	3-bits	Lower performance (but still better than rotating disks)	Low cost and high capacity NAND flash

Table 7.2: Different types of low-level technologies

And there are already new technologies, such as 3D XPoint (Intel Optane and Micron Quantx) that can provide performance much similar to DRAM, and 1,000 times faster than NAND, 10 times denser and with better endurance.

On the other hand, some applications, such as huge databases, are moving their data from disk to RAM using the in-memory paradigm, and there is also the fact that RAM memory is growing and it's becoming quite cheap. But, of course, traditional RAM is not persistent, so you still need flash or disks, although there is also the new **Dual In-Line Memory Module (DIMM)** based on a flash chip that works like RAM DIMMs, but provides data persistence. NVDIMM-N is another wave of new memory technologies referred to as **Persistent Memory (PM)**, and also as **Storage Class Memory (SCM)**.

About the connectors; for several years the SAS bus was used, usually packing the flash in a box like traditional hard disks, realizing the SAS **Solid State Disk (SSD)**. Also, the SATA bus has been used with the **Advanced Host Controller Interface (AHCI)** transport protocol. The issue is, if SSD can replace an HDD with a much faster device, the entire I/O stack remains the same with an old architecture and possible bottlenecks.

NVMe or **Non-Volatile Memory Host Controller Interface Specification (NVMHCI)** is a new logical device interface specification for accessing non-volatile memory NVE attached through a **PCI Express (PCIe)** bus instead of using an SAS bus. Supported form factors include add-in PCIe cards and M.2 and U.2 interfaces. NVE is still flash memory, but now with a stack designed to reach the best performance.

The following table summarizes the different types of transport protocols:

Transport protocol	Max number of queues	Max queue depth
AHCI (SATA)	1	32
SAS	1	254
NVMe	65.535	64.000

Table 7.3: Different types of transport protocols

NVMe reduces I/O overhead and brings various performance improvements in comparison to previous logical-device interfaces, including multiple, long command queues, and reduced latency.

As defined in http://www.esg-global.com/research:

> "ESG's 2017 European Storage Trends Survey of over 400 European IT professionals shows how NVMe deployments are here: 10% of respondent organizations are already using NVMe, 26% are planning to deploy it, and another 34% say they are interested in deploying NVMe-based technologies."

For local storage (DAS), VMware vSphere supports SAS and SATA SSD, like other disks. The only requirement is that the controller is recognized by ESXi and that it provides the RAID function at the hardware level because ESXi does not provide any *software RAID*. The only exception is vSAN, but this will be explained later. NVMe or other new technologies are also supported, but you may require additional drivers.

Storage array

The storage market has slightly changed in recent years, moving from appliance solutions (mainly based on hardware features) to software-defined solutions (some software only; others are still based on appliances).

More importantly, flash technologies have changed the storage array's components and now almost all solutions include flash devices inside each product, with two main type of arrays:

- **AFA**: This is where only flash memories are used, maybe with different types of flash devices
- **Hybrid array**: This is where both flash and HDD are used

Moving to a software-defined approach and the use of flash has made it possible to implement (in an effective way) a lot of new storage functions, such as tiering, compression, deduplication, and so on.

Also, storage architectures have evolved, especially scale-out architecture, with a new model (hyper-scaling or HCI) where each node is not only a storage array but also a computing node. We will better describe **Hyper-Converged Infrastructure (HCI)** later in this chapter.

From an integration point of view, more storage vendors are integrating management or native functions in VMware vSphere interfaces, but others are also trying to add VM visibility (and maybe manageability) on the storage side to have a VM aware storage.

Concerning the protocols used for frontend interfaces (this does not apply to HCI, but only to external shared storage), these are the main type of protocols supported in VMware vSphere and the typical use cases:

Protocol type	Type of service	Interface speed	Typical usage
SAS	Block	6 or 12 Gbps	Shared storage with limited host scaling
FC	Block	8, 16, 32 Gbps	Shared storage, typically for enterprises
FCoE	Block	10,40 Gbps	Shared storage, typically for enterprises and mid-size
iSCSI	Block	1, 10,40 Gbps	Shared storage
NFS	File	1, 10,40 Gbps	Shared storage

Table 7.4: Protocols supported in VMware vSphere and the typical use cases

If you are using FCoE, before planning any upgrade or installation on existing hardware, note that on vSphere 6.5 some FCoE drivers are not supported anymore; for example, Intel cards. For more information refer to KB 2147786—*End of Availability and End of Support for FCoE on Intel Network Controllers* at `https://kb.vmware.com/kb/2147786`.

Converged networks

FC has always been a dedicated network (a storage area network), but starting with **Internet Small Computer Systems Interface (iSCSI)** and **Fibre Channel over Ethernet (FCoE)** protocols, the storage fabric could be shared with the network infrastructure, due to the common Ethernet layer. Although, it being possible does not mean that it's always recommended; a dedicated storage network simplifies troubleshooting and can minimize throughput bottlenecks.

But if you need to use the same physical switches both for traditional networking and for storage traffic, in this case, you have to plan the solution carefully and work with new standards specific to those kinds of converged networks.

Data Center Bridging (DCB) is a set of standards and enhancements to the Ethernet protocols in order to implement a *lossless Ethernet* suitable for storage traffic. There are a lot of concepts, but the most important are:

- **Data Center Bridging Capability Exchange (DCBx)**: It is an extension of the IEEE standard 802.1AB for the **Link Layer Discovery Protocol (LLDP)** and provides capabilities, functions, and identities advertised using existing LLDP protocols
- **Priority-based Flow Control (PFC)**: It is an evolution of flow control function, originally implemented in the MAC pause feature of Ethernet (IEEE 802.3x)
- **Enhanced Transmission Selection (ETS)**: It is used to guarantee a percentage of bandwidth to a traffic class

DCB could be managed at the switch level, or also at the source and the target level; although they are usually set with **auto-discovery** (called willing mode).

Actually, VMware ESXi has a specific service dcbd for DCB protocols, usually, to manage converged networks properly, you can use specific network cards (CNA NICs) and off-load the FCoE or iSCSI traffic on them, providing DCB support. For most **Converged Network Adapter** (CNA) cards, this could be achieved by partitioning the card in multiple virtual functions using **Network Partition** (**NPAR**) and configuring some of those functions to support storage protocols. Most storage vendors already provide reference architecture and configuration guides for their storage and verified CNA cards.

The biggest issues for Ethernet storage traffic are the collisions at layer 2 (avoidable by using dedicated full rate switches), IP fragmentation (avoidable by using the right MTU on the entire communication chain), and the TCP retransmissions.

For converged networks, DCB is a must to provide the right **quality of service** (**QoS**) for your storage traffic. For dedicated storage networks, you can still benefit from using DCB; for example, in the iSCSI protocol to avoid TCP retransmissions.

VMware vSphere storage types

VMware vSphere supports different types of storage architectures, both internally (in this case the controller is crucial, that must be in the HCL) or externally with shared SAS DAS, SAN FC, SAN iSCSI, SAN FCoE, or NFS NAS (in those case the HCL is fundamental for the external storage, the fabric elements, and the host adapters).

 For local storage, with vSphere 6.x it's possible to use USB disks, not only as boot disks, but also to run VMs. But note that USB datastores are just unsupported by VMware.

Storage types at the VM logical level

There are different types of virtual disks depending on the provisioning method, pre-allocated or dynamic. The type of virtual disks are mainly the same since vSphere 4.0:

- **Eager zeroed thick Virtual Machine Disk (VMDK)**: An eager zeroed thick disk has all space allocated and wiped clean of any previous content on the physical media at creation time. Such disks may take a long time during creation compared to other disk formats. The entire disk space is reserved and unavailable for use by other VMs.

- **Thick or lazy zeroed thick VMDK**: A thick disk has all space allocated at creation time. This space may contain stale data on the physical media. Before writing to a new block, a zero has to be written, increasing the **input/output operation per second (IOPS)** on new blocks compared to eager disks. The entire disk space is reserved and unavailable for use by other VMs.
- **Thin VMDK**: Space required for the thin-provisioned virtual disk is allocated and zeroed on demand as space is used. Unused space is available for use by other VMs.

You can choose the disk provisioning type during virtual disk creation, but you can change the type using a cold VM migration across two datastores, or using Storage vMotion (if you have at least ESXi Standard edition). Note that you can also change the type of each individual disk, by choosing **Configure per disk** on the new HTML5 client shown as follows:

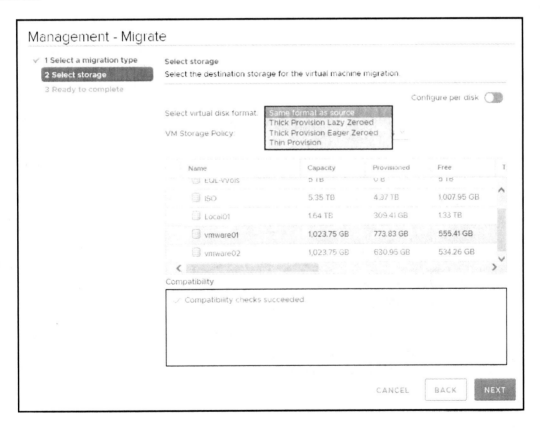

VM datastore migration

There are also **Raw Device Mapping** (**RDM**) disks where a disk at ESXi level is mapped 1:1 to a VM (like a Passthrough mode), with two different types of compatibility (virtual or physical mode). Except for building guest clusters (clusters across VMs on different hosts), there is no need to use these types of disk.

There is no significant difference in performance for sequential I/O between the different types of virtual disks. For random I/O, thin VMDKs have the worst performance and higher latency (for lazy thick, it depends if you have to write a new block).

Storage types at the VM physical level

To access a block device, such as virtual disks VMDK, virtual CD/DVD-ROM, or other SCSI devices, each VM uses storage controllers; at least one is added by default when you create a VM.

There are different types of controller available for a VM running on ESXi which are described as follows:

- **BusLogic**: This is one of the first emulated SCSI virtual controllers available in VMware ESX. Now it's a legacy controller used mainly for legacy operating systems. It does not support VMDK larger than 2 TB.
- **LSI Logic Parallel**: This was formally known as **LSI Logic** and was the other SCSI virtual controller available originally in VMware ESX, used for operating systems such as Windows Server 2003.
- **LSI Logic SAS**: This was introduced in vSphere 4.0, and is the evolution of the parallel driver, working as a SAS virtual controller and used in Windows Server 2008 or newer.
- **VMware Paravirtual** (or **PVSCSI**): This was introduced in vSphere 4.0, is an SCSI virtual controller designed to support very high throughput with minimal processing cost, working not in emulation mode, but in paravirtual mode (it requires the VMware Tools to be recognized).

Others virtual controllers are also possible in a VM, such as AHCI SATA (introduced in vSphere 5.5), IDE, and also USB controllers, but usually for specific cases (for example SATA or IDE are usually used for virtual DVD drives).

When you create a VM, the default controller is optimized for good performance and compatibility. The controller type depends on the guest operating system (usually its driver is included in the operating system), the device type, and sometimes, the VMs compatibility. But sometimes you can choose a different controller to improve the performance, like the PVSCI (useful for VMFK with high load) or a new type available in vSphere 6.5.

With ESXi 6.5 and VM virtual hardware version 13, you can now also use a virtual NVMe. Virtual NVMe devices have reduced guest I/O processing overheads (over 50% compared to AHCI SATA SCSI device), which allows more VMs per host or more transactions per minute. Each virtual machine supports 4 NVMe controllers and up to 15 devices per controller.

Virtual NVMe controllers are supported on vSphere 6.5 only on the following guest operating systems:

- Windows 7 and 2008 R2 (hotfix required, refer to `https://support.microsoft.com/en-us/kb/2990941`)
- Windows 8.1, 2012 R2, 10, 2016
- RHEL, CentOS, NeoKylin 6.5, and later
- Oracle Linux 6.5 and later
- Ubuntu 13.10 and later
- SLE 11 SP4 and later
- Solaris 11.3 and later
- FreeBSD 10.1 and later
- Mac OS X 10.10.3 and later
- Debian 8.0 and later

You can add a new NVMEe virtual controller using the vSphere Web Client (from the HTML5 web client is not yet possible) as shown in the following steps:

1. Right-click on the virtual machine in the inventory and select **Edit Settings** option
2. Click the **Virtual Hardware** tab, and select **NVMe Controller** from the **New device** drop-down menu
3. Click on **Add**

4. The controller appears in the **Virtual Hardware** devices list
5. Click **OK**

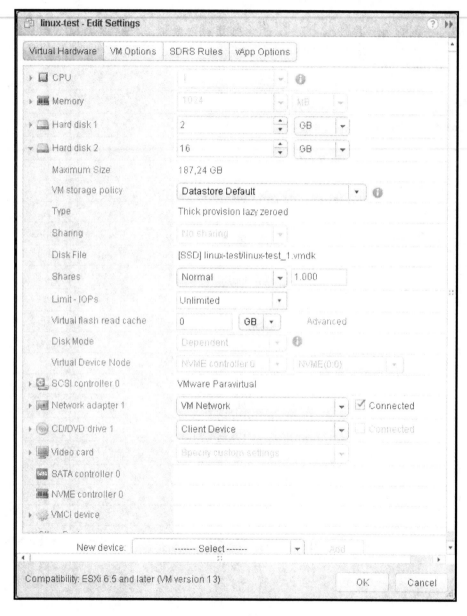

VM with an NVMe controller

For more information on NVMe, see also KB 2147714—*Using Virtual NVMe with ESXi 6.5 and virtual machine Hardware Version 13* (`https://kb.vmware.com/kb/2147714`).

For more information on PVSCI, see also KB 1010398—*Configuring disks to use VMware Paravirtual SCSI (PVSCSI) adapters* (`https://kb.vmware.com/kb/1010398`).

Storage types at the ESXi logical level

At the high level, VMware vSphere will access each storage using datastores—a logical paradigm to abstract all storage types, like a common operating system uses letters or mount points to access a filesystem.

VMware vSphere 6.x has the following four main types of datastore:

- **VMware FileSystem (VMFS) datastores**: All block-based storage must be first formatted with VMFS to transform a block service to a file and folder oriented services
- **Network FileSystem (NFS) datastores**: This is for NAS storage
- **VVol**: This is introduced in vSphere 6.0 and is a new paradigm to access SAN and NAS storage in a common way and by better integrating and consuming storage array capabilities
- **vSAN datastore**: If you are using vSAN solution, all your local storage devices could be polled together in a single shared vSAN datastore

New datastores could be provisioned from the new HTML5 client, starting from a data centre, a cluster, or a host; just right-click on the object, choose storage, and then new datastore:

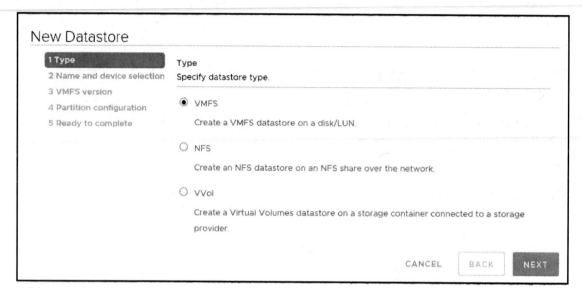

Adding a new datastore

For local disks, if you have configured the right RAID level from the controller (remember that ESXi does not provide software RAID features), you can just *format* the logical disks with a VMFS datastore.

But before external storage, before adding a new datastore, you must first configure the ESXi host, the fabric, (if present) and the storage itself. This depends on the storage type and vendor and will be discussed later. You cannot directly add a vSAN datastore; the vSAN configuration is quite different, but the final result will be a vSAN datastore with its own format.

Of course, on the same host you can have multiple datastores, also with different types:

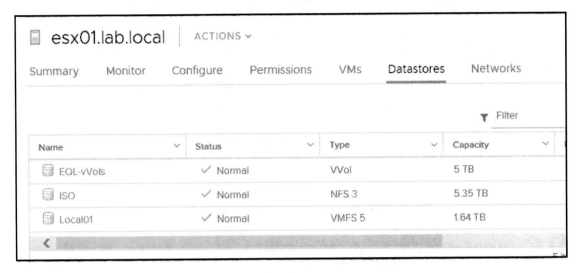

Name	Status	Type	Capacity
EQL-vVols	✓ Normal	VVol	5 TB
ISO	✓ Normal	NFS 3	5.35 TB
Local01	✓ Normal	VMFS 5	1.64 TB

Different datastores

At the datastore level, there isn't any difference between DAS or SAN, they are just block-based storage and become VMFS datastores. The functional difference is that a SAN disk could be shared across multiple hosts, not local DAS disks (but there are also shared SAS storages that are formally classified as DAS storage).

Storage types at the ESXi physical level

Excluding vSAN, which has a specific configuration, at the physical level we can have three different main types of storage:

- **Block-based storage acceded by a hardware adapter**: This includes DAS storage or a SAN FC storage.
- **Block-based storage acceded by a software adapter**: This is like the SAN iSCSI storage when the software initiator is used. In this case, you need first to properly configure the network connectivity. After that, it becomes very similar to the first case.
- **NFS storage**: This is where you have to configure first the IP network connectivity to your storage and then connect the NFS datastore.

For the physical storage adapters, VMware ESXi supports several types of protocols and technologies (refer to the hardware compatibility list to check the supported level):

- **Fibre Channel Host Bus Adapter (FC HBA)**: This is the common and historical way to implement an FC-based storage, but using a dedicated full fabric.
- **iSCSI HBA**: These are specialized PCIe cards that implement completely in hardware the entire iSCSI stack, reducing the load of the host CPU.
- **CNA adapters for FCoE or iSCSI**: These are mostly 10 Gbps (or greater) Ethernet adapters providing hardware (or hardware assisted) FCoE or iSCSI functionality on converged (or also dedicated) networks.
- **RDMA over Converged Ethernet (RoCE)**: This is a network protocol that allows **remote direct memory access (RDMA)** over an Ethernet network. Starting with vSphere 6.5, RoCE certified adapters could be used for converged networks.
- **InfiniBand HCA**: Mellanox Technologies InfiniBand HCA device drivers are available directly from Mellanox Technologies. Mostly used for the network part instead of the storage part, they could be interesting in converged networks, and also in vSAN implementation.

VMware vSphere storage configuration

For shared storage, the ESXi configuration varies a lot depending both on the storage type and the protocols used. There is a specific guide from VMware, but what's more important is to follow the specific storage vendor guides, including possible reference architectures or configuration suggestions.

Storage FC

FC is an entire high-speed network stack used to implement storage area networks. Starting with vSphere 6.0U2, ESXi supports 32 Gbps FC for all the supported HBA.

When using ESXi with FC SAN, follow the recommendations and best practices of both VMware and the storage vendor to avoid possible issues. Note that storage vendor specifications could be more restrictive than VMware's; for example, the hardware compatibility list could be smallest or restricted on specific firmware/driver versions. In those cases, it's important to use the vendor specifications.

On the ESXi side, you have only to plug the supported FC HBA (with the correct firmware and drivers) and cable them properly, usually following a full fabric topology:

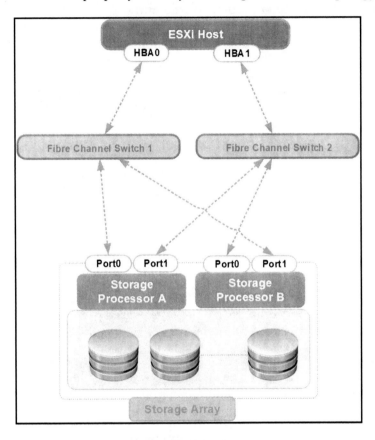

Full redundant fabric topology

VMware may support point-to-point topologies (such as a DAS storage, for a small environment), but first, you have to verify if the storage vendor supports it.

After that you have only to configure the fabric, with the correct zoning at the port level or better, at **World Wide Name (WWN)** level (again refer to what your storage vendor requires or recommends); and finally the storage with the correct LUN masking, to present the logical disks to the hosts. At this point there isn't any difference, at ESXi level, between local or remote storage, you just need to format the logical disk from one host and then re-scan the datastore from all the others. That's all!

Most storage requires that each ESXi host is registered with the array, to map correctly the hosts to the arrays and also to authorize the connections (FC does not provide strict authentication capabilities). ESXi usually performs automatic host registration by sending the host's name and IP address to the array, but if you prefer to perform manual registration, you can disable the ESXi auto-registration feature by changing the advanced settings `Disk.EnableNaviReg` to 0.

 For troubleshooting or monitoring the FC connectivity, you can use the `resxtop` or `esxtop` command-line utilities. For more information see KB 1003680—*Troubleshooting fibre channel storage connectivity* (`https://kb.vmware.com/kb/1003680`).

FC usually does not require specific tuning at the host level, except maybe the HBA settings or the queue depth for the driver (refer to the storage vendor best practices).

FCoE

FCoE encapsulates FC frames over Ethernet networks, using 10 Gbps (or higher) Ethernet networks at layers 1 and 2. But the rest remain FC protocols stacks, (note that FC is a complete network stack, so no IP, UDP, or TCP protocols are used) and you still need specific FC skills (for example, for fabric zoning), plus specific new skills for converged networks (such as DCB protocols).

For CNA cards, you can use NPAR and enable hardware assisted FCoE at ESXi level, with the right driver, you will see a new VMware storage adapter called **vmhba** acting like a traditional FC HBA. The rest of the configuration is all at the fabric and storage levels as described before.

In vSphere 5.0, VMware introduced a new software FCoE adapter, useful for NIC with a partial FCoE offload. In this case, you also need to configure the virtual switches part to bind a VMkernel port to a virtual switch connected to this NIC. FCoE traffic does not go through the virtual switch, but to manage DCB and other control traffic, you need this network configuration to forward Ethernet frames to the `dcbd` service in the user world.

Storage iSCSI

The iSCSI is a different way to implement SAN storage; instead of using a dedicated network stack FC, iSCSI relies on the standard TCP/IP stack. Like FC protocols, there are two different main roles—the **initiator** (at host side) and the **target** (at storage side). And, of course, the fabric, that is a traditional Ethernet network (maybe with new protocols, such as DCB).

ESXi can be one of the following iSCSI initiator types:

- **Software iSCSI adapter**: Use one or more VMkernel network interfaces and the virtual switches to manage the entire iSCSI traffic. With the software iSCSI adapter, you can use iSCSI technology without purchasing specialized hardware.
- **Dependent hardware iSCSI adapter**: iSCSI management and configuration are managed by VMware, and it may also be the part of the network that must be implemented at the virtual switch level. Ethernet NIC with the iSCSI offload capabilities falls in this category. At ESXi level, those NICs are presented with two different components—a hardware iSCSI adapter and a corresponding standard networking NIC.
- **Independent hardware iSCSI adapter or iSCSI HBA**: This is like the FC HBA, all the network stack is implemented in hardware inside the adapter. On the ESXi side, you just see one or more vmhba like with all other block storage adapters. Network configuration must be performed at card level, using BIOS management, or specific tools (there are also plugins for vCenter to manage the configuration inside vSphere).

CNA cards could appear fully independent or dependent on hardware adapters, but usually using NPAR as a real HBA.

The main difference between one mode and another is on how the network is configured; for independent hardware iSCSI you just configure at the adapter firmware level, for software initiator you have to build a proper virtual network configuration. Performance can change slightly across those modes, but in most cases could remain similar; not so with the host CPU load, which usually decreases when moving from software to HBA mode.

Both the virtual network and the physical network configurations depend on your storage vendor configuration and the type of adapter (for the virtual network).

Some iSCSI storage arrays work with a network topology exactly like FC fabric, two different switches with isolated networks. That means two different logical networks and two different IP classes. This is the solution that does not require any inter-switch connection and provides a better resiliency (switches are fully independent and isolated from each other). For example, the iSCSI version of Dell-EMC VNX or Compellent storage works in this way. If you are using a software initiator, you need at least two different VMkernel interfaces, one on each logical network.

But there is also another possibility, a single flat network on both layer 2 and layer 3. That means that the physical switches (to provide resiliency and redundancy you want at least two) must be in the same broadcast domain and must be (directly or indirectly) interconnected. For example, Dell-EMC EqualLogic needs this kind of network configuration. Using stacking or a virtual chassis, or similar functions to build a single logical switch, could be an option, especially to simplify the management. But plan it carefully to ensure the right network resiliency (for example, some stacked switches need to reboot all the switches during a firmware upgrade). Also in this kind of network topology, using a software initiator, more VMkernel may be needed, but in this case, you have to bind all of them to the iSCSI adapter:

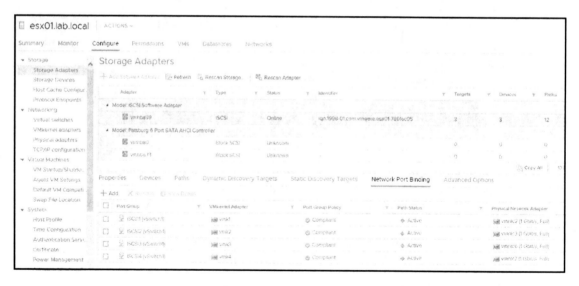

iSCSI NIC binding

There isn't a specific service type for VMkernel interface to tag it for iSCSI network traffic; the choice of the proper interface is done depending on your routing table; for this reason, be sure to use dedicated network ranges for iSCSI only when you have more interfaces on the same network. You need the iSCSI NIC binding, otherwise, only one interface will be used.

As compared to FC storage, there are several different possible tweaks and optimizations for iSCSI, but check what your storage vendor recommends:

- **Jumbo frames (9000 bytes for Ethernet frames)**: iSCSI traffic can usually benefit from jumbo frames, but is only enabled end-to-end across initiator and target; that means at the VMkernel and virtual switch level (configuration is possible under MTU settings), at the physical switch level (for all the ports used by iSCSI), and at the storage level.
- **DCB**: If you use converged networks and your storage supports them, DCB can provide **Quality of Service (QoS)** for storage traffic. Usually configured, on the ESXi side, on CNA adapters.
- **iSCSI initiator Advanced Setting delayed ACK**: Some storage vendors suggest disabling this.
- **iSCSI initiator Advanced Setting login timeout**: The default value is quite low, some storage vendors suggest increasing it (for example, to 60 seconds).
- **TSO and LRO of the physical NICs**: Sometimes you have to change these settings using KB 2055140—*Understanding TCP Segmentation Offload (TSO) and Large Receive Offload (LRO) in a VMware environment* (`https://kb.vmware.com/kb/2055140`).
- **TCO of the physical NICs**: Sometimes you have to change this setting using KB 2052904—*Understanding TCP Checksum Offloading (TCO) in a VMware Environment* (`https://kb.vmware.com/kb/2052904`).

Note that iSCSI can provide initiator (and also target) authentication in different ways:

- **IP based**: With some storage arrays you can simply add a list of authorized IPs (or networks).
- **iSCSI Qualified Name (IQN)**: Each initiator and target has at least one IQN that can be used for authorizing specific hosts. Note that the default ESXi software initiator identifier is based on the hostname (when you activate the software iSCSI adapter) followed by a random string like `iqn.1998-01.com.vmware:esx01-789fac05`, but you can change it (this requires a host reboot), or add an alias to use a different string.

- **Challenge Handshake Authentication Protocol (CHAP)**: This is a real authentication using a shared password, and can also be mutual, so that not only does the storage authenticate the host, but the host can also authenticate the storage.

Storage NFS

The only types of **network-attached storage (NAS)** supported by ESXi are those with NFS protocols, NFS 3, or NFS 4.1 (starting with vSphere 6.0), both over TCP (by default NFS is on the UDP transport protocol). Like software iSCSI, an ESXi host needs a proper VMkernel and virtual network configuration to access a remote NFS server.

Note that there isn't a specific type of VMkernel interface for NFS traffic; depending on your routing table the right interface is chosen properly.

To add a new NFS datastore, proceed with the following steps:

1. Choose **Add new datastore**
2. Select **NFS** type
3. Choose the right protocol type as shown as follows:

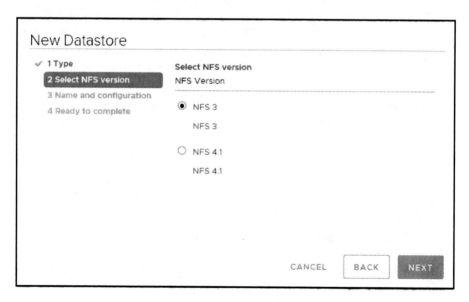

Add a new NFS datastore

4. Provide the storage information; that is, at least, a folder of the share (usually, is the full path), and the name or IP of the storage shown as follows:

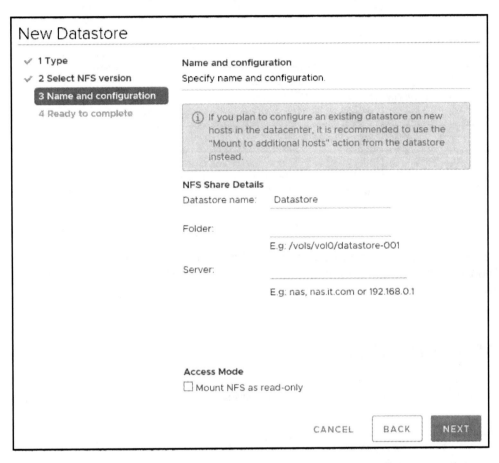

New Datastore

✓ 1 Type

✓ 2 Select NFS version

3 Name and configuration

4 Ready to complete

Name and configuration

Specify name and configuration.

ⓘ If you plan to configure an existing datastore on new hosts in the datacenter, it is recommended to use the "Mount to additional hosts" action from the datastore instead.

NFS Share Details

Datastore name: Datastore

Folder:

E.g: /vols/vol0/datastore-001

Server:

E.g: nas, nas.it.com or 192.168.0.1

Access Mode

☐ Mount NFS as read-only

CANCEL   BACK   NEXT

Add a new NFS datastore

For a NFS 4.1 datastore, you also have to provide Kerberos authentication if needed.

NFS 3 uses one single TCP connection between client and server. For this reason, ESXi does not support multiple paths and the only solution is to work with more IPs at storage side and use link aggregation. NFS 4.1 provides multipathing for servers that support the session trunking. When the trunking is available, you can use multiple IP addresses to access a single NFS volume. Client ID trunking is not supported. Storage vendors usually detail the required configuration to provide better scalability, the best resiliency, and also if some specific tuning could be requested.

The main differences between NFS 3 and 4.1 are summarized in the following table:

Feature	NFS 3	NFS 4.1
ESXi compatibility	Since v3	Only 6.x
NFS security	AUTH_SYS	AUTH_SYS / Kerberos
Hardware acceleration	**vStorage APIs for Array Integration (VAAI) NAS** (vSphere >5.0)	VAAI NAS
Multipath	No	Yes
IPv6 support	Yes	Yes
File locking	Files are named `.lck-file_id`	Share reservations

Table 7.5: Main differences between NFS 3 and 4.1

Virtual disks created on NFS datastores are thin provisioned by default. To have thick-provisioned VMDK as well, you must have VAAI compatible storage that supports the Reserve Space operation. VAAI will be discussed later.

Storage features

The new vSphere 6.5 version, brings a lot of improvements at storage level and some new features in different areas, from VMs, to datastores, to low-level storage, as we will discuss in the next paragraphs.

VM snapshots

VM snapshots usage will be discussed in `Chapter 8`, *Advanced VM and Resource Management*, but there are some interesting improvements starting with vSphere 6.0. To perform a snapshot deletion process, the mirror driver (introduced in vSphere 5 to improve storage vMotion) is used, so that the changes to the VM are written to the active VMDK and the base disk during consolidation.

This should not only speed up the consolidation process (in the client this is called a **delete snapshot**, but formally, is a consolidation), but minimize the infamous *stun issue* where a VM can temporally freeze. For more information, see `http://cormachogan.com/2016/01/06/snapshot-consolidation-changes-in-vsphere-6-0/`.

Another improvement on VM snapshot is related to the VVoLs and vSAN use cases (both discussed later), using VVoL snapshots are offloaded to the storage level (usually more efficient in snapshot management), using vSAN a new efficient snapshot model is used.

Virtual Machine File System (VMFS) 6

vSphere 6.5 has also introduced a new filesystem, for block-based storage—vSphere VMFS 6. It adds new capabilities as compared to previous filesystems:

Feature	VMFS-3	VMFS-5	VMFS-6
Supported ESXi versions	All	5.x and 6.x	6.5
VMFS datastore up to 64 TB	Yes (using extents)	Yes	Yes
VMDK larger than 2 TB	No	Yes (vSphere >5.5)	Yes
Unified block size (1 MB)	No	Yes	Yes
Atomic Test and Set (ATS) enhancements (part of VAAI, locking mechanism)	No	Yes	Yes
Sub-blocks for space efficiency	64 KB (max ~3k)	8 KB (max ~30k)	64 KB (dynamic)
Small file support	No	1 KB	1 KB
Disk partitions type	**master boot record (MBR)**	**GUID partition table (GPT)** by default MBR (legacy)	GPT
Physical block size	512n	512n	512n or 512e
Automatic space reclamation (UNMAP)	No	No (manually)	Yes

Table 7.6: Main difference between filesystems

VMFS 6 introduces two new internal block size concepts for file creation—**Large File Block (LFB)** with a size of 512 MB and Small File Blocks (SFB) with a size of 1 MB and these are used to back files on the VMFS 6 volume. Note that the VMFS block size remains 1 MB sized. Thin disks are backed by SFBs. **Eager Zeroed Thick (EZT)** or **Lazy Zeroed Thick (LZT)** disks are backed by LFBs as much as possible; SFBs are used for the portion of the disk that does not fit into an LFB. For more information, see `http://cormachogan.com/2017/08/16/vmfs-6-large-small-file-blocks/`.

 Datastore format upgrades from VMFS-5 (or previous versions) to VMFS-6 are not supported, but ESXi 6.5 can still work with VMFS-5 datastores. Since there is no direct in-place upgrade you have to build new a datastore and migrate VMs across from the old datastores.

In VMFS 6, most of the datastore management tasks remain the same as VMFS 5, such as increasing the capacity of a datastore, resignaturing a datastore, managing the pointer block cache, and checking metadata consistency with **vSphere On-disk Metadata Analyzer (VOMA)** (for more information see the Storage Guide available on `https://storagehub.vmware.com/`).

Hot-extend for jumbo VMDK

In ESXi 5.5 and 6.0, it was possible to have a single VMDK greater than 2 TB, as described in KB 2058287—*Support for virtual machine disks larger than 2 TB in VMware ESXi 5.5.x and 6.0.x* at `https://kb.vmware.com/kb/2058287`. But virtual disks of powered-on VMs could be extended only if the final size was below 2 TB (and if the virtual disks were connected to a virtual SCSI controller). If the size of a VMDK was larger than 2 TB, or the expand operation caused it to exceed 2 TB, the hot-extend operation wasn't possible at all. Of course, it was possible to perform it when the VM was powered off.

This behavior has been changed in vSphere 6.5 and now hot-extend no longer has this limitation. It is important to note that this does not require VMFS 6 or VM hardware version 13 to work. VMFS 5 will also support this functionality as long as ESXi is the version at 6.5.

Automatic space reclaim

VAAI UNMAP was introduced in vSphere 5.0 to reclaim the free space when the VMs had to be moved or deleted from a datastore that is thin provisioned at the storage level. vSphere 6.0 introduced some improvements to UNMAP that facilitated the reclaiming of stranded space from within a guest OS.

But, in this case, the reclaim operation was performed manually, as described on KB 2057513—*Using the esxcli storage vmfs unmap command to reclaim VMFS deleted blocks on thin-provisioned LUNs* at `https://kb.vmware.com/kb/2057513`.

In vSphere 6.5 and with the new VMFS6, there is now an automated UNMAP mechanism for reclaiming the dead or stranded space on datastores. Now UNMAP runs continuously in the background if enabled at the datastore level.

There are currently two settings available—None and Low. Reclaim priority is only on or off. Low implies reclaim is enabled, whereas with None it is disabled. With the default setting of Low, the expectation is that any blocks that are no longer used will be reclaimed within 12 hours. Space reclamation settings are available both in vSphere Web Client and also in the new HTML5 client, under datastore properties:

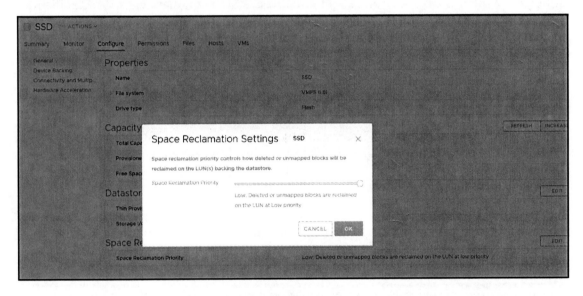

Datastore space reclamation settings

Or also from the command line, for example using `esxcli`:

```
esxcli storage vmfs reclaim config set –l Datastore _Name –p {none|low}
```

 What does it mean? Finally, you can use think provision at the storage side, and have automatic space reclaim. But note that available space could still not match between vSphere and storage view because LZT VMDKs do not use storage space unless you are writing new blocks (at storage level those virtual disks are quite similar to thin VMDKs).

In vSphere 6.0, there was limited in-guest UNMAP (note that TRIM is the ATA equivalent of SCSI UNMAP) support for reclaiming in-guest dead space natively. This was limited to Windows 2012 R2 initially, primarily because of the vSCSI version. Linux distributions check the SCSI version, and unless it is version 5 or greater, it does not send UNMAPs. With SPC-4 support, as introduced in vSphere 6.5, Linux Guest OS will now also be able to issue UNMAPs.

 What does it mean? Finally, you can use the thin provisions on the VMware side (maybe combined with the thin provision on the storage side) and have automatic space reclaim.

One way to monitor automatic UNMAP operations, is to use `esxtop`. Run this command and type *u* (switch to disk device), then *f* for define custom field, then select VAAI statistics with *o*. The DELETE column is related to UNMAP operations. Space reclaim remains manual for VMFS 5 datastores if you disable it at the datastore level, or if you disable it at the host level.

Instant clones versus linked clones

Starting with VMware Horizon 7, it's possible to choose two different ways to deliver virtual desktop pools in a space-optimized way: using **VMware Composer and Linked Clones** technology (existing from several years), or using the **VMware Instant Clones** technology introduced in vSphere 6.0.

Both technologies share a virtual disk of a parent VM between multiple VMs and therefore consume less storage than full clone VMs. It's something like differential disks in other virtualization solutions. But instant clones (also called just-in-time VM delivery or VM Fork) are significantly faster than linked clones.

Transparent page sharing is automatically enabled because clones can also share the memory of a parent VM, making them not only space efficient on the storage side, but also on the memory side. Unfortunately, there isn't a direct way to make them from the management interfaces, but only from other products. Actually, instant clones can be used in VMware Horizon Enterprise and from vSphere Integrated Containers.

Storage DRS versus storage tiering

Storage Distributed Resource Scheduler (SDRS) was introduced in vSphere 5.0 to efficiently manage a pool of datastores as a single logical datastore (a datastore cluster). VM optimization and distribution was based on two metrics—**space** and **I/O**.

SDRS fully supports VMFS and NFS datastore. However, it does not allow adding NFS datastores and VMFS datastores into the same datastore cluster. Starting with vSphere 6.0, SDRS is now aware of the storage capabilities available through VASA 2.0 and can use storage policies (see later in this chapter). It will only move or place VMs on a datastore within the datastore cluster that can satisfy specific VM's storage policies, based on several features, including the following:

- **Deduplication**: SDRS will be aware of deduplication domains, and when datastores belong to the same domain, moving a VM will have little to no effect on capacity
- **Storage tier**: SDRS will not move VMs while the storage auto-tier was just promoting or demoting blocks to a lower or higher tier
- **Thin provisioning**: SDRS can recognize if more thin-provisioned datastores have a common backing pool to avoid migrating VMs
- **Storage replica (SR)**: SDRS will recognize replica VMs and avoid resource constraints between storage vMotion and replication

Always refer to the storage vendor's guides to verify if SDRS is supported and with which settings (usually auto-tiering storage is incompatible with SDRS I/O balance). Also note that SDRS cannot replace the tiering mechanism implemented in some storage (especially hybrid storage); just because a single VMDK could only stay in one single datastore and not split across multiple datastores, there is no way for SDRS to move the *hot* blocks to a fast datastore and the *cold* blocks to a slow datastore.

Datastore cluster and SDRS management remain the same from vSphere 5, with similar considerations, like keeping disks with the same capabilities in the same datastore cluster. Although, with vSphere 6.0 you can now mix datastores with different capabilities in the same datastore cluster, using the right storage policies at VM level.

Storage I/O Control (SIOC)

SIOC was initially introduced in vSphere 4.1 to provide I/O prioritization and **quality of service (QoS)** of VM disks running on a cluster with a shared storage. It extended the shares and limits not at the host level, but at the cluster level. With vSphere 5.0, SIOC provides cluster-wide I/O shares and limits for NFS datastores, not only VMFS datastores.

With vSphere 5.1 a new SIOC feature called **stats only mode** is used to gather statistics to assist SDRS. Also, the latency threshold for SIOC has a new automatic threshold computation and the default latency threshold for SIOC (30 ms) can be reduced to as low as 5 ms.

With vSphere 6.5 there are two different SIOC:

- **SIOC V1**: It is disabled by default. It needs to be enabled on per datastore level, and it is only utilized when a specific level of latency has been reached. By default, the latency threshold for a datastore is set to 30 ms, as mentioned earlier. If SIOC is triggered, disk shares (aggregated from all VMDKs using the datastore) are used to assign I/O queue slots on a per-host basis to that datastore. In other words, SIOC limits the number of IOs that a host can issue. The more VMs/VMDKs that run on a particular host, the higher the number of shares, and thus the higher the number of IOs that particular host can issue. The throttling is done by modifying the device queue depth of the various hosts sharing the datastore. When the period of contention passes, and latency returns to normal values, the device queue depths are allowed to return to their default values on each host.

- **SIOC V2**: This can now be managed using **Storage Policy Based Management (SPBM)** policies. VM Storage Policies in vSphere 6.5 have a new option called **common rules**, used for configuring data services provided by hosts, such as SIOC and encryption.

 SIOC V1 and SIOC V2 can co-exist on vSphere 6.5.

To build a new SIOC storage policy, the first step is to enable common rules. This will then allow you to add SIOC components to the policy:

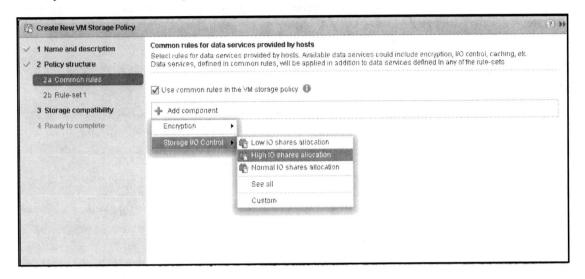

SIOC v2 VM storage policy

Note that, actually, building a new VM storage policy is possible only from the vSphere Web Client. Assigning it to a VM is possible also from the HTML5 client.

Storage integration

VMware vSphere has several different types of storage integration solutions and technologies, some started in version 4.1 (such as VAAI), others more recently (such as VVol), directed towards building a fully **software-defined storage** (SDS) stack.

VMware vSphere Storage Policy Based Management (SPBM)

SPBM is an extension of the VM Storage Policies and the foundation of the SDS control vision from VMware. SPBM enables vSphere administrators to simplify storage provisioning and management, by assigning to each virtual machine the required storage features and capabilities. VM will be automatically provisioned on the right datastore that respects these requirements.

SPBM interprets the different storage requirements and dynamically composes the different storage services, like placing the VM on the right storage tier, allocating capacity, providing snapshots, replication, and so on. To understand storage features and capabilities, **vSphere Storage APIs for Storage Awareness (VASA)** could be used, but it's not formally mandatory.

In vSphere 6.5, storage policies are used widely, also for vSAN, VVols, SIOC v2, VM encryption (see `Chapter 10`, *Securing and Protecting Your Environment*).

Actually, you can consume policies from the HTML5 client, but you need the vSphere Web Client to build new policies. Depending on your configuration, there are some default policies built-in and used for generic datastores, vSAN, or vVols.

Please consider the following points:

- Policies are stored and managed by vCenter server, but can be applied to VMs in one or more clusters.
- Each vCenter in Enhanced Linked Mode has its own set of policies.
- A maximum of 1,024 policies can exist per vCenter server.
- The storage policy name can consist of up to 80 characters. Anyway, the storage policy name is not the true identifier because, like for VM names, a unique identifier is used instead.
- Storage policy can define one or many rules regarding performance, availability, space efficiency, and so on.
- Storage policies are not additive. Only one policy (that contains one or more policy rules) can be applied per object.
- A storage policy can be applied to a group of VMs, a single VM, or even a single VMDK within a VM.

To learn more, see this blog post—*Understanding Storage Policy-Based Management* at `https:/ /blogs.vmware.com/virtualblocks/2017/01/16/understanding-storage-policy-based- management/`.

Pluggable Storage Architecture (PSA)

The PSA framework (introduced in vSphere 4.0) is a collection of VMkernel APIs that allow partners to insert specific functions into the ESXi storage layer.

Those third-party plugins fall into one of three categories:

- **Third-party Multipathing Plugin (MPP)**: Provides new multipath rules to VMware **native multipathing** (NMP)
- **Third-party Storage Array Type Plugin (SATP)**: Used to recognize some storage capabilities, not recognized by the VMware SATPs
- **Third-party Path Selection Plugin (PSP)**: Similar to the previous one, but usually used to identify the default multipath rule for a new storage

The following image summarizes the PSA architecture:

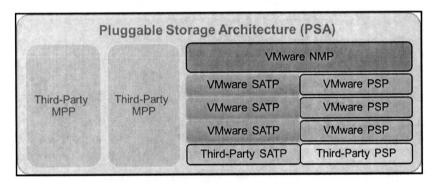

Pluggable Storage Architecture (PSA)

SATP rules are used to automatically identify SSD devices (tagged with the SSD type) or local devices. With vSphere 6.5, you can mark a disk as an SSD (or HDD) directly from the HTML5 client:

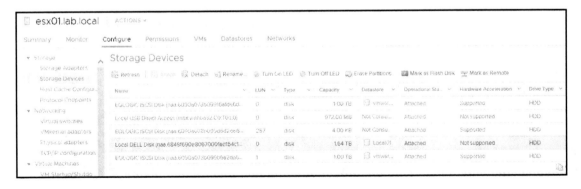

Tag a disk as a flash disk

This can be useful if the storage cannot report the type correctly (for example, if it's a multi-tier storage), and you don't want to build a manual SATP rule.

Multipathing

Multipathing is a technique that lets you efficiently and reliably use more than one physical path to transfer data between the host and an external storage array.

VMware supports different types of storage architectures as follows:

- **Active-active storage system**: All controllers (or all ports) are active; that means all the paths are active unless a path fails. In this storage, it is possible to access a LUN simultaneously through all the storage paths that are available without significant performance degradation.
- **Active-passive storage system**: Usually one controller is active (on a specific LUN) and the second is passive (but could be active on another LUN). If access through the active storage port fails, one of the passive storage processors can be activated by the servers accessing it.
- **Asymmetrical storage system**: Supports **Asymmetric Logical Unit Access (ALUA)**, where all ports could be active, but with different levels of access per port. With ALUA, hosts can determine the states of target ports and prioritize paths; some of the active paths are primary and others are secondary.
- **Virtual port storage system**: Supports access to the storage services through a single virtual port. Virtual port storage systems are active-active storage devices, but hide their multiple connections through a single port; for example with iSCSI it is possible to work with a single virtual IP instead of each IP of each port, or for FC it is possible to build a virtual WWN (if switches support NPIV). These storage systems handle port failovers and connection balancing transparently (transparent failover).

Depending on the storage type, you need specific multipath criteria. VMware ESXi has three main types of path selection policies (provided by NMP) described as follows:

- **Fixed**: The host uses the designated preferred path if it has been configured. Otherwise, it selects the first working path discovered at system boot time. This is the default policy for most active-active storage and there is also **Fixed_AP** that extends fixed functionality to active/passive and ALUA storage.

- **Most Recently Used (MRU)**: The host selects the path that it used most recently. When the path becomes unavailable, the host selects an alternative path and does not revert to the original path when that path becomes available again. This is the default policy for most active-passive storage.
- **Round Robin (RR)**: The host uses an automatic path selection algorithm, rotating through all active paths when connecting to active-passive arrays, or through all available paths when connecting to active-active arrays. This is the default for a number of arrays and can be used with both active-active and active-passive arrays to implement load balancing across multiple paths.

If the path selection for your storage is not recognized correctly or you want to change the default, you must use PSA-related commands for NMP and SATP. Refer to your storage vendor documentation and best practices for VMware vSphere.

Storage masking and filtering

Sometimes you need to hide some disks in order to protect them from possible usage. This operation is called LUN masking (at host side), and before vSphere 6.0, was also recommended before un-presenting a LUN (at storage side) to avoid the **All-Paths-Down** **(APD)** condition. Starting with ESXi 6.0 is now possible; just unmount the datastore.

For more information, see KB 1009449—*Masking a LUN from ESX and ESXi using the MASK_PATH plug-in* (https://kb.vmware.com/kb/1009449). Also note that vCenter automatically hides some LUNs; all that are already mounted or used as RDM disk, but only for hosts or VM managed by the same vCenter.

You can control this behavior using those vCenter Server advanced settings:

Advanced parameter	Description
Config.vpxd.filter.vmfsFilter	When it's set to false, it allows you to add a VMFS volume to a VM even when in use by another VM
Config.vpxd.filter.rdmfilter	When it's set to false, it allows you to add a LUN to a VM, as **Raw Device Mapping** (RDM), even when the LUN is used by another VM

`Config.vpxd.filter.SameHostandTransportsFilter`	When set to false, incompatible LUNs are allowed to be added as extents
`Config.vpxd.filter.hostRescanFilter`	When set to false, the auto rescan for all hosts is disabled after adding storage

Table 7.7: vCenter Server advanced settings

VMware VAAI

VAAI is a set of features introduced in vSphere 4.1 that provide hardware acceleration and offload functionality for some types of operations. Initially, designed only for block-based storage, with vSphere 5.0 this has also been extended to NFS datastores.

In vSphere 6.x VAAI isn't changed, but now it's available for the Standard edition. VAAI is enabled by default and you can control it with the following ESXi advanced settings:

Advanced parameter	Description
`HardwareAcceleratedLocking`	ATS that is used during creation of files on the VMFS volume
`HardwareAcceleratedMove`	Clone Blocks/Full Copy/XCOPY, that is used to copy data
`HardwareAcceleratedInit`	Zero blocks/Write Same, that is used to zero-out disk regions

Table 7.8: ESXi advanced settings

For more information, see KB 1021976—*Frequently Asked Questions for vStorage APIs for Array Integration* (`https://kb.vmware.com/kb/1021976`).

VMware vSphere APIs for IO Filtering (VAIO)

VAIO introduced in vSphere 6.0 U1, permits the adding of seamless new third-party software-based data services; the technology's partners can now put their solution directly into the I/O stream of a VM through a filter that intercepts data before it goes to the disk. It enables the secure filtering of a VM's I/O safely in the kernel, with a well-defined framework and according to storage policies. VAIO is totally storage agnostic and works with Virtual Volumes, vSAN, and legacy storage.

VAIO could be integrated both in traditional and software-defined storage as described in the following image:

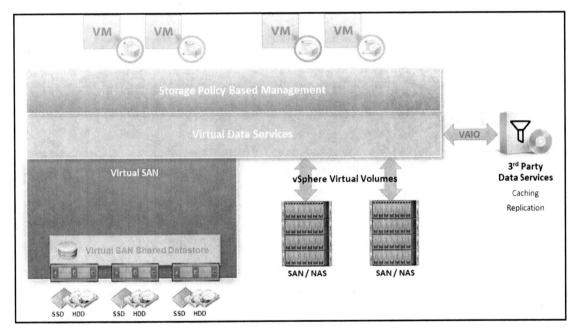

VAIO framework

Caching and replication are the initial use cases (for replication, the next version 10 of Veeam Backup & Replication will use VAIO for the new **Continuous Data Protection (CDP)** feature), but potentially can work also for anti-virus, data inspections, and other services.

VMware vCenter plugins

Several storage vendors provide a specific plugin for vCenter Server in order to integrate some storage functionalities, such as monitoring, disk provisioning, storage snapshots management, and so on. For example, the following screenshot shows the Dell-EMC EqualLogic integration with the new menu (**Volume, Protection, Recovery**) inside the vSphere Web Client. Under the **Volume and Snapshot Space,** it is possible to monitor the storage snapshots as shown in the following screenshot:

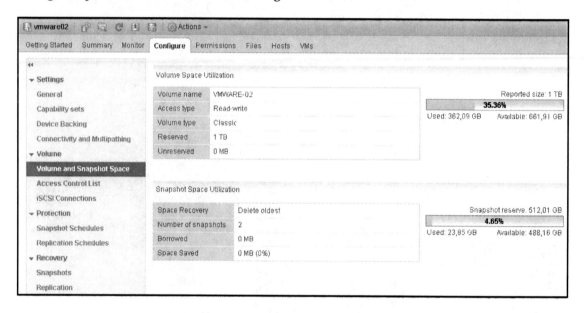

Storage plugin

Some plugins already work on the HTML5 client, others only with the vSphere Web Client. But for the future, they will have to move to HTML5 client or the VASA framework.

VASA

VASA is a set of APIs (introduced in vSphere 5.0) that will enable vCenter to see the capabilities of the datastores at storage side, making it much easier to select the appropriate datastore for virtual machine placement. Storage capabilities, such as RAID level, thin or thick provisioned, replication state, and much more can now be made visible within vCenter, without the need for a specific plugin. You just need a VASA provider (usually a web service) that exposes all of those capabilities.

VASA minimizes the need to manually manage the information of the capabilities of each LUN, usually performed by documentation or naming conventions, and makes a simple guaranteeing of the correct **Service Level Agreement (SLA)** to virtual machines.

With vSphere 6.0, a new VASA 2.0 has been introduced to manage VVols.

VVols

Introduced in vSphere 6.0, VVols is a new integration and management framework that abstracts and virtualizes SAN/NAS storage with a software-defined storage approach, based on SPBM:

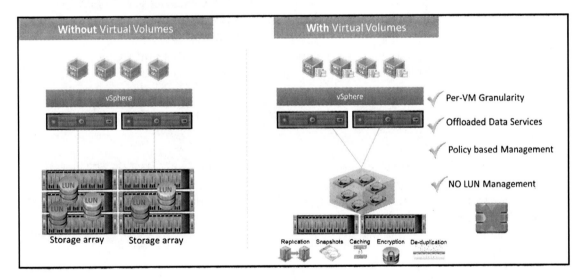

LUNs versus VVol

The VVols architecture has five major components which are described as follows:

- **VVol object**: It can be **config-VVol (metadata), data-VVol (VMDKs), mem-VVol (snapshots), swap-VVol (swap files), other-VVol (vendor solution specific)**.

- **Protocol Endpoint (PE)**: Although storage systems manage all aspects of virtual volumes, ESXi hosts have no direct access to virtual volumes on the storage side. Instead, ESXi hosts use a logical I/O proxy, called the PE, to communicate with virtual volumes and virtual disk files that virtual volumes encapsulate. ESXi uses PE to establish a data path on demand from virtual machines to their respective VVols.

- **Storage Container (SC)**: Unlike traditional LUN and NFS based vSphere storage, the VVols functionality does not require preconfigured volumes on a storage side. Instead, VVols uses an SC, which is a pool of raw storage capacity or an aggregation of storage capabilities that a storage system can provide to VVols.

- **VASA provider (2.0)**: A VVols storage provider, also called a VASA provider, is a software component that acts as a storage awareness service for vSphere. The provider mediates out-of-band communication between the vCenter Server and ESXi hosts on one side and a storage system on the other.

- **Array**: This implements VVols features; note that not all storage vendors implement VVols in the same way, so it really depends on the maturity of their solution.

For more information, see KB 2113013—*Understanding Virtual Volumes (VVols) in VMware vSphere 6.0* (`https://kb.vmware.com/kb/2113013`).

 Please note that vCenter and the VASA provider are critical for VVols and the lack of them can affect some operations, such as power-on a VM (a swap object must be created), or adding new virtual disks. For more information see this blog post at `https://cormachogan.com/2015/12/04/losing-vasa-vcenter-in-vvols/`.

With the new vSphere 6.5, there are some improvements:

- Support for storage replication (VVols replication enablement)
- SPBM for availability
- Support for Oracle **Real Application Clusters (RAC)** on VVols

But other features will be added to VVols. During VMworld 2017 the roadmap for the next release of vSphere (probably vSphere 6.7) was announced:

- **Support for Microsoft Cluster Server (MSCS) or fail-over cluster)**: Actually, it's implemented using RDMs, but VVols can provide more flexibility in the future.
- **Performance parity with VMFS**: Also, if the I/O data paths and is multipathing between a host and VVols, there are some minor changes; for example, to the path going through a PE to get to the VVols. Anyway, it seems that not all is already tuned both at storage and host side, so some speed improvement is still possible.
- **IPv6 support**: VMware vSphere already supports IPv6, but not yet on the VASA provider service.

Today, the bind operation happens out-of-band using the control path through the VASA provider, and the goal for the future is to bring it in-band to the data path through the PE instead. Still, some features, such as NFS v4.1 support and in-band binding, are not yet present (and will probably be implemented in the next major release).

 There are a lot of papers and documentation on how VVols could be useful in a vSphere environment; for example, the recent IDC research *VVols Provides Powerful Application-Aware Management for vSphere Environments* which can be found at URL `http://idcdocserv.com/ US42988017`. But there is not much data on the real adoptions in production; that seems still limited. Also, it is a technology that depends too much on the storage vendor's implementation (VMware provides just the framework).

Storage design

Choosing the right storage according to your needs could be a very long debate without a simple answer, because there are so many different types of storage solutions. As usual, you have to consider availability, scalability, performance, and manageability aspects, including some new capabilities such as data protection, data migration, security, and so on.

Traditional IOPS sizing could be too limited considering that most of the enterprise storage works with concepts more complex, such as data tiering, data reduction, and data locality; for this reason, it's always suggested you make a capacity and performance estimation using vendor-specific tools.

In most cases you will have storage with some flash technologies:

- **AFA (full flash)**: This is where performance and storage latency could be critical and you want a storage with predictable throughput and latency
- **Hybrid flash**: This is where you also need some low-cost capacity tiers (or simple capacity datastores) but still with the benefit of flash memory for hot data (or simply some datastores).

More complex is choosing between using an NAS or SAN; VMware vSphere abstracts VM with files, so both could be fine and potentially there isn't one that is better than the other. Historically, NFS datastore has got some performance issues and limits (for example, only thin disks without VAAI). But NFS storage can be more VM aware and permit a better integration (for example, see **Tintri** storage, where you have a full VM visibility also from storage side). And NFS datastore does not have the SCSI reservation issue of VMFS datastore, where you have some limitations to the number of VMs and VMDKs on each datastore, to avoid too much SCSI reservation (note that VAAI has limited this issue).

Anyway, if you are using VVols, the difference between NAS or SAN becomes quite null. If you are choosing a SAN, there can be some concerns related to the frontend protocols, especially if using FC, FCoE, or iSCSI. In case of FC protocol:

- It remains more efficient and scalable than IP protocol for storage; for example, path failover is usually less than 30 seconds, compared with less than 60 seconds for iSCSI.
- It is also a little bit more efficient, both for the protocol (8 Gbps FC could be comparable with 10 Gbps iSCSI) but also because FC uses HBA hardware; that means lower host CPU consumptions.

Anyway, the choice depends mostly on the storage type; some have limited options in frontend interface types or by your host's ability to expand; for example, blades may not have pure FC options. For converged networks, remember that you have to plan carefully the network capacity and QoS using DCB.

Converged infrastructure doesn't much change these considerations, except that you will probably always have a fixed storage solution in your stack. HCI solutions are quite different; they will be discussed later in this chapter.

VM storage layout

You can choose different VMDK provisioning as described before. EZT disks provide the best performance (also for the first writes), but they occupy the entire space including unused space, so they are not efficient with space utilization. LZT is the most common choice. Thin disks require more management attention to avoid excessive storage over-provisioning.

For more considerations of different virtual disk types in term of performance, see the blog post at `https://blogs.vmware.com/vsphere/2014/05/thick-vs-thin-disks-flash-arrays.html`.

For the different virtual storage controllers, this table recaps the different types and possible use cases:

Controller type	VM type	Minimum virtual hardware	Use cases
BusLogic	Server	-	Very old Windows OS
LSI Logic Parallel (formerly LSI Logic)	Server/Desktop	-	Legacy Windows OS (2003)
LSI Logic SAS	Server/Desktop	VH7	Windows OS (>2008)
PVSCSI	Server	VH7	Workload I/O intensive
AHCI/SATA	Server/Desktop	VH10	Large number of virtual disks, but with limited performance
NVMe	Server	VH13	Fast and low latency storage

Table 7.9: Different virtual storage controllers

Remember that you can have, in a single VM, a maximum of 4 SCSI controllers (15 devices per controller), 4 SATA controllers (30 devices per controller), and 4 NVMe (60 devices per controllers).

Use of more storage controllers has the advantage of handling different queues for the I/O request, and could be useful for specific VMDKs that require more performance (maybe using PVSCSI or NVMe controllers).

Note that adding different types of storage controllers to a VM that uses BIOS firmware can cause operating system boot issues. For more information see *SCSI and SATA Storage Controller Conditions, Limitations, and Compatibility at* https://docs.vmware.com/en/VMware-vSphere/6.5/com.vmware.vsphere.vm_admin.doc/GUID-5872D173-A076-42FE-8D0B-9DB0EB0E7362.html. VMs with EFI firmware are not affected. To manage different performance profiles for each VM, you can use shares or limits, with SIOC enabled.

VM snapshot limits

VMware recommends only a maximum of 32 snapshots in a VM chain. However, for a better performance, limit this number to only 2 to 3 snapshots and keep them for as short a time as possible, because snapshots are thin disks that can grow potentially to the same size of the base disk. VMware vSAN does not have those limitations, due to a different format for snapshots.

When using a third-party backup software, ensure that snapshots are deleted after a successful backup. Some backup programs work better than others or have specific controls for snapshot management. Avoid increasing a virtual machine disk size or virtual RDM if the VM has a snapshot, it is possible that this may corrupt snapshots and result in data loss.

For more information, see also KB 1025279—*Best practices for using snapshots in the vSphere environment* (http://kb.vmware.com/kb/1025279).

Datastore layout

If you are working with a VMFS datastore, one of the typical questions is how many LUNs will I need? Considering that each storage LUN will be formatted to become a VMFS datastore and that there is a 64 TB max limit for datastore size, potentially you may use only one LUN.

But in vSphere HA, datastore heartbeats require at least two datastores, although you can configure some vSphere HA advanced settings to use just one, or just don't use it (depending on your storage specifications).

Another aspect is related to a SCSI reservations issue for VMFS datastores; the larger your datastore, the more VMs and VMDKs and more SCSI reservations you will have. Limit the number of VMs (there isn't a magic number, but in most cases it is around 30–40 VMs) and make the number of required datastores bigger. That means more time for re-scanning and more complexity to manage them (for the second aspect, SDRS could be a good solution).

Finally, you have also to consider the different paths that you can have and remember that one per time could be used, also with a round-robin that simply distributed the requests, but at a specific time, one path is used. With more datastores, you can better distribute the active paths and increase the fabric utilization.

Permanent Device Loss (PDL) and All-Paths-Down (APD)

Starting with vSphere 6.0, in vSphere HA configurations, there is a new storage-related feature, **VM Component Protection (VMCP)**, that protects virtual machines from possible storage issues.

There are two different types of conditions that can be managed by VMCP:

- **PDL**: It occurs when the storage array issues a SCSI sense code indicating that the device is unavailable (for example, a failed LUN)
- **APD**: Usually, related to an underlying storage/networking issue, different from a PDL because the host doesn't have enough information to determine if the device loss is temporary or permanent

The configuration is available in the vSphere Web Client and also in the new HTML5 client. A typical response could be to restart the VM in the case of a PDL, just because this condition may indicate that the storage device does not expect the device to return anytime soon. But you can configure PDL with different responses:

- **Disabled**: No action will be taken to the affected VMs
- **Issue events**: No action will be taken against the affected VMs, however, the administrator will be notified when a PDL event has occurred
- **Power off and restart VMs**: All affected VMs will be terminated on the host and vSphere HA will attempt to restart the VMs on hosts that still have connectivity to the storage device

An APD condition is more of an unknown situation; when an APD occurs a timer starts. After 140 seconds, the APD is declared and the device is marked as APD time out. There are different types of responses for APD:

- **Disabled**: Same as before, no action will be taken against the affected VMs
- **Issue events**: Same as before, no action will be taken against the affected VMs, however, the administrator will be notified when a PDL event has occurred
- **Power off and restart VMs (conservative)**: vSphere HA will not attempt to restart the affected VMs unless it has determined there is another host that can restart the VMs
- **Power off and restart VMs (aggressive)**: vSphere HA will terminate the affected VMs even if it cannot determine that another host can restart the VMs

Note that there is also a **response recovery** option in order to retry before APD times out.

All settings are also available with the vSphere Client (HTML5):

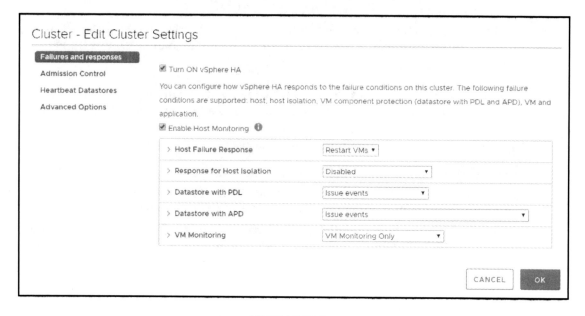

VM component protection

For more information, see also:

- *Permanent Device Loss (PDL) and All-Paths-Down (APD) in vSphere 5.x and 6.x* at `https://kb.vmware.com/kb/2004684`
- *Lost or degraded connectivity to storage device* at `https://kb.vmware.com/kb/1009553`

VVols dependencies

You can plan to use VVols and you have verified that storage vendor implementation is good, reliable, and provides major benefits.

One major benefit is the offload of the VM snapshot function directly to the storage level; this means that you minimize all the performance issues of VM snapshot and surpass also their limits.

But you have also to consider some possible risks and design considerations:

- The VASA provider is very critical. Without it, your running VMs still work, but you cannot spin up new VMs or make new operations (such as VM snapshots). If the VASA provider is a virtual appliance and does not have a specific high availability configuration, consider using not only vSphere HA but maybe also vSphere FT.
- The vCenter Server becomes more critical and cannot stay on VVols (managed by itself). If you don't have a management cluster, provide a traditional datastore for vCenter, PSC, and other VVols related dependencies (such as the VASA provider).
- Native backup can only work in network transport mode (for more information see `Chapter 14`, *Data and Workloads Protection*); actually, SAN, or virtual appliance mode are not working.

Introduction to HCI and vSAN

HCI are specific solutions that combine computing and storage (and sometimes also networking) capabilities from more hosts, to have a shared pool of resources. A vSphere cluster already does this for the computing part. Some storage products extend this to the storage part, making more external storage unnecessary, and making the HCI market a relevant trend; it is not only growing fast, with more attention from the big storage vendors, but it is also changing fast.

Some HCI products compatible with vSphere 6.5:

- **Nutanix**: This is the pioneer of HCI, actually it is the only solution that can work with all the hypervisor technologies (VMware vSphere, Microsoft Hyper-V, KVM with the custom AHV, Citrix Xen Server).
- **HPE SimpliVity**: In January 2017, HPE acquired Simplivity to bring HCI into its portfolio. Available since April, the HPE SimpliVity 380 (based on HPE ProLiant DL380) is the first HCI product after this acquisition. It offers a full suite of traditional IT functions including WAN optimization, unified global VM-centric management, data protection, cloud integration, built-in backup, disaster recovery, caching, and scale-out capabilities. In-line deduplication, compression, and optimization are applied to all data at inception.
- **NetApp HCI**: The first HCI from NetApp, based heavily on **NetApp's SolidFire** all-flash storage technology (NetApp acquired SolidFire in late 2015).
- **Pivot3 Acuity**: This is claimed to be one of the industry's first priority-aware and policy-based HCI, offering NVMe PCIe flash performance, giving customers the ability to consolidate multiple mixed-application workloads onto a single infrastructure.
- **VMware vSAN**: The only in-kernel HCI solutions for VMware vSphere, totally integrated into vCenter management; with more than 10,000 customers in all verticals and growing.

Note that there are also some specific HCI solutions for ROBO scenarios, or small clusters (usually HCI starts from at least three nodes); for example, from StarWind or StorMagic.

VMware vSAN

VMware vSAN is formally a new product from VMware, but the code is already included in all vSphere versions starting from v5.5U1. It's so tightly bound with vSphere that vSAN version depends on the vSphere versions, just because the only way to upgrade vSAN is upgrading your vSphere version.

The following table summarizes the different versions of vSphere and the related version of vSAN:

Version	Release date	Build number	Installer build number	vSAN version	vSAN disk format
ESXi 6.5 Update 1	2017-07-27	5969303	N/A	6.6.1	5
ESXi 6.5.0d	2017-04-18	5310538	N/A	6.6	5
ESXi 6.5 GA	2016-11-15	4564106	N/A	6.5	2.5, 3
ESXi 6.0 Update 2	2016-03-16	3620759	N/A	6.2	2.5, 3
ESXi 6.0 U1	2015-09-10	3029758	N/A	6.1	2
ESXi 6.0 GA	2015-03-12	2494585	N/A	6.0	2
ESXi 5.5 Update 1	2014-03-11	1623387	N/A	5.5	1

Table 7.10: Different versions of vSphere and the related version of vSAN

Like other HCI solutions, it provides a shared storage with common features from a pool of local disks. The first big difference is that each host must have at least one flash disk (SSD or also NVMe), plus other disks (HDD or other flashes); vSAN configuration could be hybrid or AFA and work with a caching tier (the faster option) or a capacity tier (the other option).

There are a lot of features such as compression, deduplication, erasure coding, but most of them can only be used in AFA configuration. It supports also the stretched cluster both for the hybrid and AFA configuration. One specific case of a stretched cluster is the two-nodes configuration useful for ROBO scenarios.

Planning and design are quite important to define your architecture, the expected performance, the capacity and how your infrastructure can scale. The HCL of vSAN is a subset of all the HCL of vSphere, just because the choice of the disks and the storage controller are very critical.

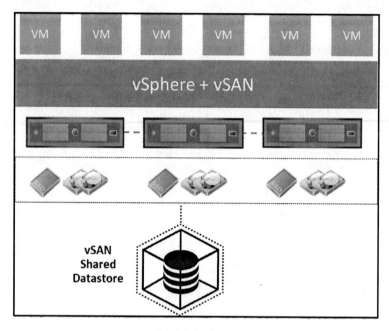

VMware vSAN

Initially, vSAN was using the same VMFS filesystem just for local storage VMFS-L, but now it is using a new filesystem, **VirstoFS**, with new capabilities. The type of vSAN disk format defines the version of the filesystem (v1 is VMFS-L).

For example, the new snapshot format introduced in VSAN 6.0 called **vsanSparse**, that replaces the traditional **VMFSsparse** format (redo logs) and adds new capabilities:

- vSAN 6.0 32 snapshots per VM
- vSAN 6.0 fully supports 32 snapshots per VMDK with the v2 on-disk format. The new snapshot mechanism on v2 uses a new vsanSparse format. However, while these new snapshots outperform the earlier version, there are still some design and sizing concerns to consider. For more information, see `https://www.vmware.com/files/pdf/products/vsan/Tech-Notes-Virtual-San6-Snapshots.pdf`.

Caching with vSphere Flash Read Cache

Flash Read Cache (vFlash) is a feature, introduced in vSphere 5.5 and available in the Enterprise Plus edition, that can improve virtual machine storage performance by using host local flash devices as a cache. The performance boost depends on your workload type and working set size. Only read-intensive workloads, with working sets that fit into the cache size, can really benefit from the Flash Read Cache feature. vSphere Flash Read Cache offers legacy support for the swap-to-SSD feature introduced in vSphere 5.0; that was a previous way to use a local SSD to host VM-related swap files.

You can reserve a Flash Read Cache for any individual virtual disk that is created only when a virtual machine is powered on; it is discarded when a virtual machine is suspended or powered off. When you migrate a virtual machine, you can migrate the cache (default option); otherwise, if you do not migrate the cache, the cache is rewarmed on the destination host. Flash Read Cache does not support RDMs in physical compatibility. Virtual compatibility RDMs are supported with Flash Read Cache as also vSphere HA and DRS; but not FT.

VM cache configuration could be managed also from the vSphere Client (HTML5), but without the advanced settings, available only in the vSphere Web Client:

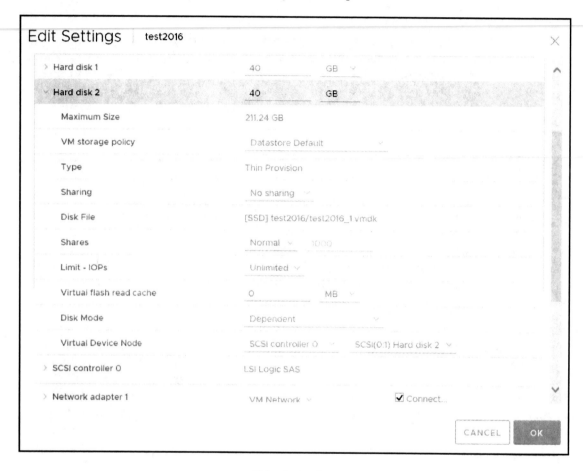

Flash read cache settings

Host configuration can only be managed with vSphere Web Client. You need to add a free local SSD disk to the capacity pool.

Virtual flash resource management

Flash Read Cache supports only write-through or reads caching; write-back, or write caching are not supported at all. But there are other products that can support it.

Other solutions

The first caching solution to provide write-back capability was **PernixData FVP**. Finally, there is a specific framework VAIO to simplify the introduction of new features in the I/O storage path. Actually, there is a list of solutions designed and certified for VAIO, available in the document at `http://partnerweb.vmware.com/comp_guide2/pdf/vi_vaio_guide.pdf`.

- **SanDisk FlashSoft 4.0**: This was the first host-based caching software to achieve VMware Ready™ certification for guaranteed compatibility, reliability, and support. It also introduces support for VMware-supported datastores, virtual disk acceleration, improved performance and stability, and integrated management through the vSphere web client GUI. But with the acquisition of SanDisk by Western Digital, the future of FlashSoft is not so clear.

- **Infinio Accelerator 3.0**: A software-based server-side cache that provides high performance to any storage system in a VMware environment. It increases IOPS and decreases latency by caching a copy of the hottest data on server side resources such as RAM and flash devices. Native inline deduplication ensures that all local storage resources are used as efficiently as possible, reducing the cost of performance. Results can be seen instantly following the non-disruptive, 15 minute installation that doesn't require any downtime, data migration, or reboot. Infinio supports both VMware vSphere ESXi 6.0 and 6.5 (Standard, Enterprise, or Enterprise Plus) and works with any VMware supported datastore, including a variety of SAN, NAS, and DAS hardware supporting VMFS, VVols, and vSAN.

- **PrimaryIO**: This is an emerging provider of performance optimization solutions for business-critical applications, that on March 2016 announced the first version of the **Application Performance Acceleration (APA)** solution. PrimaryIO APA was probably the first product born directly on the VAIO framework and seems very promising. It has also a cluster-wide caching where one host can use the SSD cache from another host in a better way.

There are also other solutions, not based on VAIO filtering, that use kernel modules, such as with Pernix FVP. Anyway, this approach is less flexible compared to VAIO filtering, because a kernel update can break the custom kernel modules.

Summary

This chapter was dedicated to the storage part of a virtual infrastructure, starting from local block-based storage and extending into shared block storage with FC, FCoE, and iSCSI protocols and NFS-based NAS storage.

For each of them, we considered the different optimization techniques, integration, and storage features provided by vSphere. Other types of storage architectures were also considered, especially HCI solutions. To learn more, a great source of information for storage aspects is the VMware StorageHub at `https://storagehub.vmware.com/`.

In this chapter, we introduced the main storage concepts and features, described how to manage local, block, and NAS storage and how to configure vSphere to use them. Also, we explained how to integrate vSphere with storage using VAAI, VASA, vVols, storage profiles, vCenter plugins, and so on.

In the final part, there was a short introduction to HCI and vSAN, and caching options in vSphere.

8
Advanced VM and Resource Management

Once the setup of the vSphere environment has been completed, the deployment of VMs is the final step to fire up your virtual infrastructure. When the hosts and vCenter Server are in place, they provide physical resources to the VMs that physically reside on the storage device shared among the environment.

The chapter will drive you into the structure of VMs and their configuration to better understand how they work and what options to configure to obtain best performance. The use of templates is a key point in the management of VMs since it simplifies the management of the environment, allowing easier creation and faster deployment of new VMs. Relying on a ready-to-run machine, admins just need to do a minor setup. As compared to physical machines, VMs deployed from a template don't need to be installed from scratch and this allows you to save time.

The ability to manage the available resources for VMs is an important factor for the global performance of the infrastructure because a bad design will negatively affect the VM behavior and the whole environment.

In this chapter, we will cover the following topics:

- Understanding VM components, properties, and options
- Deploying, configuring, and managing VM and templates
- Managing VM snapshots
- Managing resources and affinity rules for better performance
- VM migrations and conversion

VM components

A VM behaves in exactly the same way a physical computer does, but it's actually a software computer that runs an OS and applications supported by the host's provided resources. A VM supports all the functionalities and presents the same devices as a physical machine, but it's easier to manage and more secure.

Typically, a VM can be configured to run on ESXi hosts, datacenters, clusters, or resource pools and includes three main core components:

- Virtual and hardware resources
- OS
- VMware Tools

Virtual hardware

When you create a VM, the ESXi host presents the hardware as a specific set of resources to the VM. The hardware type provided by the configuration wizard has been selected by VMware to ensure the highest level of compatibility for the supported OS.

Every VM has a CPU, memory, and disk resources. Virtual devices in the VM perform the same functions as the hardware on a physical computer. You can configure most of the virtual devices present in the VM but some elements cannot be modified or removed, such as the device part of the virtual motherboard, for example:

Virtual hardware configuration for a VM

When you create a VM, specific virtual hardware is presented to the VM that needs some adjustments in order to meet the requirements. To access the virtual hardware configuration, you just need to right-click the VM and select the **Settings** option.

Let's walk-through the main components you need to configure in a VM.

vCPUs

One or more virtual processors can be defined in the VM but cannot exceed the logical processors (sockets x cores x 2 if hyperthreading is enabled) present in the host. The number of vCPU sockets specified in the configuration determines the number of cores available. One VM could have virtual sockets and virtual cores, but this choice is mostly for the licensing of OS per application limitation (for example, the latest SQL Express can work with more cores, but not with more sockets).

With more than eight vCPUs, **virtual NUMA (vNUMA)** is enabled and ESXi distributes the VMs in more NUMA nodes, if it is not possible to fit in just one. Now, memory hot-add also works well with vNUMA. For more information, see `https://blogs.vmware.com/performance/2017/03/virtual-machine-vcpu-and-vnuma-rightsizing-rules-of-thumb.html`.

The maximum supported vCPUs per VM is 128.

Memory

A default amount of RAM is configured based on the selected guest OS. The specified RAM is the memory the OS will present to its system and it's also the maximum amount of RAM the VM can claim from the physical memory installed on the host.

Memory optimization techniques remain the same as the previous version, with a big change, starting from vSphere 6.0, in **Transparent Page Sharing (TPS)**; page sharing is enabled by default within VMs (intra-VM sharing), but is enabled between VMs (inter-VM sharing) only when those VMs have the same salt value (described in the next section). This change was made to ensure the highest security between VMs. For more information, see KB 2080735—*Security considerations and disallowing inter-Virtual Machine Transparent Page Sharing* at `https://kb.vmware.com/kb/2080735`.

In vSphere 6.5, a VM supports a maximum of 6,128 GB of RAM (with the latest virtual hardware versions).

Network adapter

During the VM configuration, you must select the adapter type and the network it will connect. Depending on the VM compatibility and the guest OS, the supported NIC types are the following:

- **E1000E**: Default adapter for Windows 8 and Windows Server 2012, it emulates the Intel 82574 Gigabit Ethernet NIC.
- **E1000:** Driver is available in most newer guest OS and emulates the Intel 82545EM Gigabit Ethernet NIC.
- **Flexible**: Identifies itself as a Vlance adapter, an emulated version of the AMD 79C970 PCnet32 LANCE NIC. Most 32-bit guest OS have the driver for this NIC type. When installing VMware Tools, the adapter changes to the higher-performance VMXNET adapter.
- **VMXNET**: Optimized for VM performance, it requires VMware Tools installed to provide the driver.
- **VMXNET 2 (Enhanced)**: Based on the VMXNET adapter, it provides high-performance features such as jumbo frames and hardware offloads. It's supported by a limited set of guest OS.
- **VMXNET 3**: This offers all the features available in VMXNET 2 and it's a paravirtualized NIC designed for performance. Multiqueue support (known as RSS in Windows), IPv6 offloads, and MSI/MSI-X interrupt delivery are some of the additional features offered by this adapter. It requires VM hardware version 7 or later, and it is supported by a limited set of guest OS:

Available adapter types in vSphere 6.5

Virtual disks

A virtual disk stores the actual VM data and the VM can be configured to use a new disk, attach an existing disk, or map SAN LUN. A LUN to a VMFS map is referred to as a **Raw Device Mapping (RDM)** that points to the raw LUN. In this case, the .vmdk file (.vmdk files will be discussed later in the file structure) doesn't store data (data is stored on the LUN) but it contains only the mapping to the LUN disk information.

Virtual disks can be moved across different datastores connected to the host on which the VM runs. When a new disk is created, it can be provisioned in three different formats depending on the requirements:

- **Thick provision lazy zeroed**: The default format; space on the datastore is allocated when the VM is created and data on the physical device is not erased.
- **Thick provision eager zeroed**: The format used to support specific configuration, such as vSphere FT or some SQL installations; it allocates space on the datastore when the disk is created. As compared to lazy zeroed format, data on the physical device is zeroed out at creation time. Thick provision eager zeroed format takes a longer time to be provisioned.
- **Thin provision**: This is used to save space on the storage; it's the fastest method to create a new disk. This format doesn't allocate all the requested disk space at creation, but at the beginning, it only uses the space required by the initial operations of the disk, growing in size until the maximum configured size is reached.

The disk format of a VM can be changed using the vSphere Storage vMotion feature:

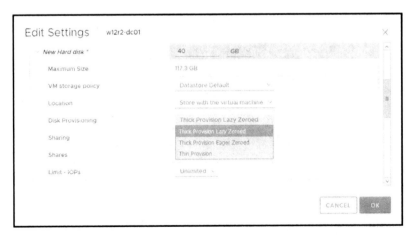

A VM disk can be configured in three formats

Storage controller

Added by default during VM creation, the storage controller is used to access virtual disks, CD/DVD devices, and SCSI devices. Storage controllers are presented to VMs as different types of storage controllers—BusLogic Parallel, LSI Logic Parallel, LSI Logic SAS, VMware Paravirtual SCSI, AHCI, SATA, and NVMe, as described in Chapter 7, *Advanced Storage Management*.

Generally, the default controller optimized for best performance is assigned to the VM based on the guest OS selection, device type, and VM compatibility. A maximum of four SATA, four SCSI, and four NVMe controllers are supported for each VM. If during the VM creation, the Windows Server 2008 or 2012 guest OS is selected, for example, the LSI Logic SAS controller is assigned by the system.

When a VM is created, two storage controllers are assigned by default:

- **SATA:** This controller is assigned to access CD/DVD devices and supports up to 30 devices. If you have multiple disks, to distribute the load and improve performance, you can add up to four controllers per VM. An AHCI SATA controller is supported for VMs with ESXi 5.5 and later compatibility. A SATA controller is supported by most guest OS and is assigned by default to CD/DVD devices.
- **SCSI**: Depending on the guest OS, many VMs have this controller configured by default. A single controller supports up to 15 devices. If you have multiple disks, to distribute the load and improve performance, you can add up to four controllers per VM. In the new SCSI controller, you can enable **SCSI bus sharing** to allow the virtual disk to be shared by the VM, for example, for building a guest cluster. There are three possible options available:

    None: Virtual disk cannot be shared
    Physical: Virtual disk can be shared by VM on the same host
    Virtual: Virtual disk can be shared by VM on any host

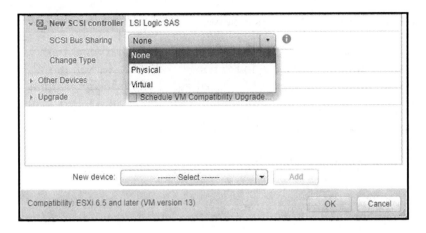

Available SCSI bus sharing options

File structure

A VM is composed by several files that typically reside on a datastore in the VMs folder. Settings of VMs are managed through vSphere Client but you can also use the command line using PowerCLI, vCLI, or the vSphere Web Services SDK. PowerCLI and vCLI were discussed in Chapter 5, *Configuring and Managing vSphere 6.5*.

The core files that compose a VM are as follows:

- .vmx: This is a plain-text file that stores the configuration of the VM. The file contains information related to the hardware that resides in the VM, such as processor number, amount of RAM, disks, MAC address, virtual hardware version, number of NICs connected, virtual disk location, and so on:

```
 7  pciBridge4.present = "TRUE"
 8  pciBridge4.virtualDev = "pcieRootPort"
 9  pciBridge4.functions = "8"
10  pciBridge5.present = "TRUE"
11  pciBridge5.virtualDev = "pcieRootPort"
12  pciBridge5.functions = "8"
13  pciBridge6.present = "TRUE"
14  pciBridge6.virtualDev = "pcieRootPort"
15  pciBridge6.functions = "8"
16  pciBridge7.present = "TRUE"
17  pciBridge7.virtualDev = "pcieRootPort"
18  pciBridge7.functions = "8"
19  vmci0.present = "TRUE"
20  hpet0.present = "TRUE"
21  floppy0.present = "FALSE"
22  svga.vramSize = "8388608"
23  memSize = "4096"
24  tools.upgrade.policy = "manual"
25  scsi0.virtualDev = "lsisas1068"
26  scsi0.pciSlotNumber = "160"
27  scsi0.present = "TRUE"
28  sata0.pciSlotNumber = "33"
29  sata0.present = "TRUE"
30  scsi0:0.deviceType = "scsi-hardDisk"
31  scsi0:0.fileName = "w12r2-dc01.vmdk"
32  scsi0:0.present = "TRUE"
33  sata0:0.startConnected = "FALSE"
34  sata0:0.deviceType = "atapi-cdrom"
35  sata0:0.clientDevice = "TRUE"
36  sata0:0.fileName = "CD/DVD drive 0"
37  sata0:0.present = "TRUE"
38  vmci0.pciSlotNumber = "32"
39  ethernet0.virtualDev = "vmxnet3"
40  ethernet0.networkName = "VM Network"
41  ethernet0.addressType = "generated"
42  ethernet0.pciSlotNumber = "192"
43  ethernet0.uptCompatibility = "TRUE"
44  ethernet0.present = "TRUE"
45  displayName = "w12r2-dc01"
46  guestOS = "windows8srv-64"
47  disk.EnableUUID = "TRUE"
48  toolScripts.afterPowerOn = "TRUE"
```

The .vmx file contains the configuration of the VM

The `.vmx` file contains a list of keys and related values that identify the components configured in the selected VM. To determine, for example, the configured RAM or the installed OS in the VM, you need to scroll down the list and identify the keys, `memSize` and `guestOS`, that indicate the requested information. The `.vmx` file is only the configuration file of the VM and doesn't store any data from the guest OS. Responsible for storing actual data of the VM is the virtual hard disk file with a `.vmdk` extension.

- `.vmdk`: This identifies the virtual hard disk of the VM that holds the data of the guestOS instance. A VM can have one or more `.vmdk` files depending on the disks configured in the `.vmx` file. For instance, if you configure disks **C:** and **D:** in a VM running Windows OS, you will have two `.vmdk` files, one for each configured drive.

If you browse the datastore where the VM resides, you are able to see only a single `.vmdk` file (if the VM is configured with a single drive). Technically, the virtual hard disk is composed by two files with the same extension—a VMDK descriptor and a VMDK flat. *What is their role?* Let's have a look.

The `.vmdk` file is the descriptor file, a plain-text file that contains the configuration information and pointers to the flat file. Generally, the `.vmdk` descriptor file is a small file in size. The `-flat.vmdk` is generally a large binary file that contains the actual data of the VM where its size is defined in the `.vmx` configuration file. The `.vmdk` file can start from a few GB in size and growing up to 62 TB (the maximum size supported in vSphere 6.5 Update 1). To see both `.vmdk` and `-flat.vmdk` files, you need to access the command line, navigating into the datastores folder where the VM resides and running the command `ls -lh`:

```
[root@esxi01:/vmfs/volumes/599ecc3b-a52c195f-15b4-000c296a6341/w12r2-dc01] ls -lh
total 17376320
-rw-r--r--   1 root     root      383.5K Aug 24 17:21 vmware-1.log
-rw-r--r--   1 root     root      680.3K Aug 30 06:45 vmware-2.log
-rw-r--r--   1 root     root      259.2K Sep  2 12:48 vmware-3.log
-rw-r--r--   1 root     root      251.7K Sep  2 20:58 vmware.log
-rw-------   1 root     root      110.0M Sep  2 16:21 vmx-w12r2-dc01-2701646168-1.vswp
-rw-------   1 root     root        4.0G Sep  2 21:18 w12r2-dc01-a107d958.vswp
-rw-------   1 root     root       30.0G Sep  2 21:23 w12r2-dc01-flat.vmdk
-rw-------   1 root     root        8.5K Sep  2 16:06 w12r2-dc01.nvram
-rw-------   1 root     root         552 Sep  2 16:06 w12r2-dc01.vmdk
-rw-r--r--   1 root     root           0 Aug 24 16:56 w12r2-dc01.vmsd
-rwxr-xr-x   1 root     root        2.6K Sep  2 16:06 w12r2-dc01.vmx
-rw-------   1 root     root           0 Aug 24 20:29 w12r2-dc01.vmx.lck
-rw-------   1 root     root        3.1K Aug 24 20:36 w12r2-dc01.vmxf
-rwxr-xr-x   1 root     root        2.6K Sep  2 16:06 w12r2-dc01.vmx~
[root@esxi01:/vmfs/volumes/599ecc3b-a52c195f-15b4-000c296a6341/w12r2-dc01]
```

To identify the .vmdk and -flat.vmdk files you need to run the ls -lh command from the console

The flat file does not exist on a vSAN datastore.

- `.nvram`: This is a binary file that cannot be edited and contains the VM BIOS or EFI configuration. If you delete this file, it will be automatically recreated when the VM is powered on.
- `.log`: This is saved in the same directory as the VM configuration files and contains the logs of the VM activities. It can be used for troubleshooting if you encounter a problem.
- `.vswp`: For each powered-on VM, there are two files that are used as swap files in case of huge RAM contentions. The biggest is usually the size of the vRAM of the VM minus the vRAM reservation.

Snapshot-related files will be described later.

Changing the default file position

By default, all VM-related files are in a single folder with the original VM name (or the VM name after a VM storage migration). You can change this behavior for different type of files and for different reasons:

- **VMDK files**: Having virtual disks in different datastores allows you to choose the proper type of disks with the proper performance and service level. You can choose a new location when you add a new virtual disk, or simply choose different locations for each VMDK when you apply a storage migration.
- **Swap file**: Migrating VM swap (`.vswp`) files to a different datastore is possible and described in KB 2003956—*Migrating virtual machine swap (.vswp) files from one datastore to another* (`https://kb.vmware.com/kb/2003956`). You can also use an SSD datastore for this purpose, but usually the need for a different position occurs when storage array replication is used and you need to avoid swap file replication.
- **Log files**: By default, ESXi/ESX hosts store VMs specific logging in the same directory as the VM configuration files. VM logs can be reconfigured to archive at different intervals, with different names, in different volumes, or when the log reaches a specific size. For more information, see KB 1007805—*Locating virtual machine log files on an ESXi/ESX host* (`https://kb.vmware.com/kb/1007805`).

- **Snapshot files**: All files comprising snapshots are created in the VM working directory, that, by default, is the same directory as that of the VM. The working directory can be changed with KB 1002929—*Creating snapshots in a different location than default virtual machine directory for VMware ESXi and VMware ESX* (`https://kb.vmware.com/kb/1002929`).

VMware Tools

VMware Tools is a set of utilities installed on the guest OS that improves the overall performance and gives better control of the VM, making administration easier. VMware Tools is not installed by default.

Although, a guest OS can run without VMware Tools, the management of power controls and other features is not available until you install VMware Tools. Shutdown or restart options, for example, are not available without VMware Tools. An improved graphic interface, a better mouse control, and the ability to copy and paste files are some of main benefits you notice at first sight after the installation.

VMware Tools delivered with vSphere 6.5 introduces some enhancements that improve the manageability experience:

- **Signed ISO images**: VMware Tools is distributed as ISO images to be mounted to individual VMs to install or upgrade. To increase security, in ESXi 6.5, the ISO images are cryptographically verified each time they are read. Additional files with appropriate signatures have been included in the VMware Tools distributions to help this verification.
- **Bifurcation of VMware Tools for legacy and current guests**: vSphere 6.5 delivers two versions of VMware Tools, 10.1 and 10.0.12 described as follows:
  - Version 10.1 is available for OEM-supported guest OS only
  - Version 10.0.12 is offered as frozen VMware Tools that won't receive further enhancements for guests no longer supported by their vendors
- **Bundling of tools for most popular guests only**: ESXi 6.5 includes VMware Tools for the most widely used guest OS but VMware also provides tools for other guests (see download at `https://my.vmware.com/web/vmware`).

For more information on VMware Tools, see the blog post at https://blogs.vmware.com/vsphere/2017/11/every-vsphere-admin-must-know-vmware-tools.html.

A recommended practice is to upgrade to the latest VMware Tools version included in your ESXi. VMware vSphere 6.5 Update 1 includes VMware Tools version 10.1.7.

Open VM Tools (OVT)

OVT is an open source implementation of VMware Tools specific for Linux that allows you to bundle the tools into the guest OS, avoiding the management of the VMware Tools lifecycle. OVT is delivered with RPM packages or with yum or apt.

To install OVT in a VM, access the system console and run the following command:

```
# yum install open-vm-tools
```

```
[root@lx6-vsftp01 /]# yum install open-vm-tools
Loaded plugins: fastestmirror, presto
Setting up Install Process
Loading mirror speeds from cached hostfile
 * base: it.centos.contactlab.it
 * epel: mirror.daniel-jost.net
 * extras: centos.mirror.iphh.net
 * rpmforge: mirror.chpc.utah.edu
 * updates: it.centos.contactlab.it
Resolving Dependencies
--> Running transaction check
---> Package open-vm-tools.x86_64 0:10.1.5-6.el6 will be installed
--> Processing Dependency: xmlsec1-openssl for package: open-vm-tools-10.1.5-6.e
16.x86_64
--> Processing Dependency: libfuse.so.2(FUSE_2.6)(64bit) for package: open-vm-to
ols-10.1.5-6.el6.x86_64
```

The yum command used to install the Open VM Tools

At the time of writing, OVT is available for the following OS:

- Fedora 19 and later releases
- Debian 7.x and later releases
- openSUSE 11.x and later releases
- Recent Ubuntu releases (12.04 LTS, 13.10 and later)
- Red Hat Enterprise Linux 7.0 and later releases
- CentOS 7.0 and later releases

- Oracle Linux 7.0 and later releases
- SUSE Linux Enterprise 11 SP4, 12 and later releases

Deploying VMs

The creation of VMs in vSphere 6.5 is a core task and different methods are available for deployment. The most suitable deployment method to use depends on the goal of the VM, the configuration, and the type of infrastructure the VM will run on.

You can create a VM with the following methods:

- **Creating a VM from scratch**: If you need a VM with a specific configuration, OS, or application and it's not already present in your environment.
- **Using templates**: If a VM has the requirements you need and it's often deployed, the use of a template (a master copy of a VM) is the option to consider. This option requires a minor setup after the deployment and allows you to save time.
- **Cloning**: If similar VMs are deployed in your environment, the cloning option requires less time than creating and configuring a VM from scratch.
- **Virtual appliance**: A VM with an OS and applications already installed is distributed in **Open Virtual Machine Format** (**OVF**) and it's a ready-to-run VM. Several vendors offer their applications as virtual appliances in OVF format in order to have a fully working, ready-to-run VM.

To identify what method is suitable for your environment, let's have a closer look at these options to better understand the differences and use cases.

Creating a new VM

You create a new VM when you need a VM with a specific configuration and with a specific OS, and it is not already installed on your virtual infrastructure. When the VM is created from scratch, you are able to define the virtual hardware to use (CPU, RAM, hard disks). The default disk assigned to the VM can be removed adding a new one, selected from an existing disk or added as RDM.

To create a new VM, follow this procedure:

1. From vSphere Client, access vCenter Server and right-click a valid parent object from the inventory (it can be a datacenter, cluster, resource pool, or host) then select **New Virtual Machine...** option.

2. From the **New Virtual Machine Wizard**, select the **Create a new virtual machine** option to proceed with a new installation.

3. Enter a VM name and specify the location for the VM then click **Next**. If you place the VM into a cluster with DRS disabled or set in manual mode, you need to specify the host on which to create the VM.

4. Select a compute resource (cluster, host, or resource pool) the VM will access for taking the resources and click **Next**. In this step, a compatibility check is performed against the selected location to avoid compatibility issues. If the checks succeeded, you can proceed with the next step.

5. Select the datastore or datastore cluster to store the configuration and virtual hard disk files that meet the VM requirements (performance, size). Make sure you have enough space for VM creation and operations related to the VM operations (for example, snapshots). Click **Next**.

6. Select the VM compatibility from the **Compatible with** drop-down menu to specify the version of ESXi the machine can run on. This setting determines the virtual hardware (hardware version is covered later in this chapter) available to the VM, such as available virtual PCI slots, maximum number of CPUs, maximum RAM config, and so on:

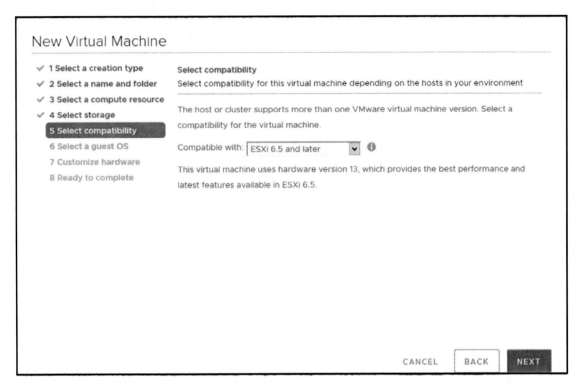

New Virtual Machine

✓ 1 Select a creation type
✓ 2 Select a name and folder
✓ 3 Select a compute resource
✓ 4 Select storage
5 Select compatibility
6 Select a guest OS
7 Customize hardware
8 Ready to complete

Select compatibility
Select compatibility for this virtual machine depending on the hosts in your environment

The host or cluster supports more than one VMware virtual machine version. Select a compatibility for the virtual machine.

Compatible with: | ESXi 6.5 and later | ▾ | ⓘ

This virtual machine uses hardware version 13, which provides the best performance and latest features available in ESXi 6.5.

CANCEL   BACK   NEXT

Select the compatibility to specify the version of the ESXi the machine can run on

7. Select the OS family(Windows, Linux, other) and the version of the guest OS the VM will run. The OS selection determines the supported devices and the vCPU number available for the VM.

When the OS is selected, by default, BIOS or EFI are assigned to the VM depending on the supported firmware by the OS (you can change the default from the **Option** tab). macOS X Server guest supports EFI only (macOS X Server must run on Apple hardware). Make your selection and click **Next**.

Because the guest OS partitions the disk based on the firmware it was booted from, don't change the firmware when the OS has been installed otherwise the guest won't boot.

8. In the **Customize hardware** screen, you have the option to customize the virtual hardware presented to the VM. You can adjust the number of vCPUs to use, specify the amount of RAM, add a new NIC, add a new virtual disk or remove a device not needed (for example, floppy drive), and so on. The hardware available and the maximum supported are determined by the VM compatibility settings. Click **Next** when done.

9. Review the VM settings and click **Finish** to create the VM. Keep in mind that you are creating the configuration only while the OS hasn't been installed yet. Once created, the VM will appear in the vCenter Server inventory:

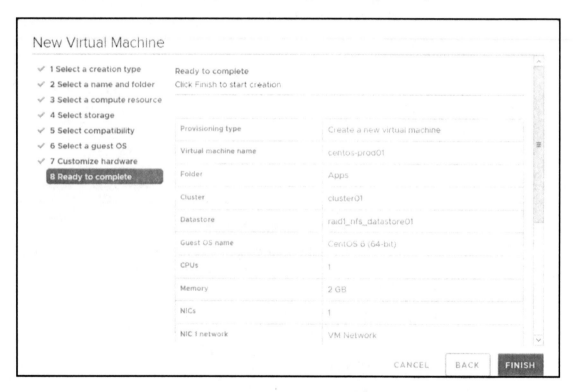

The summary window displays the settings used in the virtual machine

Hardware version

The hardware version defines the virtual hardware available to the VM that corresponds to the physical hardware available on the host. vSphere 6.5 introduces hardware version 13 and supports VMs created with previous hardware versions. Each hardware version supports at least five major or minor vSphere releases. By default, the compatibility of the VM is given by the host version on which the VM is created, or by the inventory object on which the default VM compatibility is set.

A question you might have is—*"what hardware version should I use?"*. The hardware version to use depends on what version of ESXi your environment uses. If you have multiple hosts with different versions, you should choose the correct hardware version to match the lowest version host used in the infrastructure (for example, hardware version 13 is not supported by ESXi 5.5 or 6.0).

However, a lower version will have a reduced functionality and a VM with a higher hardware version configured won't be supported by a VMware product with a lower version. If your environment runs vSphere 6.5, the suggestion is to configure the running VM with the highest hardware version available to take the benefit of the latest features.

Different VM versions can be created, edited, and run on a host if the host supports that version. Actions on a host are limited or the VM has no access to the host if the VM's configured hardware version is greater than the version supported by the host.

VM hardware versions can be summarized in the table as:

	Hardware version						
ESXi/ESX version	Version 13	Version 11	Version 10	Version 9	Version 8	Version 7	Version 4
ESXi 6.5	Create, Edit, Run	Create, Edit, Run	Create, Edit, Run	Create, Edit, Run	Create, Edit, Run	Create, Edit, Run	Create, Edit, Run
ESXi 6.0	Not Supported	Create, Edit, Run	Create, Edit, Run	Create, Edit, Run	Create, Edit, Run	Create, Edit, Run	Create, Edit, Run
ESXi 5.5	Not Supported	Not Supported	Create, Edit, Run	Create, Edit, Run	Create, Edit, Run	Create, Edit, Run	Create, Edit, Run
ESXi 5.1	Not Supported	Not Supported	Not Supported	Create, Edit, Run	Create, Edit, Run	Create, Edit, Run	Create, Edit, Run
ESXi 5.0	Not Supported	Not Supported	Not Supported	Not Supported	Create, Edit, Run	Create, Edit, Run	Create, Edit, Run
ESXi/ESX 4.x	Not Supported	Not Supported	Not Supported	Not Supported	Not Supported	Create, Edit, Run	Create, Edit, Run
ESX 3.x	Not Supported	Not Supported	Not Supported	Not Supported	Not Supported	Not Supported	Create, Edit, Run

Table 8.1: Virtual machine hardware version

The chosen version determines not only the hardware available to the VM but also the supported OS. That is, during the deployment of the VM, the OS supported depends on the hardware version configured.

 To run Windows Server 2012, you need at least virtual hardware version 8, otherwise the Windows Server 2012 guest OS option won't be available.

Setting the default hardware version

By default, the VM compatibility is configured to use the datacenter settings and host version. In vCenter Server, you can define a default hardware version for VM creation on a host, cluster, or datacenter.

To configure the default hardware version, perform these steps:

1. From vSphere Client, log in to vCenter Server and right-click the object to configure and select **Edit Default VM Compatibility**.
2. From the **Compatible with** drop-down menu, select the hardware version to use and click **OK** to confirm. When a VM is created in this cluster, the default compatibility setting is used:

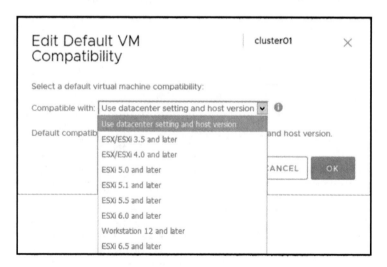

The default compatibility of a VM can be changed to meet the requirements

Installing the OS

Once the VM has been created, you need to install the OS as you would do for a physical machine. There are two methods available to install the OS on a VM:

- **Using PXE**: You don't need any installation media for this installation type and the guest OS you install must support PXE installation.
- **From media**: You install the guest OS from CD/DVD media or from an ISO image. The use of ISO images is generally faster.

To select what mode the VM should boot, you need to adjust the boot order. To change the boot order, you need to edit the VM BIOS:

1. Edit the VM settings and expand the option **Boot Options** under the **VM Options** tab.
2. Enable the **Force BIOS setup** option to access the BIOS setup screen the next time the VM boots and click **OK**.

Using an ISO image is generally the fastest method to install a VM OS:

1. After downloading the ISO image file, upload the guest OS media to install on a VMFS or NFS datastore accessible by the host. Alternatively, you can also use a Content Library (this will be discussed later in this chapter) to store the ISO image file.

2. From vSphere Client, right-click the virtual machine to install and select **Edit Settings**. Access the **Virtual Hardware** tab and expand the **CD/DVD drive 1** to specify the installation method:

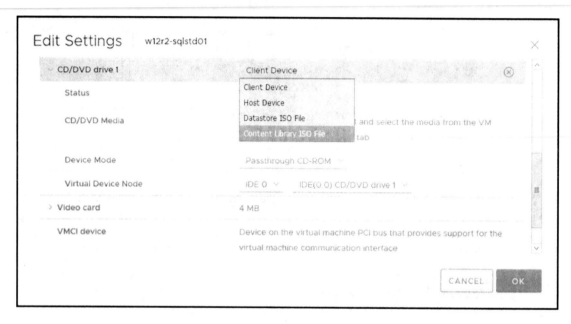

The installation method to use is selected from the Virtual Hardware tab

3. From the **CD/DVD drive 1** drop-down menu, select the installation method you want to use from the available options:

- **Client Device**: The CD-ROM of your machine will be accessed to install the guest OS
- **Host Device**: The CD-ROM of ESXi will be accessed to install the guest OS
- **Datastore ISO File**: The ISO image file of the guest OS is selected from the datastore on which you previously uploaded the file
- **Content Library ISO File**: Select the ISO image to mount from the Content Library (the creation of a Content Library is discussed later in this chapter)

Select the method to use and click **OK** to confirm.

4. Right-click the VM to install and select **Power | Power On**. Make sure you have set the correct boot order.

5. Follow the installation options of the guest OS to complete the installation.

Installing VMware Tools

Although a VM can run without VMware Tools, VMware highly recommends installing the latest version to enable advanced features (graphic, networking, mouse, storage, and so on). If a VM doesn't have VMware Tools installed, a warning message is displayed in the VM **Summary** tab.

Again, if a VM doesn't have VMware Tools, it's strongly recommended you install it to take advantage of the added features to improve performance and global functionality:

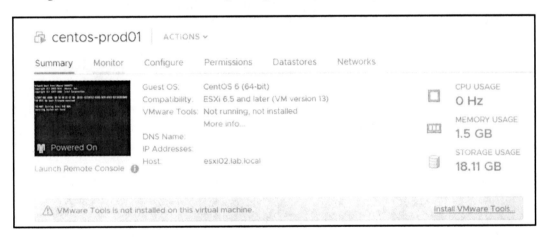

A warning message is displayed when the installed VMware Tools is outdated

The installation of VMware Tools can be performed in three ways:

- **Using vSphere Client**: You can install or upgrade VMware Tools on a single VM at a time
- **Using VUM**: If more VMs need to install or upgrade VMware Tools, you can automate the process using VUM (VUM will be covered in `Chapter 11`, *Lifecycle Management, Patching, and Upgrade*)

- **Using other tools**: You can also use tools such as a Linux repository or a standalone version of VMware Tools, downloadable from the **Driver** and **Utilities** tab

To install the VMware Tools, the steps are the following:

1. From vSphere Client, right-click the running VM to process and select **Guest OS | Install VMware Tools** to mount the disk image in the virtual CD/DVD of the VM
2. Access the guest OS and proceed with the installation

The installation takes a few seconds and may require the reboot of the VM.

 A quick way to perform the installation is by clicking the **Install VMware Tools** link from the warning message in the **Summary** tab of the VM.

VMware Tools is included in the ESXi distribution and the bundled tools ISO image files are located in the `/locker/packages/` directory. If you want a central repository on a shared datastore, look at VMware KB 2129825—*Installing and upgrading the latest version of VMware Tools on existing hosts* (`https://kb.vmware.com/kb/2129825`).

Deploying a VM from a template

The deployment of a VM from a template is performed by creating a new VM from a copy of a template configured with specific virtual hardware and software. Template deployment is the recommended option, if you need to deploy several machines with the same requirements. Proceed with the steps as follows:

1. Go to the **VMs and Templates** inventory view and right-click the template from which to deploy the new VM.
2. Select **New VM from This Template...** to create a new VM based on the selected template:

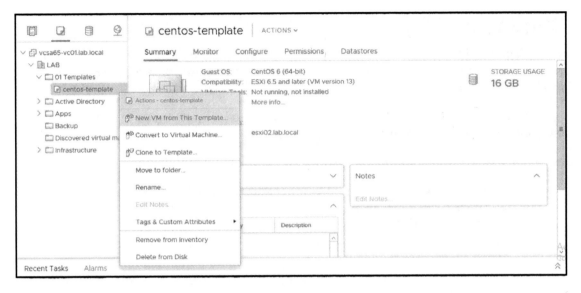

A VM created from a template

3. Specify a name of the VM and specify the location in which to place the VM by selecting a datacenter or folders, depending on your organizational needs. Click **Next**.

4. Select a compute resource to allow the VM to access the resources of the selected object. If the chosen location causes compatibility issues, a warning message is displayed in the compatibility area. If the checks succeed, click **Next** to continue.

5. Select the datastore in which to store the VM files. You can specify the format of the virtual disk (we talked earlier about disk format in the *Virtual disks* section) you want to configure then click **Next**.

6. In **Select clone options**, you can customize the guest OS to prevent conflicts due to a duplicate computer name or IP address and automatically power on the virtual machine once deployed. The guest OS customization allows you to modify the computer name, license, and network settings. When the desired option has been selected, click **Next**.

7. In the summary window, click **Finish** to deploy the new VM based on the selected template.

Cloning a VM

A VM deployed by cloning another VM creates an exact copy of the original VM. Cloning is the fastest method to deploy a new VM if an existing VM has the same features and applications you need for the new installation.

This procedure allows you to save time during deployment because you just need to clone and configure a few parameters.

To deploy a new VM by cloning an existing one, follow the steps as:

1. From vSphere Client, log in to vCenter Server and access the inventory view. Right-click the VM to clone and select **Clone** | **Clone to Virtual Machine** to create a new VM.
2. Enter a name of the virtual machine and select the location in which to deploy the VM then click **Next**.
3. Select a compute resource to allow the VM to access the resources of the selected object. If the compatibility checks succeed, click **Next** to continue.
4. Select the storage in which to store the configuration and disk files. Make sure you have sufficient space in the selected datastore. Specify the virtual disk format and click **Next**.
5. In **Select clone options**, you can customize the guest OS to prevent conflicts (duplicate computer name or IP address already in use) and automatically power on the VM once deployed. Click **Next**.
6. In the summary window, click **Finish** to begin the cloning process of the selected VM.

Deploying Open Virtual Format (OVF) and Open Virtual Appliance (OVA) templates

Virtual machines can be exported in OVF and OVA formats and deployed in the same or different environments. OVA and OVF are compressed file packages that enable faster deployment and may contain more than one VM. As compared to previous releases, in vSphere 6.5, the installation of the CIP is no longer required to import and export OVF or OVA templates.

The procedure to deploy a VM from an OVF or OVA file is similar to the deployment from a template:

1. From vSphere Web Client, right-click a valid inventory object (host, datacenter, cluster, or resource pool) and select **Actions** | **Deploy OVF Template...** option:

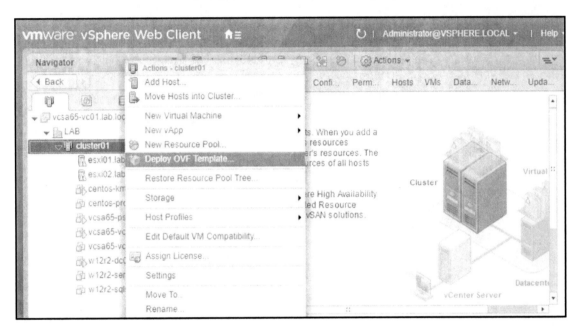

A virtual machine can be deployed from an OVF or OVA file

2. Click the **Browse...** button to specify the `.ovf` file to use then click **Next**.
3. Enter a name and select a location to deploy the VM. Click **Next**.
4. Select the resource to run the deployed appliance and click **Next**. A validation check is performed.
5. Review the details to verify whether the configuration is correct. Click **Next** to define the storage to use.
6. Specify the virtual disk format (*do you remember that we have three formats available?* thick lazy zeroed, thick eager zeroed, and thin) and select the location in which to store the files. Click **Next** to continue.
7. Select the network to use from the **Destination Network** drop-down menu then click **Next**.
8. Click **Finish** to begin the deployment of the VM.

The OVF template can also be used to export a captured state of the VM in a compressed and sparsed format. The procedure to export an OVF template requires that the VM is powered off before proceeding:

1. From vSphere Client, right-click the VM to export and select the **Template | Export OVF Template** option.
2. Specify the virtual machine name and, optionally, an annotation that can be useful to better identify the VM configuration. To include additional information or configurations, such as BIOS UUID or MAC addresses, tick **Enable advanced options**. Be careful if you enable these options because the portability will be limited. Click **OK** to proceed with the export:

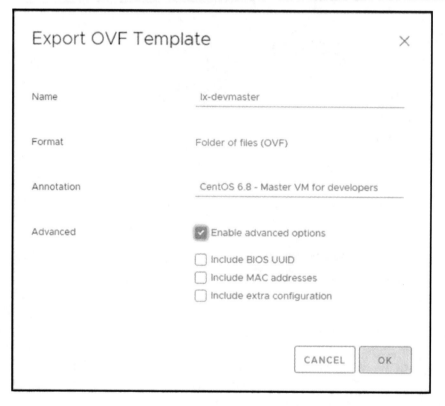

A VM can be exported to be used in a different environment

3. Specify where to save each file associated with the template.

Creating a Content Library

A **Content Library** is a container object to store templates, vApps, or other files that can be shared across multiple vCenter Server instances in the same or different locations to ensure consistency and compliance within the infrastructure.

vSphere 6.5 introduced new features and some enhancements that improve performance and recoverability. You can now mount an ISO directly from the Content Library, apply a guest OS customization during VM deployment, and update existing templates. The Content Library is now included in the vSphere 6.5 backup/restore service as well as the VC HA feature set. A VM template, a vApp template, or another type of file in a library is defined as a *library item* that can contain a single or multiple files (ISO, OVF, and so on).

You can create two types of Content Library:

- **Local**: This is used to store items on a single vCenter Server instance that can be published to allow other users from other vCenter Servers to subscribe
- **Subscribed library**: This is created when you subscribe to a published library and can be created in the same vCenter Server of the published library or in a different vCenter Server instance

If the subscribed library is created in a different vCenter Server, the option to download all contents or metadata only can be configured in the Create Library wizard. To keep the content of a subscribed library up to date, the subscribed library automatically synchronizes to the source published library on a regular basis. Synchronization of the subscribed library can also be done manually.

To create a Content Library, proceed as follows:

1. From vSphere Client, access vCenter Server and from the menu, select **Content Libraries** and click on the create a new library icon with the **+** sign to open the Create Library wizard.
2. Enter a name and a description in the note field then click **Next**.
3. Specify the type of Content Library you want to create (local or subscribed) then click **Next**.
4. Select the datastore used to store the library's content and click **Next**.
5. Review the settings and click **Finish** to create the library.

6. Right-click on the created Content Library and select the **Import item** option to import content to the library:

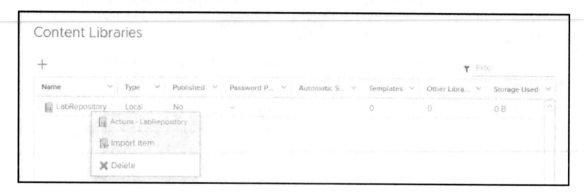

The Import item option used to import content to the library

7. You can import contents by specifying a URL or a local file. If you import the content from a local file, you locate the file through the **Browse...** button. You can also edit the name of the item to better identify the template. Click **OK** to import the required item.

8. If more than an item has been imported into the library, the **Templates** or **Other Library Items** columns display the number of actual items available.

Managing VMs

When VMs have been deployed in your infrastructure, you can start the administration using the available tools and features offered by vSphere Client. Several actions can be performed on VMs to keep a clean inventory and a healthy infrastructure. Let's have a look at some common procedures an administrator performs on a regular basis.

Adding or registering an existing VM

VM can be created or deployed using the different methods shown previously. In some circumstances, you might need to put in your production environment a pre-created VM from another source. You may wonder *how do I deploy this virtual machine?*. The procedure is not complicated at all; let's see.

First, using vSphere Client, you need to upload the VM files (generally the .vmx and .vmdk files) to an attached datastore reachable by the hosts. When the files are in the datastore, you have to register the VM to add it to the vCenter Server or ESXi host inventory. Once the VM has been added to the inventory, you can start using and managing the VM.

To register a VM to the inventory, follow this procedure:

1. From vSphere Client, log in to vCenter Server and select the **Storage** view.
2. Select the storage and the folder in which the VM has been stored.
3. From the available files in the selected folder, select the file with the extension .vmx and click **Register VM** to register the VM to the inventory:

Adding a VM to the inventory

4. By default, the system populates the **Virtual machine name** field, reading the info from the .vmx file. Enter a different name if you want to change the default instead. Specify a location in which to run the VM and click **Next**.
5. Select the compute resource the VM will access to get resources. If the compatibility checks succeed, click **Next** to continue.
6. When you are ready to complete, click **Finish** to register and add the VM to the inventory.

When the VM has been added to the inventory, you can power it on and manage it as you would do with other VMs.

Removing or deleting a VM

Removing and deleting a VM are two simple but different procedures that lead to different results. Removing a VM from the inventory doesn't delete the VM (the files still remain in the same location on storage), but removes its view from the inventory and it won't be listed any more. Removing a VM from the inventory can be useful if you want to remove a no longer used VM but you want to keep the data.

In order to remove a VM, the VM must be powered off. The procedure is quite simple:

1. Right-click the VM to remove and select the **Remove from Inventory** option
2. Click **Yes** to confirm the removal

When you delete a VM, instead, all VM files are removed from the datastore with no way to recover them if the deletion is done by mistake. *How do we recover a VM that has been deleted accidentally?* Backup.

The deletion procedure is similar to what we have done previously:

1. Right-click the powered-off (option will be grayed out if the VM is still running) VM to delete and select the **Delete from Disk** option
2. Click **Yes** to confirm the deletion

Managing the power state of a VM

In vSphere 6.5, you can change the VM power state in different ways. To change the power state, right-click the VM and select **Power** followed by the type of the state.

You have the following states available:

- **Power On** and **Power Off**: This function powers the VM on or off immediately without any interaction with the guest OS. Be careful when powering off the VM because the process doesn't perform a clean shutdown of open files and there is the risk of corrupting some files that are not closed properly.
- **Suspend**: This feature suspends the VM, freezing its current state. When the VM is resumed, it starts from the state that was suspended.
- **Reset**: This command emulates the reset button of a physical computer.
- **Shut Down Guest OS**: This is the correct command to use to shut down the guest OS since it provides the correct shutdown of the OS, avoiding data corruption. This function is available if VMware Tools is installed on the VM.

- **Restart Guest OS**: This command is available only if VMware Tools is installed on the VM and it allows a graceful restart of the guest OS:

Power states available to VM

Managing VM snapshots

A snapshot takes a specific point in time state of a VMs you can revert from at any time. You can have several snapshots (points in time) in a VM and, depending on the changes that have occurred, you may decide to keep changes by deleting the snapshots or discard changes by reverting to a previous snapshot.

A snapshot is taken on a per-VM basis and can be used for different situations. When a new patch is released from a vendor for the guest OS running on a VM, if something goes wrong during the upgrade process, the VM can become unresponsive and sometimes the blue screen of death may be displayed, in the case of a Windows guest OS. *What to do then*? If the guest OS can't be recovered, the backup is the only lifeline you have that allows a quick recovery of the VM. If the failure occurs on a core VM and the restore from backup process requires a lot of time, users are not happy and services won't be available for a while.

Taking a snapshot before applying a patch is a trick that allows you, if something goes wrong for any reason, to immediately revert to the working state of the VM before the patch was applied, with limited service disruption.

However, the use of snapshots has some limitations:

- Raw disks and **Raw device mapping (RDM)** physical mode disks are not supported. RDM with virtual compatibility mode is supported.
- Independent disks are supported only if the VM is powered off.
- VMs configured for bus sharing are not supported.
- You can have a maximum of 32 snapshots in a chain and a single snapshot should not be kept for more than 72 hours to avoid the snapshot storage location running out of space.
- Keeping snapshots for a long time may negatively impact the VM performance.
- For disks larger than 2 TB, a snapshot creation can require a lot of time to complete.
- Snapshots should not be used as backup because if the files of the VM are lost or the storage itself fails, the snapshot files are lost as well.

Creating a snapshot

To create a snapshot, follow these steps:

1. From vSphere Client, right-click the VM you want to process and select **Snapshots | Take Snapshot**.
2. Enter a name and provide a description. If the VM is powered on during the snapshot creation, you have the option to **Snapshot the virtual machine's memory** (grayed out if the VM is off). If this option is enabled, the RAM of the VM is also included in the snapshot.

Not implemented in the HTML5-based client yet, vSphere Web Client has an additional **Quiesce guest file system (Needs VMware Tools installed)** option that brings the on-disk data into a state suitable for backups, ensuring consistent and working backups. This option is available if VMware Tools is installed on the VM:

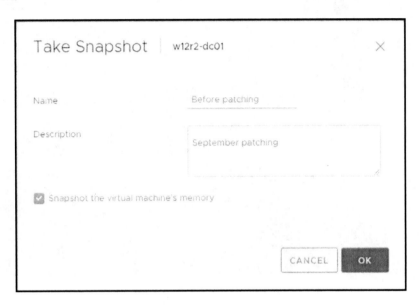

Assign a meaningful name to easily identify the snapshot

3. Click **OK** to take a snapshot of the selected VM.

When a snapshot is taken, multiple new files are created in the VM folder—.vmdk, -delta.vmdk, .vmsd, and .vmsn files:

```
[root@esxi01:/vmfs/volumes/599ecc3b-a52c195f-15b4-000c296a6341/w12r2-dc01] ls -lh
total 30221376
-rw-r--r--   1 root     root      286.5K Sep 21 06:34 vmware.log
-rw-------   1 root     root      110.0M Sep  8 10:13 vmx-w12r2-dc01-2701646168-1.vswp
-rw-------   1 root     root      110.0M Sep 21 06:37 vmx-w12r2-dc01-2701646168-2.vswp
-rw-------   1 root     root        1.9G Sep 21 06:33 w12r2-dc01-000001-sesparse.vmdk
-rw-------   1 root     root         338 Sep 20 14:37 w12r2-dc01-000001.vmdk
-rw-------   1 root     root      140.0M Sep 21 06:44 w12r2-dc01-000002-sesparse.vmdk
-rw-------   1 root     root         345 Sep 21 06:33 w12r2-dc01-000002.vmdk
-rw-------   1 root     root        4.0G Sep 20 14:38 w12r2-dc01-Snapshot1.vmem
-rw-------   1 root     root        1.2M Sep 20 14:38 w12r2-dc01-Snapshot1.vmsn
-rw-------   1 root     root        4.0G Sep 21 06:34 w12r2-dc01-Snapshot2.vmem
-rw-------   1 root     root        1.2M Sep 21 06:34 w12r2-dc01-Snapshot2.vmsn
-rw-------   1 root     root        4.0G Sep 21 06:33 w12r2-dc01-a107d958.vswp
-rw-------   1 root     root       30.0G Sep 20 14:37 w12r2-dc01-flat.vmdk
-rw-------   1 root     root        8.5K Sep 21 06:34 w12r2-dc01.nvram
-rw-------   1 root     root         552 Sep 20 11:01 w12r2-dc01.vmdk
-rw-r--r--   1 root     root         834 Sep 21 06:35 w12r2-dc01.vmsd
-rwxr-xr-x   1 root     root        2.7K Sep 21 06:33 w12r2-dc01.vmx
-rw-------   1 root     root           0 Sep 20 11:01 w12r2-dc01.vmx.lck
-rw-------   1 root     root        3.1K Aug 24 20:36 w12r2-dc01.vmxf
-rwxr-xr-x   1 root     root        2.7K Sep 21 06:33 w12r2-dc01.vmx~
[root@esxi01:/vmfs/volumes/599ecc3b-a52c195f-15b4-000c296a6341/w12r2-dc01] 
```

Files created when a snapshot is taken

Let's have a look at the files created when a snapshot is taken and the role they have:

1. `vmname-00000#.vmdk`: This is a text file that contains info about the snapshot and snapshot disks. For every snapshot taken, the file is created for each of the `.vmdk` files.

2. `vmname-00000#-delta.vmdk`: This is the delta disk file that represents the difference between the current state of the VM and the state at the time of snapshot creation.

3. `vmname.vmsd`: This file holds snapshot information such as names, descriptions, and relationships between snapshots.

4. `vmname.snasphot#.vmsn`: This stores the memory state of the VM when the snapshot is taken and it is created each time you take a snapshot.

Committing changes

To commit changes and the current state of the VM, delta disks are merged with the base disks. The operation is done using the delete options in **Snapshot Manager**:

- **DELETE**: Deletes the selected snapshot from a chain, consolidating the changes that occurred between the state of the snapshot and the previous disk state to the parent snapshot
- **DELETE ALL**: All snapshots are deleted from the VM, consolidating, and writing the changes occurred between snapshots and previous delta disks to base disks, merging them with the base VM disks:

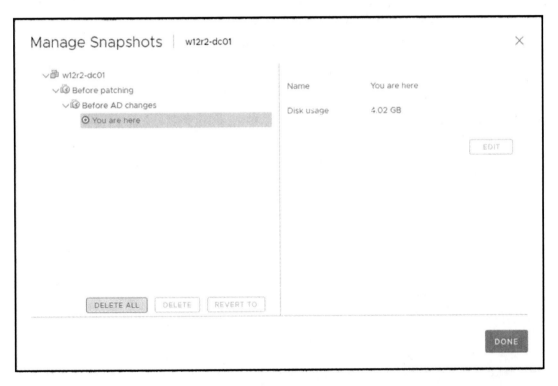

Changes are committed by deleting the snapshots from the VM

Snapshot consolidation

Snapshot consolidation is a procedure that can be used when the delete or delete all operations fail. For example, a consolidation may be required if backup software that utilizes the snapshot technology is not able to remove redundant delta disks. If the snapshots are not removed, the VM performance may suffer and the storage could run out of space. Performing a consolidation, these redundant delta disks are removed, keeping the VM in a healthy status.

To determine whether a VM requires consolidation, from vSphere Client, select the vCenter Server, cluster, or host and click the **VMs** tab. If the **Needs Consolidation** column is not visible, click the arrow on the right side of the column head and select **Show/Hide Columns...** and tick the **Needs Consolidation** option:

A VM that needs consolidation is marked with a warning

Resource management

The number of VMs that can run on ESXi is not infinite and the optimization of the resources ensures best performance. As compared to the physical world, where each server is often equipped with more resources than it actually needs, in a virtualized environment, you can allocate suitable resources to a VM based on its role and function.

An FTP server, for example, doesn't need to be equipped with a dual processor and 6 GB of RAM because the resources will be underutilized. Allocating a suitable amount of RAM and a correct number of CPUs, you can obtain best performance, saving resources for other VMs. Understanding how to manage and reallocate resources is then a key point to avoid overcommitment of resources (more demand than available capacity) that can compromise the entire infrastructure functionality.

Hosts and clusters (a group of hosts where overall CPUs and RAM are owned by the cluster) as well as datastore clusters (a group of datastores) provide physical resources to the infrastructure. Default settings configured on a VM during creation are generally suitable, but sometimes may not ensure a correct allocation of resources. You can always edit the VM settings later on to adjust assigned resources to avoid issues due to lack of resources.

Memory resources

Shares, reservation, and limit are settings used to allocate and manage memory resources for VM:

- **Shares**: Specifes the priority of a VM to get resources during a period of contention. When resources in a ESXi host are limited and the VMs compete to access resources, the VMs configured with higher shares will have higher priority to access more of the host's resources. Shares can be specified as **High**, **Normal**, or **Low** with a ratio of 4:2:1 and should be used for resource pools or sibling VMs (sibling VMs have the same parent in the resource pool hierarchy).
- **Reservation**: Specifies the minimum allocation guaranteed to a VM. When the VM is powered on, the server assigns resources based on the specified minimum reservation regardless of whether the physical server is heavily loaded. Resources are allocated only when requested by the VM and if the host's unallocated resources don't meet the reservation requirements, the VM cannot be powered on. Default reservation is set to 0.

- **Limit**: Specifies the maximum amount of resources a virtual machine can use. If the limit is not set, a VM cannot consume more resources than what is configured in its setup; if a VM is configured with 2 GB of RAM, it will be limited to consume no more than 2 GB. The default limit value is set to Unlimited.

To configure shares, reservation, and limit parameters, proceed as follows:

1. Right-click the VM to configure and select **Edit Settings**
2. Access the **Virtual Hardware** tab and expand the **Memory** item
3. Set the appropriate values then click **OK** to confirm:

Memory settings are configured in the Virtual Hardware tab

CPU resources

As for memory configuration, shares, reservation, and limit parameters can also be configured for the CPU:

- **Shares**: This parameter allows you to prioritize access to resources during resource contention. Similar to memory shares, it determines how much CPU will be provided to a VM in case of contention with other VMs.
- **Reservation**: Used to specify the minimum CPU cycles guaranteed for a VM and you can't reserve more CPU cycles than the ESXi is capable of delivering. The host must have enough physical CPU capacity to satisfy the reservation, otherwise the VM won't be able to power on.
- **Limit**: Used to prevent a VM accessing additional CPU cycles even if they are available to be used. The VM won't use more CPU cycles than specified in the limit.

To configure shares, reservation, and limit CPU parameters, follow these steps:

1. Right-click the VM to configure and select **Edit Settings**
2. Access the **Virtual Hardware** tab and expand the **CPU** item
3. Configure the parameters you need, then click **OK** to confirm:

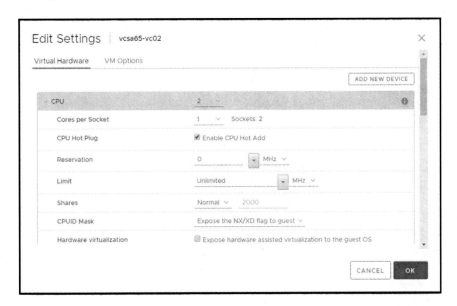

CPU settings are configured by editing the virtual hardware of the VM

To improve resource management, CPU configuration can be enhanced by enabling additional components and parameters:

- **Multicore processors**: All modern servers are equipped with multicore processors, that is, processors that combine two or more processor cores into a single circuit, referred to as a socket. This solution enables the improvement of performance, providing benefits for hosts that provide multitasking of VMs.
- **Hyperthreading**: This is a technology that allows a single physical processor core to behave like two logical processors. With this technology, a single processor core is able to execute two independent threads simultaneously, improving performance.
- **CPU affinity**: This is a configuration that assigns a specific VM to a specific physical CPU core and can be used for compliancy to license requirements. CPU affinity should be used carefully because it can introduce potential issues, such as interfering with the ESXi host's ability to meet the reservation and shares specified for a VM.

Resource pools

Resource pools are special containers used to allocate resources to a group of VMs. Previously, we have seen that the use of shares, reservation, and limit parameters allows the assignment of resources to a single VM. Unfortunately, this cannot be considered the most efficient approach for resource management, especially in large environments where the number of VMs can be high.

The use of resource pools improves resource management and can be useful to compartmentalize the resources available in a cluster, adding scalability for the control of resources for groups of VMs. Resource pools can be created in an ESXi host or in a DRS-enabled cluster.

To create a resource pool in a cluster (the procedure is similar also for the single ESXi host), proceed as follows:

1. Right-click the cluster and select the **New Resource Pool** option.
2. Specify a name for the resource pool giving a meaningful name useful to better identify the resource scope.

3. Specify how CPU and RAM resources should be allocated then click **OK**. When the resource pool has been created, you can start adding VMs to it. Share values set as **High**, **Normal**, or **Low** specify share values in a 4:2:1 ratio:

During resource pool creation, shares and reservation must be configured accordingly to assign desired resources

You may ask *how do resource pools work?*. To explain how they work, take a look at the following example. Two resource pools have been created that correspond to two different departments—**RP-DEV**, configured with CPU shares and memory set to *High*, and **RP-SALES**, with both set to *Normal*. The host can provide 6 GHz of CPU and 3 GB of memory that must be shared between the RP-DEV and RP-SALES departments:

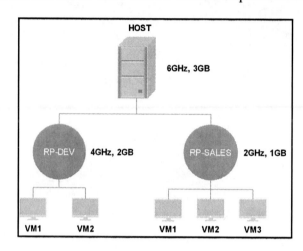

How resource pools work

Until RP-DEV doesn't use all resources, RP-SALES can use available resources. In the case of resource contention, RP-DEV will get 4 GHz of CPU and 2 GB of memory while RP-SALES will get 2 GHz and 1 GB.

Using resource pools, resources assigned to a group of VMs can be adjusted from a single point with no need to edit every single VM.

Managing resource pools

Once created, you can edit, delete, add, or remove VMs from the resource pools:

- **Edit a resource pool**: From vSphere Client, right-click the object and select **Edit Resource Settings**. Change the CPU and RAM settings then click **OK** to confirm.
- **Delete a resource pool**: From vSphere Client, right-click the resource pool and select **Delete**. Click **OK** to confirm deletion. Deleting a resource pool doesn't delete the VM it contains.

- **Adding a VM**: A VM can be added to a resource pool during the creation process, using the **Migrate...** functionality or using the drag and drop feature.
- **Removing a VM**: From a resource pool, right-click the VM to remove, and select the option **Migrate...** to move it to another resource pool. Use the drag and drop feature to move a VM off the resource pool instead.

Creating a DRS cluster

As discussed in Chapter 5, *Configuring and Managing vSphere 6.5*, a vSphere cluster is a collection of ESXi hosts that shares resources and the management interface. One of the vSphere features available only when a cluster is created is the capability to automatically balance loads across the ESXi hosts of the cluster. This feature is called **vSphere Distributed Resource Scheduler (DRS)** and provides two main functions:

- Executing the placement of the just-powered-on VM on a specific host in the cluster
- Periodically (every 5 minutes by default), DRS checks the load on the cluster, providing recommendations for migration or automatically vMotion the VM for having a balanced cluster

 If you have a DRS-enabled cluster and one of the hosts is heavily loaded compared to other host members, you might notice DRS doesn't vMotion any running VM off the host, leaving the workload unchanged. Until the ESXi host is able to satisfy resource demand from the VM, DRS doesn't perform any action. DRS ensures the cluster is balanced regardless of the workloads distributed on individual host members. To have balanced clusters and host members, there are third-party applications that provide real-time automation to efficiently allocate resources.

When a VM in a DRS-enabled cluster is powered on, the vCenter Server checks whether the cluster has enough resources to support the VM, that is, it performs admission control. If the available resources in the cluster are not sufficient to power on the VM, a warning message appears. If the resources are sufficient to support the VM, a recommendation on which host the VM should run is generated by the DRS and, based on the automation level configured in the cluster, one of the following actions is taken:

- Placement recommendation is executed automatically
- Placement recommendation is displayed, leaving the user with the option to accept or override

When DRS is disabled, no recommendations are provided and VMs are not moved among the cluster's hosts.

To enable DRS in a cluster, proceed as follows:

1. From vSphere Client, log in to vCenter Server and right-click the cluster in which you want to enable DRS and select **Settings**.
2. Under **Services**, select **vSphere DRS** and click the **Edit...** button.
3. Enable the **Turn ON vSphere DRS** option and from the **DRS Automation** drop-down menu, select the level of automation you want to apply to the cluster:

    - **Manual**: Placement and migration recommendations are displayed, but must be applied manually
    - **Partially Automated**: The initial placement is performed automatically but migration recommendations are only displayed without running
    - **Fully Automated**: Placement and migration recommendations run automatically:

DRS automation has three levels of automation

 If DRS is disabled, resource pools configured in the cluster are removed.

Virtual network-aware DRS

Virtual network-aware DRS is a new feature introduced in vSphere 6.5, where DRS now also considers the network utilization when it generates the migration recommendations. If a host has Tx and Rx rates utilization of the connected physical uplinks greater than 80%, the virtual machine won't be placed on that host. Network utilization is an additional check to evaluate whether a specific host is suitable for the VM.

Managing DRS rules

VM placement can be controlled using **affinity rules**. Affinity rules are useful for the administrators to control how specific VMs should be placed in the host members of the cluster for performance and security reasons.

Let's have a look at the DRS-supported affinity rules.

VM-VM affinity rule

The VM-VM affinity rule is used to specify that selected VMs should run on the same host. You could configure this rule to improve performance. The anti-affinity rule behaves in exactly the opposite way and it's used to ensure some VMs are kept on different hosts.

Anti-affinity can be applied to AD domain controllers, for example, to keep them on different hosts to avoid AD issues in case one host fails. Only the DC running on the failed host is not available, while the others won't be affected, continuing to provide the authentication service with no interruption.

You can't enable two affinity rules if they clash. For example, if one rule is configured to keep VMs together and another rule keeps the same VMs separated, you can't enable both. In the event of a conflict between two affinity rules, the older rule takes precedence and the newer rule is disabled.

To create a VM-VM affinity rule, perform these steps:

1. From vSphere Client, right-click the cluster to configure and select **Settings** options.
2. Under **Configuration**, select **VM/Host Rules** and click the **Add...** button.
3. Enter a name and select from the type drop-down menu one of the available options:

   - **Keep Virtual Machines Together**: The specified VMs are kept together on the same host
   - **Separate Virtual Machines**: The specified VMs are separated on different hosts

4. Click the **Add...** button to specify the VMs that must run with the specified rule. Click **OK** to save the configuration:

Affinity rules are used to keep VMs together on the same host or separated in different hosts

VM-Host affinity rule

The VM-Host affinity rule allows you to control which hosts in the cluster can run which VMs and requires that at least one VM DRS group and at least one host DRS group are created before managing host affinity rules.

To create a VM-Host affinity rule, proceed as follows:

1. From vSphere Client, right-click the cluster to configure and select the **Settings** option.
2. Under **Configuration**, select **VM/Host group** and click on the **Add...** button to create a VM group and a host group.

3. Specify a name and select from the type drop-down menu the value **VM Group**. Click the **Add...** button to add members to this group then click **OK** to save the configuration.

4. Repeat steps 2 and 3 to create a host group.

5. Now, under **Configuration**, select **VM/Host Rules** and click the **Add...** button.

6. Enter a name and select from the type drop-down menu the value **Virtual Machines to Hosts**. Specify a VM Group and the rule (for example, **Must run on hosts in group**), select the host group to associate and click **OK** to save the rule:

VM-Host affinity rule to specify which hosts in the cluster can run which VM

The options available for the rule can be one of the following:

- **Must run on hosts in group**: VMs in the selected VM Group must run on host members of the specified host group
- **Should run on hosts in group**: VMs in the VM Group should run on hosts of the specified host group but it is not required
- **Must not run on hosts in group**: VMs in the VM Group must never run on host members of the specified host group
- **Should not run on hosts in group**: VMs in the VM Group should not, but might, run on hosts of the specified host group

Managing power resources

Based on cluster resource utilization, a DRS-enabled cluster can reduce its power consumption by powering on or off ESXi hosts through the vSphere **Distributed Power Management (DPM)** feature.

Memory and CPU resources demanded by VMs in the cluster are compared with the total resource capacity available from the hosts in the cluster. If the cluster is providing excessive resources, one or more hosts are placed in standby mode by DPM and powered off after migrating the VM to other hosts. When the capacity provided is deemed not sufficient, DRS powers hosts on, bringing them out of standby mode and vMotion the VMs to them.

vSphere DPM can use three protocols to bring a host out of standby mode:

- **Intelligent Platform Management Interface (IPMI)**
- Hewlett Packard **Integrated Lights-Out (iLO)**

- **Wake-On-LAN (WOL):**

Power consumption of the cluster can be managed through the DPM feature

vSphere DPM can put a host in standby mode only if at least one protocol is supported. If a host supports multiple protocols, the following order is used: IPMI, iLO, WOL.

Managing storage and network resources

vSphere 6.5 includes additional resource management features that are useful to optimize the virtual infrastructure performance and the efficiency of hardware components, such as storage devices and network resources.

Storage I/O Control (SIOC), **Storage DRS (SDRS)**, **Storage Based Policy Management (SBPF)**, and other storage-related features (they were covered in Chapter 7, *Advanced Storage Management*), are used to control and optimize storage performance and resource availability.

Network resources can be allocated and controlled through the vSphere Network I/O Control feature to solve situations of resource contention. Network resources were discussed in `Chapter 6`, *Advanced Network Management*.

VM migration

In vSphere 6.5, VMs can be moved from one host or storage to another using hot or cold migration. Wherever possible, hot migration is the preferred option to use to avoid service disruption because it performs a live migration of the VMs:

- **Hot migration**: A powered-on VM can be moved to a different host or datastore without service disruption using the vMotion or Storage vMotion features.
- **Cold migration**: This is the migration of a powered-off or suspended VM. You can move associated disks from one datastore to another and VM are not required to be on shared storage. A cold migration can be performed manually or by scheduling a task.

The migration of a VM is performed by following this procedure:

1. From vSphere Client, log in to vCenter Server, right-click the VM to move, and click the **Migrate...** option.
2. In the **Migrate** window, select the migration type to perform, choosing from the following options:

    - **Change compute resource only**: The VM is moved to a different compute resource, such as host, cluster, resource pool, or vApp. A powered-on VM is moved using vMotion.
    - **Change storage only**: The VM disks are moved to a different datastore on the same host. The storage vMotion feature is used to move a powered-on VM to a new datastore.

- **Change both compute resource and storage**: Virtual disks are moved to a new datastore and computer resources to another host. Cold or hot migration can be used to change the host and datastore. If the network of the VM is moved between distributed switches, network configuration, and policies are transferred to the target switch:

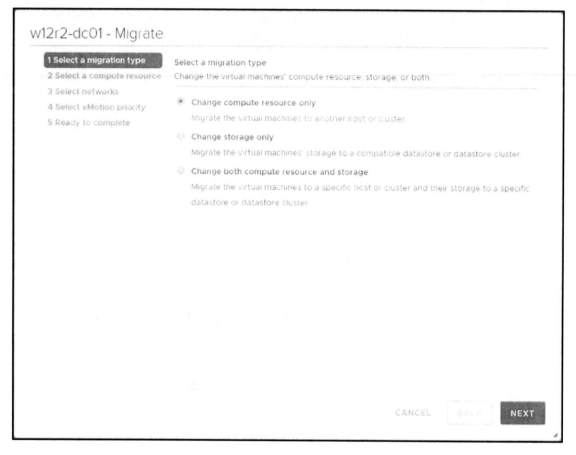

VM can be hot or cold migrated to a different host or storage

3. Based on the migration type selected, you must then specify compute resource, storage location, and vMotion priority (high or normal) to finalize the migration.

Starting from vSphere 6.0, vMotion has been enhanced, introducing new functionalities such as Cross vSwitch vMotion, **Cross vCenter vMotion (xVC-vMotion)**, and **Long Distance vMotion (LD-vMotion)**:

- **Migrate to another virtual switch**: VM can be migrated to a different type of virtual switch (standard or distributed) without reconfiguring the physical and virtual network. You can move the VM from a standard to a standard or distributed switch and from a distributed to another distributed switch.
- **Migrate to another datacenter**: During the migration, you can specify the target datacenter to move the VM between datacenters. In the target datacenter, you can specify a dedicated port group on a distributed switch for networking settings.
- **Migrate to another vCenter Server system**: VMs can be moved between vCenter Servers if they are connected in Enhanced Linked Mode and also between vCenter Servers located a long distance from each other.

vMotion without shared storage

To perform vMotion, environments with shared storage are not required. For example, you can vMotion VMs between ESXi hosts with only local storage. Migrating a VM cross-cluster, the target cluster VM might not have access to the source cluster's storage.

vMotion without shared storage can be useful during infrastructure administration tasks, such as the following:

- **Host maintenance**: You can move VMs to a different host to allow maintenance of the host
- **Storage maintenance and reconfiguration**: VMs can be moved to another storage to allow maintenance or reconfiguration without VM downtime
- **Storage load redistribution**: To improve performance or to balance capacity, VMs can be redistributed to different storage volumes

Converting VMs

There are some situations where you might need to convert a physical machine to a VM or import a VM from a third party to take advantage of the scalability, reliability, security, and features provided by the vSphere platform, released from hardware constraints. If you have old physical machines or physical machines running specific applications, OS, and configurations that require time for a fresh reinstallation, and service downtime for a long period is not tolerated, conversion to a VM might solve the problem.

You may also be requested to import in vSphere VMs created for different virtual platforms, and to run those VMs in a VMware environment, they must be converted in a supported format.

To migrate the OS, applications, and data to the virtualization platform, the VMware *vCenter Converter* tool (available to download from the VMware website at the URL `https:/ /www.vmware.com/products/converter.html`), is the solution you should use to import a physical or VM into the vSphere environment.

You can perform two types of conversion:

- **Physical to virtual (P2V)**
- **Virtual to virtual (V2V)**

P2V

P2V conversion is a procedure used to convert a physical computer to a VM. VMware vCenter Converter allows conversion from physical machines running Windows and Linux and supports both desktop and server editions. With the supported hot cloning feature, admins can convert a running machine in a non-disruptive way, with no downtime or reboot requirements.

V2V

V2V conversion refers to the migration of an OS, application programs, and data from a VM or disk partition to another VM or disk partition. VMware vCenter Converter supports the conversion from third-party VMs such as Hyper-V and KVM to vSphere.

Summary

In this chapter, we talked about VMs, that is, a software computer composed by a file structure that specifies the configuration (.vmx) and the virtual disk used to store data (.vmdk) and core components, such as virtual and hardware resources, OS, and VMware Tools. A VM can be deployed using different methods (created from scratch, clone, templates, and OVF/OVA) depending on the features requested. The use of a Content Library can simplify the deployment process.

We have seen that, once installed, a VM can be added or removed from the inventory, keeping the VM data. Snapshots can be used to take a specific point in time of a VM in order to quickly revert at any time in case of need. A typical use case is the patching process; before applying a new patch, taking a VM snapshot allows you to quickly revert in case of problems. Snapshots can be created and deleted, but sometimes a consolidation is required when snapshot deletion fails.

The chapter explained how to allocate resources to VMs in an efficient way to avoid overcommitment of resources that can compromise performance and the infrastructure functionality. VMs can be hot or cold migrated to different hosts or different storage devices using the vMotion and Storage vMotion features. Keep in mind that shared storage is not a requirement for vMotion.

The next chapter will cover virtual infrastructure monitoring, essential to keep your environment under control and avoid service disruption due to a failure you are not aware of. Monitoring the infrastructure allows the optimization of the infrastructure for best performance. Although vSphere is a stable and robust platform, failures, and problems may occur at any time. The chapter will explain the correct approach to troubleshoot a problem to quickly find a fix, minimizing the service downtime.

9
Monitoring, Optimizing, and Troubleshooting

Virtualization and VMware technologies are consolidated, usually very stable, and in most cases, they work very well. However, of course, there is a chance that a problem or an issue will occur in the VMware infrastructure.

In this chapter, we will show how it is possible to monitor, repair, optimize, and troubleshoot your VMware world. Maybe you will not become a troubleshooting master, but you will learn enough to be ready for the journey through GUI and CLI tools. This chapter will cover the native tools used to monitor and troubleshoot performance and other issues in order to improve the virtual environment and workloads. This chapter focuses on monitoring different critical resources, such as computing, storage, and networking, across the ESXi hosts, the resource pools, and clusters. Other tools, such as vRealize Operations and third-party tools, will also be described briefly.

In this chapter, we will see:

- An example of useful CLI commands for ESXi hosts and vCSA
- A brief introduction to PowerCLI
- Log management for troubleshooting purposes
- Specific hints on how to troubleshoot different components

What is troubleshooting?

Troubleshooting (TRBL) is a complete process where you (with the role of VMware administrator) identify an issue, try to find the origin of the problem, and define the way to resolve it.

The main steps involved during the troubleshooting process are therefore the following:

1. Defining the problem
2. Identifying the cause of the problem
3. Resolving the problem

The complexity of VMware environments is that different layers are involved and the problem could impact any of the sources due to different reasons:

- Hardware failures
- Software problems
- Network problems
- Resources contention
- Mistakes in configuration

A big mistake that occurs quite often, is considering TRBL only when your environment has totally failed, for example, with a **Purple Screen of the Death (PSOD)** error. NO! TRBL is about all problems and you should start troubleshooting when there is a problem or when users report problems in terms of performance, reliability or usability. The first step of every TRBL process is collecting all the symptoms. Here, you must be careful because symptoms and the origin of the problem can be totally different. This stage is very important for gathering additional information to define the problem.

The typical questions could be— *Can the problem be reproduced? What is the scope? Was the system changing before the notification of the problem? Is the problem documented in the KB VMware?* and so on.

There is a good new for you, yes, it is possible to repeat the problem then you can concentrate directly on the issue. For example, if only hosts with **Serial-Attached SCSI Host Bus Adapter (SAS HBA)** don't work, successfully applying a new firmware for FC HBA can be the solution.

When you have all the information, you can start TRBL from the following three components:

- You start on the VM OS level and continue down to hardware
- You start at the hardware level and continue up to the VM OS level
- You can start in the middle, at the VMkernel level, and continue up or down

After identifying the cause, you must specify the level of the problem to be fixed for your production environment, assigning a priority:

- **High**: Resolve as fast as a possible
- **Medium**: Resolve during the first possible window
- **Low**: You can wait for the next maintenance window

Solutions levels can be classified as follows:

- **Short**: Typical workaround
- **Long**: Reconfigure or change the advanced configuration and so on
- **Impact**: Apply available patches from VMware or other vendors

A problem resolution may require the use of different solutions together. But I think the theory is done, and we can start with real examples of how to troubleshoot your production.

Monitoring a virtual environment

How can we monitor the environment? You can use two ways: the first from a OS VM perspective and the second from a third-party tools perspective.

We can use two views to monitor the environment:

- **Inside the Guest OS tools**: Task Manager or top
- **Outside the Guest OS tools**: vCenter Server performance charts or esxtop

As per my point of view and experience, CLI is better and more helpful than GUI tools. However, of course, you can find any GUI that you love.

CLI usage

CLI is the most useful option for TRBL. There are a lot of CLIs available that are used for TRBL in a VMware environment:

- vSphere ESXi shell: `esxcli` which is the new CLI
- vSphere command-line interface vCLI: `esxcfg-*` which is the old CLI

Both CLIs can be used directly from an ESXi host and the ESXi shell must be enabled in the **Direct Console User Interface (DCUI)**. You can access the DCUI from the physical console of the host or also remotely using a specific hardware vendor cards, like iDRAC for Dell or iLO for HP. When you want to use the CLI using a remote SSH session (PuTTy is a popular SSH client you can use), SSH protocol must be enabled from the DCUI. The second place where the configuration can be set is through vCenter Server in the **Security Profile** tab. The final place where it is possible to use it is through **vSphere Management Assistant (vMA**).

ESXCLI commands

How do we use esxcli? When you write the basic `esxcli` command and press *Enter*, you will see all the possible commands:

```
[root@esxi1:~] esxcli
Usage: esxcli [options] {namespace}+ {cmd} [cmd options]
Options:
--formatter=FORMATTER
Override the formatter to use for a given command. Available formatter:
keyvalue, xml, csv
--debug             Enable debug or internal use options
--version           Display version information for the script
-?, --help          Display usage information for the script
Available Namespaces:
device          Device manager commands
elxnet          elxnet esxcli functionality
esxcli          Commands that operate on the esxcli system itself allowing
users to get additional information.
fcoe            VMware FCOE commands.
graphics        VMware graphics commands.
hardware        VMKernel hardware properties and commands for configuring
hardware.
iscsi           VMware iSCSI commands.
network         Operations that pertain to the maintenance of networking on an
ESX host. This includes a wide variety of commands to manipulate virtual
networking components (vswitch, portgroup, etc) as well as local host IP,
```

```
DNS and general host networking settings.
nvme          VMware NVMe driver esxcli extensions
rdma          Operations that pertain to remote direct memory access (RDMA)
protocol stack on an ESX host.
sched         VMKernel system properties and commands for configuring
scheduling related functionality.
software      Manage the ESXi software image and packages
storage       VMware storage commands.
system        VMKernel system properties and commands for configuring
properties of the kernel core system and related system services.
vm            A small number of operations that allow a user to Control
Virtual Machine operations.
vsan          VMware vSAN commands
```

We can continue by adding the next command `network` and once more pressing *Enter*. We see the next possible commands. ESXCLI is just a kit composed of a sequence of commands. Type `esxcli network` and press *Enter*:

```
[root@esxi1:~] esxcli network
Usage: esxcli network {cmd} [cmd options]
Available Namespaces:
firewall             A set of commands for firewall related operations
ip                   Operations that can be performed on vmknics
multicast            Operations having to do with multicast
nic                  Operations having to do with the configuration of
Network Interface Card and getting and updating the NIC settings.
port                 Commands to get information about a port
sriovnic             Operations having to do with the configuration of
SRIOV enabled Network Interface Card and getting and updating the NIC
settings.
vm                   A set of commands for VM related operations
vswitch              Commands to list and manipulate Virtual Switches on
an ESX host.
diag                 Operations pertaining to network diagnostics
```

When you want to know the IP address of all the VMkernel ports, you can use this `esxcli` command:

```
[root@esxi1:~] esxcli network ip interface ipv4 address list
Name   IPv4 Address    IPv4 Netmask     IPv4 Broadcast    Address Type
Gateway   DHCP DNS
-----  --------------  ---------------  ----------------  ------------  -----
--  --------
vmk0   10.10.70.11     255.255.255.0    10.10.70.255      STATIC
0.0.0.0     false
vmk3   10.10.90.159    255.255.255.128  10.10.90.255      STATIC
0.0.0.0     false
```

vmk4	169.254.1.1	255.255.255.0	169.254.1.255	STATIC
0.0.0.0	false			
vmk5	10.10.70.222	255.255.255.0	10.10.70.255	STATIC
0.0.0.0	false			
vmk7	169.254.3.169	255.255.0.0	169.254.255.255	DHCP
0.0.0.0	false			
vmk2	10.200.10.10	255.255.255.0	10.200.10.255	STATIC
0.0.0.0	false			
vmk6	169.254.36.156	255.255.0.0	169.254.255.255	DHCP
0.0.0.0	false			
vmk1	10.200.10.12	255.255.255.0	10.200.10.255	STATIC
0.0.0.0	false			

Once you have found the VMkernel port IP address, you need to know where the TCP/IP stack is. To achieve this, we type the following command:

```
[root@esxi1:~] esxcli network ip interface list
vmk0
Name: vmk0
    MAC Address: 44:a8:42:22:a0:fe
    Enabled: true
    Portset: vSwitch0
    Portgroup: Management Network
    Netstack Instance: defaultTcpipStack
    VDS Name: N/A
    VDS UUID: N/A
    VDS Port: N/A
    VDS Connection: -1
    Opaque Network ID: N/A
    Opaque Network Type: N/A
    External ID: N/A
    MTU: 1500
    TSO MSS: 65535
    Port ID: 33554436
...
vmk2
    Name: vmk2
    MAC Address: 00:50:56:66:2a:ef
    Enabled: true
    Portset: DvsPortset-0
    Portgroup: N/A
    Netstack Instance: vxlan
    VDS Name: DSwitch-SDN10GB
    VDS UUID: f3 37 15 50 4e ec 3a 6c-b9 4c 10 6e f3 d2 a5 9f
    VDS Port: 124
    VDS Connection: 964602202
    Opaque Network ID: N/A
Opaque Network Type: N/A
```

```
     External ID: N/A
         MTU: 9000
   TSO MSS: 65535
   Port ID: 134217736
   . . .
```

It's good to know IP and stack, which is very good information to check, for example, the correct configuration of vMotion `vmk` or VTEP `vmk`. Why is it good? Because when you want to ping a different stack, you need a name and `vmk x` number. For example, if we want to ping VMkernel for NSX VTEP we specify `vxlan` stack and interface `vmk2` as follows:

```
[root@esx1:~] vmkping ++netstack=vxlan -I vmk2 10.200.10.11
PING 10.200.10.11 (10.200.10.11): 56 data bytes
64 bytes from 10.200.10.11: icmp_seq=0 ttl=64 time=0.196 ms
64 bytes from 10.200.10.11: icmp_seq=1 ttl=64 time=0.170 ms
64 bytes from 10.200.10.11: icmp_seq=2 ttl=64 time=0.173 ms
--- 10.200.10.11 ping statistics ---
3 packets transmitted, 3 packets received, 0% packet loss
round-trip min/avg/max = 0.170/0.180/0.196 ms
```

To avoid problems in the production environment, I recommend trying all available CLI commands for storage, device, and so on in a lab environment or using the VMware **Hands-on Lab (HoL)**.

VMware **Hands-on-Lab (HoL)** is free and available online at `http://labs.hol.vmware.com`.

ESXCFG-

There is also another set of CLI commands that start with `esxcfg-*`. Those commands are a little bit older but still very useful. They can be used from the ESXi host's shell or also via vMA and, in this case, they will start with `vicfg-*`.

In the following example, you see duplicated CLI for the same output as `esxcli`. Yes, any CLI duplicates `esxcli`.

We can show the same as with `esxcli`.

To see all the available commands, you can type `esxcfg-` followed by a double hit of the *Tab* button. You will be able to see all possible `esxcfg-` CLI commands:

```
[root@esxi1:~] esxcfg-
esxcfg-advcfg esxcfg-hwiscsi esxcfg-ipsec esxcfg-nas esxcfg-resgrp esxcfg-
swiscsi esxcfg-vswitch
esxcfg-dumppart esxcfg-info esxcfg-module esxcfg-nics esxcfg-route esxcfg-
vmknic
esxcfg-fcoe esxcfg-init esxcfg-mpath esxcfg-rescan esxcfg-scsidevs esxcfg-
volume
```

Using the `esxcfg-vmknic -l` command, you can find all `vmk` IP address and netstack in an easier way compared to `esxcli`:

```
[root@esxi1:~] esxcfg-vmknic -l
Interface Port Group/DVPort/Opaque Network IP Family IP Address Netmask
Broadcast MAC Address MTU TSO MSS Enabled Type NetStack
vmk0 Management Network IPv4 10.10.70.11 255.255.255.0 10.10.70.255
44:a8:42:22:a0:fe 1500 65535 true STATIC defaultTcpipStack
vmk0 Management Network IPv6 fe80::46a8:42ff:fe22:a0fe 64 44:a8:42:22:a0:fe
1500 65535 true STATIC, PREFERRED defaultTcpipStack
vmk3 IPSstorage IPv4 10.10.90.159 255.255.255.128 10.10.90.255
00:50:56:6e:57:64 1500 65535 true STATIC defaultTcpipStack
vmk3 IPSstorage IPv6 fe80::250:56ff:fe6e:5764 64 00:50:56:6e:57:64 1500
65535 true STATIC, PREFERRED defaultTcpipStack
vmk4 vmservice-vmknic-pg IPv4 169.254.1.1 255.255.255.0 169.254.1.255
00:50:56:6b:57:d4 1500 65535 true STATIC defaultTcpipStack
vmk4 vmservice-vmknic-pg IPv6 fe80::250:56ff:fe6b:57d4 64 00:50:56:6b:57:d4
1500 65535 true STATIC, PREFERRED defaultTcpipStack
vmk5 54 IPv4 10.10.70.222 255.255.255.0 10.10.70.255 00:50:56:62:0c:5d 9000
65535 true STATIC defaultTcpipStack
vmk5 54 IPv6 fe80::250:56ff:fe62:c5d 64 00:50:56:62:0c:5d 9000 65535 true
STATIC, PREFERRED defaultTcpipStack
vmk7 VMkernel IPv4 169.254.3.169 255.255.0.0 169.254.255.255
00:50:56:66:e1:7a 1500 65535 true DHCP defaultTcpipStack
vmk7 VMkernel IPv6 fe80::250:56ff:fe66:e17a 64 00:50:56:66:e1:7a 1500 65535
true STATIC, PREFERRED defaultTcpipStack
vmk2 124 IPv4 10.200.10.10 255.255.255.0 10.200.10.255 00:50:56:66:2a:ef
9000 65535 true STATIC vxlan
vmk2 124 IPv6 fe80::250:56ff:fe66:2aef 64 00:50:56:66:2a:ef 9000 65535 true
STATIC, PREFERRED vxlan
vmk6 16 IPv4 169.254.36.156 255.255.0.0 169.254.255.255 00:50:56:61:ba:8d
9000 65535 true DHCP Mastering_Stack
vmk6 16 IPv6 fe80::250:56ff:fe61:ba8d 64 00:50:56:61:ba:8d 9000 65535 true
STATIC, PREFERRED Mastering_Stack
vmk1 61 IPv4 10.200.10.12 255.255.255.0 10.200.10.255 00:50:56:63:8d:20
9000 0 false STATIC vxlan
```

Next, a very good CLI to use is esxcfg-vswitch –l, which lists all vswitch and vDS:

```
[root@esxi1:~] esxcfg-vswitch -l
Switch Name Num Ports Used Ports Configured Ports MTU Uplinks
vSwitch0 4352 10 128 1500 vmnic0
PortGroup Name VLAN ID Used Ports Uplinks
VM Network 0 6 vmnic0
Management Network 0 1 vmnic0
Switch Name Num Ports Used Ports Configured Ports MTU Uplinks
vSwitch1 4352 4 128 1500 vmnic1
PortGroup Name VLAN ID Used Ports Uplinks
IPSstorage 0 1 vmnic1
Switch Name Num Ports Used Ports Configured Ports MTU Uplinks
vmservice-vswitch 4352 3 16 1500
PortGroup Name VLAN ID Used Ports Uplinks
vmservice-vshield-pg 0 1
vmservice-vmknic-pg 0 1
Switch Name Num Ports Used Ports Configured Ports MTU Uplinks
vSwitch2 4352 1 128 1500
PortGroup Name VLAN ID Used Ports Uplinks
Space 0 0
Switch Name Num Ports Used Ports Configured Ports MTU Uplinks
Mastering_New_vSS 4352 5 1024 1500 vmnic2,vmnic3
PortGroup Name VLAN ID Used Ports Uplinks
VLAN100 100 0 vmnic2,vmnic3
Switch Name Num Ports Used Ports Configured Ports MTU Uplinks
vSwitch3 4352 2 128 1500
PortGroup Name VLAN ID Used Ports Uplinks
VMkernel 0 1
DVS Name Num Ports Used Ports Configured Ports MTU Uplinks
DSwitch-SDN10GB 4352 21 512 9000 vmnic5,vmnic4
DVPort ID In Use Client
8 0
9 0
12 1 vmnic4
13 1 vmnic5
124 1 vmk2
54 1 vmk5
16 1 vmk6
137 1 EDGE-VIP-1.eth0
196 1 EDGE-B-0.eth0
135 1 EDGE-B-0.eth1
172 1 DB01.eth0
164 1 App01.eth0
168 1 App02.eth0
180 1 Web01.eth0
212 1 desktop-ubuntu.eth0
```

```
136 1 EDGE-VIP-0.eth0
39 1 Guest Introspection (2).eth0
```

vSphere Management Assistant

All these CLIs can be used not only in your lab environment or in the hands-on lab, but they are also available using the vMA.

You can download vMA from My VMware and deploy the appliance to your environment adding the vCenter Server and the ESXi host as a target.

 vMA 6.5 is the last version of this product, so the next release of vSphere will be deprecated. See further information at https://blogs.vmware. com/vsphere/2017/04/vsphere-management-assistant-deprecation. html.

vMA includes esxcli, vicfg-* (same as a esxcfg-*), and the very old vmware -cmd.

I won't spend much time on vMA since it is a deprecated product.

Ruby vSphere console

The next CLI that is very useful in real life is the Ruby vSphere console. Ruby vSphere console is a part of the vCenter Appliance 6.5 accessible typing rvc.

You can install rvc in your notebook or use a docker. rvc command is often used for TRBL vSAN. You can find a great post at the address: https://blogs.vmware.com/kb/2016/10/ tips-tricks-ruby-vsphere-console-rvc-managing-virtual-san-environment.html.

```
Command> rvc
Install the "ffi" gem for better tab completion.
Host to connect to (user@host): localhost
Using default username "administrator@vsphere.local".
password:
Welcome to RVC. Try the 'help' command.
0 /
1 localhost/
> cd localhost/
/localhost> ls
0 SDN_PRAHA (datacenter)
/localhost> cd 0
/localhost/SDN_PRAHA> ls
0 storage/
```

```
1 computers [host]/
2 networks [network]/
3 datastores [datastore]/
4 vms [vm]/
/localhost/SDN_PRAHA> cd 4
/localhost/SDN_PRAHA/vms> ls
0 ESX Agents/
1 vSEC lab/
2 Discovered virtual machine/
3 NSX_3_Tier_App: cpu 0.00/-0.00/normal, mem 0.00/-0.00/normal
4 LogInsight: poweredOn
5 vRealize-Operations-Manager: poweredOn
6 vrni-platform: poweredOn
7 vrni-proxy: poweredOn
8 desktop-ubuntu: poweredOn
9 NSX_Controller_3bfd388a-fd5d-4f43-b0d3-693ef5a5ef43: poweredOn
10 NSX_Controller_e9e75c82-58d1-4a2f-bc92-ad7bf5847a3c: poweredOn
11 NSX_Controller_f93b5405-2516-4dd1-adc8-ccd10183bf99: poweredOn
12 vrealize-automation: poweredOn
13 vrealize-orechestrator: poweredOn
14 DLR-0: poweredOn
15 EDGE-A-0: poweredOn
16 EDGE-B-0: poweredOn
17 EDGE-VIP-0: poweredOn
18 EDGE-VIP-1: poweredOn
19 NSX_Manager: poweredOn
20 desktop-nsx: poweredOff
21 Web03: poweredOn
22 Debian_template: poweredOff
/localhost/SDN_PRAHA/vms> cd 20
/localhost/SDN_PRAHA/vms/desktop-nsx> ls
0 datastores/
1 networks/
2 files/
3 snapshots
4 devices/
5 vmprofiles/
6 host [esxi2.sipovecs.local] (host): cpu 2*6*2.40 GHz, memory 205.00 GB
7 resourcePool [Resources]: cpu 44.63/44.63/normal, mem
373.16/373.16/normal
```

VIM-CMD

The `vim-cmd` command could be a very good CLI when you need to start a VM, for example, the vCSA:

```
[root@esxi1:~] vim-cmd
Commands available under /:
hbrsvc/ internalsvc/ solo/ vmsvc/
hostsvc/ proxysvc/ vimsvc/ help
```

For example, with the `vmscv` namespace you can manage the power status of a VM:

```
[root@esxi1:~] vim-cmd vmsvc/
Commands available under vmsvc/:
acquiremksticket get.snapshotinfo
acquireticket get.spaceNeededForConsolidation
createdummyvm get.summary
destroy get.tasklist
device.connection getallvms
device.connusbdev gethostconstraints
device.ctlradd message
device.ctlrremove power.getstate
device.disconnusbdev power.hibernate
device.diskadd power.off
device.diskaddexisting power.on
device.diskextend power.reboot
device.diskremove power.reset
device.getdevices power.shutdown
device.nvdimmadd power.suspend
device.nvdimmremove power.suspendResume
device.toolsSyncSet queryftcompat
devices.createnic reload
get.capability setscreenres
get.config snapshot.create
get.config.cpuidmask snapshot.dumpoption
get.configoption snapshot.get
get.datastores snapshot.remove
get.disabledmethods snapshot.removeall
get.environment snapshot.revert
get.filelayout snapshot.setoption
get.filelayoutex tools.cancelinstall
get.guest tools.install
get.guestheartbeatStatus tools.upgrade
get.managedentitystatus unregister
get.networks upgrade
get.runtime
```

The first step is to list all VMs because we need the **VM identificator (VMID)** to power it on:

```
[root@esxi1:~] vim-cmd vmsvc/getallvms
Vmid Name File Guest OS Version Annotation
31 App02 [esxi1_datastore1] App02/App02.vmx debian7_64Guest vmx-10
32 DB01 [esxi1_datastore1] DB01/DB01.vmx debian7_64Guest vmx-10
33 Web01 [esxi1_datastore1] Web01/Web01.vmx debian7_64Guest vmx-10
35 App01 [esxi1_datastore1] App01/App01.vmx debian7_64Guest vmx-10
83 LogInsight [esxi1_datastore1] LogInsight/LogInsight.vmx sles11_64Guest
vmx-09 VMware vRealize Log Insight
84 vrni-platform [esxi1_datastore1] vrni-platform/vrni-platform.vmx
ubuntu64Guest vmx-10 VMware vRealize Network Insight Platform VM
85 desktop-ubuntu [esxi1_datastore1] desktop-ubuntu/desktop-ubuntu.vmx
ubuntu64Guest vmx-13
```

When we know the correct VMID, we can power on the VM:

```
[root@esxi1:~] vim-cmd vmsvc/power.on 85
Powering on VM:
```

With `vim-cmd`, you can try a lot of further commands.

In the next example, the following command is used to get details of network information for VM 85:

```
[root@esxi1:~] vim-cmd vmsvc/get.network 85
Networks:
(vim.Network.Summary) {
network = 'vim.Network:HaNetwork-VM Network',
name = "VM Network",
accessible = true,
ipPoolName = "",
ipPoolId = <unset>
}
(vim.Network.Summary) {
network = 'vim.dvs.DistributedVirtualPortgroup:DVPG-f3 37 15 50 4e ec 3a
6c-b9 4c 10 6e f3 d2 a5 9f-dvportgroup-509',
name = "vxw-dvs-36-virtualwire-5-sid-5004-Client",
accessible = true,
ipPoolName = "",
ipPoolId = <unset>
```

VCSA – CLI

The next CLI is part of the vCSA, and you can use the `api` command:

```
Command> api com.vmware.appliance.version1.
com.vmware.appliance.version1.access.consolecli.get
com.vmware.appliance.version1.networking.ipv6.list
com.vmware.appliance.version1.access.consolecli.set
com.vmware.appliance.version1.networking.ipv6.set
com.vmware.appliance.version1.access.dcui.get
com.vmware.appliance.version1.networking.proxy.delete
com.vmware.appliance.version1.access.dcui.set
com.vmware.appliance.version1.networking.proxy.get
com.vmware.appliance.version1.access.shell.get
com.vmware.appliance.version1.networking.proxy.set
com.vmware.appliance.version1.access.shell.set
com.vmware.appliance.version1.networking.proxy.test
. . . . . . .
```

See the following example:

```
Command> api com.vmware.appliance.version1.networking.interfaces.list
Interfacesinfo:
1:
Status: up
Mac: 00:0c:29:29:d2:f8
Name: nic0
```

In real life, a VMware administrator needs other commands on the vCSA to restart components, such as the vSphere Web Client:

```
Command> service-control --list
vmware-vpostgres (VMware Postgres)
vmware-imagebuilder (VMware Image Builder Manager)
vmware-cm (VMware Component Manager)
vmware-vpxd (VMware vCenter Server)
vmware-sps (VMware vSphere Profile-Driven Storage Service)
applmgmt (VMware Appliance Management Service)
vmware-statsmonitor (VMware Appliance Monitoring Service)
vmware-rhttpproxy (VMware HTTP Reverse Proxy)
vmware-vapi-endpoint (VMware vAPI Endpoint)
vmware-stsd (VMware Security Token Service)
lwsmd (Likewise Service Manager)
vmafdd (VMware Authentication Framework)
vmware-psc-client (VMware Platform Services Controller Client)
vmware-vsm (VMware vService Manager)
vmonapi (VMware Service Lifecycle Manager API)
vmware-perfcharts (VMware Performance Charts)
```

```
vmware-updatemgr (VMware Update Manager)
vmware-vmon (VMware Service Lifecycle Manager)
vmware-vsan-health (VMware VSAN Health Service)
vsphere-client (VMware vSphere Web Client)
vmware-sts-idmd (VMware Identity Management Service)
vmcad (VMware Certificate Service)
vmware-eam (VMware ESX Agent Manager)
vmware-cis-license (VMware License Service)
vmcam (VMware vSphere Authentication Proxy)
pschealth (VMware Platform Services Controller Health Monitor)
vmdird (VMware Directory Service)
vmware-mbcs (VMware Message Bus Configuration Service)
vmware-vcha (VMware vCenter High Availability)
vsphere-ui (VMware vSphere Client)
vmware-content-library (VMware Content Library Service)
vmdnsd (VMware Domain Name Service)
vmware-sca (VMware Service Control Agent)
vmware-netdumper (VMware vSphere ESXi Dump Collector)
vmware-vpxd-svcs (VMware vCenter-Services)
vmware-rbd-watchdog (VMware vSphere Auto Deploy Waiter)
```

Restarting the vSphere web client service is quite easy from the command line:

```
Command> service-control --stop vsphere-client
Command> service-control --start vsphere-client
```

Another interesting command is `software-packages`, which is useful for updating your vCSA (it can be a better option than using the GUI via port 5480).

```
Command> software-packages -h
usage: software-packages [-h] {stage,unstage,validate,install,list} ...
optional arguments:
-h, --help show this help message and exit
sub-commands:
{stage,unstage,validate,install,list}
stage Stage software update packages
unstage Purge staged software update packages
validate Validate software update packages
install Install software update packages
list List details of software update packages
```

You must know basic Linux commands such as `tail`, `vi`, `more`, `less`, `grep`, and `ls` for the TRBL process.

PowerCLI

We can't miss PowerCLI, of course. Those who are lovers of PowerShell will love PowerCLI or PowerNSX:

```
Welcome to VMware PowerCLI!
Log in to a vCenter Server or ESX host: Connect-VIServer
To find out what commands are available, type: Get-VICommand
To show searchable help for all PowerCLI commands: Get-PowerCLIHelp
Once you've connected, display all virtual machines: Get-VM
If you need more help, visit the PowerCLI community: Get-PowerCLICommunity
Copyright (C) VMware, Inc. All rights reserved.
PS C:\>
```

Connect to vCenter Server with the `Connect-VIServer` command:

```
PS C:\> Connect-VIServer 10.10.70.17
Name Port User
---- ---- ----
10.10.70.17 443 VSPHERE.LOCAL\Administrator
```

You can easily get information about hosts with the command `Get-VMHost` command:

```
PS C:\> Get-VMHost
Name ConnectionState PowerState NumCpu CpuUsageMhz CpuTotalMhz
MemoryUsageGB MemoryTotalGB Version
---- --------------- ---------- ------ ----------- -----------
- ------------- -------
esxi1.sipovecs... Connected PoweredOn 12 2782 28764 69,518 191,778 6.5.0
esxdell2.sipovecs... Connected PoweredOn 12 1604 28764 56,332 191,778 6.5.0
```

 We already discussed in Chapter 5, *Configuring and Managing vSphere 6.5* how to install and work with PowerCLI. Additional info can be found at https://blogs.vmware.com/PowerCLI/2017/04/powercli-install-process-powershell-gallery.html.

The last one is PowerNSX, that is, PowerCLI for NSX. You can use PowerNSX to install or configure or TRBL NSX. PowerNSX is great to use with the PowerOps tool. Only one book is available about PowerNSX and can be found at https://powernsx.github.io/.

I think that now your brain is full of CLI and commands. However, at this moment, it is not important to remember every CLI. We need to know and remember what it is possible to do and which CLI can be used for the different parts of the TRBL process.

Logs

For TRBL it is very important to know where the logs are located. In vCSA log files are stored in /var/log/.

The way to access the bash using the shell command is as follows:

```
Command> shell
Shell access is granted to root
root@vc [ ~ ]# cd /var/log/vmware
root@vc [ /var/log/vmware ]# ls
applmgmt content-library perfcharts procstate-20171026.gz rbd sca vcha
vmcam vmware-imagebuilder vpxd-svcs
applmgmt-audit eam procstate procstate-20171027.gz rhttpproxy sso vctop
vmdir vmware-sps vsan-health
cis-license journal procstate-20171023.gz procstate-20171028.gz rsyslogd
syslog vmafd vmdird vmware-updatemgr vsm
cloudvm mbcs procstate-20171024.gz procstate-20171029.gz rsyslogd-2068
upgrade vmafdd vmdnsd vpostgres vsphere-client
cm netdumper procstate-20171025.gz psc-client rsyslogd-2078 vapi vmcad vmon
vpxd vsphere-ui
root@vc [ /var/log/vmware ]#
```

A way to easily check logs online is through the command tail with the parameter –f. vpxd.log is a key log for TRBL vCSA:

```
root@vc [ /var/log/vmware ]# tail -f vpxd/vpxd.log
2017-10-29T22:01:14.820Z info vpxd[7F3C9E6CD700] [Originator@6876
sub=vpxLro opID=1b500487] [VpxLRO] -- FINISH lro-1440671
2017-10-29T22:01:14.820Z info vpxd[7F3C9EBD7700] [Originator@6876
sub=vpxLro opID=22594913] [VpxLRO] -- FINISH lro-1440672
```

Detailed log locations and descriptions can be found in the VMware KB at https://kb.vmware.com/s/article/2110014?language=en_USr=2 Quarterback.validateRoute=1KM_Utility.getArticleData=1KM_Utility.getArticleLanguage=2KM_Utility.getArticle=1.

ESXi host logs

The ESXi host log files are very similar to vCSA logs and can be found in the /var/log directory of the host:

```
[root@esx1:/var/log] ls
Xorg.log epd.log iofilter-init.log rabbitmqproxy.log upitd.log vmware
auth.log esxcli-software.log iofiltervpd.log rhttpproxy.log usb.log
vobd.log
boot.gz esxcli.log ipmi sdrsinjector.log vdpi.log vprobe.log
clomd.log esxupdate.log jumpstart-stdout.log shell.log vitd.log vpxa.log
cmmdsTimeMachine.log fdm.log kickstart.log smbios.bin vmauthd.log
vsanmgmt.log
cmmdsTimeMachineDump.log hbrca.log lacp.log storagerm.log vmkdevmgr.log
vsansystem.log
configRP.log hostd-probe.log netcpa.log swapobjd.log vmkernel.log
vsanvpd.log
ddecomd.log hostd.log nfcd.log sysboot.log vmkeventd.log vsfwd.log
dfwpktlogs.log hostdCgiServer.log osfsd.log syslog.log vmksummary.log
vvold.log
dhclient.log hostprofiletrace.log pktcap-agent.log tallylog vmkwarning.log
```

When you use the command ls -la, you may notice an important key point about ESXi logs; all logs on the host are symbolic links to /scratch/log. When you install the ESXi host on an SD card, a warning message related to a *Non persistent storage* may appear when the installation has completed. To fix this matter you must create a datastore and redirect the logs to that datastore (we covered scratch partition in chapter 5, *Configuring and Managing vSphere 6.5*).

 Check also VMware KB 2032823—*System logs are stored on non-persistent storage* at the address https://kb.vmware.com/s/article/2032823?language=en_US.

```
[root@esxi1:/var/log] ls -la
total 488
drwxr-xr-x 1 root root 512 Oct 29 20:27 .
drwxr-xr-x 1 root root 512 Oct 13 09:29 ..
-rw-rw-rw- 1 root root 2722 Oct 29 21:57 .vmsyslogd.err
-rw-rw-rw- 1 root root 9884 Oct 29 20:27 .vmsyslogd.err.1
-rw-rw-rw- 1 root root 9884 Oct 29 13:27 .vmsyslogd.err.2
-rw-rw-rw- 1 root root 9884 Oct 29 06:27 .vmsyslogd.err.3
-rw-rw-rw- 1 root root 9884 Oct 28 23:27 .vmsyslogd.err.4
-rw-rw-rw- 1 root root 9884 Oct 28 16:27 .vmsyslogd.err.5
lrwxrwxrwx 1 root root 21 Oct 13 09:30 Xorg.log -> /scratch/log/Xorg.log
lrwxrwxrwx 1 root root 21 Oct 13 09:30 auth.log -> /scratch/log/auth.log
```

```
-rw-rw-rw- 1 root root 62226 Oct 13 09:30 boot.gz
lrwxrwxrwx 1 root root 22 Oct 13 09:30 clomd.log -> /scratch/log/clomd.log
lrwxrwxrwx 1 root root 33 Oct 13 09:30 cmmdsTimeMachine.log ->
/scratch/log/cmmdsTimeMachine.log
lrwxrwxrwx 1 root root 37 Oct 13 09:30 cmmdsTimeMachineDump.log ->
/scratch/log/cmmdsTimeMachineDump.log
-rw-r--r-- 1 root root 38291 Oct 13 09:30 configRP.log
lrwxrwxrwx 1 root root 24 Oct 13 09:30 ddecomd.log ->
/scratch/log/ddecomd.log
lrwxrwxrwx 1 root root 27 Oct 13 09:30 dfwpktlogs.log ->
/scratch/log/dfwpktlogs.log
lrwxrwxrwx 1 root root 25 Oct 13 09:30 dhclient.log ->
/scratch/log/dhclient.log
lrwxrwxrwx 1 root root 20 Oct 13 09:30 epd.log -> /scratch/log/epd.log
-rw-r--r-- 1 root root 2631 Oct 13 09:29 esxcli-software.log
-rw-r--r-- 1 root root 1975 Oct 29 12:51 esxcli.log
lrwxrwxrwx 1 root root 26 Oct 13 09:30 esxupdate.log ->
/scratch/log/esxupdate.log
lrwxrwxrwx 1 root root 20 Oct 13 09:30 fdm.log -> /scratch/log/fdm.log
lrwxrwxrwx 1 root root 22 Oct 13 09:30 hbrca.log -> /scratch/log/hbrca.log
lrwxrwxrwx 1 root root 28 Oct 13 09:30 hostd-probe.log ->
/scratch/log/hostd-probe.log
lrwxrwxrwx 1 root root 22 Oct 13 09:30 hostd.log -> /scratch/log/hostd.log
lrwxrwxrwx 1 root root 31 Oct 13 09:30 hostdCgiServer.log ->
/scratch/log/hostdCgiServer.log
lrwxrwxrwx 1 root root 33 Oct 13 09:30 hostprofiletrace.log ->
/scratch/log/hostprofiletrace.log
-rw-r--r-- 1 root root 966 Oct 13 09:30 iofilter-init.log
lrwxrwxrwx 1 root root 28 Oct 13 09:30 iofiltervpd.log ->
/scratch/log/iofiltervpd.log
```

As a first step, I recommend to check the log file `vmkernel.log`:

```
[root@esxi1:/var/log] tail -f vmkernel.log
2017-10-29T21:07:29.055Z cpu16:66338)ScsiDeviceIO: 2948:
Cmd(0x439d008344c0) 0x1a, CmdSN 0x4bbb8 from world 0 to dev
"naa.644a8420210904001cc39b5814256147" failed H:0x0 D:0x2 P:0x0 Valid sense
data: 0x5 0x24 0x0.
2017-10-29T21:16:42.527Z cpu15:10960912)Throttled.nsx-vsip:
VSIPNDSnoopTx:1942: Filter nic-10960911-eth1-vmware-sfw.2: Processing ND Tx
packet
```

There are also other ways to check ESXi logs. One way is using the DCUI from the ESXi console. Another way is using a web browser and point it at your ESXi host using the URL `https://ESXi_IP/host`. After providing the correct ESXi credentials, you will see something like this:

Home		
Configuration files		
Name	**Last Modified**	**Size**
auth.log	10-Nov-2017 13:35	21954
castore	13-Oct-2017 09:29	2356
configRP.log	04-Nov-2017 17:05	38985
dhclient.log	16-Nov-2017 19:45	278255
esx.conf	10-Nov-2017 08:17	61442
esxupdate.log	16-Nov-2017 19:15	117097
fdm.log	13-Oct-2017 09:30	56
hostAgentConfig.xml	07-Jul-2017 03:55	28018
hostd-probe.log	16-Nov-2017 19:40	422878
hostd.log	06-Nov-2017 01:30	10024546
hostdCgiServer.log	13-Oct-2017 09:30	5875
hostprofiletrace.log	13-Oct-2017 09:30	56
hosts	13-Oct-2017 09:29	228
issue	07-Jul-2017 03:55	0
lacp.log	08-Nov-2017 08:48	1906
license.cfg	13-Oct-2017 09:29	310
motd	07-Jul-2017 03:55	543

ESXi log files

When you want to collect all logs in one place to simplify the management, you can use the vSphere Syslog Collector. Syslog collector is part of the vCenter Server Appliance.

GUI Tools

Another solution which is very popular in recent months is vRealize Log Insight. This tool is very cool and can be used as a single location to collect and analyze all logs (not only VMware related). You can find additional information about vRealize Log Insight at the page `https://www.vmware.com/products/vrealize-log-insight.html`:

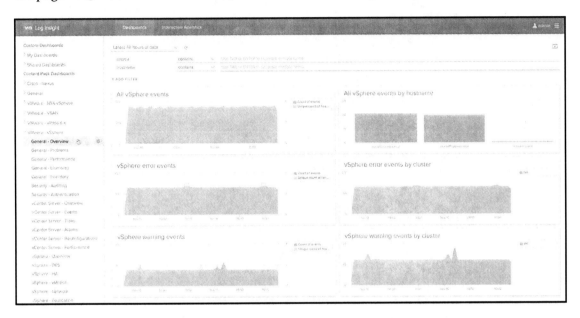

vRealize Log Insight dashboard

You can use this tool also for Microsoft, Veeam, and NetApp solutions only if the content pack is installed from the Marketplace:

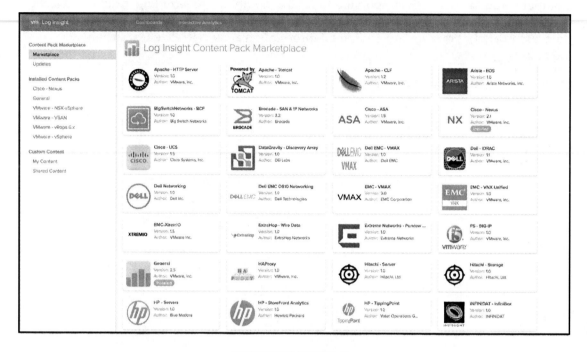

vRealize Log Insight-Marketplace view

We can close the Logs topic finishing with the next available and useful GUI tools.

vRealize Operations Manager

The first one is **vRealize Operations Manager** (vRO), which helps you to monitor and report your environment. vRO is a powerful tool which collects complex information about all objects in your VMware environment.

You can quickly identify the problematic parts of your infrastructure and start with the TRBL process. vRO can describe and recommend a solution (For more information refer to `https://www.vmware.com/products/vrealize-operations.html`).

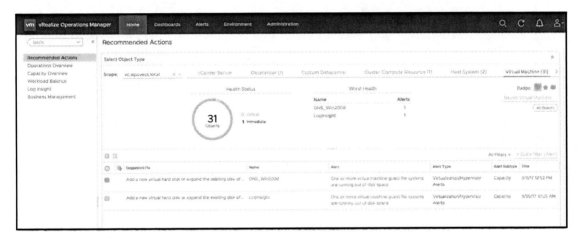

vRealize Operations Manager

You can also integrate vRealize Log Insight with vRO where a very important feature useful for troubleshooting is the reporting:

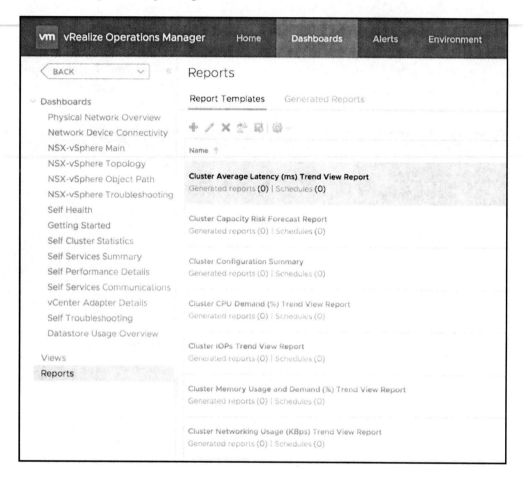

vRealize Operations Manager - Reports view

For a vRealize Log Insight, you can add vRO packs. For example, in the following screenshot, we see a Management Pack for NSX for vSphere. Additional information are available at the following website: `https://marketplace.vmware.com/vsx/solutions/management-pack-for-nsx-for-vsphere-3-5-1`:

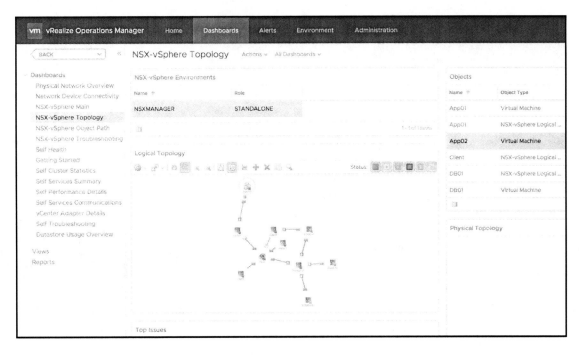

vRealize Operations Manager - NSX Pack view

We could write a book just about vRO, but the best way to learn the product is to download the trial and play with it. For the scope of the book, let's stay with the vRealize family.

vRealize Network Insight is a product for monitoring network and NSX environments. vRNI uses the tool NetFlow for collecting and it is a big friend for all NSX administrators because it allows tracing traffic and NSX components easily. Additional details are available at the address `https://www.vmware.com/products/vrealize-network-insight.html`.

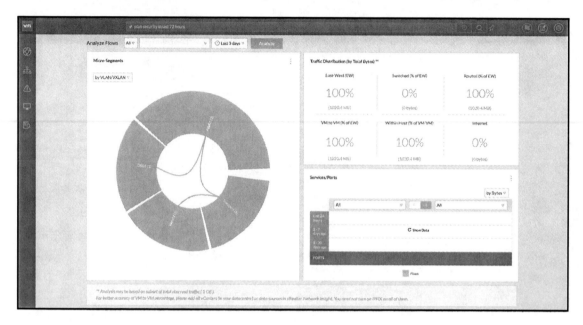

vRealize Network Insight

We discussed the tools available from the vRealize suit and more details can be found at the website: `https://www.vmware.com/products/vrealize-suite.html`. Still, it is possible to use the GUI for TRBL through the vSphere Web Client **Monitors** and **Performance** tabs. **Issues** and **Task & Events** tabs as well:

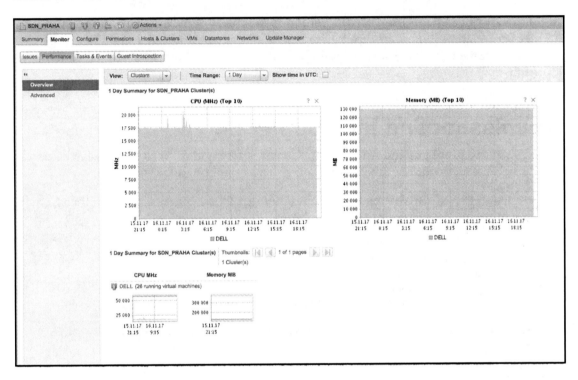

Performance vCenter view

Troubleshooting

Now that we have learned a lot about CLI or GUI commands and tools, we can start with specific troubleshooting aspects.

Troubleshooting can be focused on different infrastructural parts, like the ESXi hosts or the vCenter Server, the network, or the storage part or directly performed at the VM level. Depending on the different issues, it could be better to adopt a bottom-up or top-down approach.

Troubleshooting the vCenter Server

Troubleshooting problems and errors with vCenter Server and ESXi or Cluster can be very easy. Possible issues could be simply that some services are no longer working.

The first action to perform during the troubleshooting of a problem occurred in the vCenter Server, is to restart the service using the `service-control` command:

```
Command> service-control --list
vmware-vpostgres(VMware Postgres)
vmware-imagebuilder(VMware Image Builder Manager)
vmware-cm (VMware Component Manager)
vmware-vpxd (VMware vCenter Server)

Command> service-control --stop vmware-vpxd and service-control --start
vmware-vpx
```

When you see a problem in `vmkernel.log`, you can check the next important component, that is the vCenter Server database. Typical problems are disk capacity, CPU, and RAM. With vCSA, the database that can be used is only PostgreSQL, but with the Windows version of vCenter Server both Microsoft SQL Server or Oracle can be used.

For the vCenter Server Windows-based, you may use the available monitoring tools as a part of the database used, such as the Management Studio for MS-SQL or SQL Developer for Oracle. When you are using the vCSA, life is more much easier and you can use the new management console VAMI accessible through browser typing the address `https://vc.vsphere.local:5480`:

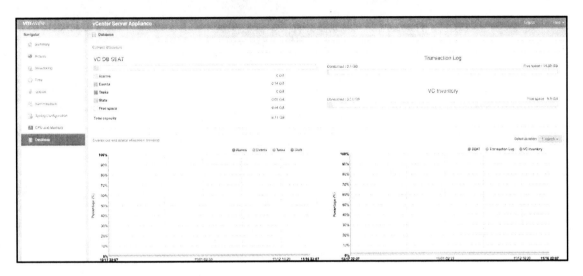

Database utilization - vCenter Server Appliance port 5480 view

To verify the size of the database, you can go to the **Database** tab of the VAMI and check the reported value.

You can also check the KB 2007388 - *Determining if vCenter Server rollup jobs are processing performance data* at `https://kb.vmware.com/s/article/2007388`.

Next step to solving the problem related to the database is trying to restart the vPostgresSQL using the command `service-control`. Next, it is usually useful to restart the problematic vSphere web client.

You can use a backup feature available only for the vCSA to restore the database. vCSA native backup will be discussed in `Chapter 14`, *Data and Workloads Protection*.

TRBL with ESXi host

A typical problem you may face with ESXi host, is the fatal error PSOD purple diagnostic screen:

Purple diagnostic screen

This crash is a problem that can be related to CPU, RAM, modules, hardware, or a software bug. When you see this error through iDRAC or iLO, you should take a photo or screenshot to support VMware. You can also try checking the VMware KB to find a resolution. *Did you experience PSOD after an ESXi upgrade?* A possible quick solution to fix the error is to perform an ESXi downgrade. This problem may also occur when you change RAM or firmware in HBA. All these situations can be potentially problematic for ESXi.

Another way to troubleshoot the problem is to gather maximum information from PSOD, such as last changes in the environment, and restart the ESXi host to create the log bundle requested by the VMware support. The log bundle can be created through GUI or through CLI with the command `vm-support`.

Question for you: *Is the PSOD occurred only on one ESXi host or all ESXi hosts with Qlogic FC HBA? Is it a specific ESXi build affected by the problem?* You must know this information because it can help to resolve the root problem.

The worst situation you can face is when the VMKernel is in stopped status and the ESXi host is not responding. When the VMkernel is busy and doesn't work correctly, as a possible solution you can try is the reboot of the host. After rebooting the ESXi is very important to gather logs and performance statistics for the support.

Troubleshooting cluster HA or DRS

Problems with cluster HA or DRS may occur at any time. If you have a problem with vSphere HA, you must first check the HA logs stored in the `/var/log/fdm.log` directory. A typical problem can occur during the installation of the `fdm` agent (HA agent) to the ESXi host. Logs where to check are located in `/var/log/esxupdate.log`.

If you have a problem with the `/root` partition space, it is possible to control the partition through CLI through the command `vdf`.

Other possible problems in the cluster can be related to VMkernel ports, VMs reservation on the target host and wrong network time. If the time is not synced in the VMware environment you can have issues. Another typical vMotion issue is often due to misconfiguration of the IP address, VLANs, and so on.

To check the VMkernel, you can use the command `ping` but when using the vMotion stack you should use the parameter `++netstack=vmotion`.

A problem with vMotion can be caused also by DRS. Keep in mind that DRS uses vMotion for balancing resources. Sometimes a problem is simply due to DSR misconfiguration (manual or fully automated setup) or related to DRS rules.

To get more information for a specific problem, the `esxtop` is a great tool you can use to monitor components like CPU or memory. Use the `esxtop` command specifying the `c` parameter for CPU and the `m` parameter for memory:

```
10:48:14pm up 34 days 13:19, 955 worlds, 14 VMs, 33 vCPUs; CPU load
average: 0.47, 0.47, 0.47
PCPU USED(%): 2.9 45 65 1.9 9.0 5.7 4.5 2.7 4.4 3.6 1.1 108 4.3 4.3 8.4 3.3
108 0.5 5.7 3.2 3.3 2.9 0.8 108 AVG: 21
PCPU UTIL(%): 3.4 44 58 2.4 8.1 5.6 4.5 2.8 4.8 3.9 2.1 99 4.4 4.4 8.0 3.3
99 1.1 5.7 3.4 3.4 3.0 1.4 99 AVG: 19
CORE UTIL(%): 46 60 13 6.9 7.8 99 8.5 11 99 8.7 6.0 99 AVG: 39

ID GID NAME NWLD %USED %RUN %SYS %WAIT %VMWAIT %RDY %IDLE %OVRLP %CSTP
%MLMTD %SWPWT
705902 705902 vrni-platform 16 461.94 434.55 0.10 1235.07 0.20 1.22 399.24
0.32 1.05 0.00 0.00
708709 708709 vrealize-automa 15 12.92 12.58 0.06 1500.00 0.00 0.20 405.57
0.05 0.00 0.00 0.00
42640 42640 NSX_Controller_ 12 11.07 11.45 0.10 1200.00 1.04 0.48 405.67
0.04 0.00 0.00 0.00
83831097 83831097 desktop-ubuntu 10 10.13 9.48 0.01 1000.00 0.00 0.11
202.62 0.01 0.00 0.00 0.00
50799 50799 NSX_Controller_ 12 9.87 10.22 0.11 1200.00 0.00 0.68 408.55
```

```
0.05 0.00 0.00 0.00
176174615 176174615 esxtop.22975861 1 5.09 4.06 0.00 100.00 - 0.00 0.00
0.00 0.00 0.00 0.00
712324 712324 LogInsight 12 4.90 5.03 0.08 1200.00 0.00 0.37 203.76 0.04
0.00 0.00 0.00
717682 717682 App02 9 1.91 1.76 0.01 900.00 0.52 0.03 102.23 0.00 0.00 0.00
0.00
716883 716883 App01 9 1.51 1.40 0.01 900.00 0.62 0.05 102.47 0.00 0.00 0.00
0.00
1 1 system 326 1.28 2012.73 0.00 31553.25 - 497.38 0.00 1.34 0.00 0.00 8.47
717706 717706 Web01 9 1.06 1.04 0.01 900.00 0.00 0.03 104.12 0.00 0.00 0.00
0.00
10737 10737 vpxa.67848 52 1.04 1.04 0.00 5200.00 - 0.09 0.00 0.00 0.00 0.00
0.00
6039 6039 hostd.67222 34 0.92 0.93 0.00 3400.00 - 0.06 0.00 0.00 0.00 0.00
0.00
24914 24914 EDGE-VIP-0 10 0.52 0.50 0.01 1000.00 0.08 0.06 103.94 0.00 0.00
0.00 0.00
33673 33673 EDGE-B-0 11 0.30 0.31 0.01 1100.00 0.09 0.05 104.09 0.00 0.00
0.00 0.00
15715 15715 EDGE-VIP-1 9 0.29 0.30 0.01 900.00 0.00 0.03 104.67 0.00 0.00
0.00 0.00
113730056 113730056 netcpa.14846937 30 0.27 0.32 0.00 3000.00 - 0.11 0.00
0.00 0.00 0.00 0.00
```

Troubleshooting virtual network

Every administrator around the world may have problems with the network connection and the first action to begin the troubleshooting process is the use of the command `ping`. Yes, an easy ping can help you but you have to ping from all directions: ESXi to vCSA and vCSA to ESXi. A typical possible TRBL scenario is when the network configuration is bad, VLAN is bad, NIC Teaming is not configured correctly, a port on a switch can be down, or there is a hardware problem with a vmnic or with a physical switch.

The following CLIs can help you to identify the problem:

```
esxcfg-vswitch
esxcfg-vmknic
esxcli network
esxcfg-nics
```

When you need a real change in the management network, you can repair it through DCUI.

From the DCUI, access the **Configure Management Network** section:

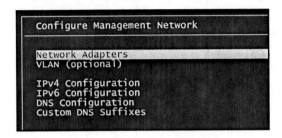

Configure Managment Network - DCUI detail

There is an option for a total restore of the network settings and the configuration can be done once more through DCUI.

In TRBL you must, of course, understand what vSS or vDS is. The problem can be anywhere, from the virtual machines to the physical network, software or hardware.

A very good CLI command for TRBL network is `esxcli network`. For example, a command which can be used to enable or disable a vmnic is `vmnic` followed by `up` or `down` parameters:

```
esxcli network nic down -n vmnic2
esxcli network nic up -n vmnic2
```

Network cards can be checked and listed using the command `esxcli network nic list`:

```
Name PCI Device Driver Admin Status Link Status Speed Duplex MAC Address
MTU Description
------ ------------- ------ ------------- ----------- ----- ------ ----------
------- ---- --------------------------------------------------------
vmnic0 0000:02:00.0 ntg3 Up Up 1000 Full 44:a8:42:22:a0:fe 1500 Broadcom
Corporation NetXtreme BCM5720 Gigabit Ethernet
vmnic1 0000:02:00.1 ntg3 Up Up 1000 Full 44:a8:42:22:a0:ff 1500 Broadcom
Corporation NetXtreme BCM5720 Gigabit Ethernet
vmnic2 0000:03:00.0 ntg3 Up Down 0 Half 44:a8:42:22:a1:00 1500 Broadcom
Corporation NetXtreme BCM5720 Gigabit Ethernet
vmnic3 0000:03:00.1 ntg3 Up Down 0 Half 44:a8:42:22:a1:01 1500 Broadcom
Corporation NetXtreme BCM5720 Gigabit Ethernet
vmnic4 0000:04:00.0 ixgbe Up Up 10000 Full 00:10:86:82:26:e8 9000 Intel(R)
82599 10 Gigabit Dual Port Network Connection
vmnic5 0000:04:00.1 ixgbe Up Up 10000 Full 00:10:86:82:26:e9 9000 Intel(R)
82599 10 Gigabit Dual Port Network Connection
```

A typical problem due to misconfiguration is the selection of a bad virtual machine's port group. Changing to the correct VLAN fix the problem.

Firewall and ports can raise a problem causing the block as well, but ports can be controlled referring to the VMware KB 1012382—*TCP and UDP Ports required to access VMware vCenter Server, VMware ESXi and ESX hosts, and other network components* at `https://kb.vmware.com/s/article/1012382`.

You must be very careful with the vCenter Server Windows-based when the internal firewall is used, UDP port `902` must be open to ensure the access to the vCenter Server. Since the Windows version has been deprecated, it is recommended to migrate all Windows-based vCenter Servers to vCSAs.

When you change the IP address of your management network, you can see an error message where you find text rolled back. This error is not an error but is your guard and name is **Rollback**. Rollback detects configuration changes on the MGMT network. If the configuration of the management network is bad (the change results in losing the host connection to the vCenter server), the change is rolled back automatically to the previous configuration. For additional information, check the VMware KB 2032823—*Understanding network rollback and recovery in vSphere 5.1 and later at* `https://kb.vmware.com/s/article/2032908`

`esxtop` tool can also be used to monitor the network using the parameter n:

```
PORT-ID USED-BY TEAM-PNIC DNAME PKTTX/s MbTX/s PSZTX PKTRX/s MbRX/s PSZRX
%DRPTX %DRPRX
33554433 Management n/a vSwitch0 0.00 0.00 0.00 0.00 0.00 0.00 0.00 0.00
33554434 vmnic0 - vSwitch0 392.15 4.05 1352.00 222.78 0.20 117.00 0.00 0.00
33554435 Shadow of vmnic0 n/a vSwitch0 0.00 0.00 0.00 0.00 0.00 0.00 0.00
0.00
33554436 vmk0 vmnic0 vSwitch0 10.68 0.04 431.00 9.54 0.00 65.00 0.00 0.00
33554437 72177:NSX_Controller_e9e75c82- vmnic0 vSwitch0 885.58 7.83 1158.00
780.68 4.45 746.00 0.00 0.00
33554438 73259:NSX_Controller_3bfd388a- vmnic0 vSwitch0 578.31 4.27 968.00
512.50 3.82 978.00 0.00 0.00
33554439 159714:vrni-platform vmnic0 vSwitch0 0.00 0.00 0.00 0.00 0.00 0.00
0.00 0.00
33554440 160131:vrealize-automation vmnic0 vSwitch0 0.19 0.00 42.00 0.19
0.00 60.00 0.00 0.00
33554441 160597:LogInsight vmnic0 vSwitch0 0.19 0.00 42.00 2.86 0.01 290.00
0.00 0.00
33554444 10960911:desktop-ubuntu vmnic0 vSwitch0 0.95 0.00 74.00 0.76 0.00
68.00 0.00 0.00
33554445 18573682:Guest Introspection ( vmnic0 vSwitch0 0.00 0.00 0.00 0.00
0.00 0.00 0.00 0.00
```

```
50331649 Management n/a vSwitch1 0.00 0.00 0.00 0.00 0.00 0.00 0.00 0.00
50331650 vmnic1 - vSwitch1 8.58 0.09 1407.00 8.58 0.01 121.00 0.00 0.00
50331651 Shadow of vmnic1 n/a vSwitch1 0.00 0.00 0.00 0.00 0.00 0.00 0.00
0.00
50331652 vmk3 vmnic1 vSwitch1 8.58 0.09 1407.00 8.58 0.01 121.00 0.00 0.00
67108865 Management n/a vmservice-vswit 0.00 0.00 0.00 0.00 0.00 0.00 0.00
0.00
67108866 vmk4 void vmservice-vswit 0.00 0.00 0.00 0.00 0.00 0.00 0.00 0.00
67108868 18573682:Guest Introspection ( void vmservice-vswit 0.00 0.00 0.00
0.00 0.00 0.00 0.00 0.00
83886081 Management n/a vSwitch2 0.00 0.00 0.00 0.00 0.00 0.00 0.00 0.00
100663297 Management n/a Mastering_New_v 0.00 0.00 0.00 0.00 0.00 0.00 0.00
0.00
100663298 vmnic2 - Mastering_New_v 0.00 0.00 0.00 0.00 0.00 0.00 0.00 0.00
100663299 Shadow of vmnic2 n/a Mastering_New_v 0.00 0.00 0.00 0.00 0.00
0.00 0.00 0.00
100663300 vmnic3 - Mastering_New_v 0.00 0.00 0.00 0.00 0.00 0.00 0.00 0.00
100663301 Shadow of vmnic3 n/a Mastering_New_v 0.00 0.00 0.00 0.00 0.00
0.00 0.00 0.00
117440513 Management n/a vSwitch3 0.00 0.00 0.00 0.00 0.00 0.00 0.00 0.00
117440514 vmk7 void vSwitch3 0.00 0.00 0.00 0.00 0.00 0.00 0.00 0.00
134217729 Management n/a DvsPortset-0 0.00 0.00 0.00 0.00 0.00 0.00 0.00
0.00
134217730 LACP_MgmtPort n/a DvsPortset-0 0.00 0.00 0.00 0.00 0.00 0.00 0.00
0.00
134217731 lag10gb n/a DvsPortset-0 0.00 0.00 0.00 0.00 0.00 0.00 0.00 0.00
134217732 vmnic4 - DvsPortset-0 1.14 0.00 124.00 0.38 0.00 146.00 0.00 0.00
134217733 Shadow of vmnic4 n/a DvsPortset-0 0.00 0.00 0.00 0.00 0.00 0.00
0.00 0.00
134217734 vmnic5 - DvsPortset-0 1.34 0.00 124.00 0.00 0.00 0.00 0.00 0.00
134217735 Shadow of vmnic5 n/a DvsPortset-0 0.00 0.00 0.00 0.00 0.00 0.00
0.00 0.00
134217736 vmk2 lag10gb* DvsPortset-0 0.00 0.00 0.00 0.00 0.00 0.00 0.00
0.00
134217737 vmk5 void DvsPortset-0 0.00 0.00 0.00 0.00 0.00 0.00 0.00 0.00
134217738 vmk6 lag10gb* DvsPortset-0 0.00 0.00 0.00 0.00 0.00 0.00 0.00
0.00
134217739 vdr-vdrPort lag10gb* DvsPortset-0 33.38 0.04 160.00 0.00 0.00
0.00 0.00 0.00
134217740 68676:EDGE-VIP-1.eth0 lag10gb* DvsPortset-0 0.00 0.00 0.00 0.00
0.00 0.00 0.00 0.00
134217741 69855:EDGE-VIP-0.eth0 lag10gb* DvsPortset-0 11.06 0.02 180.00
12.97 0.02 191.00 0.00 0.00
134217742 71005:EDGE-B-0.eth1 lag10gb* DvsPortset-0 0.00 0.00 0.00 0.19
0.00 90.00 0.00 0.00
134217743 71005:EDGE-B-0.eth0 lag10gb* DvsPortset-0 0.00 0.00 0.00 0.00
0.00 0.00 0.00 0.00
134217745 161231:App01.eth0 lag10gb* DvsPortset-0 7.06 0.01 141.00 6.87
```

```
0.01 117.00 0.00 0.00
134217746 161512:App02.eth0 lag10gb* DvsPortset-0 4.96 0.01 145.00 4.77
0.00 131.00 0.00 0.00</strong>
134217747 161521:DB01.eth0 lag10gb* DvsPortset-0 3.43 0.00 96.00 3.81 0.00
79.00 0.00 0.00
134217748 161534:Web01.eth0 lag10gb* DvsPortset-0 6.87 0.01 178.00 5.15
0.01 223.00 0.00 0.00
134217751 10960911:desktop-ubuntu.eth0 lag10gb* DvsPortset-0 0.19 0.00
74.00 0.19 0.00 102.00 0.00 0.00
```

Troubleshooting storage

When you want to quickly resolve problems with the storage, you must understand the architecture. There is a big difference between NFS and VMFS filesystems or if DAS, FC, FCoE, iSCSI or new vSAN or VVOL are used. A great friend will be `esxcli storage` and `esxcli iscsi` for special use with iSCSI storage only.

A problem you may need to analyze is the space occupied on the datastore. Use the command `df -h`:

```
[root@esxdell1:~] df -h
Filesystem Size Used Available Use% Mounted on
VMFS-5 1.8T 406.2G 1.4T 22% /vmfs/volumes/esxdell1_datastore1
VMFS-5 900.0G 828.5G 71.5G 92% /vmfs/volumes/NETAPP_NSX_iSCSI
vfat 285.8M 205.9M 80.0M 72% /vmfs/volumes/5559de5a-7b1a20ef-
ed91-0010868226e8
vfat 249.7M 178.5M 71.3M 71% /vmfs/volumes/8f8f587c-516422b7-
d925-07d7806f7725
vfat 249.7M 178.3M 71.4M 71%
/vmfs/volumes/2ecc137e-08e991b9-05cf-022195dd8353
vfat 4.0G 512.0K 4.0G 0% /vmfs/volumes/59863b3d-88e9d712-04c5-0010868226e8
```

To solve a problem with the LUN or LAN connectivity the `esxtop` tool is what you can use with parameters u, d or v.

- With parameter u, the output will be as follows:

```
10:21:00pm up 34 days 12:52, 956 worlds, 14 VMs, 33 vCPUs; CPU
load average: 0.50, 0.47, 0.46

DEVICE PATH/WORLD/PARTITION DQLEN WQLEN ACTV QUED %USD LOAD
CMDS/s READS/s WRITES/s MBREAD/s MBWRTN/s DAVG/cmd KAVG/cm
naa.60a98000534b487558353737756324f2f - 128 - 0 0 0 0.00 4.58
0.19 4.39 0.00 0.01 0.73 0.0
naa.644a8420210904001cc39b5814256147 - 32 - 0 0 0 0.00 583.46
0.57 582.89 0.00 20.21 16.52 2.3
```

- With parameter d, the output will be as follows:

```
ADAPTR PATH NPTH CMDS/s READS/s WRITES/s MBREAD/s MBWRTN/s
DAVG/cmd KAVG/cmd GAVG/cmd QAVG/cmd
vmhba0 - 1 11.44 0.00 11.44 0.00 0.07 0.27 0.01 0.28 0.00
vmhba1 - 0 0.00 0.00 0.00 0.00 0.00 0.00 0.00 0.00 0.00
vmhba2 - 0 0.00 0.00 0.00 0.00 0.00 0.00 0.00 0.00 0.00
vmhba64 - 1 7.63 0.00 7.63 0.00 0.03 0.51 0.01 0.51 0.00
```

- With parameter v, the output will be as follows:

```
GID VMNAME VDEVNAME NVDISK CMDS/s READS/s WRITES/s MBREAD/s
MBWRTN/s LAT/rd LAT/wr
15715 EDGE-VIP-1 - 2 2.86 0.00 2.86 0.00 0.02 0.000 2.159
24914 EDGE-VIP-0 - 2 1.53 0.00 1.53 0.00 0.00 0.000 0.673
33673 EDGE-B-0 - 2 1.14 0.00 1.14 0.00 0.00 0.000 0.708
42640 NSX_Controller_ - 1 5.53 0.00 5.53 0.00 0.06 0.000 2.688
50799 NSX_Controller_ - 1 118.64 0.00 118.64 0.00 0.97 0.000
24.871
705902 vrni-platform - 1 15.26 0.00 15.26 0.00 0.13 0.000 1.740
708709 vrealize-automa - 4 14.31 0.00 14.31 0.00 0.12 0.000
0.691
712324 LogInsight - 3 34.33 0.19 34.14 0.00 0.38 29.899 2.275
716883 App01 - 1 0.00 0.00 0.00 0.00 0.00 0.000 0.000
717674 DB01 - 1 0.00 0.00 0.00 0.00 0.00 0.000 0.000
717682 App02 - 1 0.00 0.00 0.00 0.00 0.00 0.000 0.000
717706 Web01 - 1 0.00 0.00 0.00 0.00 0.00 0.000 0.000
83831097 desktop-ubuntu - 1 0.00 0.00 0.00 0.00 0.00 0.000
0.000
142397216 Guest Introspec - 1 0.00 0.00 0.00 0.00 0.00 0.000
0.900
```

To change in the configuration view, use the parameter `f` and set what you need to see.

A quick overview of the ESXTOP command in pdf format is available at `http://www.running-system.com/wp-content/uploads/2015/04/ESXTOP_vSphere6.pdf`.

Troubleshooting VMs

The last component you may need to troubleshoot is the VMs. Typical issues are related to power-on, delete, misconfiguration, and resources.

To list the files belonging to a specific VM you use the command `ls -lh`:

```
[root@esxdell1:/vmfs/volumes/55c2fd45-d88e90e6-ae16-
e41f13b3b2d0/WEB_Server_01] ls -lh
total 5899280
-rw------- 1 root root 1.0G Aug 12 13:47 WEB_Server_01-ecc960d0.vswp
-rw------- 1 root root 20.0G Oct 13 06:46 WEB_Server_01-flat.vmdk
-rw------- 1 root root 8.5K Aug 12 13:47 WEB_Server_01.nvram
-rw------- 1 root root 533 Aug 12 13:47 WEB_Server_01.vmdk
-rw-r--r-- 1 root root 0 Nov 3 2015 WEB_Server_01.vmsd
-rwxr-xr-x 1 root root 2.7K Aug 12 13:47 WEB_Server_01.vmx
-rw------- 1 root root 0 Aug 12 13:47 WEB_Server_01.vmx.lck
-rw------- 1 root root 150 Nov 18 2015 WEB_Server_01.vmxf
-rwxr-xr-x 1 root root 2.7K Aug 12 13:47 WEB_Server_01.vmx~
-rw-r--r-- 1 root root 226.8K Nov 18 2015 vmware-1.log
-rw-r--r-- 1 root root 203.6K Feb 9 2016 vmware-2.log
-rw-r--r-- 1 root root 180.8K Feb 9 2016 vmware-3.log
-rw-r--r-- 1 root root 152.1K Feb 12 2016 vmware-4.log
-rw-r--r-- 1 root root 177.0K May 29 23:16 vmware-5.log
-rw-r--r-- 1 root root 196.7K Aug 11 20:02 vmware-6.log
-rw-r--r-- 1 root root 167.8K Aug 12 13:47 vmware.log
-rw------- 1 root root 110.0M Aug 12 13:47 vmx-
WEB_Server_01-3972620496-1.vswp
```

During the TRBL process, the `vmware.log` is the virtual machine's log file that helps to better understand the problem. In this log, you see all the details about the problem. The name of the log file `vmware.log` is the same for each VM.

A problem that quite often may occur to your VMs is the error message related to a locked file. When you click on power-on VM option, the system displays the error *the file is locked*. For this situation there is the command `vmkfstools -D` to manage the file lock. The important modes are as follows:

- `mode 0`: No lock
- `mode 1`: Exclusive lock
- `mode 2`: Read-only lock

To solve the lock file error, proceed as follow:

1. Run the command `vmkfstools -D <locked disk>`, you can identify the mode type in use (for example, `mode 1`: exclusive lock) and the MAC Address of the ESXi host that holds the VM lock (you have to look at the last part of the number, `0010868226e2` as in the following example).

```
vmkfstools -D WEB_Server_01-flat.vmdk
Lock [type 10c00001 offset 226893824 v 301, hb offset 3751936
gen 635, mode 1, owner 598e133a-a788d32f-337a-0010868226e2 mtime 17138
num 0 gblnum 0 gblgen 0 gblbrk 0]
Addr <4, 526, 148>, gen 282, links 1, type reg, flags 0, uid 0, gid 0, mode
600
len 21474836480, nb 4619 tbz 0, cow 0, newSinceEpoch 4619, zla 3, bs
1048576

vmnic4  0000:04:00.0  ixgbe    Up             Up            10000  Full
00:10:86:82:26:e2  9000  Intel(R) 82599 10 Gigabit Dual Port Network
```

2. When you know which host holds a lock, connect the ESXi through SSH to remove the lock.
3. Run the command `lsof | grep <file_of_locked_file>` to obtain the PID of the process for the VM.
4. The final step is to use the command `kill -9 PID` to kill the process. If the problem is not solved, you may try rebooting the host.

In the following example, we will get the PID of a VM (using the step 3), and then use this PID to kill the VM (as explained in step 4):

```
[root@esxdell2:~] lsof | grep WEB_Server_01-flat.vmdk
5065291 less FILE 4 WEB_Server_01-flat.vmdk
[root@esxdell2:~] kill -9 5065291
```

A lot of problems are due to resources, resource pools, and vApp thus you should be very careful. If it is not a requirement, don't use reservations or limits for VMs.

Although troubleshooting can fix most of the problems, there are situations where the VM restore from the backup is the only possible solution. Backup is an essential part of the vSphere management.

Great! You are now ready for basic TRBL operations.

Summary

This chapter covered the vSphere native tools that can be used to monitor and troubleshoot performance and other issues in a virtual environment.

Monitoring and troubleshooting are really important tasks to improve the virtual environment and the workloads for performance and efficiency. The chapter focuses on monitoring different critical resources, such as computing, storage, and networking, across the ESXi hosts, the resource pools, and clusters.

In order to help monitoring and troubleshooting, there are also other tools, complementary to the vSphere suite, such as vRealize Operations and several third-party tools specific to those tasks.

In the next chapter, we will discuss security aspects and how to improve the security of a vSphere environment.

10
Securing and Protecting Your Environment

One of the pillars of virtualization is the VM isolation property that can protect the host layer from the VM, effectively. Although some possible attacks have been found, virtualization remains an interesting approach to improve the security of your infrastructure.

But the isolation property doesn't work for the network layer, which remains potentially weak from a security point of view, even though standard and distributed virtual switches have some specific security features. VMware NSX tries to provide better security with micro-segmentation.

A new trend is now also to protect VMs from the underlying infrastructure; for example, in the case of a public cloud service, consumers may have some concerns about the security and privacy of their data.

This chapter will cover the following topics:

- Tuning and hardening guidelines
- Working with encryption and securing VMs

Regulations and compliance

Industry and regulatory compliance standards help protect computing assets from various security vulnerabilities and misconfiguration, and minimize the risk in various execution environments, such as development, test, and production.

There are different standards such as the following:

- **Payment Card Industry (PCI)**: `https://www.pcisecuritystandards.org/`
- **Health Insurance Portability and Accountability Act (HIPAA)**: `http://www.hhs.gov/ocr/privacy/`
- **Federal Information Security Management Act (FISMA)**: `http://csrc.nist.gov/groups/SMA/fisma/faqs.html`
- **Department of Defense Information Assurance Certification and Accreditation Process (DIACAP)**: `http://www.diacap.net/`
- **Federal Risk Authorization Management Program (FedRAMP)**: `https://www.fedramp.gov/`
- **Gramm Leach Bliley Act (GLBA)**: `https://en.wikipedia.org/wiki/Gramm-Leach-Bliley_Act`

The VMware Compliance Reference Architecture Framework and the Secure and Compliance Capable Platform help customers to improve their security and IT strategies by matching compliance and governance requirements. The VMware Compliance Reference Architecture Framework defines independently validated programs for creating secure and compliant environments for different standards. For more information, see `https://www.vmware.com/solutions/compliance-cyber-risk.html`.

Security and hardening concepts in vSphere

Security is a complete process flow with an entire lifecycle; depending on the model that will be used, the first part of the process is usually product agnostic, but then there is a part dependent on the different products and their features and capabilities.

Following VMware's vision, the five pillars of cyber hygiene are as follows:

- **Least privilege**: This is the common and most reasonable approach, that applies for user accounts, service accounts, and services in general (for example, used ports).
- **Micro-segmentation**: Using NSX, it's finally possible to bring network control at VM level with granular security rules. Considering also the new product VMware AppDefense, VM security can be enforced at both network and application levels.
- **Encryption**: Data must be protected at each level, and for the physical level, encryption is the only way to ensure good protection. We will discuss this later in the chapter.

- **Multi-factor authentication**: Authentication is usually the weakest part, mostly due to passwords that are too simple (or passwords that are not changed periodically). We will discuss this later in the chapter.
- **Patching**: Keeping your software components up to date is crucial for the security aspect, but it's also very important for implementing new features. We will discuss this more in `Chapter 11`, *Lifecycle Management, Patching, and Upgrade*.

Hardening vSphere

Hardening is the process of securing a system, a service, or an entire infrastructure, by reducing the attack surface and minimizing the possible vulnerabilities. VMware has built some *Security Hardening Guides*, which can found at `https://www.vmware.com/security/hardening-guides.html`, to provide prescriptive guidance for customers on how to deploy and operate VMware products in a secure manner.

The *vSphere 6.5 Security Configuration Guide* is a spreadsheet file with several guidelines classified with a risk profile, useful as a checklist for your tuning, with rich metadata for guideline classification and risk assessment. There are also some example scripts for enabling security automation. For more information on how to read them and how the guidelines have changed since the previous release, see `https://blogs.vmware.com/vsphere/2017/04/vsphere-6-5-security-configuration-guide-now-available.html`.

> The *vSphere 6.5 Security Configuration Guide* isn't a compliance tool; it can be used to reach compliance, but it's not automatically enforced. It's mostly a set of guidelines that attempt to explain security risks, but there can also be more solutions to mitigate them. Also, the guidelines may or may not be applicable to specific customer cases.

Host hardening

To protect the ESXi hosts against unauthorized intrusion and misuse, consider the following options for improving infrastructure security:

- **Limit user access**: This is done by restricting user access to the management interface and enforcing access security policies such as setting up password restrictions. Lockdown Mode could be used to limit access to the hosts to all users, otherwise a centralized authentication could be useful to manage security groups and related roles (for example, with AD).

- **Limit shell access**: ESXi Shell (locally, but also through ESXi SSH access) has several privileged accesses to certain parts of the host. Therefore, provide only trusted users with ESXi Shell login access. Usually, it is safe to keep both ESXi Shell and SSH access disabled, to prevent direct access to the ESXi CLI. In this case, you can still use `esxcli` remotely or another remote CLI.

- **Limit services**: You can run ESXi essential services only. Some hardware vendors have specific agents that can run on ESXi hosts, but check their support and security level before running any third-party agents or services on ESXi hosts.

- **Limit network connections**: ESXi has a personal firewall (starting from ESXi 5.0) and, by default, is closed on most ports. When you enable a service, it also opens the right ports. Although you can manually open ports with the predefined firewall rules, or you can also build new custom ESXi firewall rules, it could be better to try to keep the ESXi firewall rules management totally automatic. The personal firewall does not protect you from DoS attacks, so still keep your ESXi VMkernel interfaces on protected networks and still use perimeter firewalls.

- **Use secure connections**: By default, weak ciphers are disabled and all communication from clients is secured by SSL. The exact algorithms used for securing the channel depend on the **SSL handshake**. VMware vSphere 6.0 introduces a certification authority to help in certification management. Starting with vSphere 6.5, the **Transport Layer Security (TLS)** protocol versions 1.0, 1.1, and 1.2 are enabled by default.

- **Patch your hosts**: Use only VMware sources to upgrade or patch ESXi hosts. VMware does not support upgrading these packages from any source other than a VMware source.

- **Check VMware Security Center:** VMware monitors all security alerts that could affect ESXi security and, if necessary, issues a security patch. If you regularly check the VMware Security Center site, you can find any alerts that might impact the environment.

Lockdown Mode

When you connect ESXi to vCenter, to increase the host's security, it can be put in **Lockdown Mode**. When enabled, Lockdown mode prevents remote users from logging directly onto this host. The host will only be accessible through the local console or an authorized centralized management application. It is possible to modify lockdown mode configuration in the host settings, or (usually) from the **Direct Console User Interface (DCUI)**.

In vSphere 6.5, Lockdown Mode has multiple settings and a user exception list. This allows users and solutions to be excluded from the lockdown mode settings. The following are the different configuration options available:

- **Disabled**: Lockdown Mode is disabled.
- **Normal**: DCUI is not blocked. Privileged user accounts can still log in to the ESXi host console and exit lockdown mode.
- **Strict**: DCUI is stopped and is only accessible through vCenter:

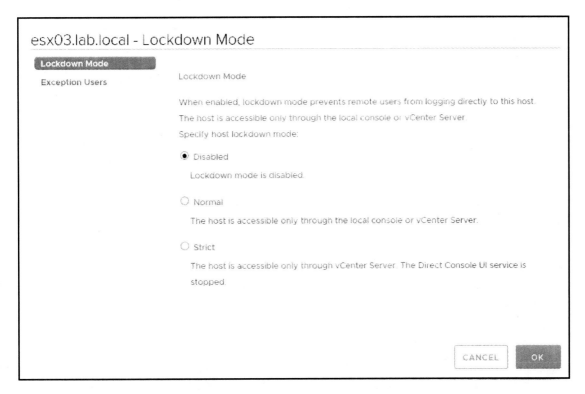

ESXi Lockdown mode

Strict mode dramatically reduces the manageability of the hosts because CLI commands cannot be executed from an administration server or script. Exception users is a list of accounts that still keep their permissions when the host enters lockdown mode; for example, the accounts are used by third-party solutions and external applications that must continue their function in lockdown mode. To keep lockdown mode uncompromised, you should add only user accounts that are associated with applications.

Networking

If you are using distributed virtual switches, there are some specific network security configurations that can be managed only from the host advanced settings. For example, to enable the **Bridge Protocol Data Unit (BPDU)** filter, you must use a host advanced setting **Net.BlockGuestBPDU** as described in KB 2047822—*Understanding the BPDU Filter feature in vSphere* at https://kb.vmware.com/kb/2047822.

Of course, the security policies (promiscuous mode, MAC address change, and forge packets) for the virtual switches are still important, but for distributed virtual switches, they are just all rejected (starting with vSphere 5.1).

Virtual switches do not provide firewall functions (ESXi personal firewall works only on VMkernel ports); to implement micro-segmentation, you need solutions such as NSX.

Transparent Page Sharing (TPS)

Recent academic research has demonstrated that it is theoretically possible to leverage TPS to gain unauthorized access to data under certain highly controlled conditions. For more information, see https://blogs.vmware.com/security/2014/10/transparent-page-sharing-additional-management-capabilities-new-default-settings.html.

For this reason, in vSphere 6.x, TPS is disabled across different VMs, but is still working inside individual VMs. It is still possible to enable it on the entire ESXi, by following KB 2097593—*Additional Transparent Page Sharing management capabilities and new default settings* at https://kb.vmware.com/kb/2097593.

VIB acceptance levels

By default, ESXi only allows signed **vSphere Installation Bundle (VIB)**, because an unsigned VIB represents untested code installed on an ESXi host. You can change the acceptance level for each host, in the **Configure, System, Security Profile** menu, under the **Host Image Profile Acceptance Level** option:

Host image profile acceptance level

The host image profile supports the four acceptance levels:

- **VMware Certified**: VIBs created, tested, and signed by VMware.
- **VMware Accepted**: VIBs created by a VMware partner but tested and signed by VMware.
- **Partner Supported**: VIBs created, tested, and signed by a certified VMware partner.
- **Community Supported**: VIBs that have not been tested by VMware or a VMware partner. Community Supported VIBs are not supported and do not have a digital signature. To protect the security and integrity of your ESXi hosts, do not allow unsigned Community Supported VIBs to be installed on your hosts.

VM hardening

The hardening guide describes a lot of specific VM options but, starting with ESXi 6.0 Patch 5, many of the VM advanced settings are now set to be *Secure By Default*. This means that the desired values in the *Security Configuration Guide* are the default values for all new VMs and you don't have to manually set them anymore.

For more information, see the blog post at `https://blogs.vmware.com/vsphere/2017/06/secure-default-vm-disable-unexposed-features.html`.

For virtual networking, NSX can provide the micro-segmentation capability to enforce network security directly at VM virtual NIC level. Also, at VMworld 2017, a new product was announced—**VMware AppDefense**, a data center endpoint security product that protects applications running in virtualized environments. AppDefense works *inside* the VMs (as compared to NSX that works only at the network level) and understands how applications are supposed to work *normally* and monitors all changes to that behavior state that indicate a threat.

VMware vCenter hardening

By using the vCSA, as also suggested by VMware, you can use the same VM hardening suggestions and also benefit from a hardened OS. By default, shell access is disabled. SSH can be enabled during deployment but you still access the vCSA with a limited set of commands (anyway, enabling the full shell is quite easy).

PSC security best practices are quite simple and are as follows:

- **Check password expiration**: The default vCenter SSO password lifetime is 90 days.
- **Configure NTP**: This ensures that all systems use the same relative time source (including the relevant localization offset). Synchronized systems are essential for vCenter SSO certificate validity, and for the validity of other vSphere certificates.

Authentication and identity

The vCenter SSO authenticates a user in an identity source (configured in the vCenter SSO). **Identity Sources** define how and where to verify user credentials, for this reason, are a possible authentication backend, and vSphere supports the following:

- **Active Directory (native)**: When the PSC is joined to an AD domain, it is possible to use the domain or the forest as an authentication source
- **LDAP (Active Directory)**: If you don't want to join the PSC to the AD domain, or if you are using a lightweight active directory

- **LDAP (OpenLDAP)**: If you have an open source based LDAP server (such as OpenLDAP)
- **Local OS**: The user defined in the SAM (for a Windows-based PSC) or the `/etc/passwd` and `/etc/shadow` file (for a Linux-based PSC)

The SSO domain is always enabled and included in the identity sources shown as follows:

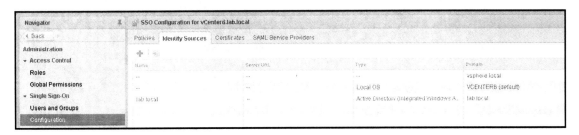

SSO identity sources

You can add new sources, but actually only from the vSphere Web Client (Flash). It also appears in the HTML5 client, but it's just an embedded page from the Flash client.

Users and groups could be used to define vSphere permissions at two different levels:

- **Inventory object level:** This is the traditional way, where you can add permissions by matching a user or group with a specific vSphere role on a specific object. It is useful if you need to delegate some management tasks.
- **Global level:** This is an option available with the vSphere Web Client (but now also with the HTML5 client), where you can define global permissions (with a specific role) on the entire infrastructure:

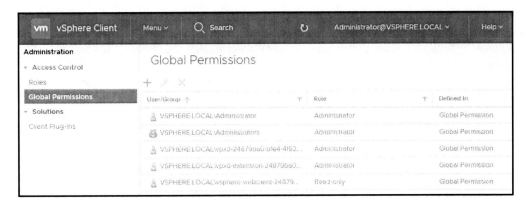

Global permissions

Global permissions are defined at PSC level, so several vCenter servers connected to the same PSC share the same global permissions.

Permissions are assigned with a role-based model, where you are going to match the object (if permission is not global), the user, or the group with the right role. A role is just a set of permissions and you can use predefined roles or build (or copy) new ones. Starting with vSphere 6.0 Update 2, you can include a login banner with your environment. You can enable and disable the login banner from the SSO configuration, and you can require that users click an explicit consent checkbox.

Password management

It is really important to use strong passwords that are not easily guessed and that are difficult for password generators. Password strength and complexity rules apply to all passwords, including hosts users (such as root).

ESXi uses the `pam_passwdqc.so` plugin to set the strength and the complexity of host's passwords. You can define the password quality using the host's advanced system settings, called `Security.PasswordQualityControl`.

ESXi 6.0 has introduced a new account lockout feature; by default, a maximum of 10 failed attempts is allowed before the account is locked. The account is unlocked after 2 minutes by default. In the host's events you will see the following row:

```
Remote access to ESXi local user account 'LOGINNAME' has been locked for
120 seconds after ### failed login attempts.
```

Account locking works for access through SSH and through the vSphere Web Services SDK. It does not apply to the DCUI and ESXi Shell. For vCenter Server (or rather the PSC component), SSO users have specific policies defined in the SSO configuration (actually only through the vSphere Web Client):

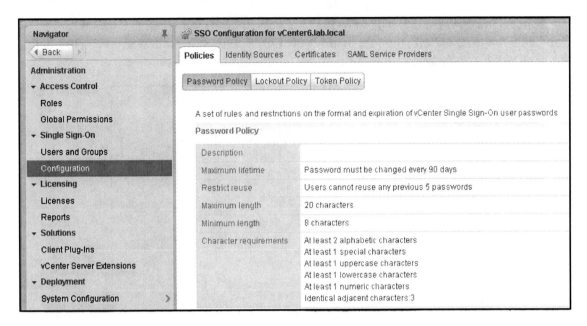

SSO configuration

 If you are using AD users, both for hosts and vCenter, then the password policies are enforced by the AD GPO.

There are also password expiration rules for the virtual appliance local users, in case you are using vCSA for vCenter and/or the PSC components. Be sure to also check those settings.

AD authentication

Using AD for user authentication simplifies permission management, ensures password complexity, and allows you to use the same security policies for the AD to minimize the risk of unauthorized access. For vCenter Server, you can add additional identity sources, as discussed; usually, the PSC component is joined to the AD domain in order to use the native AD integration.

For ESXi hosts, it is possible to set the authentication to the AD domain to eliminate the need to create and maintain multiple local user accounts. For more details, see KB 2075361—*Configuring the ESXi host with Active Directory authentication* at `https://kb.vmware.com/kb/2075361`.

You can use the vSphere Web Client or the vSphere Client (HTML5) and choose the **Configure** tab on the ESXi , then the **Authentication Services** menu, followed by clicking on **Join Domain** button:

ESXi AD Join Domain

 All users and groups that are assigned as members of the AD group ESX Admins will have full administrative access to all ESXi hosts in the domain.

If you use host profiles to configure AD authentication for your hosts, then the AD credentials are saved in the host profile and are transmitted over the network. You can use the vSphere Authentication Proxy to avoid storing AD credentials in a host profile and to avoid transmitting them over the network.

Multi-factor authentication (MFA)

MFA grants user access only after successfully presenting several separate pieces of evidence to an authentication mechanism, usually at least two of the following categories—knowledge (something they know), possession (something they have), and inherence (something they are).

Two-factor authentication (2FA) is a type of MFA where just two components are used.

Starting with vSphere 6.0 Update 2, it is possible to have a 2FA using the following:

- Smart card (UPN-based Common Access Card or CAC)
- RSA SecurID token

vCenter SSO supports only native SecurID and does not support RADIUS authentication.

Smart cards

A smart card is a small plastic card with an embedded integrated circuit chip that can be read by a smart card reader (many laptops may have one integrated). To enable smart card authentication for vCenter authentication, you must first set up your clients before users can log in using a smart card:

- With vSphere 6.0, verify that the Client Integration Plugin is installed
- With vSphere 6.5, verify that the Enhanced Authentication Plugin is installed

Then the configuration of the PSC is a little different in versions 6.0 and 6.5. For the latest version, before you can enable smart card authentication, you must properly configure the reverse proxy from the command line on the PSC (or the vCenter if you have an embedded deployment). You have to create a trusted client **Certificate Authority (CA)** store, that contains the trusted issuing CA's certificates for the client certificate.

For a Linux-based PSC, these are the possible commands:

```
cd /usr/lib/vmware-sso/

openssl x509 -inform PEM -in xyzCompanySmartCardSigningCA.cer >>
/usr/lib/vmware-sso/vmware-sts/conf/clienttrustCA.pem
```

Then you have to modify the `config.xml` file with the following changes:

```
<http>
<maxConnections> 2048 </maxConnections>
<requestClientCertificate>true</requestClientCertificate>
<clientCertificateMaxSize>4096</clientCertificateMaxSize>
<clientCAListFile>/usr/lib/vmware-sso/vmware-
sts/conf/clienttrustCA.pem</clientCAListFile>
</http>
```

And finally restart the service:

```
/usr/lib/vmware-vmon/vmon-cli --restart rhttpproxy
```

Then verify that an enterprise **Public Key Infrastructure (PKI)** is set up in your environment and that certificates meet the following requirements:

- A **User Principal Name (UPN)** must correspond to an AD account in the **Subject Alternative Name (SAN)** extension
- The certificate must specify **Client Authentication** in the **Application Policies** or **Enhanced Key Usage** fields or the browser does not show the certificate

At this point, you can simply enable smart card authentication from the SSO configuration menu.

Starting with ESXi 6.0, it's also possible to use smart card authentication to log in to the ESXi DCUI by using a **Personal Identity Verification (PIV)**, CAC, or SC650 smart card instead specifying a username and password. Under **Configure | System**, select **Authentication Services** (described before for AD authentication) and you will see the current smart card authentication status and a list of imported certificates.

In the **Smart Card Authentication** panel, you can click **Edit...** and select the **Certificates** page in order to add trusted CA certificates, for example, root and intermediary CA certificates.

RSA SecurID

SecurID setup is supported only from the command line on vCenter Server version 6.0 or later. The configuration is well explained in the following blog post at https://blogs.vmware.com/vsphere/2017/07/using-vcenter-login-banner-rsa-securid-support.html.

Then the integration is quite simple on the Web Client authentication page:

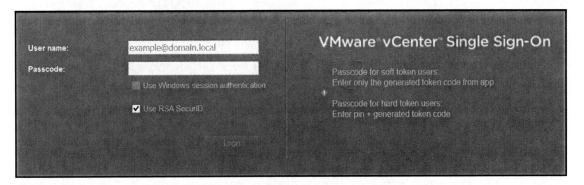

RSA SecurID authentication

RSA Authentication Manager requires that the user ID is a unique identifier that uses 1 to 255 ASCII characters. The characters ampersand (&), percent (%), greater than (>), less than (<), and single quote (`) are not allowed. Also, the RSA SecurID agent that is integrated into the PSC component of vCenter does not support PIN resets.

Other security aspects

There are several other aspects that should be considered for security purpose, for example, log management and system monitoring; both of them are useful not only for the security of your environment, but also for the manageability.

Another common aspect that will be discussed is the certification management, that has been widely improved starting with vSphere 6.0 version.

Log management

All ESXi hosts run a syslog service (`vmsyslogd`), that logs messages from the VMkernel and other system components to log files. The log destination can be configured from the vSphere Client; select the host and click **Configure | Settings | Advanced System Settings**. By default, the `Syslog.global.logDir` parameter is set to `[] /scratch/log`.

ESXi can be configured to store log files on an in-memory filesystem. This occurs when the host's /scratch directory is linked to /tmp/scratch. When this is done, only a single day's worth of logs is stored at a time. For more information on ESXi partitions, see Chapter 5, *Configuring and Managing vSphere 6.5*.

You can also set a syslog server, both with the GUI (under the advanced settings) or with the CLI, for example, from ESXi Shell:

```
esxcli system syslog config set –loghost tcp://SYSLOG_SERVER:514
esxcli system syslog reload
```

You can use more syslog servers, using a comma, or also use SSL connections instead of clear TCP (or UDP); in this case, you must use the syntax ssl://SYSLOG_SERVER:1514.

For more information, see KB 2003322—*Configuring syslog on ESXi at* https://kb.vmware.com/kb/2003322.

You can use an external third-party syslog server or the following VMware solutions:

- **VMware Syslog Collector**, included in vCenter Server. It supports TLS protocol versions 1.0, 1.1, and 1.2. But it does not have a simple way to analyze the log.
- **VMware vRealize Log Insight server**, a dedicated product also used to correlate different logs and get to the root cause of issues more quickly and efficiently.

vRealize Log Insight 3.3.2 and above, will accept the vCenter Server Standard 6.x or 5.x license key and provide 25 OSI pack (syslog sources).

For more information on Log Insight, see the VMware KB 2144909—*FAQ: Log Insight for vCenter Server* at http://kb.vmware.com/kb/2144909.

Monitoring protocols

By default, SNMP is not enabled on hosts, either as a service or as a configured node. If you want to enable the SNMP service, in order to use this protocol, then, for each host, the proper trap destination should be configured as also a correct community.

ESXi 5.1 and later, supports SNMPv3, which provides stronger security than SNMPv1 or SNMPv2, including key authentication and encryption.

Also on vCenter Server, you can enable sending traps on different alarms, but the SNMP receivers must be set in the general configuration. If SNMP is not being used, it might be better to keep it disabled; if it is not properly configured, monitoring information can be collected from a malicious host that can then use this information to plan an attack.

Certification management

Starting with vSphere 6.0, the new PSC component includes not only the SSO part, but also a certification authority, **VMware Certificate Authority (VMCA)**, for certification management of all vSphere infrastructure elements (unfortunately, it is not yet being used by all the other VMware products). This simplifies not only the certification management (with auto-enrollment for expired certificates) but also the trust between the different connections.

In this environment, the vSphere certificates are generated and issued by the VMCA and stored by the **vSphere Endpoint Certificate Store (VECS)**. But to avoid browser warnings, you need to trust on the VMware's CA by adding at your certification chain. First of all, you need to gain the CA root certificate. You can simply download it from the vCenter home page, under **Download trusted root CA certificates**:

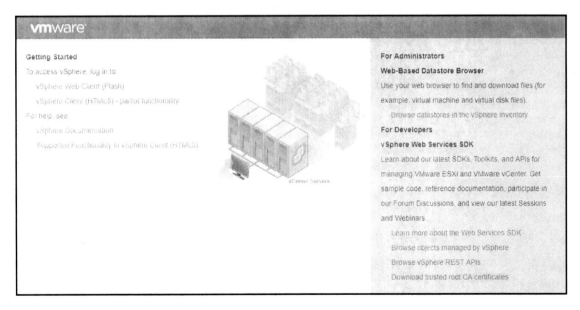

Default web page of vCenter Server

You will download a simple `download.zip` file that contains both the CA certificate and the revocation list.

In order to import the certificate, you can use different approaches for a Windows system:

- **Import manually**: For Internet Explorer, Edge, and Chrome, you can simply double-click on the certificate and import it into the trusted CA. Firefox has a different certificates repository.
- **Import by using GPO**: Under **Computer Configuration | Windows Setting | Security Settings | Public Key Policies | Trusted Publishers**, you can import existing certificates. Be sure to import it into the **Trusted Root Certification Authorities** store.
- Add as an intermediate CA in your existing CA authority.

Otherwise, you can replace the CA certificate of VMCA, or just don't use it at all and manage all the certificates as in the past. For more information, see VMware KB 2097936—*How to use vSphere 6.x Certificate Manager* described in (`https://kb.vmware.com/kb/2097936`).

New security options in vSphere 6.5

VMware vSphere 6.5 has several improvements for the security aspects; a new vCenter linked mode, VM encryption, VM Secure Boot, and enhanced logging. And of course, several improvements and bug fixes.

For more details, see also `https://blogs.vmware.com/vsphere/2016/10/whats-new-in-vsphere-6-5-security.html`.

VMware vCenter federations

You can join multiple vCenter Server systems using vCenter Linked Mode (introduced in vSphere 4.0) to build a single pane of glass and share information between vCenter instances, such as views, and manage the inventories of all the vCenter Server systems that are linked. With vSphere 6.0, a new vCenter **Enhanced Linked Mode (ELM)** was introduced to replace the existing Linked Mode capability that was based on Microsoft ADAM technology. In this way, it was finally possible to have Linked Mode capability for both Windows-based vCenter Server as well as the vCSA, with new features and functions, such as the cross-vCenter vMotion.

With ELM, it is possible to use a single SSO domain for all vCenters with single-pane-of-glass management (HTML5 client is also supported), with a maximum of 15 vCenters (with vSphere 6.5 U1). A PSC must be deployed externally; embedded vCenter Server is not supported. Roles, global permissions, licenses, certificates, vSphere tags, and VM storage policies are automatically replicated across all vCenter instances.

You have to configure ELM during installation of PSC and vCenter Server; post-deployment is not supported.

But with the new **VMware Cloud on AWS (VMC)** offering, there is also a new **Hybrid Linked Mode (HLM)**, with a completely different implementation and some differences from ELM:

- SSO domains will be different between on-premises and VMC; however, it is a 1:1 relationship.
- Instead of a two-way trust, a one-way trust is established, where the *cloud part* trusts the on-premises vCenter Server and data is synced unidirectional from on-premises to the cloud.
- It can be configured at any point in the on-premises vCenter Server, not only during the initial installation.
- Actually, it requires that the on-premises vCenter Server is an embedded deployment; an external PSC is not supported. It will be interesting to see whether it will be changed in the future.

For more information about the differences between ELM and HLM, see `http://www.virtuallyghetto.com/2017/09/enhanced-linked-mode-elm-vs-hybrid-linked-mode-hlm.html`.

 Actually, in vSphere 6.0 and 6.5, it is not possible to merge SSO domains or migrate easily from an embedded PSC to an external deployment or vice versa.

Protecting the data at rest

There are different possible options to store your data securely which are as follows:

- **Encryption at storage physical level:** This is done by using **self-encrypting drives (SED)** using full disk encryption, also known as hardware-based **full-disk encryption (FDE)**. Opal Storage Specification is a set of specifications for SED developed by the Trusted Computing Group. But those types of disks are quite costly and also require controllers or storage that support this feature.
- **Encryption at storage logic level:** This is done by using vSAN encryption that uses an AES 256 cipher and eliminates the extra cost, limitations, and complexity associated with purchasing and maintaining self-encrypting drives. vSAN datastore encryption is enabled and configured at the datastore level. In other words, every object on the vSAN datastore is encrypted when this feature is enabled.
- **Encryption at VM level**: This is a new feature of the vSphere 6.5 Enterprise Plus edition. Previously, it was only possible with third-party products.
- **Encryption inside the VM:** Consider, for example, using Microsoft BitLocker, or using a Linux-encrypted filesystem (with `losetup` or other tools).

For more information, see also the official vSphere 6.5 Encryption FAQ at `https://blogs.vmware.com/vsphere/2017/10/vsphere-6-5-encryption-faq-now-available.html`.

VM encryption

A new feature introduced in vSphere 6.5 is the encryption of VMs, that secures the VMDK virtual disks (also `.vmx` and `swap` files are encrypted), making the stored data unreadable.

To take benefit of encryption, you need to connect vCenter Server to a working **Key Management Server (KMS)** that provides the necessary keys to encrypt and decrypt VMs using the **Key Management Interoperability Protocol (KMIP)** protocol. To establish the connection between KMS and vCenter Server, the KMS performs a certificate exchange.

The components required to allow VM encryption features are the following:

- **KMS**: Generates and stores the keys passed to the vCenter Server to encrypt and decrypt the VMs.
- **vCenter Server**: This is the only component that can log in to the KMS to obtain the keys and push them to ESXi hosts. KMS keys are not stored in vCenter Server, which keeps a list of keys IDs only.

A KMS cluster configured in vCenter Server requires that all KMS instances added to the cluster are from the same vendor and must replicate keys. If you use different vendors in different environments, you can create a KMS cluster for each KMS specifying the default cluster. The first cluster added becomes the default cluster.

At the time of writing, there are three following KMS providers certified by VMware:

- **HyTrust KeyControl**: `https://www.hytrust.com/`
- **Dell-EMC CloudLink**: `http://www.cloudlinktech.com/data-security-products/secure-vm/`
- **IBM Security Key Lifecycle Manager**: `http://www-03.ibm.com/software/products/en/key-lifecycle-manager`
- **Thales Vormetric Data Security Manager:** `https://www.thalesesecurity.it/products/data-encryption/vormetric-data-security-manager`
- **Gemalto SafeNet KeySecure**: `https://safenet.gemalto.com/data-encryption/enterprise-key-management/key-secure/`

Additional vendors are going through certification.

A KMS is required to enable and use vSAN encryption. Multiple KMS vendors are compatible, including HyTrust, Gemalto (SafeNet), Thales e-Security, CloudLink, and Vormetric.

Access to the encrypted virtual disk requires a correct key owned only by the VM that manages the virtual disk. An unauthorized VM that tries to access the encrypted VMDK without the correct key will receive only meaningless data. No additional hardware is required for the encryption/decryption operation and performance is improved if the used processor supports the AES-NI instruction set because encryption is CPU-intensive. AES-NI should be enabled in your BIOS.

The encryption and decryption process of VMs is controlled by storage policies and the VM needs to be powered off before proceeding.

To encrypt VMs, you first need to configure a KMS in vCenter Server:

1. From the vSphere Web Client, select vCenter Server in the inventory and select the **Configure** tab. Expand **More** and select **Key Management Servers** to access the KMS management section.

2. Click the **Add KMS** icon to add the KMS server (you must have one in your network). Specify the required parameters and click **OK** to save the configuration:

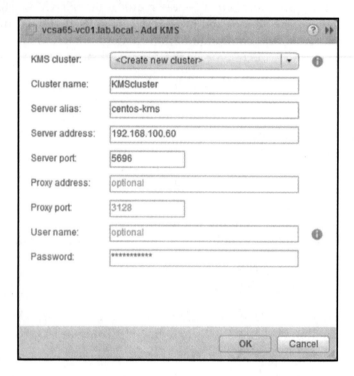

Adding a KMS to vCenter

3. Once the KMS server is successfully added to vCenter Server, the **Connection Status** column is displayed as **Normal**. Once you have configured the KMS server, you can start encrypting VMs:

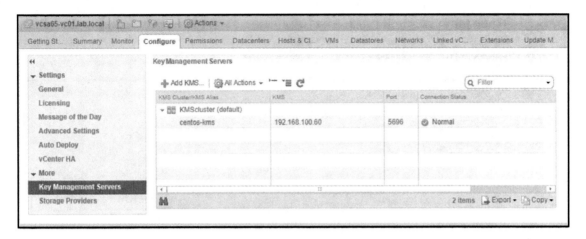

Checking the KMS configuration

Change the storage policy of a VM by following this procedure:

1. From the vSphere Client, access vCenter Server and right-click the VM to encrypt. Select **VM Policies** | **Edit VM Storage Policies**.

2. From the **VM storage policy** drop-down menu, select the **VM Encryption Policy** option to encrypt the VM and click **OK**:

VM encryption policy

3. When the encryption process has completed, the VM Hardware area in the VMs **Summary** tab displays the **Encryption** field that indicates which components are encrypted:

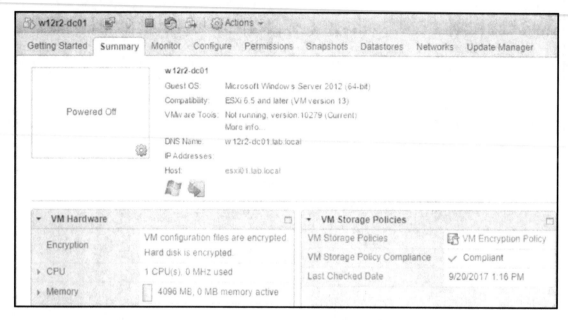

Encrypted VM

Here are some recommendations for using encrypted VMs:

- PSC and vCenter Server VMs should not be encrypted.
- The support bundle used to decrypt a core dump is generated using the ESXi host key. If the host is rebooted, the host key may change and the support bundle can no longer be generated with a password or decrypt core dumps in the support bundle with the host key. For this reason, if the host crashes, you should retrieve the support bundle as soon as possible.
- Since `.vmx` files and `.vmdk` descriptor files contain the support bundle, do not edit these files, otherwise the VM becomes unrecoverable.

Encryption and decryption of a VM can also be performed using PowerCLI.

- To encrypt a VM, run the following command:

```
Get-VM -Name <vmname> | Enable VMencryption
```

- To decrypt a VM, use the following command:

  ```
  Get-VM -Name <vmname> | Disable VMencryption
  ```

 Encrypted VMs can be a potential challenge for native backup programs, but there is a way to permit backup of those encrypted files in a clear format, to permit indexing and granular restore. Several backup products already support this feature.

Also, you have to consider the following caveats:

- vSphere FT, vSphere Replication, and content library do not work with VM encryption.
- Snapshot operations have some limitations; for example, you cannot select the **Snapshot the virtual machine's memory** checkbox.
- Cloning an encrypted VM or performing a Storage vMotion operation and changing the disk format may not work. For example, if you clone a VM and attempt to change the disk format from lazy zeroed thick format to thin format, the VM disk keeps the lazy zeroed thick format.
- You cannot encrypt a VM and its disks by using the **Edit Settings...** menu. You have to use the storage policy.
- When you detach a disk from a VM, the storage policy information for the virtual disk is not retained.
- OVF export is not supported on an encrypted VM.
- You can use vSphere VM Encryption with IPv6 in mixed mode, but not in a pure IPv6 environment.
- The vCenter Server become more critical; only vCenter Server has the credentials for logging in to the KMS. Your ESXi hosts do not have those credentials. vCenter Server obtains keys from the KMS and pushes them to the ESXi hosts.

Protecting data in motion

Protecting the stored data is only a part of the data security; you also need to encrypt or make secure the network connections and how data is moved. Data in motion is trickier to protect. The best way is always to use secure channels and communication.

At VM level, it is a problem that is addressed and managed as in any physical environment. Do not only use VLAN (or VXLAN) to segregate traffic but use the right network traffic rules (in this case, NSX can help with micro-segmentation) and try to avoid clear text network communication.

But you have also the infrastructure part to consider. VMware vSphere management traffic is already on SSL connections since version 3.5, but other types of traffic are usually not encrypted, such as vMotion (until vSphere 6.5), or FT logging or storage traffic based on IP, such as iSCSI or NFS traffic.

Encrypted vMotion

The vMotion encryption feature isn't simply an encrypting of the entire network channel for the vMotion traffic. There aren't certificates to manage.

The encryption happens on a per-VM level; when the VM is migrated, a randomly generated, one-time-use 256-bit key is generated by vCenter (it does not use the KMS). In addition, a 64-bit *nonce* (an arbitrary number used only once in a crypto operation) is also generated. The encryption key and nonce are packaged into the migration specification sent to both hosts. At that point, all the VM vMotion data is encrypted with both the key and the nonce, ensuring that communications can't be used to replay the data:

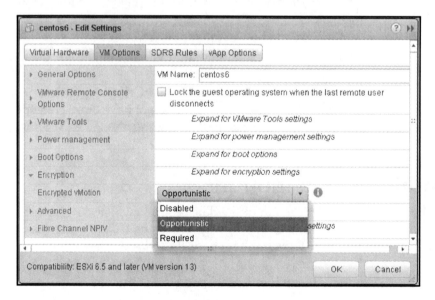

Encrypted vMotion

You can disable vMotion encryption, unless the VM is encrypted; in this case, it is always enforced.

Secure boot

Unified Extensible Firmware Interface (UEFI) is a replacement for the traditional BIOS firmware that has its roots in the original IBM PC. With secure boot, the UEFI firmware validates the digital signature of the OS and its bootloader to ensure that only a properly signed system will boot.

With vSphere ESXi 6.5, you can have secure boot in both ESXi and VM.

ESXi secure boot

For ESXi, secure boot is possible using the digital signature of all VIB components, like a cryptographic assurance. By leveraging that digital certificate in the host UEFI firmware, at boot time, the validated ESXi VMkernel will subsequently validate each VIB against the same certificate:

Secure boot

 When ESXi secure boot is enabled, you will not be able to forcibly install unsigned code on ESXi.

For more information on how to enable this feature and some possible issues such as during the upgrade process, see the following post at `https://blogs.vmware.com/vsphere/2017/05/secure-boot-esxi-6-5-hypervisor-assurance.html`.

VM secure boot

In an OS that supports UEFI secure boot, each piece of boot software is signed, including the bootloader, the OS kernel, and OS drivers.

VM secure boot has some important requirements:

- Virtual hardware version 13 or later
- EFI firmware in the VM boot options
- Guest OS that supports UEFI secure boot

Some examples of supported OS are Windows 8 and Windows Server 2012 or newer, VMware ESXi 6.5 and Photon OS, RHEL/Centos 7.0, and Ubuntu 14.04.

You can enable secure boot, using the vSphere Web Client, in the **VM Options** of the selected VM:

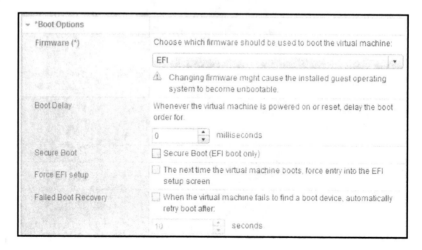

VM boot options

You cannot upgrade a VM that uses BIOS boot to a VM that uses UEFI boot. Only if a VM already uses UEFI boot and the OS supports UEFI secure boot can you simply enable secure boot.

Enhanced logging

vSphere logs have traditionally been focused on troubleshooting and not on being security or even IT operations oriented, until vSphere 6.5 with the introduction of the newly enhanced logging.

VMware vSphere 6.5 offers enhanced audit-quality logging capabilities to provide detailed information about all user actions and track *who*, *what*, *when*, and *how*.

Summary

Security has become a critical part of any implementation, also for the virtual environment. In addition to the security and hardening aspects of vSphere, the new 6.5 version introduces some important new features related to this aspect, such as audit-quality logging of vSphere events, VM encryption, encrypted vMotion, secure boot support for VMs, and secure boot plus Cryptographic Hypervisor Assurance for ESXi.

In this chapter, we have explained some security topics, such as security and hardening concepts in vSphere, new security options in vSphere 6.5, and how to design for security.

In the next chapter we will discuss other administrator tasks, somehow related also with security aspects; how to patch and manage the lifecycle of the different infrastructural components of a vSphere environment.

11
Lifecycle Management, Patching, and Upgrading

vSphere 6.5 simplifies and enhances the capabilities for patching and upgrading ESXi hosts and vCSAs. vSphere 6.5 introduces a lot of new features and improvements, such as the vCSA with the integrated VUM, vCenter HA, and so on, that make migration to the latest release a recommended task.

The VUM service is now fully integrated in the vCSA and no longer requires an additional external Windows server. The embedded VUM can also benefit from the vCenter HA feature for redundancy. VUM is enabled by default and only a minor configuration is required to have a system ready to handle patches and upgrade tasks. This chapter will discuss how to patch ESXi hosts using the command line when no vCenter Servers are available in the network.

vSphere 6.5 includes a migration tool that allows administrators to easily and quickly upgrade from version 6.0 to 6.5. With the release of Update 1, now vSphere 6.0 Update 3 installations can also be upgraded to vSphere 6.5 Update 1.

In this chapter, we will cover the following topics:

- Lifecycle management improvements in vSphere 6.5
- Patching ESXi hosts with the command line and VUM
- Patching vCenter Server using **vCenter Server Appliance Web Console (VAMI)** and **vSphere Update Manager (VUM)**
- Configuring VUM and baseline creation
- Upgrade workflow and procedures
- Migration from previous vSphere versions using the migration tool

Updating or patching ESXi hosts and vCSAs

Keeping ESXi hosts and vCenter Servers up-to-date is not only an essential best practice, but it's strongly recommended to ensure the correct functionality of the virtual platform and protection from bugs. Several ways are available to patch ESXi hosts using—VUM, (this will be discussed later in the chapter) to update all hosts automatically or, if no vCenter Servers are present in the network, using the command line. Also, the vCSA can be patched in different ways that will be analyzed later on.

Updating or patching ESXi hosts through the command line

Patches and updates for ESXi are combined in a bundle provided by VMware in a `.zip` format that includes some VIBs (ESXi software packages) containing fixes and updates. To proceed with the update, you need to obtain the latest available patches from the VMware website at the URL `https://my.vmware.com/group/vmware/patch`. Patches and upgrades are cumulative and the patch bundle is provided including all the previous security and critical updates.

Once the patch bundle has been downloaded, proceed with the following steps:

1. From vSphere Client, log in to the ESXi host in order to upload the downloaded bundle to a local datastore reachable by the host. In the **Navigator** area, select **Storage** then select **Datastores** on the right side.
2. From the available datastores, select the location on which you want to upload the patch and click **Datastore browser**.
3. Create a new folder or select an existing folder then click the **Upload** button to upload the patch. Click **Close** when the upload has completed.

> Alternatively, you can use a tool such as WinSCP to copy the patch bundle directly to a local datastore on the ESXi host. This may be an option if ESXi hosts to be patched in the network don't have access to the same shared storage.

4. SSH the host using a tool such as PuTTY and log in to the host by entering the root credentials. If the SSH shell is not enabled, from vSphere Client, right-click the **Host** item and select **Services | Enable Secure Shell (SSH)** or enable the SSH service directly from the DCUI as discussed in `Chapter 5`, *Configuring and Managing vSphere 6.5*.

5. Before patching the host, it can be useful to identify the currently installed build version by running the following command:

```
esxcli system version get
```

```
[root@esxi01:~] esxcli system version get
    Product: VMware ESXi
    Version: 6.5.0
    Build: Releasebuild-4564106
    Update: 0
    Patch: 0
[root@esxi01:~]
```

esxcli command used to get the system version

6. Before applying the patch, the host must be put in Maintenance Mode in order to migrate running VM off the host and preventing new VMs to be placed in the hypervisor. To enter the host in Maintenance Mode, from the command line, run the following command:

```
esxcli system maintenanceMode set --enable true
```

7. Make sure the ESXi is in Maintenance Mode, then proceed with the update procedure by running the following command:

```
esxcli software vib update -d
/vmfs/volumes/datastore/patch_bundle.zip
```

```
[root@esxi01:~] esxcli software vib update -d /vmfs/volumes/local_vmfs01/patches
/update-from-esxi6.5-6.5_update01.zip
Installation Result
    Message: The update completed successfully, but the system needs to be reboot
ed for the changes to be effective.
    Reboot Required: true
    VIBs Installed: VMW_bootbank_ehci-ehci-hcd_1.0-4vmw.650.0.14.5146846, VMW_boo
tbank_i40en_1.3.1-5vmw.650.1.26.5969303, VMW_bootbank_igbn_0.1.0.0-14vmw.650.1.2
6.5969303, VMW_bootbank_ixgben_1.4.1-2vmw.650.1.26.5969303, VMW_bootbank_misc-dr
ivers_6.5.0-1.26.5969303, VMW_bootbank_ne1000_0.8.0-16vmw.650.1.26.5969303, VMW_
bootbank_ntg3_4.1.2.0-1vmw.650.1.26.5969303, VMW_bootbank_nvme_1.2.0.32-4vmw.650
.1.26.5969303, VMW_bootbank_pvscsi_0.1-1vmw.650.1.26.5969303, VMW_bootbank_qlnat
ivefc_2.1.50.0-1vmw.650.1.26.5969303, VMW_bootbank_sata-ahci_3.0-26vmw.650.1.26.
5969303, VMW_bootbank_usbcore-usb_1.0-3vmw.650.1.26.5969303, VMW_bootbank_vmkata
_0.1-1vmw.650.1.26.5969303, VMW_bootbank_vmkusb_0.1-1vmw.650.1.26.5969303, VMW_b
```

ESXi can be updated using esxcli commands

8. When the patch has been applied successfully, you may need to reboot the host. Run the following command to reboot the host:

```
reboot
```

9. When the ESXi host has rebooted, exit the host from Maintenance Mode with the following command:

```
esxcli system maintenanceMode set --enable false
```

The ESXi is now patched and available to host VMs.

 To quickly put the host in Maintenance Mode using vSphere Client, right-click the **Host** item and select **Enter Maintenance Mode**.

10. Check the host version after the update to confirm the update was successful by running the following command:

```
esxcli system version get
```

Updating hosts using vSphere Client

The ESXi host can also be updated using the new HTML5 vSphere Client:

1. Log in to the hypervisor to update, select **Manage** in the **Navigator** area and go to the **Packages** tab.
2. Select the updates to install and click the **Install update** button:

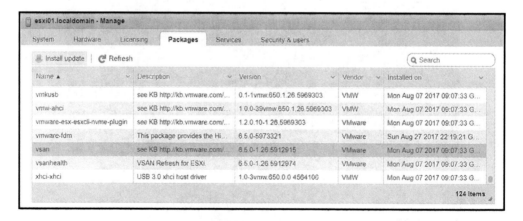

List of available patches from vSphere Client

3. You are prompted to enter the URL or datastore path of the selected VIB. Click **Update** to apply the selected update.

Updating the vCSA through the command line

In vSphere 6.5, upgrading the vCSA has also been simplified. There are two ways to patch the vCSA—VAMI introduced in vSphere 6 or using the command line. From the VMware website, download the latest vCenter Server update provided in ISO format and save it anywhere in your computer. The ISO image containing the patches must be uploaded to shared storage accessible from the vCSA present in the network. The ISO image can also be attached to the CD/DVD drive of the vCSA.

 Before proceeding with the update, take a snapshot of the vCSA to quickly revert to a working state in case something goes wrong during the patching process.

Staging and remediating patches

Patches from the ISO file previously downloaded from the VMware website can be staged to the vCSA to update by attaching the ISO image to the CD/DVD drive of the vCSA or specifying a datastore ISO file.

 Staging patches is useful procedure to speed up the remediation process because patches are already available locally on the vCSA and the downtime during remediation is reduced.

Mount the ISO image patch to the vCSA 6.5 VM and SSH the vCSA using a tool such as PuTTY. Enter the root credentials to log in to the vCSA and proceed with the upgrade procedure of the vCSA.

To stage the patches from the attached ISO image, run the following command:

```
software-packages stage --iso
```

Staged patches information can be checked with the following command:

```
software-packages list --staged
```

```
Command> software-packages list --staged
 [2017-10-02T11:48:22.275] :
        category: Security
        kb: https://docs.vmware.com/en/VMware-vSphere/6.5/rn/vcenter-server-appl
iance-photonos-security-patches.html
        vendor: VMware, Inc.
        name: VC-6.5.0U1a-Appliance-FP
        tags: [u'']
        summary: Patch for vCenter Server Appliance 6.5 with security fixes for
PhotonOS
        version_supported: [u'6.5.0.10000']
        thirdPartyInstallation: False
        releasedate: September 21, 2017
        TPP_ISO: False
        version: 6.5.0.10100
        buildnumber: 6671409
        rebootrequired: True
        productname: VMware vCenter Server Appliance
        eulaAcceptTime: 2017-10-02 11:47:35 UTC
        severity: Critical
Command>
```

Staged patches can be checked before applying

If a mistake is made during the patch staging procedure, you can always unstage the staged patches by running the following command:

```
software-packages unstage
```

To install staged patches, run the following command from the command line:

```
software-packages install --staged
```

Staging patches is not a requirement and updates can be installed directly from an attached ISO image. To install patches directly from the ISO image, run the following command:

```
software-packages install --iso
```

The patch installation process requires a few minutes to complete and a reboot may be necessary.

Updating the vCSA with VAMI

To make the overall procedure simpler, the vCSA can also be updated using the UI through the VAMI. To access the VAMI, type `https://<VCSA_IP>:5480` into your favorite browser and enter the root credentials.

Perform the following steps to install available updates from the repository or from the ISO image:

1. Access the **Update** tab and select the **Check Updates** | **Check Repository** option in order to check available updates from the default VMware repository.

2. If the ISO image has been mounted to the vCSA 6.5 VM, from the **Update** tab, select the **Check Updates** | **Check CDROM** option to install available updates directly from the ISO image.

3. If a new update is detected, the **Available Updates** area displays the information related to the available update but the current release doesn't provide a list of patches that will be installed in the system. Click **Install Updates** to proceed with the update installation:

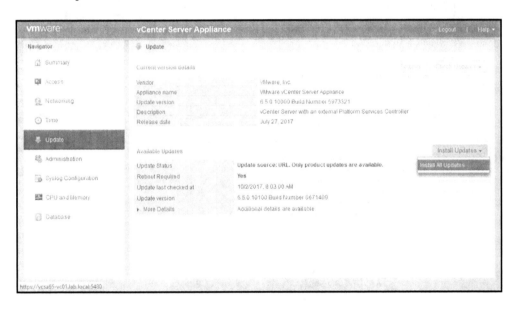

vCSA updates can be applied using VAMI that provides a simple and intuitive GUI

4. The installation requires a few minutes to complete and a reboot of the vCSA may be required to complete the update process. Click **OK**:

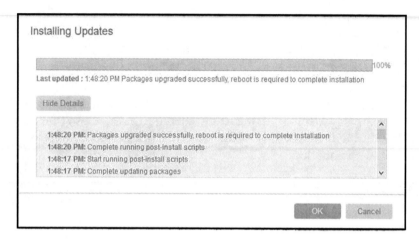

Installing Updates

100%

Last updated : 1:48:20 PM Packages upgraded successfully, reboot is required to complete installation

Hide Details

1:48:20 PM: Packages upgraded successfully, reboot is required to complete installation
1:48:20 PM: Complete running post-install scripts
1:48:17 PM: Start running post-install scripts
1:48:17 PM: Complete updating packages

OK   Cancel

With a single click, available patches are automatically installed in the vCSA

If a vCSA in your network is configured with PSC, patches or updates must be applied first to the PSC and its replicating partners then, if installed, in the vCenter SSO domain. For the correct update sequence, there is a dedicated KB article 2147289—*Update sequence for vSphere 6.5 and its compatible VMware products* in the VMware KB at the URL `https://kb.vmware.com/kb/2147289`.

If a proxy is enabled in the network configuration of your vCSA, you might experience a generic *Download failed* error (both PSC and vCenter Server are affected) when you try checking updates online through VAMI.

To quickly fix the issue, perform the following steps:

1. From the vCSA UI, enable the **Proxy Settings** in the **Networking** area
2. SSH the vCSA and edit the `/etc/sysconfig/proxy` file and manually enter a valid HTTP proxy address in the `HTTPS_PROXY` line, for example:

```
HTTPS_PROXY="https://proxy.domain.com:3128/"
```

VUM

VUM service is a tool available in vSphere 6.5 that allows you to easily manage patches and updates for VM, hosts, and vApps installed in the virtual environment. As compared to previous versions, VUM no longer requires the installation of an additional external Windows server because in vSphere 6.5, the Update Manager server and client components are now part of the vCSA.

VUM is installed during the vCSA installation procedure and it's enabled by default. VUM uses a PostgreSQL database that is bundled with the appliance to store its data. Although both vCenter Server and VUM share the same PostgreSQL database, they use a different database instance.

 In vSphere 6.5, a Windows based Update Manager 6.5 instance cannot be connected to a vCSA 6.5 during the installation procedure because it will fail with an error.

If the Update Manager doesn't have access to the internet, you can install the optional module **Update Manager Download Service (UMDS)** to download virtual appliance upgrades, patch binaries, patch metadata, and notifications. UMDS must be installed on a machine with internet access and, in version 6.5, it's available for both Windows and Linux based OS.

Configuring VUM

Default settings configured during the vCSA installation can be modified from the Update Manager administration area and changes are applied only to the Update Manager instance specified. If you have multiple Update Manager instances in your SSO domain, changes are not propagated to other instances in the group. To specify the Update Manager instance to work with, you have to select the name of the vCenter Server on which the Update Manager instance is registered.

Update Manager uses some specific TCP ports for its communications. If you experience conflicts with other applications, you can change the port number, assigning a new value.

The following table shows default ports used by Update Manager:

TCP port number	Description
80	Used by VUM to connect to vCenter Server
9084	ESXi hosts use this port to access host patch downloads over HTTP
902	Used to push host upgrade files
8084	Update Manager Client plugin uses this port to connect to the Update Manager SOAP server
9087	HTTPS port used by Update Manager Client plugin to upload host upgrade files

Table 11.1: Update Manager default ports

To configure VUM from vSphere Web Client, select **Home** I **Update Manager** and specify the vCenter Server instance to edit. In the **Manage** tab, you can specify the following VUM configuration settings:

- **Network Connectivity**: From this tab, you can only change the IP address or the hostname for the patch store.
- **Download Settings**: Edit this area to specify the patch type to download and additional custom URLs to specify third-party patch repositories. By enabling the **Use a shared repository** option, you can specify the URL of the UMDS instance used to centralize the downloads. If a proxy is used to access the internet, edit the **Proxy Settings** area to specify the correct parameters. Patches in ZIP format can also be imported in the repository using the **Import Patches...** button.

 Since the service strongly relies on DNS resolution, use an IP address whenever possible to avoid any potential DNS resolution problems. If you use a DNS name, make sure that the specified DNS name can be resolved by vCenter Server and from all ESXi hosts managed by the Update Manager.

- **Download Schedule:** In this area, you specify the frequency of patch downloads with the option of sending a notification email (SMTP settings must be configured in vCenter Server by accessing the **Configure** I **General** area).

- **Notification Check Schedule**: To specify the frequency used by Update Manager to check the VMware repository for notifications about patch recalls, new fixes, and alerts.
- **VM Settings**: You can specify whether a snapshot of the VM should be taken before applying the patch. In case the remediation fails, you can quickly roll back to the state before applying the patch. Since snapshots affect the VM performance, it's strongly recommended that a snapshot retention policy is defined to delete the created snapshots, saving precious storage space:

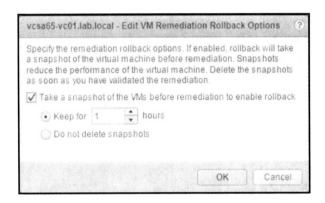

To avoid performance issues snapshots should be removed from the VM by configuring a suitable retention

- **Host/Cluster Settings**: This area allows the control of the operations required during remediation. To apply the updates, the target host must be put in Maintenance Mode and running VM must be migrated to other hosts of the cluster to ensure availability. The operation can be automated if vSphere vMotion is configured and DRS is enabled in the cluster. You can also specify to install patches on PXE booted hosts, but updates are lost after the host reboots.

The configuration of these settings may vary depending on the setup of your infrastructure but, as a general guideline, you can configure host and cluster settings as follows:

- **Disable any removable media devices**: Removable devices may prevent the host entering in Maintenance Mode
- **Disable admission control**: It is suggested this parameter is disabled to make additional resources available to the cluster, especially if you have a few hosts

- **Disable FT**: This is required if you have two hosts only:

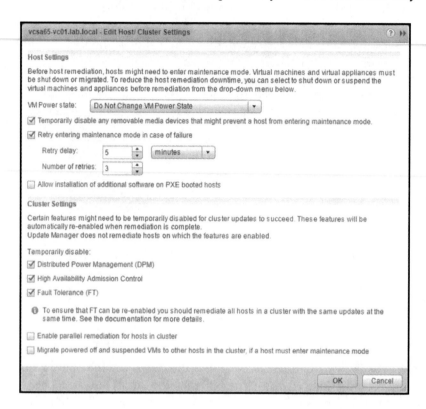

Host and cluster can be configured to automate the upgrade process

When a new ESXi patch is available, make sure to update the image used for PXE booted hosts as soon as possible to have the patch applied in a persistent way.

- **vApp Setting**: Enabled by default, this allows you to specify the use of the smart reboot feature to reboot the virtual appliances, maintaining the correct startup dependencies.

Working with baselines

To upgrade objects in your vSphere environment, you can use predefined hosts and VMs baselines created during the installation of the vCSA. Baselines are used during the scan of the VM to determine the compliancy level of scanned objects (hosts, VM, and virtual appliances).

While host baselines can be customized, you cannot create custom VM or VA baselines.

 In vSphere 6.5 Update 1, VUM has been integrated into vSAN, providing an automated update process to ensure a vSAN cluster is up-to-date with the best available release to keep your hardware in a supported state.

VUM provides some predefined baselines that can only be attached or detached to the inventory objects, without the ability to edit or delete them:

- **Hosts Baselines**: It provides for **Critical Host Patches** and **Non-Critical Host Patches** options
- **VMs/VAs Baselines**: It provides **VMware Tools Upgrade to Match Host**, **VM Hardware Upgrade to Match Host**, and **VA Upgrade to Latest**

To create a new Host baseline, proceed as follows:

1. From vSphere Web Client, select **Home | Update Manager** and select the vCenter Server instance on which Update Manager is registered.
2. Select **Manage | Hosts Baselines** and click **New Baseline**.
3. Enter a name in the **Name** field and description in the **Description** field for the new baseline and specify the **Baseline type** area from the three available options. Click **Next**.
4. Specify the type of baseline patch you want to use and click **Next**. You have two baseline types to choose from:

    - **Static baseline**: The baseline doesn't change even if new patches are added to the repository. You can create a static baseline to ensure a specific patch is applied to all hosts of your environment.
    - **Dynamic baseline**: This is useful to keep systems current, as patches change over time. Dynamic baselines specify a set of patches that meet the criteria specified during the configuration, adding, or removing some specific patches.

5. If a dynamic baseline type has been specified, you have to define the criteria to determine what patches to include in the baseline. For example, to create a host baseline specifically for critical bug fixes, you can select in the **New Baseline** wizard the parameters that meet your needs. You can also specify a **Release date** range to restrict patches to include:

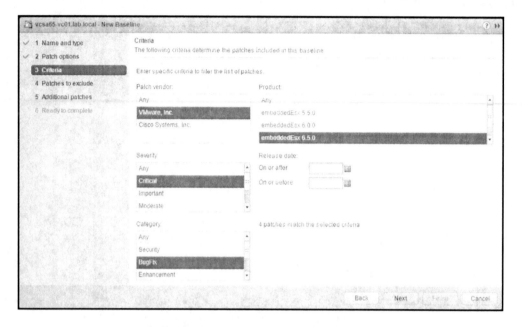

Based on selected criteria, matching patches are included in the baseline

6. Select patches to exclude from the baseline and click **Next**.
7. Specify additional patches, if any, to include in the baseline and click **Next**.
8. When the parameters have been defined, click **Finish** in the summary window to create the new baseline:

Created baselines are listed in the corresponding tab of the Update Manager

To verify which hypervisor is not compliant with the parameters configured in the created baseline, the new baseline must be attached to the ESXi hosts executing the scan procedure (host scans will be discussed later in the chapter).

Baseline groups

In addition to baselines, you can define baseline groups used to put together different existing baselines to meet specific needs for your environment. For example, baseline groups can be used if you want to update ESXi hosts in your environment, ensuring that a specific patch is applied during remediation. You can create a baseline group combining a dynamic baseline for patches and a static baseline with the specific patch you want to apply. To install the latest updates and host extensions to ESXi hosts, using a baseline group allows you to combine different baseline types, performing the task in a single step, simplifying the overall procedure.

To create a new baseline group, from vSphere Web Client, select **Home** | **Update Manager** and click the **Manage** tab. The following steps are to be followed:

1. Select **Hosts Baselines** and click the **New Baseline Group** button. Enter name and description then click **Next**
2. Specify the upgrades to apply, if any, then click **Next**
3. Select the patch baseline to use and click **Next**
4. Select the extension to apply to the hosts then click **Next**

5. In the summary window, click **Finish** to create the new baseline group:

Use baseline groups to put different existing baselines together

To edit or delete a baseline, right-click the baseline to process and select the **Edit Baseline** or **Delete Baseline** option accordingly.

Attaching or detaching baselines

Once a baseline or a baseline group has been created, you must attach it to a host or VM to scan to determine whether the object is compliant. Attaching a baseline at a higher level in vCenter Server, it will also be applied also to child objects. You can attach different baselines at different levels if you need to apply specific baselines to specific objects.

To attach or detach baselines or baseline groups to hosts or VM, proceed with the steps as follows:

1. Using vSphere Web Client, select from the inventory view the object level on which you want to attach the baseline or baseline group and select the **Update Manager** tab
2. Click the **Attach Baseline...** button to select the baselines to use from the list then click **OK**
3. To detach a baseline, right-click the baseline or baseline group to remove and click the **Detach Baseline** button

Use **Hosts and Clusters** view to attach baselines to ESXi hosts, and the **VMs and Templates** view to attach baselines to VMs.

Scanning VMs and hosts

The scanning process allows the identification of hosts, VM, or virtual appliances not compliant with the attached baselines and baseline groups.

Object scans can be initiated manually or scheduled to automate the process. To perform a manual scan, select the vCenter Server, data center, cluster, or the host object then select the **Update Manager** tab:

- To scan hosts, click the **Scan for Updates...** button to open the dialog box. Select **Patches and Extensions and Upgrades** as types of updates to scan for, then click **OK**.
- To scan VMs and vApps, the procedure to follow is similar to what is performed for hosts. Click the **Scan for Updates...** button and select any of the three available options—**Virtual appliance upgrades**, **VMware Tools upgrades**, and **VM Hardware upgrades**. Click **OK** to proceed with the scan.

The **Compliance Status** column indicates whether the scanned objects are **Compliant** or **Non-Compliant** against the attached baselines and baseline groups. If the value reported is **Non-Compliant**, you need to perform the remediation of missing patches or updates:

Scanned objects marked as Non-Compliant need to be updated

Staging and remediating patches

If the scanned hosts are marked as non-compliant, you need to remediate them in order to apply missing patches or updates. You have the option to stage or remediate patches and updates.

Let's see the differences between the two processes:

- **Staging**: Patches are copied from the Update Manager to the ESXi hosts across the network and this allows you to reduce the remediation time. Staging host patches is not a required step and it is not necessary to put hosts in Maintenance Mode while patches are staged. If you have hosts connected to the Update Manger over slow WAN, staging patches can reduce the ESXi outage required for remediation.

  To proceed with staging, from vSphere Web Client, click the **Stage Patches...** button in the **Update Manager** tab and follow these steps:

  1. Select the baselines to attach and click **Next**
  2. Specify the hosts on which you want to stage patches then click **Next**
  3. Select patches and extensions to be staged in the selected hosts and click **Next**
  4. Review the settings selection then click **Finish** to begin the staging process:

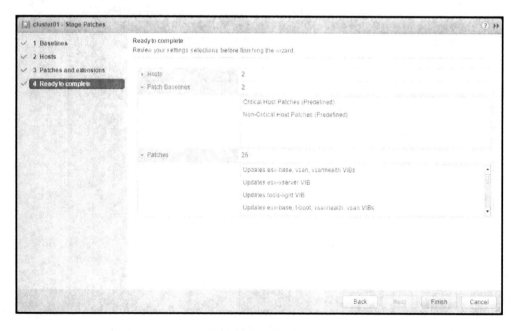

Staging patches configuration

- **Remediating**: The remediation process applies patches and upgrades to the objects that are non-compliant with the attached baseline.

To remediate hosts, from vSphere Web Client, click the **Remediate...** button in the **Update Manager** tab and follow this procedure:

1. Select the baseline to apply to the hosts and click **Next**.
2. Select the hosts to remediate and click **Next**.
3. Select patches and extensions to apply to selected hosts and click **Next**.
4. In the **Advanced options** step, you can schedule the remediation task by specifying the name of the task, description of the task, and remediation time. You can also specify to ignore warnings for unsupported hardware devices that may stop the remediation procedure. Click **Next**:

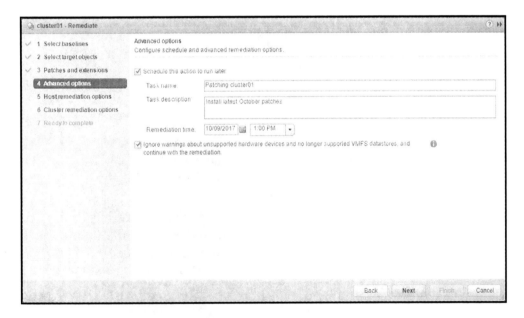

Remediation can be scheduled to avoid service disruption during working time

5. In the **Host remediation options**, be sure to leave the VM power state set as **Do Not Change VM Power State** to avoid VM downtime, allowing the system to vMotion the VMs to other hosts. Also tick the **Disable any removable media devices connected to the virtual machines on the host** option then click **Next**.

6. Specify the **Cluster remediation options** to apply to the selected cluster during remediation. Disable DPM, FT (if you have only two hosts in the cluster), and HA admission control (if you have a few hosts in the cluster), and click **Next**.

 By default, the remediation process runs sequentially for host members of a cluster. You can enable the remediation in parallel by ticking the option in the **Cluster remediation options** step.

7. After reviewing the settings selection, click **Finish** to begin the remediation procedure for the selected hosts. When the remediation process is complete, ESXi hosts will be patched/upgraded and ready to host VM.

Upgrading hosts with VUM

VUM allows you to upgrade an ESXi host from a previous supported version to the current version.

The first step is the creation of the baseline to attach to hosts to upgrade:

1. From vSphere Web Client, select **Home | Update Manager** and select the vCenter Server instance to configure. Select the **Manage** tab.
2. Navigate to **ESXi Images** and click the **Import ESXi Image...** button to import the image file used to upgrade the ESXi hosts.
3. From the wizard, click on the browser button and select the ISO file to use for the upgrade then click **Next** to upload the image into VUM.
4. When the upload has completed, a review of the ESXi image information is displayed. Click **Close** to exit the import wizard. The uploaded image listed in the ESXi images tab will be used to create the baseline:

ESXi image is imported into VUM to automate the upgrade process of hosts

5. Go to the **Hosts Baselines** tab and click the **New Baseline** button. In the wizard, enter the name of the new baseline and, optionally, add a description, that are useful to better identify the baseline scope. Under **Baseline Type**, select **Host Upgrade** then click **Next**.

6. Select the ESXi image to use for the upgrade then click **Next**.

7. A review of settings selection is displayed. Click **Finish** to create the baseline and exit the wizard.

8. Click the **Go to compliance view** button to attach the new baseline to the hosts to upgrade.

9. In the **Update Manager** tab, click the **Attach Baseline...** button to specify the baseline to attach to the object level (cluster) that contains the ESXi hosts you need to upgrade to the new version and click **OK**.

10. Click the **Scan for Updates...** button to verify the host's compliance against the attached baseline. In the **Confirm Scan** wizard, specify **Upgrades** as the scan for option then click **OK**.

11. Click the **Remediate...** button and select the created baseline to apply to the ESXi hosts. Click **Next** to continue.

Before starting the remediation process of the hosts, back up the current ESXi configuration to quickly restore the hypervisor in case something goes wrong with the upgrade.

12. Select the target ESXi hosts to remediate then click **Next**.

13. Accept the EULA and click **Next** to continue the upgrade procedure.

14. Follow the remediation steps as discussed previously. As a result of the remediation procedure, the processed ESXi hosts will now be compliant against the applied baseline:

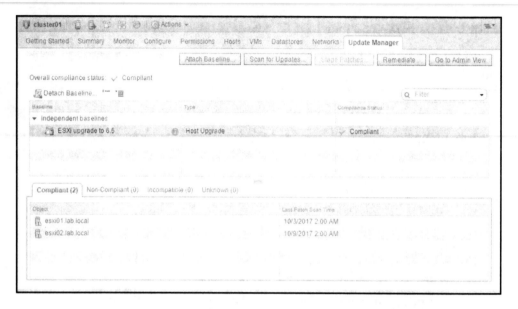

When the remediation procedure has completed successfully, processed hosts will be marked as Compliant

 If you are upgrading host members of a cluster, it is suggested to upgrade one host at a time to prevent cluster failure in the event of problems during the remediation process.

Upgrading VM hardware

Another useful feature of VUM is the option to automate and schedule the upgrade of VM hardware version. VM with an outdated hardware version cannot take advantage of new features introduced in the latest VMware vSphere release. VUM allows admins to easily identify VM that doesn't have a current hardware version and upgrade it automatically.

VUM comes with a predefined VM hardware baseline you can't change or delete but you should use to upgrade the VM hardware to the current version (vSphere 6.5 introduces hardware version 13).

 Hardware upgrades can be performed only while the VM is powered off. If you plan a hardware upgrade of your VM, you should consider that this process will cause downtime.

The hardware upgrade steps are similar to what we have discussed already:

1. From vSphere Web Client, go to **VMs and Templates** inventory view and select the object level (data center for example) on which you want to attach the baseline.
2. Select the **Update Manager** tab and click the **Attach Baseline...** button. Select the **VM Hardware Upgrade to Match Host** baseline and click **OK**.
3. Click the **Scan for Updates...** button to check the VM's compliance against the attached baseline. In the Scan for Updates wizard, specify **VM Hardware upgrades** as the scan option to allow VUM to detect outdated VM hardware then click **OK**.
4. Now click **Remediate...** to configure the task to upgrade the hardware version for outdated VM.
5. The remediation procedure requires the selection of the baseline to attach and the selection of the objects to remediate.

6. The remediation task can be scheduled to be executed in the correct maintenance window where the downtime due to the upgrade has a minor impact on the production environment. By defining a task name and a task description, you can remediate the VM on power cycle or you can specify three different schedules depending on the state of the VM—powered on, powered off, or suspended. By default, all three options are configured to run the action immediately so you should pay attention before confirming the remediation execution. Click **Next** to continue:

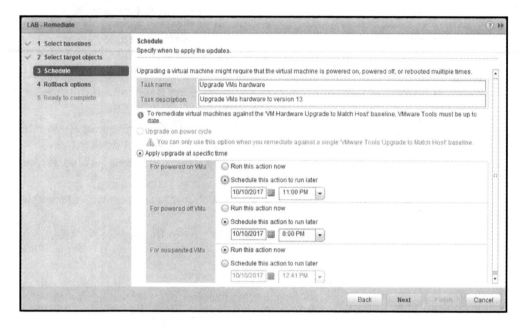

Upgrade procedure can be scheduled to avoid downtime during working hours

7. Specify the remediation **Rollback options** step in order to revert the VM to the state before the remediation if something goes wrong during the upgrade process. It's recommended to configure a snapshot retention in order to delete the snapshot after a specified time to avoid performance issues. Click **Next** to go to the final step.

8. Review your settings selection and click **Finish** to execute or schedule the remediate task.

Upgrading VMware Tools

VUM can also be used to automate the VMware Tools upgrade process for the VM in the inventory. During the power on or the restart of a VM, Update Manager can be configured to check the VMware Tools version installed in the VM and perform the upgrade to the version supported by the host that is running the VM. The upgrade of VMware Tools can be scheduled to avoid VM downtime during working hours.

The procedure is the same as that used to upgrade the hardware version of a VM:

1. From vSphere Web Client, go to the **VMs and Templates** inventory to attach the requested baseline.

2. Once the **VMware Tools Upgrade to Match Host** baseline has been attached (through the **Attach baseline...** button), click **Scan for Updates**, selecting VMware Tools upgrades as the option to check the VM's compliance against the attached baseline. Click **OK**.

3. To remediate non-compliant VM, click the **Remediate...** button to configure the task to upgrade the VMware Tools for outdated VM:

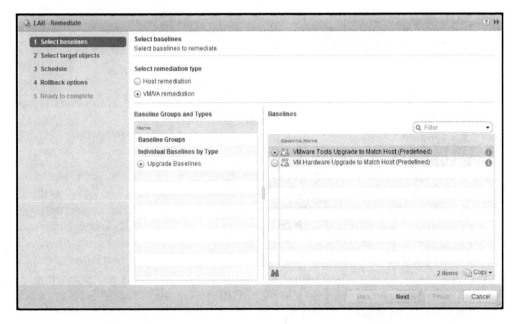

To upgrade VMware Tools, the correct baseline must be selected from the list

4. Now follow the steps used previously to upgrade the hardware version to complete the remediation procedure.

VM where the VMware Tools upgrade is performed on power cycle cannot rolled back to a previous version in case of problems because VUM doesn't take a snapshot of the VM.

Upgrading and migrating to vSphere 6.5

The latest version of the VMware virtual platform, vSphere 6.5 Update 1, comes with interesting new features and improved capabilities that bring tremendous benefits for the network in terms of improved functionality, management, security, and more, which were not available in previous versions.

The entire upgrade process needs to follow a specific sequence and flow; first, all PSCs, then all vCenters, then all ESXis. But if you have more VMware products, the entire sequence could be much complicated. For more information, see KB 2147289—*Update sequence for vSphere 6.5 and its compatible VMware products* at `https://kb.vmware.com/kb/2147289`.

Why migrate to version 6.5?

There are several reasons why it's worth migrating to version 6.5 Update 1:

- A migration tool has been introduced in version 6.5 as part of the installation media to support and make the migration simpler.
- Migration to vSphere 6.5 Update 1 is now supported from vSphere 6.0 Update 3 and from vSphere 5.5 Update 3b.
- VMware vCSA 6.5 provides better performance and scale and includes advanced features such as native vCenter HA, file-based backup and recovery, and embedded VUM. The security level of the virtual platform has been incremented, introducing new features such as the encrypted vMotion, ESXi secure boot, and VM encryption. The management of the infrastructure is now performed with a responsive and easy-to-use new HTML5-based vSphere Client interface.
- vSphere 6.5 Update 1 is the final release that supports third-party vSwitch, such as Cisco Nexus 1000V, Cisco VM-FEX, HPE 5900v, and IBM DVS 5000v, and those switches must be migrated off prior to upgrading to any future release. The introduction of REST-based APIs makes task automation easier.

- Another good reason to migrate to the new version is the extended period for the General Support of version 6.5 that will now end on November 15, 2021. If your virtual platform still runs vSphere 5.5, be careful because the General Support for version 5.5 will end on September 19, 2018.
- In addition, upgrading to vSphere 6.5 Update 1 prepares the environment for the hybrid cloud solution VMware Cloud on AWS.

 Before migrating your infrastructure, keep in mind that vCenter Server needs to be running 6.5 Update 1 before upgrading the ESXi hosts to 6.5 Update 1.

Upgrading the workflow and procedure

For a successful migration to the new version, the overall procedure must be carefully planned with a clear and well-executed workflow to avoid potential issues, such as service disruption or compatibility issues with running components.

The migration procedure plan can be split into three main steps:

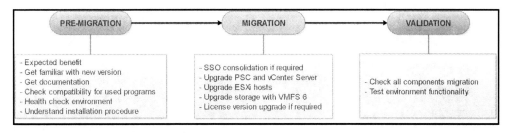

Migration workflow

Step 1 – Pre-migration

The pre-migration step includes a plan of the tasks that should be done before starting the actual migration. An analysis of the expected benefits of the new features should be done to determine the added value to your business and justify the investment to the management. Try to obtain as much documentation as you can, such as guides, release notes, tips of the new release, to limit possible problems. How the new release and the new features should be implemented and configured is also an essential key point for a successful migration.

Make sure that running programs in the current vSphere environment are also supported in the release you are going to install. If other VMware products are used in your network, validate the compatibility of each product by using the *VMware Product Interoperability Matrices* available on the VMware website at the URL `https://www.vmware.com/resources/compatibility/sim/interop_matrix.php`:

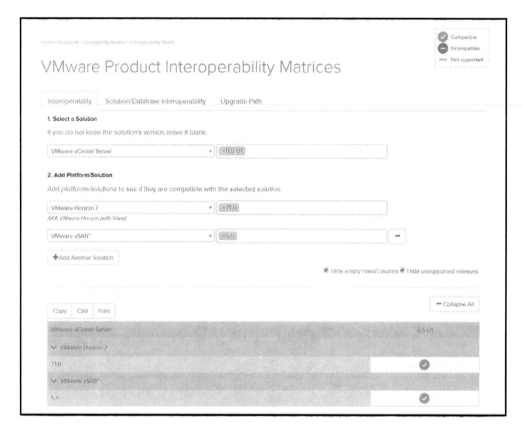

VMware Product Interoperability Matrices page is used to verify the compatibility of installed products with the release you are installing

Make sure the backup solution in use supports the new version to ensure the protection of your workload. In the event of incompatibility, take all the necessary actions (upgrades, replacement) to ensure full support before migrating.

Before migrating, it's also useful to determine obsolete VM and services no longer required that don't need to be migrated. Performing a health assessment of your current vSphere environment is useful to detect objects that are no longer needed but are still consuming resources, and to fix misconfigurations to avoid issues during the migration cleaning up the network.

There are several tools available on the market that allow you to perform a health check of the vSphere environment. In addition to solutions that require a license, some free tools can also be used to health check your virtual platform.

Here, some examples of commercial and free products you can use for the health check of your environment:

- **Licensed**: VMware vRealize Operations Manager, vSphere Optimization Assessment, Runecast Analyzer, Opvizor Health Analyzer
- **Free**: Turbonomic Virtual Health Monitor, HPE **Virtualization Performance Viewer (vPV)**, Veeam One Free Edition, RVTools

Step 2 – Migration

Plan all the involved steps accordingly, evaluating the impact of new features and the improvements that can be applied to the current environment. An upgrade order of the virtual components should be established to avoid potential problems. For example, the vSphere platform requires first upgrading the vCenter Server then the ESXi hosts to avoid communication issues within vSphere components.

If you need to consolidate an SSO domain, this can be done only on vSphere 5.5 and involves a change of architecture since you need to deploy the PSC from embedded to external. Check out the VMware KB 2033620—*How to repoint and re-register vCenter Server 5.1 / 5.5 and components* at `https://kb.vmware.com/kb/2033620` for SSO consolidation. PSCs are the first components to upgrade, then go ahead with vCenter Servers. If you migrate from vSphere 5.5, before starting the upgrade procedure, you need to break Linked Mode if configured in your network.

Since VMware has deprecated the Windows-based version of vCenter Server, it's worth migrating directly to the Linux-based vCSA, taking advantage of the new features introduced in version 6.5, such as embedded VUM, VCHA, built-in file-based backup restore, available in the vCSA only. If you have vCenter Servers with external PSCs, get both components on the same version to take advantage of new features. vSphere 6.5 provides a Migration Tool in the installation media that supports migration from vSphere 5.5 and 6.0 environments.

The vCSA installation can also be performed through script using CLI commands that allows the automation of the installation procedure, making the process faster:

```
G:\vcsa-cli-installer\win32>vcsa-deploy.exe --help
Usage: vcsa-deploy.exe [-h] [--version] [--supported-deployment-sizes]
                       {migrate,upgrade,install} ...

optional arguments:
  -h, --help              Show this help message and exit.
  --version               Show the version and exit.
  --supported-deployment-sizes
                          Display all of the supported deployment options from the
                          OVA in default location. If the OVA package is not
                          found, default values are displayed

Available sub-commands. Use vcsa-deploy [subcommand] --help for a list of subcommand-specific arguments:
  {migrate,upgrade,install}
    install               Deploy vCSA to a remote host.
    upgrade               Upgrade an existing vCSA.
    migrate               Migrate an existing Windows installation of vCenter
                          Server to a vCSA.

G:\vcsa-cli-installer\win32>
```

vCSA can be installed using CLI commands to speed up the process

When PSCs and vCenter Servers have been upgraded, you can start migrating ESXi hosts. Although ESXi 5.5 is supported in version 6.5, new vSphere features won't be enabled until hosts are upgraded as well. vSphere 6.5 introduces VMFS 6 as a storage filesystem that brings a lot of improvements, such as **Automatic Space Reclamation (ASR)** and the support for 4K Native Drives in 512e mode, enhancing the core storage space performance.

The vSphere Storage vMotion feature can be used to move VM to other datastores while you upgrade the existing datastore to VMFS 6. To identify the VMFS version used in your datastores, in addition to vSphere Client (select the vCSA object and go to the **Datastores** tab), you can use esxcli commands from the ESXi command line:

```
esxcli storage filesystem list
```

The same information can be retrieved using PowerCLI:

```
Get-Datastore | ft Name, Type, FileSystemVersion
```

```
PS C:\> Get-Datastore | ft name, Type, FileSystemVersion

Name                    Type FileSystemVersion
----                    ---- -----------------
ts421_nfs01             NFS  3.0
nfs_drstorage           NFS  3.0
local_esxi01_disk1      VMFS 6.81
local_esxi02_disk1      VMFS 6.81
ts421_lun02             VMFS 5.61
ts421_lun03             VMFS 5.61
ts421_lun01             VMFS 5.61


PS C:\>
```

PowerCLI can be used to get the VMFS version of attached datastores

If you come from a vSphere 5.x environment, licenses must be upgraded to version 6. Keep in mind that if you have a 60-day, fully working trial when you install vSphere then your environment will continue working while you upgrade the licenses.

For large environments, you could schedule the upgrade in different maintenance windows by upgrading the vSphere environment in stages. You can start by upgrading all PSCs, followed by the vCenter Servers, then the ESXi hosts. Planning the upgrade process in different steps, reduces the maintenance of the environment in three shorter time frames limiting the downtime. To avoid issues, upgrade each vCenter Single Sign-On or PSC one at a time.

Step 3 – Validation

Ensure the upgrade has been completed successfully and all components work as expected. Verify the full functionality of the infrastructure and provided services according to plan. Once the validation has succeeded, the migration procedure is complete.

Migrating from previous releases

VMware made a big effort to simplify the migration process to vSphere 6.5, introducing a Migration Tool that allows an easy upgrade of an existing vCSA and PSC Appliance 6.0 or a Windows-based vCenter Server to the new version. The tool supports vCenter Servers running version 5.5 Update 3 or 6.0.

The upgrade process is composed of following two stages:

- vCSA deployment
- Copy of the configuration from source vCenter Server

The automated upgrade process requires the DRS feature in the cluster in which the source vCenter Server resides to not be set to fully automated. To migrate a Windows-based vCenter Server or an external Update Manager requires the installation of the Migration Assistant, a tool that facilitates the migration of the two components and the database to the new upgraded vCSA.

The upgrade procedure is straightforward and guided through a simple and clear UI where you must specify source and target network parameters in the Migration Tool when requested. If the tool is not installed on the source server, you receive an error message that stops the migration. You need to install the tool on the source system and start the procedure from the beginning.

Stage 1 of the procedure deploys the new vCSA to the target host, assigning a temporary IP address specified in the Migration Tool wizard:

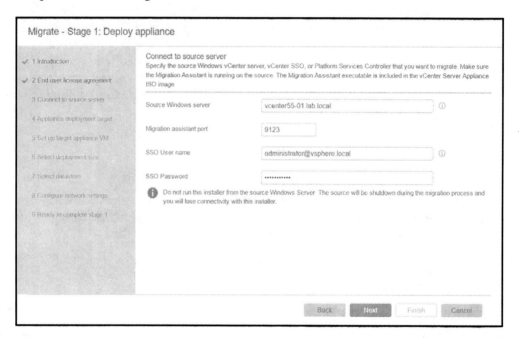

Temporary IP address must be assigned to the new vCSA during the migration

Once the vCSA 6.5 is deployed, the upgrade process continues with stage 2, where data is copied from source vCenter Server to the target vCSA and can be finalized in two ways:

- Using the vCSA Installer
- Accessing the vCenter Server Appliance Management Interface by typing into your favorite browser the address `https://<VCSA_IP>:5480`

Before proceeding with stage 2 of the migration procedure, take a snapshot of the newly deployed vCSA 6.5 to quickly resume the migration in case of problems.

As a result of the migration procedure, the new vCenter Server will have the same hostname and IP address of the source vCenter Server without any service disruption.

The migration process doesn't delete the old vCenter Server and its configuration, but simply copies data to the new vCSA and then powers the source vCenter off. This allows you to quickly restore the old vCenter Server if the upgrade process fails.

Troubleshooting

During the copy process in stage 2, an error related to the `vmidentity-firstboot.py` may occur that stops the procedure at 5% while the system tries starting the VMware Identity Manager service. Even clicking on the **Retry** button does not solve the problem and the same error occurs again:

The vmidentity-firstboot.py error occurred during the copy process step

This error doesn't give you any chance to continue the upgrade and the entire procedure must be started again from the beginning (if you created a snapshot at the end of stage 1, you can resume the migration from that point, saving a lot of time).

To fix the problem, follow this procedure:

1. Add `localhost.localdom localhost` in the `/etc/hosts` file of the new vCSA before stage 2 takes place. When stage 1 has completed, from the vSphere Web Client of the source vCenter Server, right-click the new vCSA 6.5 and select **Open Console**.

2. Press *Alt + F1* and log in with root credentials. Run the following commands:

   ```
   ssh.set --enabled true
   echo "::1 localhost.localdom localhost" >> /etc/hosts
   ```

3. Continue with stage 2 of the deployment. As soon as stage 2 begins processing step 2, *Set up target vCenter and start services*, add immediately the entry `localhost.localdom localhost` to the `/etc/hosts` file once again to prevent the error.

Another error may occur in stage 2 during importing VMware vSphere Update Manager data that requires starting the overall upgrade procedure from the beginning once again:

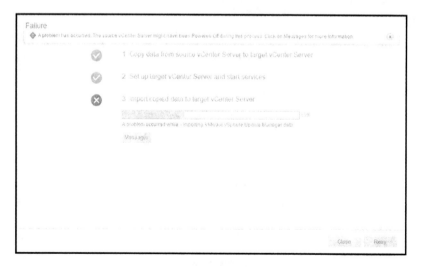

An error may occur during the import of VUM's data

To avoid this issue, make sure the VMware vSphere Update Manager Service in the VUM server runs with a dedicated account and not as a local system.

Summary

To keep the infrastructure healthy, ESXi hosts and vCenter Servers must be patched on a regular basis.

ESXi hosts can be patched and updated using the command line if a vCenter Server is not available in the network. The vCSA can be patched and updated using the command line by staging and remediating the mounted ISO image patch file or through the VAMI that provides a graphic UI.

We talked about VMware Update Manager, a tool used to automate the patching and upgrading procedures of the ESXi hosts installed in the network as well as to install VMware Tools and upgrade the hardware version of the VM.

The chapter explained the upgrade and migration procedures to vSphere 6.5. Both processes must be carefully planned to ensure the compatibility of the used programs and the correct upgrade procedure. The upgrade process can be split into three stages—pre-migration, migration, and validation. The Migration Tool provided with vSphere 6.5 simplifies the migration of vSphere vCenter Servers from version 5.5 Update 3 and 6.0 to version 6.5.

The next chapter will explain the business continuity concepts and the implementation of the disaster recovery strategy to ensure data and service availability, avoiding downtime in case of dramatic failures.

12

Business Continuity and Disaster Recovery

Business Continuity (BC) ensures that an organization can continue (or restart) operations after service interruptions due to serious incidents, issues, or disasters. Typical disasters include unexpected natural disasters such as fires, floods, earthquakes, or also unnatural incidents, like terrorist attacks.

As defined on *Disaster Recovery Journal website* (`https://www.drj.com/`) states that:

> *"A disaster is a sudden, unplanned calamitous event that brings about great damage or loss. Any event that creates an inability on the organization's part to provide the critical business functions for some undetermined period of time."*

But you also have to consider accidents by key personnel in the business, server crashes, and security breaches. All these can impact the business from the infrastructure level to the application and service level. Natural disasters are just the smallest part of the causes of information unavailability, as demonstrated in this graph from the EMC introduction course for BC:

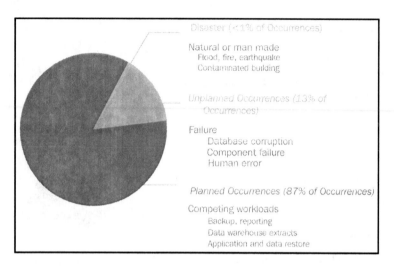

Causes of information unavailability

BC is about having a complete plan to deal with Murphy's law or critical situations, to minimize the downtime and the impact of possible issues and service disruptions, and all business (directly or indirectly) related risks. It doesn't matter what kind of business we are talking about; it could be a large enterprise, a public sector, or a non-profit organization. All must know how they can keep going under any circumstances, the related costs of a service interruption, and of course, the costs of prevention.

Each organization has to define which risks will be managed, and as a final result how to recover to an operational state within a (from the business point of view) reasonable period. Disasters also happen to large organizations and big cloud providers, as history has widely demonstrated in the past. For example, see *Top 10 business continuity disasters over last 12 months* (http://www.itspecialists.uk.com/top-10-business-continuity-disasters-over-last-12-months/).

From the 2014 survey of Uptime Symposium, 46% of companies using their own data center had at least one business-impacting data center outage over 12 months, and 7% had 5 or more outages.

Formally, part of this analysis should be included as part of the planning and design phase of a virtual infrastructure. For more information see also `Chapter 2`, *Design and Plan a Virtualization Infrastructure.*

In this chapter, we will cover the following topics:

- Understand different business continuity solutions
- Describe the differences between MetroCluster and DR solutions

BC concepts

BC is a process, so there will be a full life cycle, with some periodical iterations and improvements. **BC planning** or **BC and resiliency planning** is the process of defining solutions to prevent and recover from potential issues or threats related to business operativity and functionality. The result of this process is typically the **Business Continuity Plan (BCP)** that recognizes potential risks and provides a way to mitigate them.

The BCP life cycle is like other flows—starts from an analysis, follows with a solution design, the implementation, testing and validation and a maintenance phase, as described in the following figure:

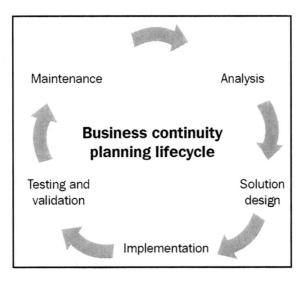

Business continuity planning lifecycle

Business continuity includes at least three following key elements:

- **Resilience**: All critical business functions and the supporting infrastructure must be designed with the right specific solution to increase availability levels, also in the case of failures. Usually, the use of redundancy, spare capacity, or cluster are some ways to achieve this goal.
- **Recovery**: In case of service, system, or data disruptions there should be some arrangements to recover or restore critical (and maybe also less critical) business functions.
- **Contingency**: Each organization must establish a generalized capability and readiness to cope effectively with whatever major incidents and disasters occur. Contingency preparations constitute a last-resort response if resilience and recovery arrangements should prove inadequate in practice. Usually, you have to also include those cases that were not, and perhaps could not have been, foreseen.

Different approaches and technical solutions can be used to provide better business continuity, but in most cases, we have to consider at least these three areas:

- **HA**: Solutions and technologies, including redundant or standby hardware and software components, that enable a system to recover quickly from a failure
- **Data protection**: The ability to preserve information and data accessibility and integrity, usually achieved through backup solutions and products
- **Disaster recovery**: The set of processes, policies, and procedures that define how critical services and the related infrastructures recover from a disaster.

For HA and data protection, more details will be provided in the next two chapters, especially for specific VMware features and VM protection and backup.

The rest of this chapter describes high-level concepts for BC and provides more information about the disaster recovery aspect.

BC metrics

The two industry standard measurements of DR solutions are:

- **Recovery Point Objective (RPO)**: This is the point in time to which systems must be recovered after an outage. This measurement defines the amount of data loss an organization can endure. Different services may have varying RPO requirements. Sometimes you may also need multiple RPOs to restore not only the latest data (that means the closest point from a time point of view), but also the oldest; in this case, we are talking about the type of retention that is required.
- **Recovery Time Objective (RTO)**: This refers to how long it takes to recover services after the disaster. This measurement defines the amount of downtime an organization can endure. Recovery time includes fault detection, recovering data, and bringing applications back online.

Different solutions, like backup and replicas, can reach different types of RPO and RTO, as described in the following figure:

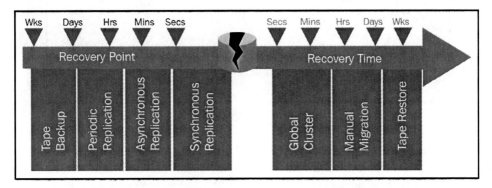

RPO and RTO

Another aspect of BC is availability, where different types of availability can be required and provided:

- **HA**: The system or application is available during specified operating hours with no unplanned outages. This is the most common way to manage availability at the infrastructure level and is usually measured in the availability level.
- **Continuous operations**: This means that a system is committed to constant availability, with no unscheduled downtime. To achieve this level, you must implement HA and continuous operations techniques that make the system more reliable and eliminate dependence on scheduled maintenance work that would require system downtime.

- **Continuous availability**: This is similar to the continuous operations, but the system is committed to being available always, with no scheduled or unscheduled downtime.

For the HA level, usually, a number of nines define the percentage of uptime in a given year. The following table shows the downtime that will be allowed for a particular percentage of availability:

% Uptime	% Downtime	Downtime per Year	Downtime per Week
98%	2%	7.3 days	3 hrs 22 min
99%	1%	3.65 days	1 hrs 41 min
99.8%	0.2%	17 hrs 31min	20 min 10 sec
99.9%	0.1%	8 hrs 45 min	10 min 5 sec
99.99%	0.01%	52.5 min	1 min
99.999%	0.001%	5.25 min	6 sec
99.9999%	0.0001%	31.5 sec	0.6 sec

Availability levels

Finally, the **Service Level Agreement (SLA)** is defined as an official commitment that prevails between a service provider and a service consumer. Usually, the most common component of SLA is that the services should be provided to the customer as agreed upon in the contract.

Business impact analysis (BIA)

BC must identify all business functions within an organization, and then assign a critical level to each of them. A business impact and risks analysis should be the primary method for gathering this information and, in most cases, it's part of the design phase. Each risk should be assigned a reasonable and critical means to minimize its impact and define a correct recovery point objective, a recovery time objective, and of course, an entire plan to handle this risk.

BIA can be used to identify the extent and timescale of the impact on different levels of an organization. For instance, it can examine the effect of disruption on the operational, functional, and strategic activities of an organization. Aside from current activities, the disruptive effects of major business changes, such as introducing new product or services, can also be determined by BIA.

Most standards require that a business impact analysis should be reviewed at defined intervals appropriate for each organization and whenever any of the following occur:

- Significant changes in the internal business process, location, or technology
- Significant changes in the external business environment—such as market or regulatory change

BIA has several intersections with other business and technology related processes such as:

- **Security management**: Security must be one of the top priorities when managing IT.
- **Document management**: Documentation is the knowledge of your environment and should include not only the technical references but also the high-level decision and design concepts.
- **Change management**: Regulations require that all changes to business functions must be documented and tracked for auditing purposes and for change control.
- **Audit management**: All modern business functions should be designed to automatically generate the requisite audit compliance information and documentation while conducting day-to-day business. This dramatically reduces the time and cost associated with manually producing this information.

Business continuity standard

Several BC standards have been published by various standards. They are as follows:

- **ISO/IEC 27031:2011**: Describes the concepts and principles of **information and communication technology (ICT)** readiness for BC, and provides a framework of methods and processes to identify and specify all aspects (such as performance criteria, design, and implementation) of improving an organization's ICT readiness to ensure BC.
- **ISO 22301:2012**: Specifies requirements to plan, establish, implement, operate, monitor, review, maintain, and continually improve a documented management system to protect against, reduce the likelihood of, prepare for, respond to, and recover from disruptive incidents when they arise.

- **ISO 22313:2012**: This provides guidance based on good international practices for planning, establishing, implementing, operating, monitoring, reviewing, maintaining, and continually improving a documented management system that enables organizations to prepare for, respond to, and recover from disruptive incidents when they arise.
- **ISO/TS 22317:2015**: This provides guidance for an organization to establish, implement, and maintain a formal and documented BIA process. This technical specification does not prescribe a uniform process for performing a BIA, but will assist an organization in designing a BIA process that is appropriate to its needs.
- **ASIS/BSI BCM.01-2010**: This provides auditable criteria for developing and implementing a BC management system that improves an organization's ability to prepare for, respond to, and recover from a disruptive event.
- **British Standard BS 25999-1 and 25999-2**: A two-part BC management standard which was withdrawn in 2012 when it was (in effect) replaced by ISO 22301:2012.
- **ANSI/ASIS SPC.1-2009**: This helps an organization design a balanced system to reduce the likelihood and minimize the consequences of disruptive events.
- **Australian Standard AS/NZS 5050 and AS/NZS 31000**: This provides organizations with guiding principles, a generic framework, and a process for managing risk.
- **National Fire Protection Association NFPA 1600**: This is the standard for disaster, emergency management and BC programs.
- **Continuity of Operations (COOP):** This is a United States federal government initiative, required by U.S. **Presidential Policy Directive 40 (PPD-40)**, to ensure that agencies are able to continue the performance of essential functions under a broad range of circumstances.

Common mistakes

There are some possible errors or wrong approaches in BC. The most common are as follows:

- **No BI**: There may be a BIA, but it's not complete or does not cover all the possible business-related risks.
- **Not applied**: Some cases are skipped and not considered; perhaps even the entire BC analysis just because *it can't happen to me*. As with security, all organizations need a proper BCP and all cases must be considered in some way.
- **Non-involvement of business level**: You cannot understand the risks and define the possible budget to avoid (or minimize) them without the C-levels.

- **Technology focus**: Written BC is a process, not necessarily a single technical solution. Technologies came later, and can help in some decisions, but are mostly organizational and high-level.
- **Complexity**: Simplicity usually pays and works. The more complex the solution or the documentation is, the most difficult it will be to implement the BCP in the proper way, and also to keep it updated.
- **Correlated aspects**: The BC does not include other correlated aspects, like security, maintenance and management, audit, and so on.
- **Compliances**: The BC does not consider compliances or is too focused on just complaints regulations.
- **BCP has never been applied**: BCP analysis has been done well - maybe there is even a good paper that defines BCP - but it has never been applied. It's possible to decide to ignore some risks, but at least a reasonable part of the BCP must be implemented properly.
- **Too dependent on people or automation**: You need a good BCP solution that is balanced with regard to how it can be automated and how it can be humanly controlled (for example, the decision to activate the DR site). It's not realistic to have something totally automated or too human dependent (in this case it would also be difficult to have a deterministic RTO).
- **Not enough training or no training at all**: All people should be trained, of course, with the right level of detail depending on their role.

Disaster recovery (DR)

A disaster is any event that halts business activity on a large scale. In most cases, we are thinking about natural disasters, but there are also man-made disasters and all of them can happen at any time without warning. Technologies and all IT services could be impacted by these kinds of disasters. Of course, there are other and more important aspects; like human life that can also be at risk, but for BC, we put the main focus on the business-critical services and applications.

DR provides BC in the event of a disaster, and may be just localized on equipment (like a single server) or globally on an entire site. Business will be recovered by following a specific DR plan; it is just a subset of the BCP. In the worst case of a disaster that impacts an entire site or region, usually, the recovery process uses a remote location called a **disaster recovery site**.

DR is essential to ensure the continuation of business after a disaster. DR can also be required in several regulatory compliances. Effective DR is a critical part of a BCP that must address the following three organizational requirements:

- **Minimize risks**: Having a BC plan does not eliminate all risks if you cannot be certain that the plan is reliable or practicable. The DR plan could be difficult to implement, and for several organizations it may have some business impacts and possible risks.
- **Minimize downtime**: The consequences of extended downtime can be critical for business, recognition, and productivity. For most companies, a service disruption of ten or more days could be a total disaster and lead to the closing of the company itself.
- **Control costs**: Traditional disaster recovery plans are often limited in scope because of the cost, but you must find a tradeoff between the costs and risk mitigations.

Although everyone realizes the importance of a DR plan, some organizations do not have the proper level of DR protection that they need. Only after a real disaster does they fully understand the importance of DR and the real impact that a disaster can have on their business.

Legacy solutions and processes to activate applications in the DR site usually requires complex runbooks and manual procedures to execute the failover process. They may require highly specialized staff with vertical skills, large time investments, and high levels of coordination from several teams that are responsible for different layers of the infrastructure.

The main challenges that must be handled by DR, in order to have a successful and effective plan, are as follows:

- **Complexity**: Usually data center recovery plans are complex processes, because to guarantee the correct recovery of entire business services they must deal with all the interdependencies between applications, hosts, networks, and storage and other infrastructural and organizational aspects.
- **Lack of predictable and reliable recovery**: Recovery plans documented in run books can be incomplete and may quickly fall out of sync with rapidly evolving deployments. Most enterprises test their recovery plan only twice a year or less.
- **High cost**: Legacy DR solutions require significant capital and operating expenditures. The DR site typically requires a dedicated duplicate server infrastructure.

As defined in *Gartner, Survey Analysis: IT Disaster Recovery Management Spending and Testing Activities Expand in 2012, July 2012*:

> *"The net result is that legacy disaster recovery solutions are regarded as non-strategic and costly "insurance policies" with very questionable returns. At best, only a few mission-critical applications get the privilege of site-level protection".*

DR of a virtual data center

Protecting a virtual workload is much easier compared to protecting a physical data center, in a legacy way, for several reasons:

- Virtualization provides encapsulation, so a VM is usually a set of files that can be easily managed.
- Virtualization provides hardware independence, where a VM can run as it is (without any changes) on different hardware, maybe also with different sizing, but using the same hypervisor (or a compatible one).
- Different types of data replication can be used, from traditional storage array replication to VM replication.
- On the DR site, you can, potentially, and for a limited number of workloads, use a single server that has enough computing and storage capacity.
- Cloud **DR as a Service (DRaaS)** solutions are possible and effective.

All of the preceding benefits make it possible and convenient to provide a low RPO and a low RTO for the entire data center (or a large set of it), not just for the first tier of business-critical applications and services. Also, we have to consider that most companies are already leveraging virtualization, with a virtualization-first approach, also dictated for BC and DR requirements.

DR versus disaster avoidance

Disaster avoidance, as the name implies, is the process of preventing or significantly reducing the probability that a disaster will occur (through human errors), or ensuring that if such an event does occur (as in natural disaster) then the effects upon the organization's technology systems will be minimized as much as possible. The idea of disaster avoidance provides better resilience rather than good recovery, but to do so, you cannot rely only on infrastructure availability solutions, which are mostly geographically limited to a specific site; you also need to look at how to provide better application availability and redundancy in the wake of foreseeable disruptions.

Multi-data center (or multi-region cloud) replication is one part. The second part is having active-active data centers or having applications spread between the multiple sites that provide service availability.

Most of the new cloud-native applications are designed for this scenario. But there are also some examples of traditional applications with HA concepts at the application level that can also work geographically, such as DNS services, **Active Directory Domain Controller (ADDC)**, Exchange **database availability group (DAG)** or SQL AlwaysOn clusters. In all those cases one system can fail, but the service will not be affected because another node will provide it. Although solutions like Exchange DAG or SQL AlwaysOn rely on internal cluster services, applications designed with HA solutions usually use loosely coupled systems without shared components (except of course the network, but it can be a routed or geographical network).

An interesting example of the infrastructure layer could be the stretched cluster, or metro cluster.

DR versus stretched cluster

A stretched cluster, sometimes called as a metro cluster or metro storage cluster, is a deployment model in which two or more host servers are part of the same logical cluster but are located in separate geographical locations, usually two sites. In a stretched cluster, the two groups of servers (in each site) are usually used to provide HA and load balancing features and capabilities.

This allows the proactive behavior to avoid or minimize service outages, using disaster avoidance; if a disaster affects an entire site, the second one will manage all the resources and services. Although a stretched cluster can be used for disaster recovery and not only for disaster avoidance, there are some possible limitations on using a stretched cluster as DR as well:

- A stretched cluster can't protect you from site link failures and can be affected by the split brain scenario.
- A stretched cluster usually works with synchronous replication; that means limited distance, but also makes it difficult to provide multiple restore points with different timings.
- Bandwidth requirements are really high, to minimize storage latency. So you need not just reliable lines but also larger ones.
- A stretched cluster can be more costly than a DR solution, but of course, can also provide disaster avoidance for some cases.

In most cases where a stretched cluster is used, there could be a third site acting as a traditional DR; in this way, a multi-level protection approach is used.

VMware solutions

In the past, BC was the first driver of virtualization initiative; virtualization not only helps in server consolidation and in driving down costs across IT organizations, but can also improve availability, resiliency, and recoverability for business-critical applications and services.

There are three key features of virtualization that lead to better-managed BC:

- **Consolidation:** Server consolidation means doing more with less. You're reducing your physical footprint, which also means you can streamline your DR plans and standardize your recovery process.
- **Hardware independence:** This means being able to recover onto any x86 hardware. So, you have the flexibility to buy different servers for your recovery site, or even fewer servers. Continuing to virtualize your production site will free up additional machines that can then be moved over to your recovery site.
- **Encapsulation:** Because virtualization captures everything about a server onto just a few files on a disk, the real benefit here is mobility; the ability to move your VMs wherever you want. You can back them up in the same way you currently protect your other files. You can also replicate them to your DR site, so that they will be available when you need to recover from an outage.

VMware provides a holistic approach to protecting your IT environment and all applications running on the vSphere platform from a variety of factors that can cause application downtime, including unplanned events like server failures and even planned events such as server maintenance. These solutions provide a simple, cost-effective protection with a common solution for all your applications and services.

The VMware BC related solutions cover the following:

- **Local availability**: There are products and technologies that protect applications against the downtime of individual hosts. This includes vSphere HA and FT for unplanned downtime, as well as vMotion and Storage vMotion for planned downtime. More information will be provided in `Chapter 13`, *Advanced Availability in vSphere 6.5*.

- **Data protection**: There are solutions to back up entire VMs, including OS, application binaries, and application data, in a simple non-disruptive manner. A third-party solution can use VMware Storage APIs for data protection that enables native VM backup. More information will be provided in `Chapter 14`, *Data and Workloads Protection*.

- **Disaster recovery**: vSphere Replication is an exciting addition to the vSphere platform, providing a cost-efficient and simple way to implement a VM based replication. For DR orchestration, vCenter Site Recovery Manager leverages vSphere and vSphere Replication (or storage-based replication) to protect applications against site failures and to streamline planned migrations.

- **Disaster avoidance**: The **vSphere Metro Storage Cluster (vMSC)** is a configuration option, introduced in vSphere 5, that allows for the use of stretched clusters.

VM Replication

vSphere Replication can provide very cost-efficient, simple, and powerful replication at the VM level, using scheduled asynchronous file-based replication. It is more cost efficient because it reduces both storage costs and replication costs, and also because it's included in all editions, starting from the Essential Plus edition.

Despite its simplicity and cost efficiency, vSphere Replication is a powerful and integrated replication solution that can provide up to 15 minute RPOs, with multiple restore points, and gives the flexibility to set RPOs between 15 minutes and 24 hours.

VMware vSphere Replication uses some virtual appliances (included in vSphere from the Essential Plus edition) to provide VM based replication as described in the following figure:

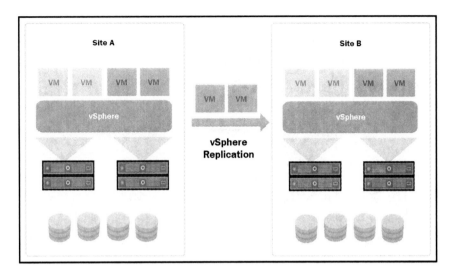

VMware vSphere Replication

One interesting aspect is that it does not use the VM snapshots at all, so it can be more flexible from this point of view. On the other side, it is strictly dependent on vCenter Server for its configuration and management.

Of course, it's not the only VM based replication solution; there are several third-party products that provide more features and capabilities. Most of the native backup products also have VM Replication features, and so, in this case, could be cost-effective solutions, especially if you already have that specific backup product.

There are also some replication products that can replicate the VMs not only across the same virtualization platform, but also across different types of hypervisors.

Stretched cluster

VMware vMSC is just a configuration option for a vSphere cluster, where half of the virtualization hosts are on one site and the second half is on a second site. Both sites work in an active-active way, and common vSphere features like vMotion or vSphere HA can be used.

The only restrictions are that vMotion must support higher latency (and this is possible in the Enterprise Plus edition), that all VMs must reside on the same layer 2 network (that means a stretched network is needed, or some other network virtualization technique), and that the storage part can provide active-active access from both sites (there are several storages certified for vMSC).

In the case of a planned migration, such as in the need for disaster avoidance or data center consolidation, using stretched storage enables zero-downtime application mobility. In the case of a site disaster, vSphere HA will provide a VM recovery on the other site.

A vMSC cluster can handle both planned and unplanned downtime as described in the following figure:

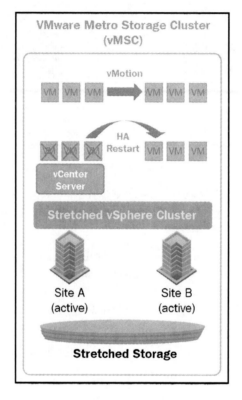

VMware vSphere Metro Storage Cluster

VMware vSAN in the Enterprise edition can also provide the stretched shared storage part; in this way, it's possible to build a complete stretched cluster using vSphere as an infrastructural foundation.

Site Recovery Manager (SRM)

As written, cross-site replication at the VM or storage level is just the first step for DR. You will then need an entire set of rules to define how to recover your VMs in case of the main site failure. SRM delivers several features and functions, including centralized recovery plans, non-disruptive testing and automated orchestration, both for fail-over (in case of DR) and fail-back (in case the original site has been recovered).

SRM 6.1 adds support for stretched storage solutions over a metro distance from several major storage partners, and integration with cross vCenter vMotion when using these solutions for disaster avoidance.

Also, adding a stretched storage to an SRM deployment fundamentally reduces recovery times; in the case of a disaster, recovery is much faster due to the nature of the stretched storage architecture that enables synchronous data writes and reads on both sites.

But note that the SRM model for active-active data centers is fundamentally different to the model used in the VMware vMSC. SRM uses two vCenter Server instances, one on each site, instead of stretching the vSphere cluster across sites.

The new version of SRM supports properly and natively stretched storage, but with two different VMware clusters as described in the following figure:

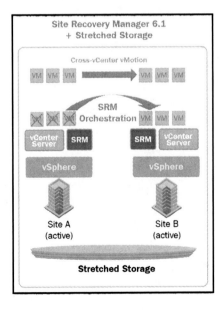

VMware SRM with stretched storage

Adding SRM to a stretched storage deployment allows users to benefit from key features of SRM that are not present in vMSC, such as centralized recovery plans, orchestrated recovery, and non-disruptive automated testing.

Summary

BC and DR are at the top of IT and data center initiatives; usually, improving BC and DR capabilities is the top priority for SMBs and one of the first for an enterprise.

This chapter has described what's behind the normal operation and maintenance, in order to define your BC requirements and match your expected services levels.

Availability, SLA, data and system protection, DR, and other basics concepts were described in this chapter, with a brief introduction to SRM and SR as a solution for DR.

In this chapter, we have introduced some BC concepts, availability, and DR metrics and the differences between availability and DR.

In the next chapters, we will give more details on availability and data protection solutions.

13
Advanced Availability in vSphere 6.5

This chapter will focus on specific availability (and resiliency) solutions in vSphere, whereas with VMware technology, it is possible to create total HA infrastructure on every level. Starting from the infrastructure level, using the new vSphere HA features, the proactive HA, or also the new vCenter HA configuration, specific for the vCSA deployment of vCenter Server.

When we think about how we can work with all the benefits of VMware solutions, we see a lot of positions and levels where it is possible to protect the infrastructure. Still, the physical and infrastructural part of your environment is really important and crucial, so a correct design and configuration is needed for your hardware parts, such as servers, switch, storage, and **host bus adapter (HBA)**, in order to design and configure all of them without a potential single point of failure.

However, only the infrastructure level is important and must be resilient, also workload needs a good HA level according to business requirements and needs. There are not only several native solutions that can be used, such as NIC teaming, multipathing for storage, vSphere **High Availability (HA)** and vSphere **Fault Tolerance (FT)**, but also other solutions typically, from the physical world, such as guest clustering.

In this chapter, we will cover the following topics:

- vSphere HA
- vSphere FT
- vCenter HA
- vSphere Replication and Site Recovery Manager

VMware vSphere HA

First, we will be speaking about vSphere HA. vSphere HA protects primary ESXi host failures. Of course, you can use vSphere HA protection for datastore failures, application failures, and network isolation. vSphere HA configuration is a part of the cluster object, so first, you must create a cluster object in your data center object.

Configuration vSphere HA is a part of the cluster configuration in vSphere Web Client; click on the **Edit...** button in the **vSphere Availability** area as shown in the following screenshot:

vSphere HA – Configuration – Edit

The configuration in the basic state is very easy; click on **Turn ON vSphere HA** checkbox and then **OK**:

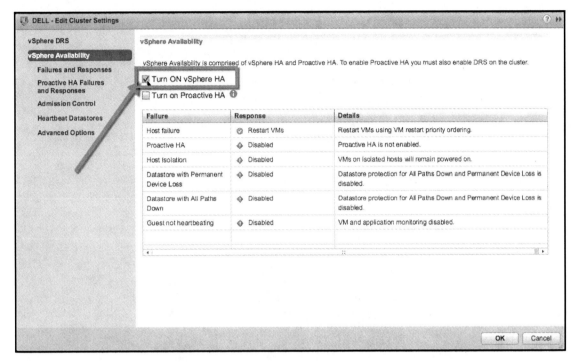

Turn ON vSphere HA

Under the **Recent Tasks** area, you can see **Configuring vSphere HA** on each host, so wait for the success on all hosts of the cluster:

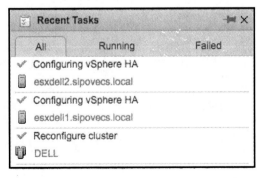

Recent Tasks – Configuration HA

When you click **Turn ON** on every ESXi host in the cluster, a special agent called **Fault Domain Manager** (**FDM**) is installed. In case of a failure, probably, this agent has not been installed on a host. You can check the VIB installation (package is named VMware-fdm) in /var/log/esxupdate.log:

```
2017-11-18T14:48:34Z esxupdate: 249378: LiveImageInstaller: DEBUG: done
2017-11-18T14:48:34Z esxupdate: 249378: LiveImageInstaller: DEBUG: Starting
to enable VIBs: VMware_bootbank_vmware-fdm_6.5.0-5973321
2017-11-18T14:48:34Z esxupdate: 249378: LiveImageInstaller: DEBUG: Live
installing vmware-fdm-6.5.0-5973321
2017-11-18T14:48:34Z esxupdate: 249378: LiveImageInstaller: DEBUG: Trying
to mount payload [vmware-fdm]
2017-11-18T14:48:34Z esxupdate: 249378: LiveImageInstaller: DEBUG: Mounting
vmware_f.v00...
2017-11-18T14:48:34Z esxupdate: 249378: vmware.runcommand: INFO: runcommand
called with: args = 'mv /tmp/img-stg/data/vmware_f.v00 /tardisks/', outfile
= 'None', returnoutput = 'True', timeout = '0.0'.
2017-11-18T14:48:34Z esxupdate: 249378: LiveImageInstaller: INFO:
Extracting etc/opt/vmware/fdm/hostlist from state.tgz
2017-11-18T14:48:34Z esxupdate: 249378: LiveImageInstaller: INFO:
Extracting etc/opt/vmware/fdm/vmmetadata from state.tgz
2017-11-18T14:48:34Z esxupdate: 249378: LiveImageInstaller: INFO:
Extracting etc/opt/vmware/fdm/clusterconfig from state.tgz
2017-11-18T14:48:34Z esxupdate: 249378: LiveImageInstaller: DEBUG: Enabling
VIBs is done.
2017-11-18T14:48:34Z esxupdate: 249378: LiveImageInstaller: DEBUG: Running
[/sbin/secpolicytools -p]...
2017-11-18T14:48:34Z esxupdate: 249378: vmware.runcommand: INFO: runcommand
called with: args = '/sbin/secpolicytools -p', outfile = 'None',
returnoutput = 'True', timeout = '0.0'.
2017-11-18T14:48:34Z esxupdate: 249378: LiveImageInstaller: DEBUG: output:
Error: More than one exception specification for tardisk /tardisks/vsan.v00
Error: Ignoring /etc/vmware/secpolicy/tardisks/vsan
2017-11-18T14:48:34Z esxupdate: 249378: vmware.runcommand: INFO: runcommand
called with: args = '['/sbin/chkconfig', '-B', '/etc/chkconfig.db', '-D',
'/etc/init.d', '-i', '-o']', outfile = 'None', returnoutput = 'True',
timeout = '0.0'.
2017-11-18T14:48:34Z esxupdate: 249378: vmware.runcommand: INFO: runcommand
called with: args = '['/sbin/chkconfig', '-B', '/etc/chkconfig.db', '-D',
'/etc/init.d', '-i', '-o']', outfile = 'None', returnoutput = 'True',
timeout = '0.0'.
2017-11-18T14:48:34Z esxupdate: 249378: LiveImageInstaller: DEBUG: Running
[['/etc/init.d/vmware-fdm', 'start', 'upgrade']]...
2017-11-18T14:48:34Z esxupdate: 249378: vmware.runcommand: INFO: runcommand
called with: args = '['/etc/init.d/vmware-fdm', 'start', 'upgrade']',
outfile = 'None', returnoutput = 'True', timeout = '0.0'.
2017-11-18T14:48:35Z esxupdate: 249378: LiveImageInstaller: DEBUG: output:
```

```
Starting vmware-fdm:Setting the memory limit for fdm resource pool on this
host to 200 MB ERROR: ld.so: object '/lib/libMallocArenaFix.so' from
LD_PRELOAD cannot be preloaded: ignored. success
```

A log specific for the FDM agent is available on each host in the `/var/log/fdm.log` file.

One of the typical problems that can block FDM agent installation can be ramdisk space which you can check before installing or upgrading the new VIB. In order to check ramdisk space, use one of these commands:
`esxcli system visorfs ramdisk list`
`vdf`

Now we have to enable HA and protect VMs. When a host fails, vSphere HA restarts the VMs on other hosts in the cluster. During the configuration, select the **master host**, and other hosts are **slave hosts**. A very important part is the configured redundant **heartbeat network**. The heartbeat network is the VMkernel port that is marked for management or vSAN.

Network redundancy has two choices—practically, first you create one VMkernel port, and on the port groups, configure NIC Teaming and use two vmnics. The second configuration is that you have two port groups and two VMkernel ports for management that are assigned to every one vmnic.

In practice, we usually use first options, in this example:

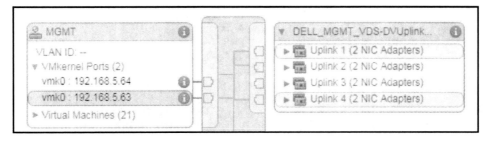

Heartbeat network – configuration

We can describe vSphere HA architecture a little bit.

In order to configure vSphere HA, we have several following requirements:

- **Right license:** Minimal Essential plus
- **Two hosts minimal:** 64 hosts, it's the maximum per cluster in vSphere 6.0 and 6.5
- **At least two share datastores**: This is required for datastore heartbeating, but you can have also a single shared datastore (in this case, you need an advanced option to remove the warning on the datastore numbers)
- **vCenter server**: Needed for configuration vSphere HA, but for running HA is not important

When the HA is enabled, FDM is started on the ESXi hosts. ESXi host says *hello, I am here in your fault domain*. A host can be only part of one fault domain. The fault domain is managed only per master host. All other hosts are slave hosts. FDM agents on slave hosts communicate with FDM on the master host. The master host sends heartbeats to the slave hosts. **Datastore heartbeating** is used as a backup to detect host heartbeats. Both network and datastore heartbeats indicate that the host is a failure. The host can be failed or isolated. The host is isolated when it follows two conditions. The host is not receiving network heartbeats and cannot ping to the isolation address. By default, it is the isolation address default gateway. It is not good, so it is recommended you define the new isolation address through advanced vSphere HA settings. The name of this advanced setting is `das.isolationaddress[0-9]`.

 For more information on the different vSphere HA advanced options, check in the *vSphere Availability* Guide at `https://docs.vmware.com/en/VMware-vSphere/6.5/com.vmware.vsphere.avail.doc/GUID-E0161CB5-BD3F-425F-A7E0-BF83B005FECA.html`.

You can set up to 10 isolation addresses. Set the address to ping to determine if a host is isolated from the network. This address is pinged only when heartbeats are dead:

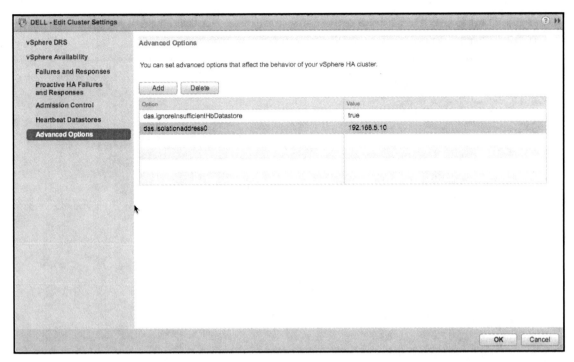

VMware vSphere HA Advanced Options

Virtual Machine Component Protection (VMCP)

VMCP is a new technology from vSphere 6.0. VMCP protects storage failures, used typically for block-based storage. Before vSphere 6.0, vSphere HA was only protecting hosts, by monitoring network failures; if the FDM agent is not able to talk with other agents, it can be considered in a fault state from the other agents, and it will be considered in an isolated state itself.

The following two types of storage failures can now be handled:

- **Permanent Device Loss (PDL)**
- **All Paths Down (APD)**

For more information about PDL and APD, read VMware KB 2004684—*Permanent Device Loss (PDL) and All-Paths-Down (APD) in vSphere 5.x and 6.x* at `https://kb.vmware.com/s/article/2004684` or in `Chapter 7`, *Advanced Storage Management*.

When you want to use VMCP, you must configure for the **Failures and Responses** part of the configuration:

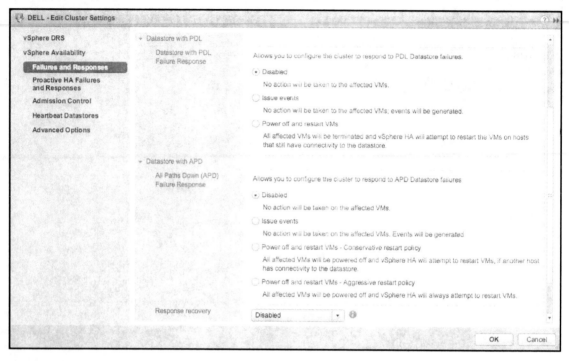

VM Component Protection – Configuration

Proactive HA

Proactive HA is a new feature integrated with server vendor monitoring systems. The cluster must use vSphere DRS for correct Proactive HA. With Proactive HA coming to the new server state **Quarantine Mode**, you must have a server vendor that supports Proactive HA and correctly configures the plugin to vSphere Web Client. For example, Proactive HA can help you when there is a problem with power supply. All VMs are moved to other hosts, and you have a chance to repair problems with the hardware.

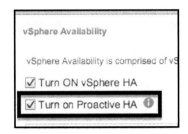

Turn on Proactive HA

In the **Proactive HA Failures and Responses** tab, here you would see the **Proactive HA-provider** option as follows:

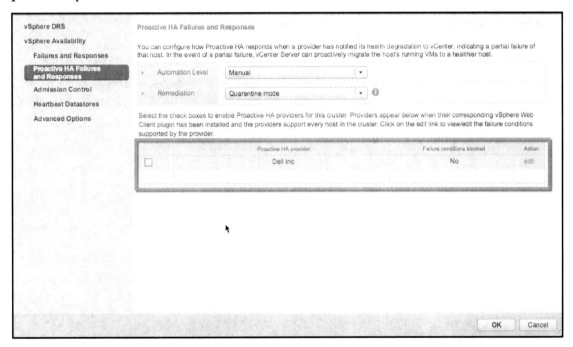

Proactive HA-provider

Admission control

Admission control guarantees vSphere HA failover by ensuring enough spare failover capacity inside the cluster. You need free resources when hosts must manage the failure for all affected VMs and admission control takes care of you.

Configuration is at the cluster level under the vSphere Availability section shown as follows:

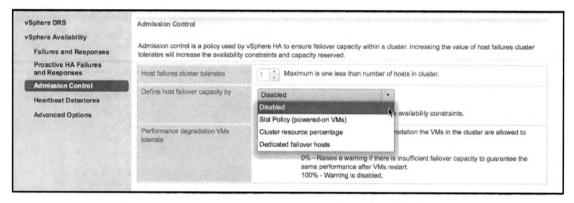

Admission Control

You can define host failover capacity using one of the following options:

- **Disabled**: This option is not a very good idea, but it is possible. For example, for a two nodes cluster, you may want to disable admission control during maintenance operation.

- **Slot Policy (powered-on VMs)**: A slot is a logical representation of memory and CPU resources. A slot is the memory and CPU reservation required for any powered-on VMs in the cluster. Slot policy can do good work in the environment where there is a very similar VM with the same CPU memory configuration. When you have a lot of small VMs and two monster VMs, it is not a very good situation because the reservation is selecting the largest value. You can change this value for CPU slot size and memory slot size through the **Advanced Options**:

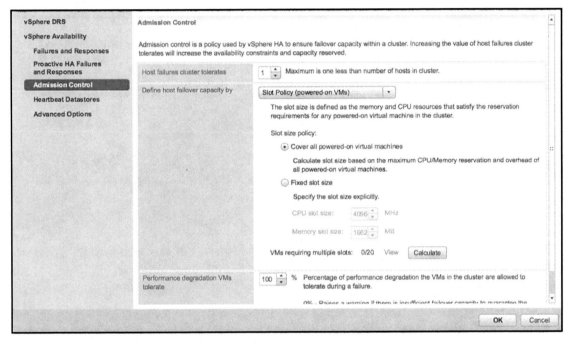

Slot Policy – Admission Control

- **Cluster resource percentage**: You can configure vSphere HA to perform admission control by reserving a specific percentage of cluster CPU and memory resources for recovery from host failures. vSphere HA calculates CPU and memory. CPU calculation uses CPU reservation for the powered-on VMs. If you don't use reservation HA, use default value 32 MHz. The memory calculates the memory reservation and memory overhead of each powered-on VM, the default value is 0 MB. You can override calculated failover capacity:

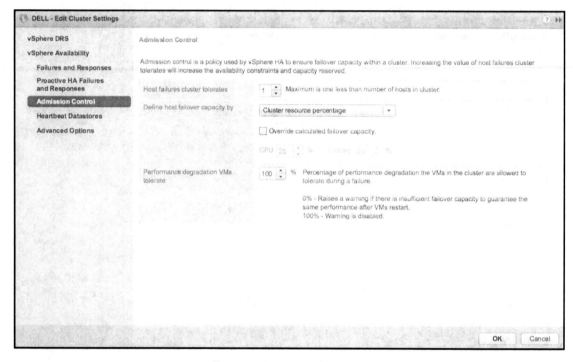

Cluster resource percentage – Admission Control

- **Dedicated failover hosts**: The last option is defined failover hosts. You can specify and dedicate failover hosts. vSphere HA uses these hosts when it needs failover actions or has insufficient resources:

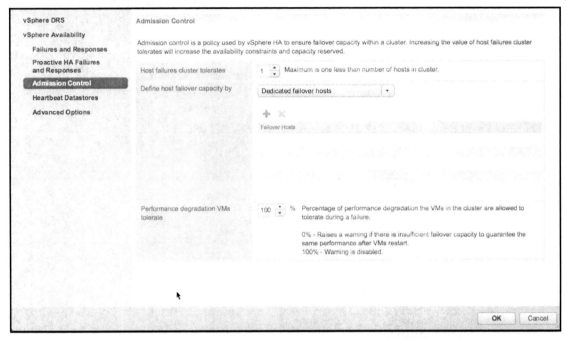

Dedicated failover hosts – Admission Control

Then, there is a new option, named **Performance degradation VMs tolerate**. This new setting in vSphere 6.5, if set, will issue a warning when a host failure would cause a reduction in VM performance based on the actual resource, not just configured reservations.

VM restart and monitoring

You can override specific vSphere HA (but also vSphere DRS) configurations for specific VMs directly from the cluster level. In the **Configure** tab, under the **Configuration** menu:

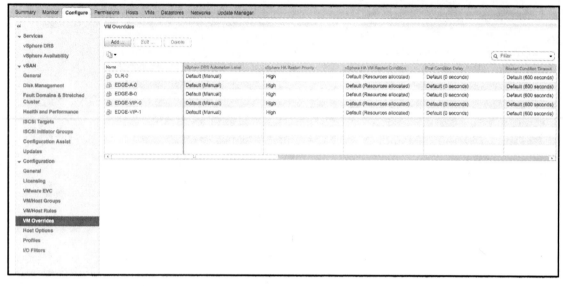

VM Overrides

The first option is the **Automation level**, but it's related to vSphere DRS. For vSphere HA, you can specify a different **VM restart priority**, shown as follows:

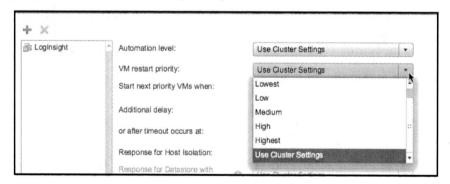

VM restart priority

Note that starting with vSphere 6.5. there are two new levels (**Lowest** and **Highest**) to provide more control. If a VM does not need to be restarted (for example, it's for test purposes), you can also disable vSphere HA. The next option is **Start next priority VMs when**, to define a condition on when restarting the next VM, for example, you can choose the **Guest Heartbeats detected** option through VMware Tools:

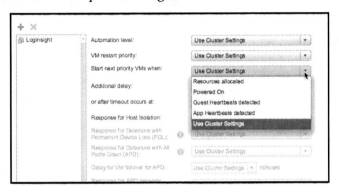

Start next priority VMs when

The next option is orchestration through VM/Host rules and **Virtual Machines to Virtual Machines** rule:

VM/Host Rule

To monitor vSphere HA, it is possible to use the **Monitor** tab, and the **vSphere HA** section on it:

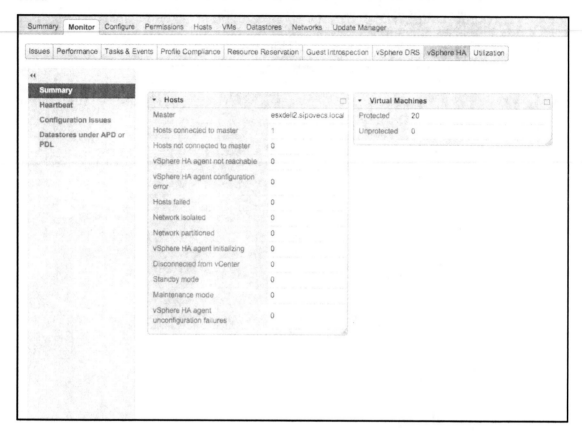

Monitor vSphere HA

A very quick overview of vSphere HA when you want a deep self-study, you can read this PDF at `https://docs.vmware.com/en/VMware-vSphere/6.5/vsphere-esxi-vcenter-server-65-availability-guide.pdf`.

There exists a great book (written by Duncan Epping) about vSphere HA, for the older version 6.0 Update 2, but still usable for deep dive study. You can get it for free at `https://www.gitbook.com/book/duncanyb/vsphere-ha-60-deepdive/details.`

VMware vSphere FT

VMware vSphere FT is a way to improve the availability level for critical VMs, with a (close to) zero-downtime technology. The protected VM is named the **primary VM**, and for each primary VM, there is a duplicate VM named **secondary VM** (or sometimes also the shadow VM).

VMware vSphere FT provides continuous availability by having two identical VMs running on separate hosts. The secondary VM execution is identical to that of the primary VM. Primary and secondary VMs are still monitoring each other's status. If primary VM failed, the secondary VM immediately replaces the primary VM.

VMware vSphere FT has also some limits—for each VM, it supports a maximum of 4 vCPU and 64 GB RAM. For each host, it supports a maximum of 4 fault-tolerant VMs. VMware vMotion migration is supported for both VMs, as also the different virtual disk formats and the native backup capability (using VM snapshots).

The requirements for vSphere FT are:

- The CPU used in hosts for FT must be compatible with vSphere vMotion or improved with **Enhanced vMotion Compatibility (EVC)**.
- The network for FT logging must use a 10 Gbps speed. A dedicated FT network is highly recommended.
- For licensing, only Enterprise Plus allows up to 4 vCPUs, with the Standard editions the maximum is 2.
- It is best to check compatibility on the VMware web page.

VMware vSphere FT can be easily activated or de-activated. To turn on this feature, just right-click on the VM:

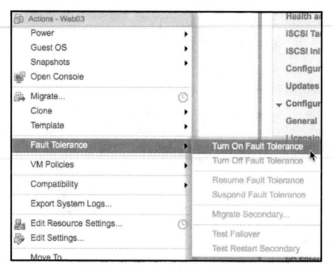

Enable vSphere FT

 For more details, refer to https://docs.vmware.com/en/VMware-vSphere/ 6.5/com.vmware.vsphere.avail.doc/GUID-7525F8DD-9B8F-4089-B020- BAA4AC6509D2.html.

VMware vCenter High Availability (VCHA)

VMware VCHA is a new feature from vSphere 6.5, and it's available only with the vCSA deployment. It's based on a multi-nodes architecture with an active-passive configuration plus a Witness node, and it's designed to reduce downtime when vCSA fails. These features support both deployment architecture, so internal or external PSC.

Deployment and configuration are easy. The first vCSA that is deployed will be the **Active node**; then, when you start to configure VCHA, one of the first processes will be the cloning of this first VM with two new VMs; the **Passive node** and the **Witness node**. During this process, not only the two clones are created, but it's created also a DRS rule for separate the nodes on different hosts for a better resiliency.

When VCHA configuration is complete, only the Active node has an active management interface. All the three nodes will use a specific network (named VCHA network) for private communication; also this network is set up during the configuration phase. Only the Active and Passive nodes are continuously replicating data. The Witness node is a light version clone of the Active node and provides a quorum to protect a split-brain situation. VCHA requires a single vCenter Server license, so don't worry.

Refer to KB 2147672—*Supported and deprecated topologies for VMware vSphere 6.5* at `https://kb.vmware.com/s/article/2147672`. Check this KB, before deploying vCenter HA, because it is good to understand supported topologies for vSphere 6.5.

To configure VCHA, proceed as follows:

1. Configure VCHA as a part configuration on vCenter through vSphere Web Client and click on the **Configure** option:

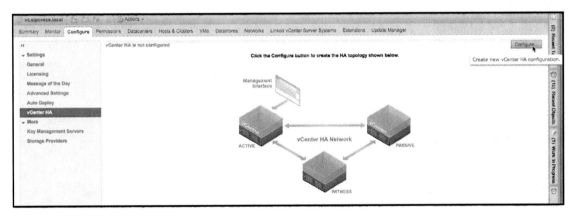

Configure VCHA

2. There are two different configuration options—the basic configuration that creates and configures the clones, and advanced configuration, where the administrator creates and configures the two clones. Let's choose the basic option:

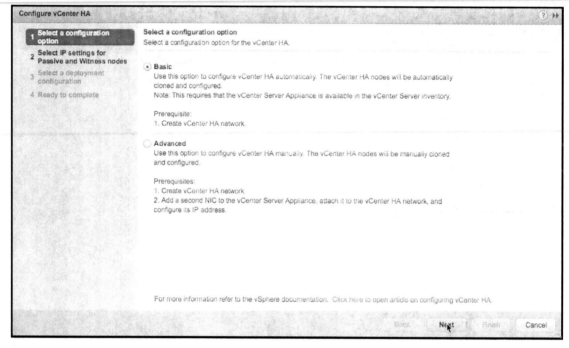

Basic configuration option for VCHA

3. The VCHA topology can be configured with a vCenter Server with an embedded PSC or a vCenter Server with an external PSC.

- The setup of the VCHA with embedded PSC is configured as follows:

  Part of the cloning process is PSC, and all services are cloned. After configuration, VCHA starts replicating Active to Passive node replication and includes PSC data. In this use case, all services and PSC are available on the Passive node:

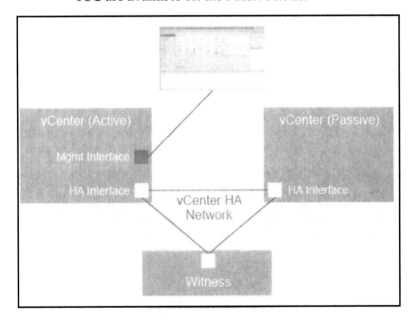

VCHA topology with an embedded PSC

Image source: https://kb.vmware.com/s/article/2147672

- The configuration of the VCHA with external PSC topology can be configured as the follows:

  It is possible to configure all with one external PSC, but it is a potential single point of failure. The correct idea is to use load balancer F5 or NSX and Netscaler to protect the PSC. If failed, one PSC load balancer directs the vCenter to a different PSC. We must configure two external PSCs, which will replicate vCenter SSO information and other PSC information. When the configuration is finished, only the vCSA is protected:

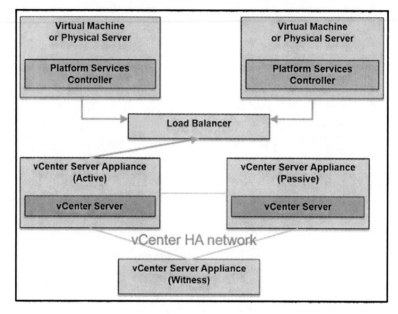

VCHA with external PSC topology using a load balancer

Image source: https://kb.vmware.com/s/article/2147672

 Check KB 2147046—*How to configuring NSX Edge Load Balancer for use with PSC 6.5* at https://kb.vmware.com/s/article/2147046.

4. Network configuration requires the setup of a dedicated VCHA network for the communication between VCHA nodes:

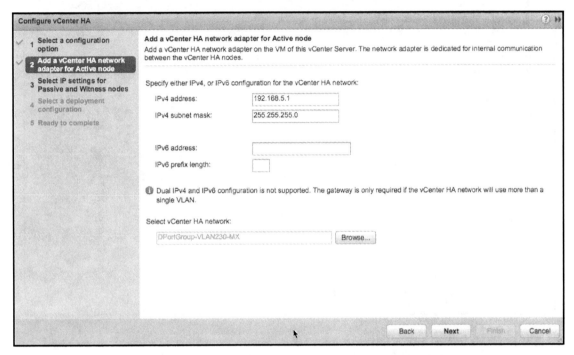

VCHA – network adapter for Active node

5. Specify IP settings for Passive and Witness nodes as follows:

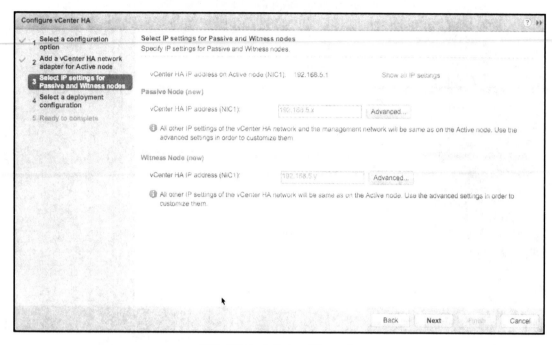

VCHA – IP Settings for Passive and Witness nodes

6. VCHA is now configured successfully as shown in the following screenshot:

VCHA – Summary

7. In the **Hosts & Clusters** view, you can see three VMs—a vc (active node), a vc-peer (passive node), and a vc-witness:

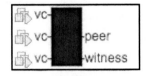

vCenter HA all VMs

VMware vSphere Replication and Site Recovery Manager (SRM)

vSphere Replication is the extension to the vCenter Server, and it provides hypervisor VM replication and recovery. This replication can be used for SRM. vSphere Replication is an alternative to storage-based replication.

When you want to use vSphere Replication, you must download and deploy the vSphere Replication appliance. This appliance provides a plugin to vSphere Web Client and a user interface for vSphere Replication. Inside is the embedded database that stores replication configuration.

The plug-in for vSphere Replication is available in the vSphere Web Client with the following icon:

vSphere Replication icon

The vSphere Replication page presents a **Getting Started** tab with the basic concepts on how VR will work:

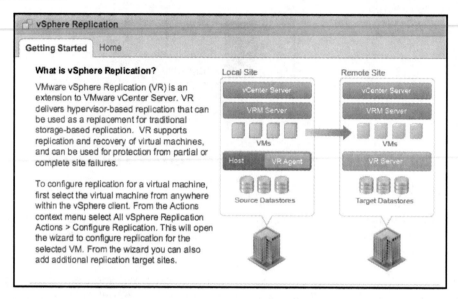

VR Getting Started page

When everything is properly configured, you can easily select the **Configure Replication...** option from the menu on every VMs:

Configure Replication

 Refer to KB 2150038—*Unable to reset the root password of vSphere Replication appliance 6.5* at `https://kb.vmware.com/s/article/2150038`.

VMware vSphere Replication can be used as a standalone VM replication solution, or can be one possible part of another VMware product—SRM.

SRM is the BC and DR solution for the customer. This solution helps you with creating test plan recovery of a VM between a protected vCenter Server site. Planned migration is possible, and you can evacuate VMs from a protected site to a recovery site. When you want to install SRM servers you need Windows OS. When you install SRM, you install the plugin to the vSphere Web Client. The SRM Server provides the embedded vPostgreSQL database, you can use external DB. You must install the SRM Server on a protected and recovery site, of course.

After installing SRM servers, you use the only configuration through the vCenter Web Client plugin:

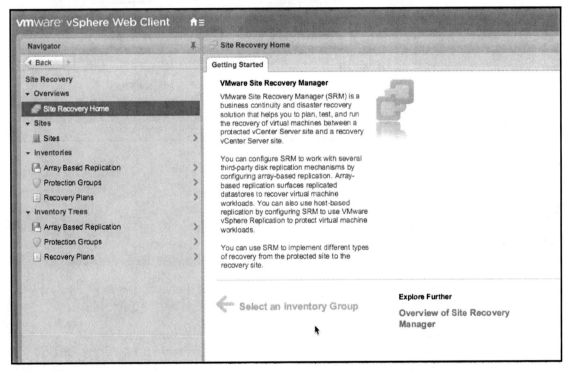

SRM GUI

The **Summary** tab shows all connection status and potential problems:

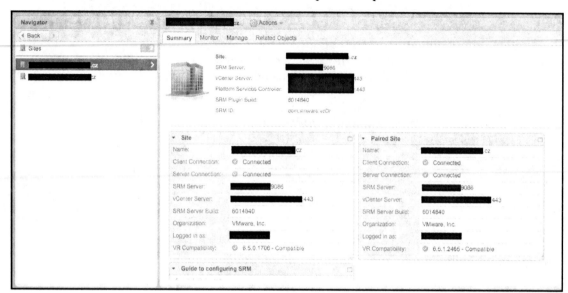

SRM Summary tab

Summary

In this chapter, we described some specific availability (and resiliency) solutions in vSphere, including the new vSphere HA features, Proactive HA, and the vCenter Server HA.

Building a reliable infrastructure is the first (crucial) part, but then also the workloads must have a reasonable availability level, according to business needs and requirements.

VMware vSphere HA can provide a basic and convenient availability level for all workloads, with minimum effort and cost. However, it's not suitable for business-critical workloads. In this case, other solutions can be used, such as vSphere FT or also traditional (from the physical world) solutions, such as guest clustering.

The next chapter will describe how to successfully back up your VMware environment.

14
Data and Workloads Protection

Data and workloads protection is a fundamental aspect that every administrator must consider to ensure data availability and BC. In each design, the protection of the infrastructure is important for having all services available with a working strategy to quickly recover vSphere components in case of failure.

This chapter will explain how to perform the setup of the backup and restore process for the ESXi host as well as the vCSA, to reduce the time required by the restore process, minimizing the service outage. Without a backup strategy, in case of failures, you will have to install and configure each ESXi host or vCSA from scratch, a time-consuming activity that creates service disruption and an extra workload.

When hosts and vCenter Servers are protected, running a VM plays a fundamental role in the infrastructure since they provide all the services to users. Ensuring VM protection and availability is the task assigned to the backup strategy design that must be reliable and scalable, and offer all the features required by modern data centers. This chapter will discuss some software backup solutions and the main features that you can use to manage data protection, thus ensuring the BC.

In this chapter we will cover the following topics:

- Backup and restore the ESXi host configuration
- How to protect the vCSA ensuring a quick restore process
- What are transport modes and how data is handled
- Understanding what backup solutions are available in the market to protect VM, and their main features
- Hyper-scale solutions

Backup technologies

The choice of suitable backup solution for an infrastructure depends on what you actually need to protect—configurations, data, VM, applications, and so on. Depending on that, backup solutions can be categorized as follows:

- **Backup with agent**: This solution is intended for the protection of a physical environment or specific configurations like VM cluster. Vendors like Arcserve or Veritas Backup Exec provide this solution type.
- **Native backup for VMware**: This is specifically developed for virtualized environments, and is the recommended solution for a virtualized environment because it takes the benefits of vSphere features (for example, snapshots technology). Veeam, Nakivo, Altaro,Vembu, HPE are some vendors that provide backup solutions for virtual infrastructure.
- **Hyper-scale backup**: Vendors like Rubrik or Cohesity provide ready-to-use backup solutions based on appliances installed in the infrastructure.

Let's discuss the protection of the infrastructure components and the tools used to guarantee maximum availability.

Backup host configuration

Every administrator knows how important a backup is, to ensure data protection and BC. ESXi host is not an exception. The server where the ESXi is installed may fail and the re-installation and configuration of the settings can be time-consuming, with the result that the host is out of service for a certain period of time. Since the installation of the ESXi only takes a few minutes, you can perform a fresh installation of the server. What really takes a long time is the host's configuration.

The option of backing up the host's configuration allows you to quickly restore the host functionality, reducing the service outage. The backup can be taken by accessing the ESXi console and following these steps:

1. SSH the ESXi host to backup and enter the root credentials.
2. Using the ESXi command line, run the following command:

```
vim-cmd hostsvc/firmware/backup_config
```

```
[root@esxi01:~] vim-cmd hostsvc/firmware/backup_config
Bundle can be downloaded at : http://*/downloads/52c2e632-4f8c-a55a-a848-576ddab
9ef6b/configBundle-esxi01.localdomain.tgz
[root@esxi01:~] █
```

The host's configuration can be backed up through the command line

The backup is saved in the /scratch/downloads directory, and because it's not recommended to store the backup on the same device, it must be transferred off the host. To transfer the backup file, you can use free tools such as WinSCP (available at the URL https://winscp.net/).

Alternatively, you can use the vSphere CLI to backup the host configuration by running the following command:

```
vicfg-cfgbackup --server=ESXi_IP_address --username=root -s
output_file_name
```

Here, ESXi_IP_address is the IP address of the ESXi host and output_file_name is the name of the backup file created.

Restoring the host configuration

To restore an ESXi after a failure, you need to reinstall the same version and build number of the failed host using one of the methods covered in Chapter 4, *Deployment Workflow and Component Installation,* and assign an IP address to the management console.

Restore the configuration to the new host by following these steps:

1. SSH the host to backup and enter the root credentials.
2. Put the host in maintenance mode by running the following command:

   ```
   vim-cmd hostsvc/maintenance_mode_enter
   ```

3. Using a tool like WinSCP, copy the backup file to a location accessible by the new host, for example to /tmp/configBundle.tgz.
4. To restore the configuration run the following command:

   ```
   vim-cmd hostsvc/firmware/restore_config /tmp/configBundle.tgz
   ```

With the old configuration applied, the host will initiate an automatic reboot:

```
[root@esxi01:~] vim-cmd hostsvc/maintenance_mode_enter
[root@esxi01:~] vim-cmd hostsvc/firmware/restore_config /tmp/configBundle.tgz
```

Configuration is restored to the new host

5. When the host is booted, exit maintenance mode and use the ESXi normally.

To restore the configuration data, both the build number and UUID of the host must match the build number and UUID of the host on the backup file. The host's UUID can be obtained using the command `esxcfg-info -u`.

To override the UUID mismatch, use numeric option 1:

`vim-cmd hostsvc/firmware/restore_config 1 /tmp/configBundle.tgz`

Using the vSphere CLI, power off all the running VM on the host and run the following command:

`vicfg-cfgbackup --server=ESXi_IP_address --username=root -l backup_file`

Here, `ESXi_IP_address` is the IP address of the ESXi host and `backup_file` is the name of the backup file.

In order to restore a backup, the build of the host must match the build of the host contained in the backup file. Therefore, you should take a backup each time you upgrade the host.

If the vSphere Host Profile feature is used in your environment to set up your hosts, the host configuration backup is not required.

File-based backup of the vCSA

Protecting the vCSA is another key point to ensure BC. Technically, vSphere can work without vCenter Server but advanced features, such as vMotion, vSphere HA, and vSphere DRS won't be available to keep your VM in a protected state.

If the vCSA gets corrupted or fails, you should restore the vCenter Server functionality as soon as possible to avoid worse problems. What happens if an ESXi host also fails? The running VM on that host will stop working, because the vSphere HA service is not available.

vSphere vCSA 6.5 introduces a new feature that allows a file-based backup of the vCSA and the PSC to be performed through the vCenter Server Appliance Management Interface. This speeds up the restore process.

The backup file includes the core vCSA configuration, inventory, and historical data of your choice. The backup file is not stored in the vCSA but streamed over FTP, FTPS, HTTP, HTTPS, or SCP to a remote system.

 If the backup is taken for a vCSA in an HA cluster, only the active node of the vCenter Server instance is backed up.

To take the vCSA backup, follow these steps:

1. Open your preferred browser and enter the address `https://<VCSA_IP>:5480` to access the vCenter Server Appliance Management Interface. Log in as root.
2. Go to the **Summary** tab and click on the **Backup** button to open the backup appliance wizard.

3. Specify the backup protocol, choosing from the HTTP, HTTPS, SCP, FTPS, and FTP options, then enter the details in the **Location** field, specifying also the credentials required to access the target destination. Enable **Encrypt Backup Data** if you want to encrypt the backup file and enter a password for the encryption. The password will be requested during the restore process. Click **Next**:

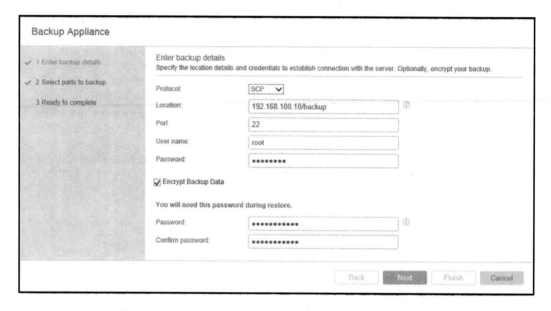

Backup Appliance

Enter backup details
Specify the location details and credentials to establish connection with the server. Optionally, encrypt your backup.

- ✓ 1 Enter backup details
- ✓ 2 Select parts to backup
- 3 Ready to complete

Protocol:	SCP
Location:	192.168.100.10/backup
Port	22
User name:	root
Password:	••••••••

☑ Encrypt Backup Data

You will need this password during restore.

Password:	••••••••••••
Confirm password:	••••••••••••

Back   Next   Finish   Cancel

vCSA 6.5 comes with a backup feature that allows us to quickly recover the appliance in case of failure

4. Specify data to backup, selecting **common** parts (inventory and configuration) and **Stats, Events, Alarms, and Tasks** to backup additional historical data in the vCenter Server database. Click **Next** to continue.

5. Review the summary information and click **Finish** to perform the backup. The progress of the backup is displayed in the **Backup Progress** window once the backup is launched. When the backup procedure is finished, click **OK** to close the window.

If for any reason the backup fails, cancel the backup job and start the process again.

To avoid service outages and to better protect the vCenter Server, vSphere 6.5 introduces a new feature available to vCSA only that provides HA to vCenter Server, called **vCenter Server High Availability (VCHA)**. VCHA was covered in Chapter 13, *Advanced Availability in vSphere 6.5*.

Restoring the vCSA from a file-based backup

To restore a failed vCSA from a file-based backup, you can use the vCSA GUI installer that will complete the process in the following two stages:

1. Deploy a new vCSA
2. Copy data from the file-based backup to the appliance

The file-based restore can be performed only if the backup has been previously taken from the vCenter Server Appliance Management Interface. Alternatively, you can deploy a new vCSA and restore the data from the file-based backup using the vCenter Server Appliance Management Interface.

> To restore a VCHA, all nodes (active, passive, and witness) must be powered off. The vCSA is restored in non **vCenter Server High Availability (VCHA)** mode and the cluster must be reconstructed once the restore procedure completes.

A file-based restore of the PSC should be performed only when the last PSC installed in the domain fails. If a PSC fails, you must decommission the failed PSC first, redeploy a new one, and join the existing SSO domain. The multi-master model of the PSC will allow the replication to update the new PSC.

To restore a vCSA, proceed with the following steps:

1. From the vCSA media, run the **vCenter Server Appliance 6.5 Installer** and select the **Restore** option.
2. Stage 1 of the restore process is the deployment of a new vCSA to replace the failed appliance. Refer to `Chapter 4`, *Deployment Workflow and Component Installation* for the installation steps. When the deployment of the new vCSA is completed, the vCSA will run on the target ESXi, but the data copy process from the backup hasn't occurred yet.
3. After the completion of the deployment, you are automatically redirected to stage 2, which completes the restore process by copying the data from the backup location.
4. Click **Next** in the introduction page of the stage 2 installer to proceed with the restore.
5. Once you have reviewed the backup details, click **Next** to go to the final step. Click **Finish** then **OK** to complete stage 2. The vCSA will be restarted to complete the restore process.

If for any reason the restore process fails, power off, delete the partially recovered VM, and try again.

> If the vCSA has the PSC embedded, the backup of the VM is already a protection solution for the vCenter Server.

Protecting the workloads

The hosts and the vCenter Server are not the only components that need to be protected in your infrastructure. Once you have fired up your virtual infrastructure, the VM deployed in your environment must be protected against failures, data loss, and service disruptions.

Transport modes

Software backup solutions use different protocols called **transport modes** to retrieve VM data from the storage. The transport mode to use for backups depends on the design of the network and the storage architecture.

There are four main transport modes that are supported for handling data:

- **Network Block Device (NBD)**: The ESXi host reads data from the storage and sends it to the application, across the network, using the NBD protocol. This mode can be used in any infrastructure configuration and is the simplest method to implement.
- **Network Block Device Secure Socket Layer (NBDSSL)**: This is the same as NBD but uses SSL to encrypt the data passed over the TCP/IP connection.
- **SCSI HotAdd**: This is a LAN free data transfer mode where the .vmdk files of a VM are attached to the backup application. Data won't go through the network but is read and written directly from/to the datastore. In a lot of environments, this is the preferred mode.
- **Direct SAN**: In this, data is read directly from the SAN or iSCSI LUN; this provides the fastest data transfer speed. Direct SAN transport mode is recommended if VM's disks are stored on shared SAN LUNs connected to ESXi host over FC, FCoE, and iSCSI.

Not all transport modes can be used in all cases: for example with Virtual Volumes, actually, Direct SAN mode is not supported.

Also, some specific backup products can implement other specific transport modes (for example Direct NFS with Veeam Backup & Replication.

VMware vSphere Data Protection (VDP)

VMware provides VDP as the backup and recovery solution for the vSphere environment, and it's managed by vSphere Web Client. However, version 6.5 has been announced as the final release of VDP and in future versions of vSphere it won't be available any longer.

The VDP workflow can be outlined as follow:

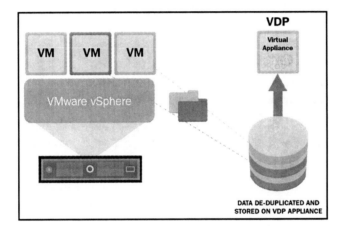

How vSphere Data Protection works

VDP takes image-level backups of VM based on snapshot technology and the deduplication takes place within the appliance. VDP takes advantage of the **Changed Block Tracking** (**CBT**) technology during image-level backups to ensure that only changed blocks are copied, making the process faster and thus saving time.

The restore procedure allows you to rename VMs to restore them in different locations.

Backup solutions for VMware vSphere

The market offers several valid solutions you can choose from, and backup product selection must consider different elements, such as infrastructure complexity, supported platforms, backup types, licensing, budget, and so forth.

Based on what you need to backup, the chosen software solution must provide specific features to meet the requirements. For example, to backup Microsoft SQL Servers, application-aware backups with log truncate features must be supported to ensure database consistency. If you are still performing backups on tapes, make sure the product supports tapes.

Since the available backup solutions provide different options, capabilities, and pricing (a complete list of the backup interoperability matrix for the VMware vSphere environment is available at http://www.vbrain.info/backup-interoperability-matrix-vsphere/), some popular backup products specific to virtual environments will now be briefly illustrated to better understand what the market is offering. The listed vendors and product ordering don't follow any classification or preference.

Veeam Backup & Replication

Veeam offers robust and powerful backup and replication features to protect entire virtual infrastructures. It's a backup solution for enterprises but also for SMBs.

The installation supports Windows OS only. The management of the application can be done through a console deployed on the administrator's computers or with a web-based console. Despite its simplicity, Veeam protects the infrastructure in a very robust and reliable way.

The main features of Veeam are as follows:

- **Backup**: Full VM backup, incremental backup, copy backup, cloud backup (AWS, Azure, Veeam Cloud Connect), tape backup, replication, cloud replication.
- **Restore**: Restore full VM, Instant File Recovery, Instant VM Recovery, Instant Object Recovery (AD, Exchange, Microsoft SQL, SharePoint, Oracle).
- **Licensing**: This is per physical CPU Socket.
- **Available in three editions**: It is available in Standard, Enterprise, and Enterprise Plus. Veeam also provides an Essential version with an affordable price that is designed for small organizations with less than 250 employees and is limited to 6 CPU sockets. A Free Edition is available but limited to full backups only and vPower, VMs replication, and scripting features are not available.

NAKIVO Backup & Replication

NAKIVO Backup & Replication is a backup solution for SMBs and enterprises, and can be deployed on both Windows and Linux OS or as a virtual appliance, allowing the saving of some Windows licenses. The management is done through a simple, easy, and intuitive HTML5-based console that guides the user through the configuration steps required by the backup or restore procedures.

The installation and usage are very simple and this product offers all the features required by modern data centers. You just need a few minutes to get the software up and running.

The main features of NAKIVO Backup & Replication are as follows:

- **Backup**: Full VM backup, incremental backup, copy backup, replication, cloud backup (AWS), cloud replication.
- **Restore**: Restore full VMs, Instant File Recovery, Instant Object Recovery (AD, Exchange), Instant VM Recovery.
- **Licensing**: This is per physical CPU Socket.
- **Available in three editions**: This is available in Basic, Pro, and Enterprise. An Essential version is also available with an affordable price for Pro and Enterprise editions, designed for SMBs and limited to a maximum of 6 socket licenses per organization. A Free Edition is available and supports up to two VMs.

Altaro VM Backup

Altaro VM Backup is a backup solution for SMBs deployed to the Windows platform. It offers all the features required by the DR to protect VMware virtual infrastructures. A dedicated Windows machine is not required and there is no need for third-party software dependencies such as Microsoft SQL. The product is easy to use, with an intuitive design, and provides full control over backup jobs across all hosts.

You can manage the application from a console that is deployed on the administrator's computers and can be used as a central monitoring station for several Altaro VM instances.

The main features of Altaro VM Backup are as follows:

- **Backup**: Full VM backup, Incremental backup, copy backup, cloud backup (Azure), replication
- **Restore**: Restore full VMs, Instant File Recovery, Instant Object Recovery (Exchange), Instant VM Recovery
- **Licensing**: This is per physical host with unlimited sockets/CPUs

- **Available in three editions**: It is available in Standard, Pro, and Enterprise. A Free Edition is also available and supports protection for two VMs.

Vembu VMBackup

Vembu is a backup and DR software solution that can be deployed on the Windows and Linux platforms or as a virtual appliance. It is suitable for data centers and small and medium businesses with enterprise level features. Backup copies of your backups can be sent to offsite storage or to Vembu Cloud, which provides data redundancy and DR.

The main features of Vembu VMBackup are as follows:

- **Backup**: Full VM backup, incremental backup, copy backup, cloud backup (Vembu Cloud), replication.
- **Restore**: Restore full VMs, Instant File Recovery, Instant VM Recovery, Instant Object Recovery (Microsoft Exchange, SharePoint, SQL, and AD).
- **Licensing**: This is per physical CPU socket.
- **Two editions available**: It is available in two editions—BDR Suite and Free. The Free Edition supports a maximum of three VMs.

Micro Focus VM Explorer

Micro Focus VM Explorer (formally, HPE) can be deployed on Windows OS. It's managed through a simple and easy web-based console. The product is oriented for SMBs and offers interesting features that make the product a good backup solution to consider during software selection. It's available in nine different languages that you can select from the configuration area.

The integration with leading storage products (such as HPE StoreOnce Catalyst, HPE StoreVirtual VSA, EMC) optimizes performance and storage use, providing a complete flexibility to your environment.

The main features of Micro Focus VM Explorer are as follows :

- **Backup**: Full VM backup, incremental backup, copy backup, cloud backup (Amazon S3, Rackspace, Microsoft Azure, Scality, and OpenStack), tape backup, replication
- **Restore**: Restore full VMs, Instant File Recovery, Instant Object Recovery (Exchange), Instant VM Recovery

- **Licensing**: This is per physical CPU socket. VM Explorer installations must be licensed with a Starter Pack available in two editions—a Professional Edition (license for 4 CPU sockets) and an Enterprise Edition (license for 6 CPU sockets).
- **Two editions available**: It is available in Professional and Enterprise. A Free edition is available and provides basic manual VM backup and restore.

Deduplication appliances

Data that needs protecting is continuously growing and the available space on storage devices is never enough. To reduce the space occupied by backup files on storage devices, deduplication technology allows a reduction in storage space consumption.

Deduplicated storage should be used mainly as secondary targets due to their design. These storage systems are often developed to optimize write operations, but random read I/O performance may suffer.

Hyper-scale solutions

Hyper-scale is an architecture capable of scaling appropriately as increased demand is added to the system. This architecture is composed of individual servers, referred to as nodes, that provide resources in terms of compute, storage, and networking, and are put together in a cluster and managed as a single entity.

The advantage of hyper-scale is having an architecture that can be expanded as demand grows simply by adding new nodes to the cluster.

Cohesity

Cohesity DataPlatform is a hyperconverged platform solution that consolidates and manages secondary data at a web scale. Cohesity offers secondary storage devices with global dedupe, compression, and encryption.

The Cohesity appliance is installed with a proprietary OS and distributed filesystem. The design allows for scaling to any capacity.

When using a Cohesity solution you have two main benefits:

- You can eliminate secondary storage silos and consolidate backups
- You can control all your secondary data operations with converged data protection

Hyperconverged Cohesity solution embeds all backup components in one box simplifying the management:

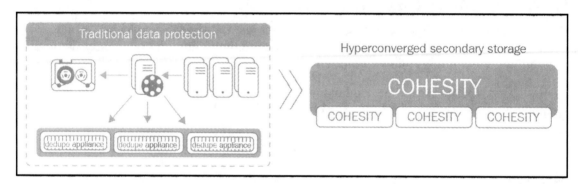

Cohesity hyperconverged platform

Rubrik

Rubrik is a cloud data management solution for protecting workloads that deliver a data management platform for enterprises in private, public, and hybrid cloud environments.

The Rubrik solution is deployed as an appliance to insert in the rack and power on. The scale-out hardware combined with a robust backup software manages, with a single platform, all data in the cloud, or on-premises for automated backup, DR, archival, search, in a simple, scale-out platform built for hybrid cloud.

The following image shows the Rubrik solution workflow:

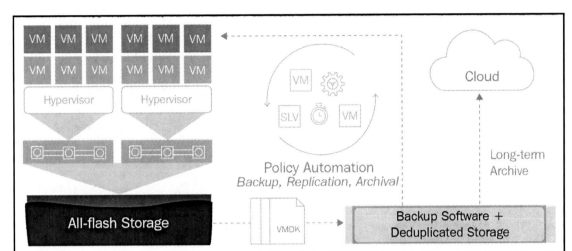

Rubrik cloud data management solution

Summary

Protection of the virtual infrastructure is an essential key point for every administrator, to limit potential services disruption.

The chapter covered how to protect ESXi hosts with a backup of the host's configuration to quickly restore a failed ESXi with minimal downtime. You just need a fresh installation of the ESXi host and to restore the configuration from the backup.

Another important key point to consider to avoid potential issues in case of failure is the backup of the vCSA. If the vCenter Server fails, vSphere features, such as vMotion and DRS, are no longer available and VM on production is not protected from potential host failures. This chapter explained how to protect the vCSA with the available backup options to quickly restore vCenter Server functionality, limiting service disruption.

Virtual servers are the most critical components of an infrastructure, since they provide services to the business. A suitable protection of VM is therefore required to ensure data protection and BC. The chapter provided a general overview of some backup solutions available in the market that protect virtual environments. Hyper-scale technology is quite a new solution that reduces the management of the workload's protection, providing appliances that are ready to go.

Index

V

CPSIA information can be obtained
at www.ICGtesting.com
Printed in the USA
LVOW09s2349220218
567654LV00003B/59/P